And the revelation was a little like what saints receive on mountains
—a further chapter in the history of the mystery...

—Diane Arbus, circa 1960

Clouds on screen at
a drive-in, N.J. 1960

Child in a nightgown, Wellfleet, Mass. 1957

REVELATIONS

Fire Eater at a carnival, Palisades Park, N.J. 1956

A young Brooklyn family going for a Sunday outing, N.Y.C. 1966

Woman with a veil on Fifth Avenue, N.Y.C. 1968

DIANE ARBUS
REVELATIONS

JONATHAN CAPE

LONDON

Images from Diane Arbus's collage wall, including a number of pictures torn from the pages of newspapers, magazines, and books, several of her own rough prints, and a framed E. J. Bellocq photograph printed by Lee Friedlander *(center, at right)*.

Killed After Kidnaping Cop.

Self-portrait pregnant, N.Y.C. 1945

the way of the monkey and the
way of cat. The ... follows the
effortless way ... the mother
cat carries her kittens. the monkey
follows the ... hard
way, since the baby monkey has
to hang on to the mothers hair.
(Salvation by works and Salvation
in faith.)
            hindu — Watts. Chicago Revue

I am in an enormous estate while
gorgeous hotel which ... ...
but the fire is ... ...
that people are still allowed to
come and go freely. I can see the
fire, but smoke hangs thinly every
where especially around the
... It is eerily pretty. I
am in a hurry and I want to photog
most awfully. I go to our room
to get what I must save and I can
not find it whatever it is. My
grandmother is around, perhaps in the
next room. I do not know what I
am looking for, what I must save, how
soon the building will collapse, what
I must do, how long I may photo if
maybe I don't even have film or can
... my camera. I am constantly
... everyone is busy
... around but the
... golden ... like the
... I am fully
... I am not
... not yet
... whole

18 EAST 68 St.
1959

I am in an enormous ornate white gorgeous hotel which is on fire, doomed, but the fire is burning so slowly that people are still allowed to come and go freely. I can't see the fire but smoke hangs thinly everywhere especially around the lights. It is terribly pretty. I am in a hurry and I want to photograph most awfully. I go to our rooms to get what I must save and I cannot find it whatever it is. My grandmother is around, perhaps in the next room. I do not know what I am looking for, what I must save, how soon the building will collapse, what I must do, how long I may photograph. Maybe I don't even have film or can't find my camera. I am constantly interrupted. Everyone is busy and wandering around but it's quiet and a little slowed. The elevators are golden. It's like the sinking Titanic...I am filled with delight but anxious and confused and cannot get to the photographing. My whole life is there. It is a sort of calm but painfully blocked ecstasy like when a baby is coming and the attendants ask you to hold back because they aren't ready. I am almost overcome with delight but plagued by the interruptions of it. There are cupids carved in the ceilings. Perhaps I will be unable to photograph if I save anything including the camera and myself. I am strangely alone although people are all around. They keep disappearing. No one tells me what to do but I worry lest I am neglecting them or not doing something I am supposed to do. It is like an emergency in slow motion. I am in the eye of the storm.

—A DREAM FROM 1959 NOTEBOOK (NO. 1)

A pile of Diane Arbus notebooks including 1959 Notebook (No. 1)
open to first page of the dream transcribed above.

"...a thing is not seen because it is visible, but conversely, visible because it is seen..."

—PASSAGE UNDERLINED BY DIANE ARBUS IN HER COPY OF THE WORKS OF PLATO,

MODERN LIBRARY EDITION, 1928, PAGE 46

Room with lamp and light fixture, N.Y.C. 1944

Boy stepping off the curb, N.Y.C. circa 1956

Carroll Baker on screen in "Baby Doll" (with silhouette), N.Y.C. 1956

Lady in a tiara at a ball, N.Y.C. 1963

Female impersonators' dressing room, N.Y.C. 1958

The Backwards Man in his hotel room, N.Y.C. 1961

Woman on the street with her eyes closed, N.Y.C. 1956

42nd Street movie theater
audience, N.Y.C. 1958

Wax museum strangler, Coney Island, N.Y. 1960

Kiss from "Baby Doll," N.Y.C. 1956

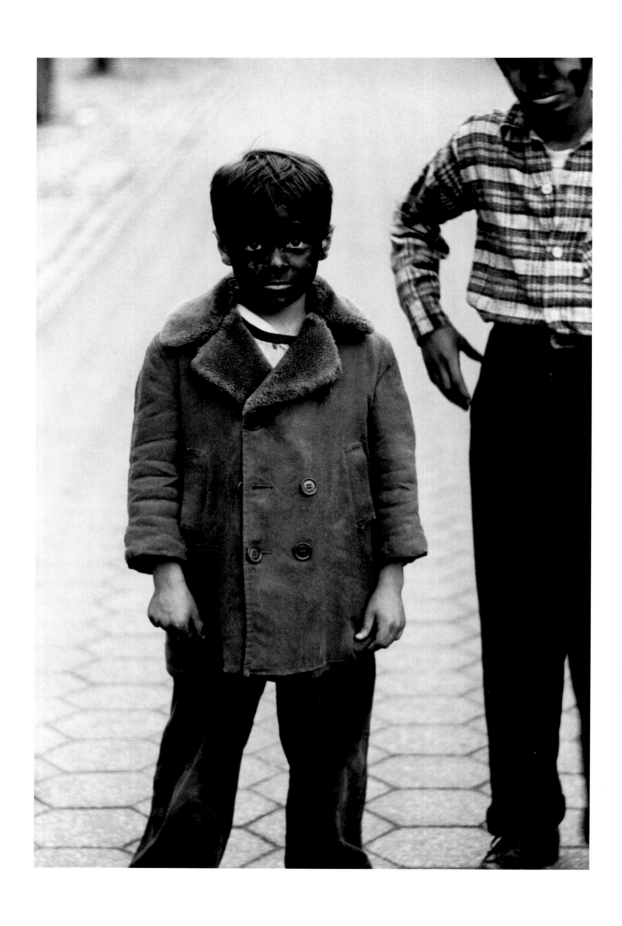

Kid in black-face with friend, N.Y.C. 1957

DIANE ARBUS
REVELATIONS

THE QUESTION OF BELIEF

SANDRA S. PHILLIPS

❖

A CHRONOLOGY

ELISABETH SUSSMAN AND DOON ARBUS

❖

IN THE DARKROOM

NEIL SELKIRK

❖

AFTERWORD

DOON ARBUS

❖

BIOGRAPHIES

JEFF L. ROSENHEIM

❖

The condition of photographing is maybe the condition of being

on the brink of conversion to anything...

—FROM A LETTER TO MARVIN ISRAEL, FEBRUARY 12, 1960

People on a bench, Central Park, N.Y.C. 1956*

Stripper with bare breasts sitting in her dressing room, Atlantic City, N.J. 1962

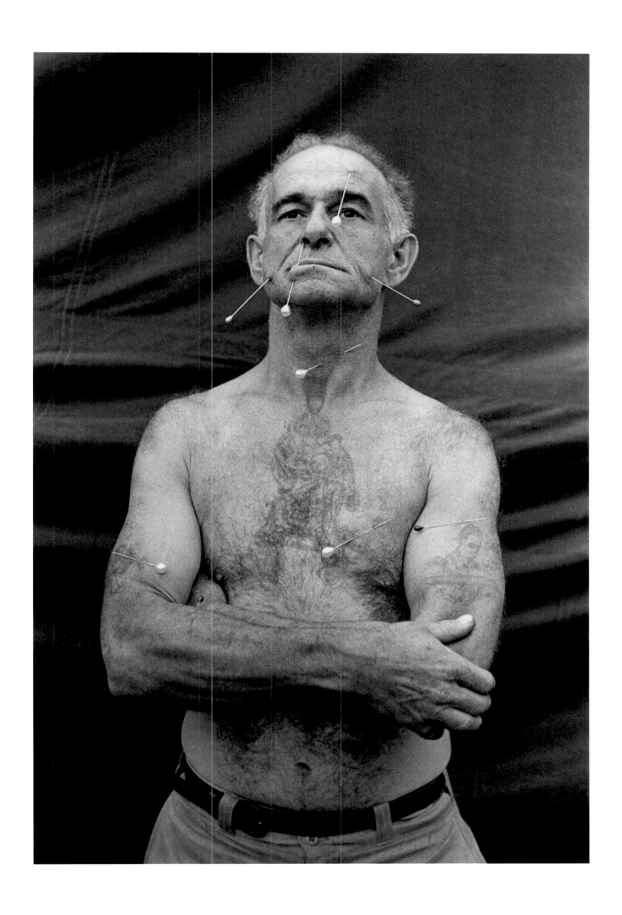

The Human Pincushion, Ronald C. Harrison, N.J. 1962

Couple on a pier, N.Y.C. 1963

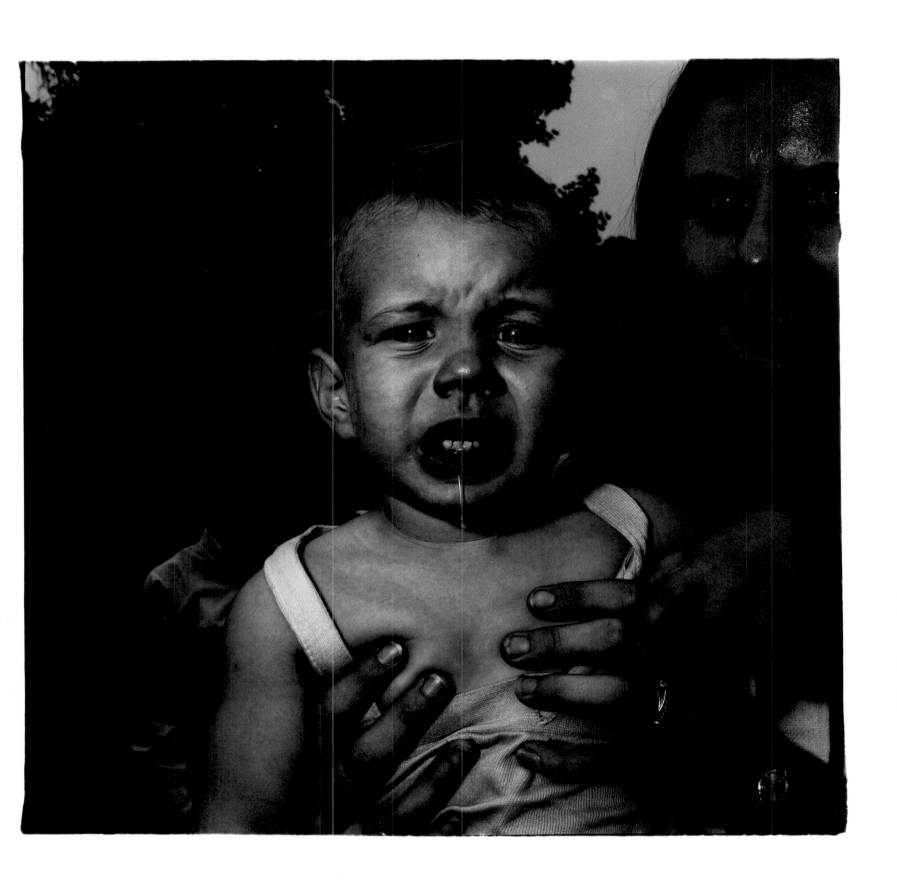

Mother holding her child, N.J. 1967

Patriotic young man with a flag, N.Y.C. 1967

Three Puerto Rican women, N.Y.C. 1963

The Junior Interstate Ballroom Dance Champions, Yonkers, N.Y. 1963

Diane Arbus

Plan for a Photographic Project

*

American Rites, Manners and Customs

I want to photograph the considerable ceremonies of our
present because we tend while living here and now to perceive only what is random and barren and formless about
it.While we regret that the present is not like the past
and despair of its ever becoming the future, its innumerable inscrutable habits lie in wait for their meaning.I
want to gather them,like somebody's grandmother putting
up preserves, because they will have been so beautiful.

There are the Ceremonies of Celebration (the Pageants,
the Festivals,the Feasts, the Conventions) and the Ceremonies of Competition (Contests,Games,Sports), the Ceremonies of Buying and Selling, of Gambling,of the Law and
the Show; the Ceremonies of Fame in which the Winners Win
and the Lucky are Chosen or Family Ceremonies or Gather-
ings (the Schools, the Clubs, the Meetings). Then there
are the Ceremonial Places (The Beauty Parlor , The Funeral
Parlor or, simply The Parlor) and Ceremonial Costumes
(what Waitresses wear, or Wrestlers), Ceremonies of the
Rich,like the Dog Show, and of the Middle Class,like
the Bridge Game.Or,for example: the Dancing Lesson, the
Graduation, the Testimonial Dinner, the Seance, the Gym-
nasium and the Picnic.And perhaps the Waiting Room,the
Factory,the Masquerade,the Rehearsal,the Initiation,the
Hotel Lobby and the Birthday Party.The etcetera.

I will write whatever is necessary for the further description and elucidation of these Rites and I will go
wherever I can to find them.

These are our symptoms and our monuments.I want simply
to save them,for what is ceremonious and curious and
commonplace will be legendary.

*

Project proposal for 1963 Guggenheim Foundation grant application.

Pin-up collection at a barber shop, N.Y.C. 1963

Girl with a cigar in Washington Square Park, N.Y.C. 1965

A widow in her bedroom, N.Y.C. 1963

Girl and boy, Washington Square Park, N.Y.C. 1965

A young man in curlers at home on West 20th Street, N.Y.C. 1966

Siamese twins in a
carnival tent, N.J. 1961

THE QUESTION OF BELIEF

BY SANDRA S. PHILLIPS

I really believe there are things which nobody would see unless I photographed them.[1]
—Diane Arbus

Diane Arbus's personal and distinctive photographic work is rooted in her sophisticated understanding of the relationship between photographer and subject. In a manner unique among her contemporaries, Arbus rendered the interaction between these two parties as a self-conscious and collaborative meeting. She found the people she photographed challenging and intriguing, and they were similarly interested in her. *For me the subject of the picture is always more important than the picture. And more complicated,*[2] she said, and Arbus's pictures evidence her deep investment in the people who inhabit them. The subjects stand often in the center of the frame; they are the focus of attention, as direct and frank as in a snapshot or a folk painting. Their posture is subordinate to the ineffable expression of who they are.

Arbus balanced this emotional investment in the subject with a documentary photographer's interest in recording the apparently incidental yet telling detail. She was fascinated by how pictures that were purportedly factual and objective could also register the intangible. Each element of the pictorial environment is deliberate and expressive of the place in which the subjects are depicted, and serves as a clue to better know them. The result is a body of work that strikes the observer with all the force of a personal encounter. Peter Bunnell, a former curator of photography at The Museum of Modern Art, noted, *It seems to me, what disturbs people more than the subjects of these pictures, is the intensity of their power to dominate us, to literally stop us in mid-life and demand we ask ourselves who we are.*[3]

While Arbus was interested in the individual people she photographed, she was also drawn to the more ephemeral and intuitive idea of belief and to the power of myth as a means of ascribing meaning to everyday existence. In an age and culture that prized rationalism and technology, Arbus was attuned to the ancient, folkloric, or talismanic aspects of contemporary life. She described some of her photographic subjects as follows: *These are...people who appear like metaphors somewhere further out than we do, beckoned, not driven, invented by belief, each the author and hero of a real dream by which our own courage and cunning are tested and tried; so that we may wonder all over again what is veritable and inevitable and possible and what it is to become whoever we may be.*[4] But the way her subjects evoke something beyond themselves was not the only remarkable aspect of her work; the sense of mystery extended to the medium itself: As she said, *There's a kind of magic power thing about the camera. You're carrying some slight magic which does something to* [the subject]. For Arbus, the camera possessed an ability to see things right, to trace a continuity with an ancient past, to reveal a mythological richness in the unexalted present.[5]

She was not a sentimentalist, nor was she isolated from the concerns of her contemporaries. In the 1967 *New Documents* show at The Museum of Modern Art, Arbus's only major museum exhibition during her lifetime, her work was shown alongside that of Garry Winogrand and Lee Friedlander. In retrospect, these three photographers may seem to have less in common than they did in 1967,

but they all participated in a culture in which photography's essential nature was being reconsidered, and in which the documentary approach was the chosen means for doing so. In the wall panel that served to introduce the work to the public, John Szarkowski, head of the Department of Photography, acknowledged the common heritage these artists had to their documentary predecessors of the 1930s: *In the past decade a new generation of photographers has directed the documentary approach toward more personal ends. Their aim has been not to reform life, but to know it. Their work betrays a sympathy—almost an affection—for the imperfections and the frailties of society.*[6]

Arbus knew the work of the two men whose photographs were exhibited with hers, but her approach was demonstrably different from theirs. The street work of Winogrand and Friedlander is less obviously composed than her photography and more engaged in the formal possibility of chance. Their photographs often play upon happenstance and the irony of finding what strange and marvelous conjunctions occur within the frame. Her photographs, however, are largely unconcerned with serendipity; rather, they are more deliberate descriptions of the people she photographed and her relationship to them as witness. Unlike most other documentary photographs of the period, her pictures depend on the subjects' active participation. She posed them or, rather, waited for them to pose themselves. She would often talk with them; sometimes she would visit their homes or return to photograph them after many years. Although she

also made portraits in the street, even single-frame, close-up pictures of strangers anonymously, in a great many cases she took a methodical approach to selecting the people she depicted: she sometimes found them through research and inquiry or looked for a kind of person she had already identified. As a consequence of this deliberateness, her photographs tend to be formally heirarchical and possess a gravitas not found in other work of the time.

When Szarkowski organized *New Documents*, he therefore introduced not a form but an approach. What characterized Arbus's work, he said, was the outlook she had toward her subjects: *The portraits of Diane Arbus show that all of us—the most ordinary and the most exotic of us—are on closer scrutiny remarkable. The honesty of her vision is of an order belonging only to those of truly generous spirit.*[7]

The origins of Diane Arbus's interests and direction can be found very early. The daughter of an upper-middle-class Jewish family that owned a Fifth Avenue clothing store, she attended Ethical Culture and Fieldston Schools. Beginning in high school and continuing throughout her life, she read seriously and even voraciously, and the literary work that interested her is a valuable record of her development.

The contents of her library suggest that she had an active interest in myth. She owned not only the volumes on Greek myths by Robert Graves but his book *The White Goddess,* his version of *The Golden Ass,* James Stephens's *The Crock of Gold,* James Frazer's seminal *The Golden Bough,* and J.R.R. Tolkien's *The Hobbit,* as well as a worn copy of

FAMILY AT EASTER, N.Y.C. 1956   WOMAN AND A HEADLESS DUMMY, N.Y.C. 1956*

Ovid's *Metamorphoses*. She also possessed works, probably acquired a little later, in which myth was examined for its psychological or philosophical implications and its relevance to contemporary society: Arbus had copies of Joseph Campbell's *The Hero with a Thousand Faces,* Sigmund Freud's *An Introduction to Psychoanalysis* and *The Psychopathology of Everyday Life;* C. G. Jung's *Modern Man in Search of a Soul;* and a number of Friedrich Nietzsche's works, including *Thus Spake Zarathustra.*[8]

Arbus became involved in photography around the time of her marriage to Allan Arbus in 1941, and though the greater part of her energies went toward their professional partnership in fashion photography, she simultaneously pursued her personal work. Before 1958, Arbus, who was working with a 35mm Nikon SLR, accepted the then prevailing notion that the negative was the field in which the artist could go hunting for the true picture by cropping closely and even deceptively for the desired image. Alexey Brodovitch, the legendary art editor for *Harper's Bazaar* (with whom Arbus briefly studied), had encouraged the technique of cropping the full frame in order to find the real picture within, and Lisette Model, Arbus's teacher and friend, often worked in this way. This practice both valorized the creative importance of the art editor and the photographer in retrospect and worked to impose a sense of immediacy, or of a privileged, almost private, view after the fact. In this way Arbus could transform a picture of a crowd into a kind of portraiture

of a single face. By about 1958, however, all evidence of cropping ceased, and Arbus thenceforth generally adhered to the full negative's larger field of vision, implicit evidence that the photograph was an unmediated document, an actual occurrence in real time. The intimacy Arbus once sought from cropping was now usually earned through a direct relationship with the subject.

By the mid-fifties she was photographing the crowds at Coney Island and people in Central Park or in the streets—subjects she shared with other New York photographers, such as William Klein, whose early pictures, grainy and aggressive, she knew.[9] Arbus's photographs of this period are more distanced than Klein's and more attentive to form. Yet she also stressed the film's grain, not as Klein did to suggest a sense of foreboding but to enhance the fabulous nature of what she found in the city: Boy stepping off the curb, N.Y.C. circa 1956 (p. 20), Woman on the street with her eyes closed, N.Y.C. 1956 (p. 25), another carrying a child like a ceremonial gift (Woman carrying a child in Central Park, N.Y.C. 1956, p. 230), and Fire Eater at a carnival, Palisades Park, N.J. 1956 (p. 7) are just a few examples.

At the same time Arbus was producing these pictures, she was also taking photographs in movie houses, portraying them as spangled dream palaces (Movie theater lobby, N.Y.C. 1958) or recording the flared beam of the projector over the hunched figures of ordinary people at the top of the balcony (42nd Street movie theater audience, N.Y.C. 1958, p. 26). Many of the movie theater pictures are details of

1959 Contact Sheet #668: An autopsy, and female impersonators backstage.

intimate or ironic moments: a close-up of a kiss (p. 29), or a picture of stilled clouds on-screen at a drive-in movie (p. 2). One photograph juxtaposes an erotic scene from the film *Baby Doll* with the shadowy profile of a man searching for a seat (p. 21). She was examining the relationship between the real and the fictional. The confrontation she posed between still photography and the moving image was part of her inquiry into the nature of photography itself: *It always seemed to me that photography tends to deal with facts whereas film tends to deal with fiction. The best example I know is when you go to the movies and you see two people in bed, you're willing to put aside the fact that you perfectly well know that there was a director and a cameraman and assorted lighting people all in that same room and the two people in bed weren't really alone. But when you look at a photograph you can never put that aside.*[10]

Arbus consciously worked to understand her craft and achieve her artistic vision. As noted earlier, she enrolled in the class for photography at the New School taught by Brodovitch, but found it generally unhelpful. She also educated herself by accumulating books and photographs.[11] The most useful and meaningful guidance came from Model, with whom Arbus studied between 1956 and 1957. Like Arbus, Model originally worked within the journalistic tradition, successfully publishing her work in magazines. By the time the two women met, however, Model had effectively ceased making photographs. Perhaps their shared interest in people who operated at the margins of society—dwarves, street people, costumed women—played a part in their

enduring friendship, one that continued long after Model was an active teaching catalyst for Arbus. Arbus attributed to Model the gradual realization of herself as a photographer: Model freed her to find her particular subject and define her own artistic voice. Arbus would later say, *My favorite thing is to go where I've never been,*[12] and *Nothing is ever the same as they said it was. It's what I've never seen before that I recognize.*[13]

Such determination to engage in the discovery of new territory provoked Arbus to think deeply about the relationship of author and subject. Embedded in the notebooks she kept in 1959 and 1960, among the lists of people she wanted to photograph and names of those who could help her find them, are pieces of texts that Arbus was reading, quotations from conversations with friends, as well as meditations, often elliptical, on the complicated and special contract between herself and the subject she chose: *Nothing human is alien to me. — Terence. To confess to someone is to implicate, involve them. — N[ancy Bellamy]. If we are all freaks the task is to become as much as possible the freak we are. — M[arvin Israel]. Vampires are a metaphor for the dependency of power. A murderer needs a victim...Freaks are a fairy tale for grownups. A metaphor which bleeds.*[14]

Arbus first appeared in print in July 1960, in an article for *Esquire* entitled "The Vertical Journey: Six Movements of a Moment Within the Heart of the City." She provided both pictures and text for the essay, although *Esquire* ultimately dispensed with her detailed descriptions of the people she photographed in favor of brief captions. The magazine was

WOMAN WITH A STUFFED DOG, N.Y.C. 1960   YOUNG MAN IN A PLAID COAT, N.Y.C. 1961

publishing a form of personalized journalism written essentially by novelists (Norman Mailer, Gay Talese, Tom Wolfe), soon to be called the New Journalism.[15] Arbus's essay included pictures of the usual figures found in the pages of popular magazines at that time—a young society woman who sponsored charity balls, a member of the Daughters of the American Revolution (D.A.R.)—but these photographs were accompanied by portraits of Hezekiah Trambles, who played "The Jungle Creep" at Hubert's Museum on Times Square (p. 147), and the midget actor Andrew Ratoucheff, who specialized in imitations of Marilyn Monroe and Maurice Chevalier. Arbus's notes for the project not only document the literary inspiration for her essay title, but also suggest that she already saw her subjects as characters in a larger, imaginative context: *Alice in Wonderland: I fell into it like Alice...The journey was vertical and dizzying like Alice's.*[16]

The first essay was followed by another on eccentrics—or, in her words, *singular people*—with pictures and text, entitled "The Full Circle" and published in *Harper's Bazaar* in November 1961.[17] *Infinity* magazine republished the article in February 1962 with a picture and accompanying text on "Miss Stormé de Larverie, The Lady Who Appears to Be a Gentleman" (p. 156), material that had been omitted in *Harper's Bazaar*. Arbus had begun to photograph female impersonators in their backstage dressing rooms about 1958 as a continuation of her interest in investigating the nature of identity. Arbus wrote that, *Stormé regards the transformation as a delicate art and has conscientiously experimented to*

perfect the cut, fit, shape, and style of her appearance as a man, without ever tampering with her nature as a woman, or trying to be what she is not. [As Stormé herself said,] *(If you have self-respect and respect for the human race you know that Nature is not a joke.) Her grocer thinks she is a man and her tailor knows she is a woman. She doesn't try to explain to strangers what she doesn't need to explain to friends, and many people who are uneasy about living in a Man's World or queasy about being in a Woman's, find her curious privilege a source of wisdom.* Stormé described herself as *slightly out of context and most at home there,* and she interested Arbus—like the other subjects of "The Full Circle"—precisely because she was a self-invention.[18]

These pictures of Stormé and of female impersonators backstage are central to Arbus's work. Since fairy tales and myth had always attracted Arbus, it was perhaps logical for her to seek, or to find, the real counterparts to the figures who so powerfully inhabit these stories.[19] She seems to have had a particularly deep interest in the hermaphrodite as a mythological ancestor to the modern transvestite and transsexual. In many ancient cultures (including that of ancient Greece), the hermaphroditic body was understood to be an ideal conjunction of two opposing forces in one divine being, a figure of great power. As such, the hermaphrodite often embodied the complex, multifaceted nature of human sexuality and, in Arbus's work, represented the complexity and interdependence of what was considered absolute and separate.[20] It is not surprising, then, that in Arbus's later accounts of the female impersonators she describes their

prosaic and quotidian lives with references to Greek mythology. Like a poet, Arbus understood not only the reverberation of irony but also the potency of metaphor, of coupling within the presumed reality of the photograph the fantastic and the actual, as if to prove the authenticity of both. Arbus's appreciation of the surprising coexistence or unification of opposites made the symbolism of the hermaphrodite especially poignant and rich for her:

Like the greatest living parody they shriek and bicker and wriggle and smile so splendidly that any real woman looks pale and dubious beside them. Sometimes they undergo a series of operations to make their noses smaller or their hips larger, their calves more delicate or their bosoms more convincing. The gradual metamorphosis of one sex to another is so [illegible] *that no one of either can fail to be stirred and dizzied and beguiled before them. For while it may not be as helpful as Prometheus, it is purely audacious to steal from Venus everything she holds most dear.*[21]

In September 1962 Arbus wrote to both Edward Steichen and Szarkowski at The Museum of Modern Art asking for references in her pursuit of a Guggenheim Foundation Fellowship grant. When she picked up her prints at the museum, Szarkowski, who had replaced Steichen as head of the Department of Photography, pulled out one of her most recent photographs, the image of the children, Junior Interstate Ballroom Dance Champions, Yonkers, N.Y. 1963 (p. 40). For Szarkowski, the picture recalled the work of August Sander, and he brought out the boxes of Sander

prints in order to show Arbus the breadth and seriousness of this photographer.

Sander's work was already known to Arbus, but this reminder must have clarified and stimulated her direction.[22] His quest, undertaken in the 1920s and 1930s, was to visualize the specific with reference to the typical, the particular within the larger ideology. Arbus was fascinated by the range of his photographic subjects, which encompassed the whole social spectrum—from peasant to landowner, industrial worker to high-level manager—and included small tradesmen and bourgeois shopkeepers, as well as artists, members of the intelligentsia, and social outcasts. Sander's great sympathy and respect for his subjects encouraged Arbus's own desire to explore the singularity of each person she photographed. Moreover, the range of his work confirmed the scope of her own ambition. No one else in her generation was able to make such personal use of Sander's sober and prescient work.

Privately, Arbus compared her photographic approach to gathering a *butterfly collection*, a metaphor that evokes both the evanescent quality of photography and its scientific objectivity.[23] She was interested in finding and revealing the defining characteristics of her subjects. As her friend Marvin Israel noted, *She was entranced by differences, the minutest variations. That from the beginning nothing, no two rooms, no two beds, no two bodies or any parts of them were ever the same. Finding those differences thrilled her, from the most*

GIRL ON A STOOP WITH BABY, N.Y.C. 1962

JACK DRACULA, THE MARKED MAN, N.Y.C. 1961

glaring ones like a giant to the smallest ones that just barely make someone unique.[24] Arbus herself would later say that *nothing is ever alike. The best thing is the difference. I get to keep what nobody needs.*[25] From the beginning it is clear that she was looking not for a typology, but for varieties of experience.

What distinguished Arbus's work from Sander's and that of her contemporaries was her intense interest in the way her subjects saw themselves and the mutability of their person-ae. As she noted, *Everybody has this thing where they need to look one way but they come out looking another way and that's what people observe. You see someone on the street and essentially what you notice about them is the flaw...Our whole guise is like giving a sign to the world to think of us in a certain way, but there's a point between what you want people to know about you and what you can't help people knowing about you. And that has to do with what I've always called the gap between intention and effect.*[26] The pre-sentation of the gap itself is a defining aspect of her work.

This phenomenon is visible in many of her photographs: A Jewish giant at home with his parents in the Bronx, N.Y. 1970 (p. 300) is closely related to A family one evening in a nudist camp, Pa. 1965 (p. 295); A family on their lawn one Sunday in Westchester, N.Y. 1968 (p. 329) to A young Brooklyn family going for a Sunday outing, N.Y.C. 1966 (p. 8). Often her subjects are accompanied by signs or symbols of their identities: the trophy won by the junior dance champions (p. 40), the grenade held by the boy (p. 104). In other pictures the self-image is implied

rather than manifested in an object, as in Arbus's portrait of the nudist couple posed like Albrecht Dürer's *Adam and Eve* (p. 118). A comparison of this image with Sander's photo-graph of a middle-aged, portly landowner couple reveals the kinship between these two artists. Both couples address the viewer directly; both are planted firmly in the center of the picture. And, in both pictures there are telling, particular details that point to the subjects' complexity and ideals: the rose held gracefully by the woman in the Sander photo-graph, or the pack of cigarettes carried by Arbus's male nudist.[27] The subjects' vision of themselves is part of the objective record of what the camera documents.

Arbus's interest in documenting the role of belief and rit-ual in everyday activity informs her 1963 grant application to the Guggenheim Foundation, in which she proposes to photograph "American Rites, Manners and Customs":

I want to photograph the considerable ceremonies of our present because we tend while living here and now to perceive only what is random and barren and formless about it. While we regret that the present is not like the past and despair of its ever becoming the future, its innumerable inscrutable habits lie in wait for their meaning...These are our symptoms and our monuments. I want simply to save them, for what is ceremonial and curious and com-monplace will be legendary.[28]

It is Arbus's great gift that she did not romanticize her subjects once she found them, or, more accurately, once she found her subjects she acknowledged their complexity. For

TWO FEMALE IMPERSONATORS, N.Y.C. 1961

GIRL AND GOVERNESS WITH BABY CARRIAGE, N.Y.C. 1962   MISS VENICE BEACH, VENICE, CAL. 1962

instance, according to Lee Friedlander Arbus was fascinated by a figure known as Moondog (p. 157), a blind street person who dressed in a Woton-like costume and could be seen on street corners near The Museum of Modern Art. A compelling and strangely insightful figure, he claimed to be the son of a Protestant minister, and his monologues, which Arbus recorded in her notebooks, revealed a canny sense of the politics of madness and the palpability of belief. Arbus wrote in a letter to Marvin Israel: *Moondog's name is Louis, and he is not especially eccentric but I had never before seen a blind person at length, and it is remarkably like being in someone else's dream in which the most definitive act you can perform would be to disappear. He lives in an atmosphere as dense and separate as an island with its own sea, so he is more autonomous and vulnerable than anyone, and the world is rendered into shadows and smells and sound as though it was being remembered even as it acts...Moondog's faith is other than ours. We believe in the invisible and what he believes in is the visible.*[29]

While Arbus's thematic concerns remain more or less constant, her work moves gradually from formal simplicity and diffuse lighting to heightened detail and greater contrast. This aesthetic move produced an apparently more objective photograph yet one which, paradoxically, introduces greater ambiguity. As she wrote in 1971, *A photograph is a secret about a secret. The more it tells you the less you know.*[30] In Identical twins, Roselle, N.J. 1967 (p. 265), she showed the bobby pins and unruly hair and paint-splattered ground on which the two girls stood. They appear as a single being,

half aloof, half engaged; or in photographing the Mexican dwarf in his hotel room (p. 66), she observed his hat, which emphasizes his nakedness, draped delicately with a towel, and recorded his kind regard, implicating our own selves as viewers when we look at the picture.

A comparative examination of two other photographs reveals a transformation from her earlier pictures to her later, more classical documentary work. In Headless man, N.Y.C. 1961 (p. 158), a male figure is seated on a chair, his vigorous, torqued body clothed in a white undershirt. Occupying the space where his head should be is an evocative, bird-like sculpture, an unnatural appendage that gives him the appearance of an Egyptian god. Arbus framed the picture to show the subject at a distance, enveloped in a half-light. It is an image of wonder, found in a cheap sideshow, the details unspecified.

The other picture, Naked man being a woman, N.Y.C. 1968 (p. 98), shows a man in what is most likely his own room—the trash underneath the bed, the discarded shoes, the hot plate. But he has parted the curtains to his bed as though revealing a mystery at once theatrical and divine, and poses with impenetrable self-consciousness, genitals concealed between his thighs as the Venus Anadyomene who sprang from the foam of the sea. Even his feet are placed like those in Botticelli's *Birth of Venus*. Arbus's flash accentuates the supple body, its extraordinary beauty, and the provocative pose with cocked hip—a gesture that also recalls antiquity and has long connoted sexual readiness.

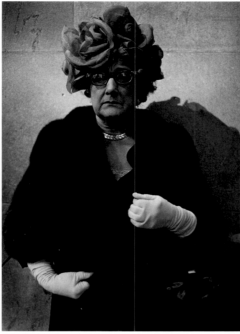

WOMAN WITH WHITE GLOVES, N.Y.C. 1963   NORMAN MAILER AT HOME, BROOKLYN, N.Y. 1963

The man's face, painted like that of a woman, is strangely remote. The precision and apparent artlessness of this picture is characteristic of Arbus's later work.

Some of the change that occurred between Headless man, N.Y.C. 1961 (p. 158), and Naked man being a woman, N.Y.C. 1968 (p. 98), can be attributed to a change in the materials and equipment Arbus chose to use. In 1962 she relinquished the 35mm Nikon SLR in favor of a 2¼ twin-lens reflex camera (she used a Rolleiflex and, later, a Mamiyaflex), which generates a larger negative and thus a sharper, more precise image. Arbus said that she changed cameras because she felt that the pictures produced with the 35mm camera were not particular enough: *In the beginning of photographing I used to make very grainy things. I'd be fascinated by what the grain did because it would make a kind of tapestry of all these little dots and everything would be translated into this medium of dots. Skin would be the same as water would be the same as sky and you were dealing mostly in dark and light, not so much in flesh and blood.*[31] A larger camera provided more clarity, and also more light: it was as though the pictures were freed from obscurity.

The 2¼ camera lent itself to a more direct relationship with the subject of the picture. The Nikon can be passed to the eye in an easy, swift balletic movement that permits the photographer to seize a picture and disengage quickly from the subject. Cartier-Bresson, who really established this practice, called the resulting photographs "images à la sauvette" (pictures on the run or on the fly), later translated

into English as "the decisive moment." This strategy of picture-making made chance and movement aesthetic features, so that finding the picture in the contact sheet became an important step, perhaps even the most important. Such agility is really not possible with the bulkier, and hence more obvious, 2¼ camera, held at waist level where the photographer must still the camera and look down into it. As a result, the making of the picture becomes a deliberate process that requires the subject's cooperation and participation.[32] Equally significant, her Rolleiflex, which was the wide-angle model, tended to isolate the center and wrap the surrounding environment in a particular, slightly exaggerated perspective. This visual effect served to emphasize the psychological component of the subject and its imagined quality. Arbus later favored the 2¼ Mamiyaflex, for which she apparently did not use a wide-angle lens.[33]

She was very aware of the photographer's ambiguous relationship with, and responsibility to, the subject, and she recognized that her intense emotional investment in her subjects had to be moderated by deliberation and dispassion. According to Arbus, *The process itself has a kind of exactitude, a kind of scrutiny that we're not normally subject to. I mean that we don't subject each other to. We're nicer to each other than the intervention of the camera is going to make us. It's a little bit cold, a little bit harsh.*[34] Or as she wrote on another occasion, *I think it does, a little, hurt to be photographed.*[35] Arbus's understanding of the productive tension between empathy and critical distance in her work represents almost a theoretical

A PUERTO RICAN HOUSEWIFE, N.Y.C. 1963

MAN FROM WORLD WAR ZERO AND HIS WIFE, N.J. 1964   REPUBLICAN RALLY, MAD

gloss on the nature of photography itself: *Now I don't mean to say that all photographs have to be mean. Sometimes they show something really nicer in fact than what you felt, or oddly different. But in a way this scrutiny has to do with not evading facts, not evading what it really looks like.*[36]

In the mid-sixties a portable strobe called the Mighty Light came on the market, and photographers working outside, like Friedlander, often used it to see into the shadows.[37] Arbus seems to have been struck by the palpable beauty of artificial light and the additional detail and clarity it provided. When she made Woman with her baby monkey, N.J. 1971 (p. 217), she described her use of flash as an aesthetic choice, but she probably also wished to recall the common symbolic nature of family snapshots, which became widespread following the introduction of the Kodak Instamatic with its built-in flash in 1963.[38] It was the factuality of photography rather than its illusionism (or the two working in concert) that interested her.

As early as 1965 she also began to print her pictures with irregular black borders that showed the complete, uncropped negative. The borders called attention to the fact that the print is an image on a two-dimensional sheet of paper rather than an "objective," window-like view onto the subject. This in combination with the use of flash helped to assert the picture as a real, tactile object made by someone, an expression of someone's point of view. For the *New Documents* exhibition, Arbus was careful to present her prints so as to reveal these borders. The presence of the

borders underscores the complexity of the transaction between subject, photographer, and viewer.[39]

Arbus's artistic embrace of ambiguity and cultural conflict, and her unvarnished presentation of the figures that represent them, presaged many of the cultural changes wrought by the generation of the sixties. This generation challenged nearly all the dominant assumptions of the preceding one: its materialism, its optimism, its ardent capitalism, its strident conformism, its bravado. Arbus's pictures find strength and the possibility of poetry in the opposite, but without accepting the convictions of the younger generation. For example, Arbus's photograph of a peace march with its tiny cluster of figures in cloaks bearing signs, gathered on the horizon like a small troupe of medieval players, illustrates the absurd and hopeless theater of their effort (p. 161). The swan that floats in the moat in Disneyland (p. 288), the facade of the house on the hill (p. 344), even the comical rocks moving on wheels (p. 248) seem as strange and political as the man with the dirty raincoat holding his hat to his chest, whose cause is not clear but who nevertheless possesses a religious gravity (p. 303). Arbus felt no need, as Richard Avedon and others had done, to photograph the figures of power that had embroiled America in enterprises as troubling as the Vietnam War. Her means were more indirect and allusive. As Szarkowski observed in 1978, *For most Americans the meaning of the Vietnam War was not political, or military, or even ethical, but psychological. It brought us to a sudden, unam-*

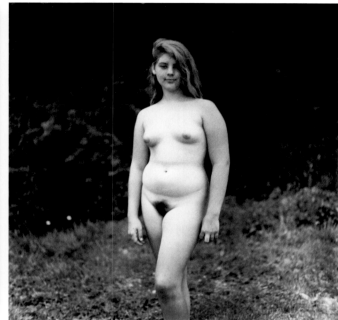

DANCING COUPLE, N.Y.C. 1965 A YOUNG GIRL AT A NUDIST CAMP, PA. 1965

biguous knowledge of moral frailty and failure. The photographs that best memorialize the shock of that new knowledge were perhaps made halfway around the world, by Diane Arbus.[40]

The clear and psychologically resonant pictures that constiture Arbus's later work were made at a time when the tradition of documentary photography was being examined and reevaluated. After the heroic period of the 1930s—when the moral authority of the witness could not be questioned, nor the intrinsic value of the subject or cause—the pictures made by the generation that followed assumed more ironic, personal, or even formal meanings.

The major place for sustained investigation of documentary photography was The Museum of Modern Art, New York. Two exhibitions organized by Szarkowski for the museum demonstrate his research into the material of photography itself. In preparing *The Picture Story*, a 1965 show that examined the relationship between caption and picture, Szarkowski was reminded that photographs did not always mean what they implied, and that a representation of an idea or a position was often ambiguous and more often imposed on a mute and rather elastic still image. For example, he came to realize that Dorothea Lange's picture *End of an Era* was not made to reveal class distinction, nor was Cartier-Bresson's picture of boys playing in ruins in Spain a depiction of the Spanish Civil War.[41] *The Picture Story* was preceded by *The Photographer's Eye*, an exhibition in which he tried to distinguish the basic constructs that applied to photography alone, without the encumbrance of

words or context. Here, he included the widest possible range of photography and commingled the work of acknowledged masters of the medium with pictures by amateurs or local practitioners. On the catalogue cover he reproduced a picture that resembled the work of Walker Evans, but was in fact made by an anonymous master. This kind of rigorous rethinking and democratic reordering of the journalistic system—in which photography was part of an armature of text and imagery orchestrated by an editorial staff—was new and liberating. It also acknowledged an aesthetic shift. Szarkowski intended the exhibition to serve as an inquiry into the nature of the medium: how it worked and where meaning might reside.[42]

Arbus was very much a part of this new engagement with documentary photography and of the renewed interest in vernacular photographs, which were often regarded as examples of a purity of content and form. In both these pursuits Evans was a central figure and an important predecessor. In the still-emerging field of photography made for expressive purposes, Evans was a defender of the non-arty and the unself-conscious, of rendering the subject over the author. He was the last remaining antagonist to Stieglitz, who in Evans's view possessed a *veritably screaming aestheticism, his personal artiness veered many young camera artists to the straight documentary style.*[43] While Evans repudiated Stieglitz's insistence on the artist's presence in the picture and asserted a more distanced approach, he did not mean to imply that the subject had less connection to the author's imaginative per-

YOUNG COUPLE ON A BENCH, N.Y.C. 1965   WOMAN WITH A BEEHIVE HAIRDO, N.Y.C. 1965   COUPLE IN BED, N.Y.C. 1966

sonality.[44] Arbus would have been familiar with the pictures Evans made with a concealed camera in the subways, photographs that Marvin Israel published while art director of *Harper's Bazaar*. They are pictures of staring, without the subject's knowledge or consent: unlike Arbus's work, they are aloof. Evans aspired to a photography without seeming affect, where the full attention of the viewer was directed toward the subject, rather than toward the photographer's report of that encounter. For Arbus, the objective documentary nature of the photograph could not be disentangled from the experience of the personal encounter.

In 1970, Szarkowski invited Arbus to help him work on an exhibition called *From the Picture Press*, which explored the ways *news photography…describes to us over and over again, with subtle but constant variations, the few simple and enduring human issues with which this medium has learned to cope — ceremonies, winners, losers, good news, alarums and conundrums, confrontations and disasters.*[45] He also wrote that the pictures *are (or seem) unimpeachably frank; they have redefined prior standards of privacy and the privilege of anonymity; they deal not with the intellectual significance of facts, but with their emotional content; they have directed journalism toward a subjective and intensely human focus. As images, the photographs are shockingly direct, mysteriously elliptical, and fragmentary, reproducing the texture and flavor of experience without explaining its meaning.*[46]

Working on this exhibition not only permitted Arbus to pursue her interest in discovering the ritualistic aspect of everyday life but also drew her into a deeper examination of the folkloric in photography itself. Just as the content of ritual impressed its meaning on her, so also she found the

unartful, impersonal, content-driven photograph a useful and meaningful artifact. Arbus had already compiled a thorough list of photographs made only for recording information or bearing witness. The 1962 list begins, *Daily News; Coney Island or Bowery; Wedding; Baby; Family; Graduation; Theatrical; Spirit.*[47] The lists that Arbus presented to Szarkowski as part of her research on *From the Picture Press* resonate with her own artistic interests and seem almost lifted from her notes to herself: *Subjects: Accident, grief, pain, crashes, death of pet animals…Contests, Winners, crying or otherwise, Beauty, Losers, Pie eating, lottery, awards, medals, Heroes.*[48]

She wrote to her daughter Amy in 1970, saying, *I have just had what I think is a realization about the form of the show [From the Picture Press] which is that it should be all anonymous photographs, no great events or famous personalities.*

Here, Arbus's interests coincided with renewed curiosity about unknown or little seen work, sometimes by naïve or unsophisticated photographers. Friedlander discovered the portraits of prostitutes by E. J. Bellocq, a journeyman photographer in New Orleans, and Avedon assisted in the publication of the forgotten work of Jacques-Henri Lartigue (p. 219). Arbus herself found James Vanderzee, a studio photographer still working in Harlem. Szarkowski also organized exhibitions of older European documentary photographers whose work was not well known or currently available in the United States. One of these was the Transylvanian artist Brassaï, whose work Arbus admired and acknowledged: *He taught me something terrific about obscurity, you know, that obscurity could be as thrilling as clarity, which for a long time I didn't realize, because I had been moving more and more towards*

WOMAN IN A TURBAN, N.Y.C. 1966   FAMILY OF THREE, BEAUFORT COUNTY, S.C. 1968

clarity for years.[49] Arbus would eventually return to this obscurity in her own work: *Lately I've been struck with how I really love what you can't see in a photograph. An actual physical darkness and it's very thrilling for me to see darkness again.*[50]

In the course of her work on *From the Picture Press*, Arbus's most revealing discovery was of the archive of Weegee, the ultimate naïf. In 1970 she wrote to Allan Arbus and Mariclare Costello in Los Angeles about seeing the full range of this artist's work:

The best thing this past week was the discovery of ALL Weegee's work in the house of an old lady he lived with, a charming lady. We went through about 4,000 prints of which I chose 383, some for the news show, some for a Weegee show which seems inevitable to me. He was SO good when he was good. Extraordinary! I came across a photograph of Lisette at about my age. Wish you could see 'em. Such wild dynamics make everybody [else] *look like an academician. People pushing, shoving, screaming, extraneous events thrust into the main one.*[51]

Arbus's enthusiasm was that of one mature artist for another, and her response to Weegee's energy and his directness—which was populist and ultimately humanist—demonstrates a fellow feeling. Though the work of Arbus and Weegee may appear unrelated, he was in fact very relevant to her own interests. He was the first to discover the real beauty of flash, the poetry of revealed, casual detail in brilliant light. He also acknowledged the beauty of darkness, not only graphically but metaphorically. Weegee's photographs record both the mystery and the banality of death and suffering. Implicit in the work of both Arbus and Weegee is an understanding, too, that the

relationship between subject and author must be at once intimate and detached. Photography, as a medium often credited with producing a "factual" or "objective" record of the world, paradoxically, in Arbus's work, reveals what is otherwise invisible: the mythic or ritualistic aspects of everyday life. Arbus's pictures challenged the presumed objectivity of the "documentary," the presumption that the author could be detached from the subject.

Arbus's livelihood as a photographer-artist, like that of most of her colleagues, had been earned working for magazines. By 1968 or the following year, it must have become evident to her that she would need other sources of income beyond journalism to sustain herself. Although her photographs continued to appear in *Harper's Bazaar, Esquire,* and elsewhere, her published work declined in volume as those magazines became less imaginative and more politically conservative. The last major grant she received was a second Guggenheim award in 1966. She began to teach at Parsons, and at Cooper Union, and later gave a master class at her home in Westbeth.

At the same time, Arbus seemed restless with her materials, anxious—with good cause, since most photographic suppliers, Kodak preeminent among them, were in the process of lowering their standards on photographic materials in order to cut costs. She devoted much concern to finding film as well as paper with sufficient silver quantity, most of which was produced in Europe. She wrote about losing her fondness for flash, about changing the atmosphere of her pictures. In 1970 Arbus began experimenting with a new 6x7 Pentax. Just as her decision to change to the

Rolleiflex had coincided with her decision to reevaluate the way she made pictures, she sought and wrestled with the challenge of this new camera, as evidenced in pictures such as A woman passing, 1971 (p. 351). Arbus described working with the Pentax in a letter to Allan:

I...must try all sorts of things, mainly sharpness at slow speeds. It makes an enormous difference in the pictures. Of course they aren't very good. It's hard to get used to a new shape. It looks like a greater degree of reality and I haven't yet learned how to use that. A little like when I switched from Nikon to Rollei. I wake at night with the excitement of it, or alternately with dread and confusion and worry and abhorrence...What it could do is make the pictures more narrative and temporal, less fixed and single and complete and isolated, more dynamics, more things happening. I'd like that. The difference knocks me out...This marvelous shape (exactly 11x14, 8x10 proportions) and clarity, focusing is fun. And turning it for horizontal or vertical is delightful, like any 35, just heavier.[52]

Arbus also continued to challenge herself with experimental subjects and situations. She wrote to Peter Crookston, an editor in London, about her interest in R. D. Laing, the innovative English psychiatrist who had a special appreciation of the power and insight of psychotic people: *He seems so extraordinary in his knowledge, his empathy for madness, that it suddenly seemed he would be the most perfect guide.*[53] She also mentioned sexologists who were eager to be of help to her, though she admitted that they, while intriguing, gave her *a funny eerie sense of mutual exploitation which I don't like...I want to do some-*

thing unfathomable, like the family.[54] In conjunction with an assignment to photograph love for Time-Life she mentioned *an incredible heart-stopping handicapped couple...he is retarded and terribly tall and thin and she is radiant, maybe 3½ ft. tall with curly red hair like Maureen O'Hara. I saw them dancing at a dance for handicapped people. Never saw anything like that. I danced with a sixty year old man who was very shy and spoke like a nine year old. He sells Good Humors in the summer.*[55]

In keeping with her long-standing interest in subcultures and the rituals of self-contained miniature societies— Masons, baton twirling clubs, female impersonators, gangs, prisons, old age homes, singles clubs, families, nudists, and other utopias—she began photographing at a home for the mentally retarded around 1969. As always, Arbus's approach was to be attentive to their individuality. In a letter to Allan she wrote, *It's the first time I've encountered a subject where the multiplicity is the thing. I mean I'm not just looking for the BEST picture of them. I want to do lots...I really adore them.*[56] And she wrote to her daughter Amy, then fifteen, *They are the strangest combination of grownup and child I have ever seen...I think you'd like them.*[57]

While undertaking this project, she began to explore a new quality in her pictures: *I am plagued by mysterious technical problems, like trying to make my sharp pictures blurred but not too much so. Having great trouble balancing strobe and daylight when used together especially on gray days but sometimes this nutty method seems just beautiful to me. And very different. It is a little agonous, a thou-*

ORIGINAL 1969 UNTITLED CONTACT SHEET #6746, INCLUDING IMAGES POSTHUMOUSLY TITLED AS FOLLOWS *(FROM LEFT, TOP TO BOTTOM): UNTITLED (28) (CLOWN MASK);* UNTITLED (31) *(CLOWN SUIT AND COAT);* UNTITLED (27) *(MASKED COAT WITH CROWD);* UNTITLED (26) *(SCARECROW);* UNTITLED (24) *(TWO IN GRASS) (NOT VISIBLE, CENTER STRIP, SECOND FROM TOP);* UNTITLED (33) *(PUMPKIN);* UNTITLED (20) *(CLOWN HAT);* AND UNTITLED (3) *(GHOST).*

sand misses but when it all of a sudden works, I recognize it is what I wanted without precisely knowing I wanted anything. I am like someone who gets excellent glasses because of a slight defect in eyesight and puts Vaseline on them to make it look like he normally sees. It doesn't seem sensible but somehow I think it's right.[58] In a later letter to Allan, she wrote, *I took the most terrific pictures, the ones at Halloween...of the retarded women...FINALLY what I've been searching for...I...have discovered sunlight, late afternoon early winter sunlight...In general I seem to have perverted your brilliant technique all the way round, bending it over backwards you might say until it's JUST like snapshots but better. I think it's going to be marvelous...They are so lyric and tender and pretty.*[59]

Another project that absorbed Arbus from 1969 to 1971 was the limited edition portfolio, also called *A box of ten photographs*, on which she began work in late 1969. The portfolio was intended to present her work as an artist in the manner of the special print editions offered by new artists' presses such as Crown Point and Universal Limited Art Editions (ULAE). This group of pictures and its presentation was a very conscious statement of what she stood for, and how she regarded her own photography. The pictures range from the relatively early ones of the nudists in their summer home (p. 353) and Xmas tree in a living room in Levittown, L.I. (p. 92), both of 1963; through the now iconic Identical twins, Roselle, N.J. 1967 (p. 265) and the Westchester couple sunning themselves on their lawn (p. 329); to the later pictures of the Jewish giant (p. 300), the Mexican dwarf in his hotel room (above), and The

King and Queen of a Senior Citizens' Dance, N.Y.C. (p. 247), all of 1970. There is clearly an attempt to be representative of the general idea, the larger plan behind her work. There is also a significant stylistic range, from the graceful daylight in the picture of the older couple in the nudist camp, to the later picture of the elderly king and queen, whom she photographed with sharp flash. She included Xmas tree, a work without human subjects.

The prints for this portfolio were selected three years after the *New Documents* exhibition, before there was thought of another show. But the pictures constituted a kind of exhibition in and of themselves, to be examined one at a time rather than all at once. From her letters we know that the idea of a clear box was very important; it was to serve as both a container and a display case, allowing the owner to reorder and display the pictures easily. Just as she had wanted the black border of the print to show in the *New Documents* exhibition, here she wished to exhibit the entire print as it appeared on the photographic paper.[60]

Most of the pictures in the portfolio either depict families or refer to the family. Even the corner of the cellophane-looking room in Levittown is made by peering over the two outstretched arms of a family armchair, posed like the trousered knees of the empty chair in the picture of the Jewish giant. The idea of the family album was a private but expressive metaphor for her.[61] As in a family album, each member is part of the larger group: they are related, perhaps even tolerated, and harmony may be rare and perhaps even

C. 1971 NEW YORK SKYLINE IN A LOBBY, ST. PETERSBURG, FLA. 1971 WOMAN IN A FLOPPY HAT, N.Y.C. 1971

uninteresting. But they are all considered with the same intelligent and human regard. She photographed the Jewish giant as a mythic figure, enclosed in a modest Bronx living room, an unconventional member of an otherwise conventional family: *I know a Jewish giant who lives in Washington Heights or the Bronx with his little parents. He is tragic with a curious bitter somewhat stupid wit. The parents are orthodox and repressive and classic and disapprove of his carnival career...They are a truly metaphorical family. When he stands with his arms around each he looks like he would gladly crush them. They fight terribly in an utterly typical fashion which seems only exaggerated by their tragedy...Arrogant, anguished, even silly.*[62]

In February 1971 Arbus wrote Szarkowski to ask him to serve as a reference for the Ingram Merrill Foundation and enclosed her proposal for a new project called *The Quiet Minorities*: *The sign for a minority is the Difference. Those of birth, accident, choice, belief, predilection, inertia. (Some are partial and temporary, others irrevocable...) Every difference is a Likeness too...Not to ignore them, not to lump them all together, but to watch them, to take notice, to pay attention.*

Because it is so compelling, thoughtful, and undeniably personal, and perhaps because it reflects not only the uncertain times in which she lived but the larger uncertainties of late modernism, Arbus's work has served to erase the boundaries that once separated the presumed "higher arts" from the more accessible one of photography, and to open the discourse between expression and form. In the chaotic time in which her work achieved greatness, minimalism, pop, and

other avant-garde movements were highly prized and much emulated. The preeminent mode of creative expression was considered by many to be art that was assertive, even arrogant, and suspicious of content beyond the practical understanding of form. In hindsight, the alternative aesthetic voice of Eva Hesse, the imaginative work of Louise Bourgeois, and the mythologies of Arbus now appear among the most sophisticated work of the time and continue to speak to artistic practice today.

Arbus's particular contribution as an artist was not in what kinds of people she approached to photograph, but in what she was able to derive from the experience. Her devotion to the principles of the art she practiced—without deference to any extraneous social or political agenda—has produced a body of work that is often shocking in its purity, in its bold commitment to the celebration of things as they are. Her refusal to patronize the people she photographed, her acceptance of the challenge of the encounter constitutes a deep and abiding humanism.[63]

Szarkowski acknowledged Arbus's originality and courage in the pursuit of her art at her 1972 retrospective: *Arbus knew that honesty is not a gift, endowed by native naiveté, nor a matter of style, or politics, or philosophy. She knew rather that it is a reward bestowed for bravery in the face of the truth. Those who have been news reporters, and have been required by their role to ask the unforgivable question, know the sense of relief with which one averts one's eyes, once perfunctory duty is done. Arbus did not avert her eyes.*[64]

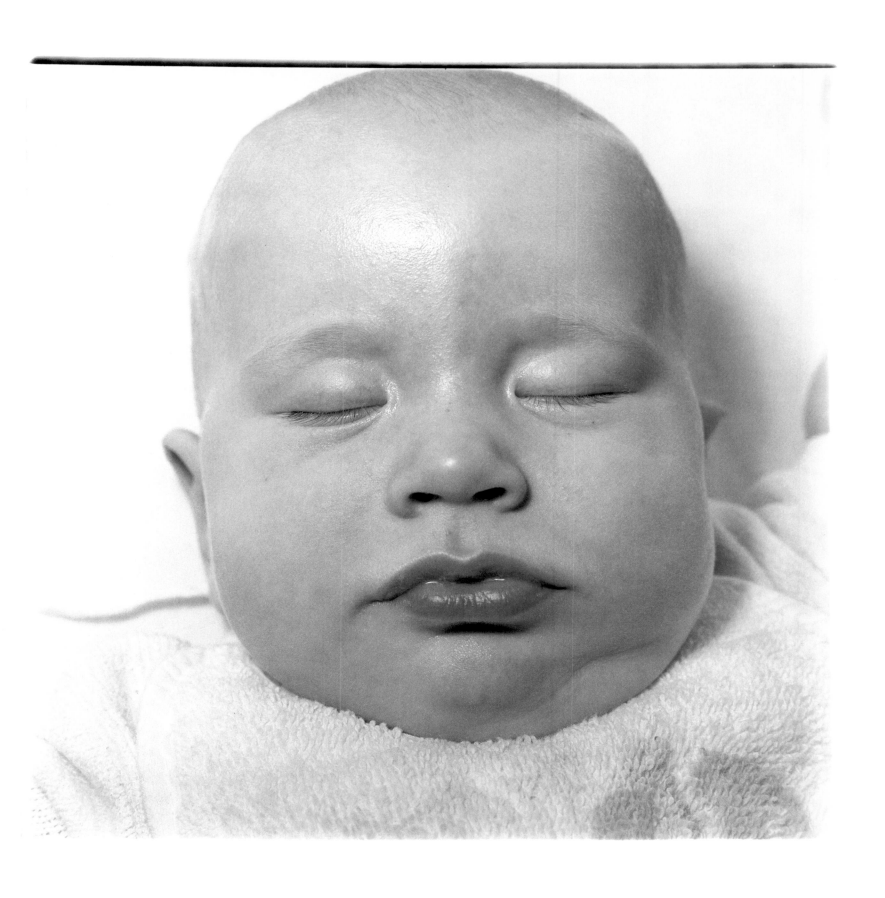

A very young baby, N.Y.C. 1968

There are and have been and will be an infinite number of things
on earth. Individuals all different, all wanting different things, all knowing
different things, all loving different things, all looking different.
Everything that has been on earth has been different from any other thing.
That is what I love: the differentness, the uniqueness of all things
and the importance of life...I see something that <u>seems</u> wonderful;
I see the divineness in ordinary things.

—November 28, 1939, paper on Plato, senior English seminar, Fieldston School

Two ladies walking in Central Park, N.Y.C. 1963

A young waitress at a nudist camp, N.J. 1963

Young man on a sofa, N.Y.C. 1966

Woman in a mink coat, N.Y.C. 1966

Two friends at home, N.Y.C. 1965

Man and a boy on a bench in Central Park, N.Y.C. 1962

Blonde girl with shiny lipstick, N.Y.C. 1967

A lobby in a building, N.Y.C. 1966

Young man and his pregnant wife in Washington Square Park, N.Y.C. 1965

We stand on a precipice, then before a chasm, and as we wait
it becomes higher, wider, deeper, but I am crazy enough to think it doesn't matter
which way we leap because when we leap we will have learned to fly.
Is that blasphemy or faith?

—FROM A POSTCARD TO MARVIN ISRAEL, DECEMBER 27, 1959

Bishop by the sea, Santa Barbara, Cal. 1964

Transvestite showing cleavage, N.Y.C. 1966

Santas at the Santa Claus School, Albion, N.Y. 1964

Puerto Rican woman with a beauty mark, N.Y.C. 1965

Triplets in their bedroom, N.J. 1963

A footprint is made by a shoe but it is not the shoe itself.

—FROM *THE WISDOM OF LAO TSE* QUOTED IN 1959 NOTEBOOK (No. 1)

Boy with a straw hat waiting to march in a pro-war parade, N.Y.C. 1967

Muscle man contestant, N.Y.C. 1968

Woman and her son, N.Y.C. 1965

Two boys smoking in Central Park, N.Y.C. 1962

Masked woman in a wheelchair, Pa. 1970

Xmas tree in a living room, Levittown, L.I. 1963

Two ladies at the automat, N.Y.C. 1966

James Brown at home in curlers, Queens, N.Y. 1966

Girl in a coat lying on her bed, N.Y.C. 1968

A Jewish couple dancing, N.Y.C. 1963

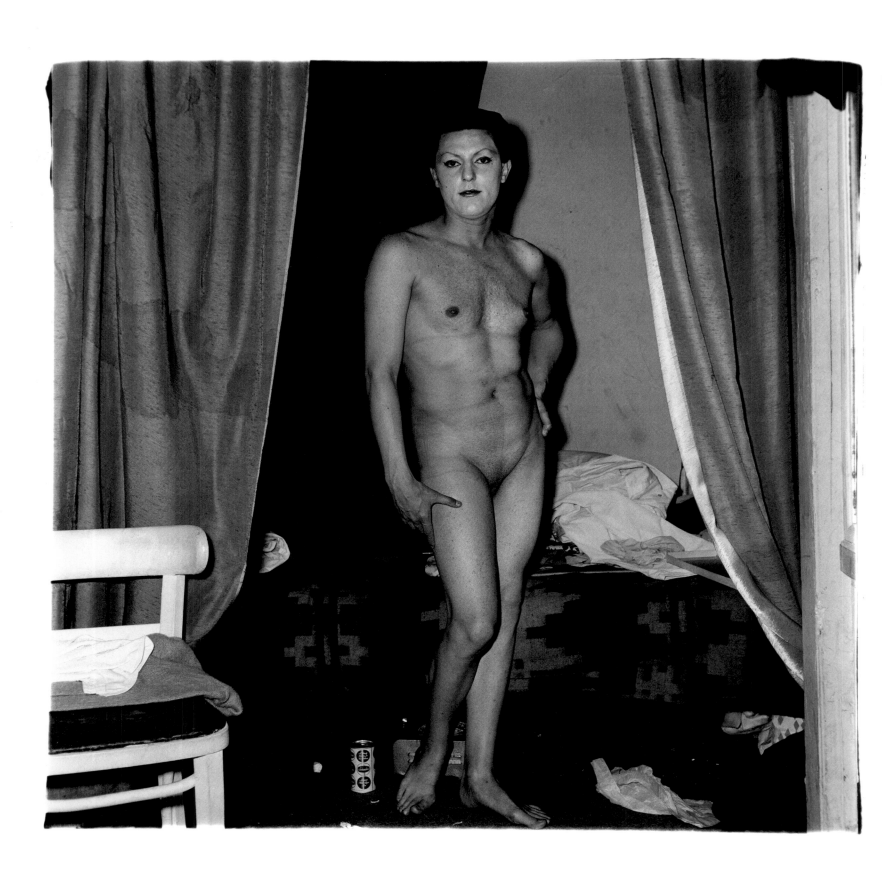

A naked man being a woman, N.Y.C. 1968

Girl in a watch cap, N.Y.C. 1965

It's like going around a mirrorless world asking everyone you meet
to describe you and everyone says endlessly, "you have a face even as I do and your
eyes are bluer and big," and even, "my smile when I look at you is you,"
but you don't believe it and then one day you bump smack into a stone wall and
no one hears you say, "ouch," and your whole problem is solved.

—FROM A LETTER TO ALEX ELIOT AND JANE WINSLOW FROM SPAIN, SUMMER 1951

Russian midget friends in a living room on 100th Street, N.Y.C. 1963

Teenage couple on Hudson Street, N.Y.C. 1963

Woman with a locket in Washington Square Park, N.Y.C. 1965

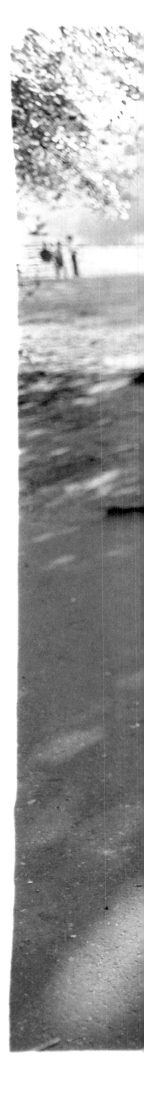

Child with a toy hand grenade in Central Park, N.Y.C. 1962

Lady in a rooming house parlor, Albion, N.Y. 1963

Masked man at a ball, N.Y.C. 1967

Dominatrix embracing her client, N.Y.C. 1970

Photographer posing communion boy, N.Y.C. 1968

The House of Horrors, Coney Island, N.Y. 1961

Girl in a shiny dress, N.Y.C. 1967

Couple under a paper lantern, N.Y.C. 1966*

Woman in a rose hat, N.Y.C. 1966

A young Negro boy, Washington Square Park, N.Y.C. 1965

Untitled (6) 1970–71

115

Mrs. T. Charlton Henry on a couch in her Chestnut Hill home, Philadelphia, Pa. 1965

Loser at a Diaper Derby, N.J. 1967

...If the fall of man consists in the separation of god and the devil

the serpent must have appeared out of the middle of the apple when eve bit like the

original worm in it, splitting it in half and sundering everything

which was once one into a pair of opposites, so the world is a Noah's ark on the sea of

eternity containing all the endless pairs of things, irreconcilable and

inseparable, and heat will always long for cold and the back for the

front and smiles for tears and mutt for jeff and no for yes with the most

unutterable nostalgia there is.

—FROM A LETTER TO MARVIN ISRAEL, CIRCA 1960

A husband and wife in the woods at a nudist camp, N.J. 1963

A CHRONOLOGY

BY ELISABETH SUSSMAN AND DOON ARBUS

The first part of my story is mostly
taken from my imagination. You also must
use some imagination. I am not born yet...

—DIANE ARBUS, 1934 AUTOBIOGRAPHY, SEVENTH-GRADE CLASS ASSIGNMENT, FIELDSTON SCHOOL

1923–1971

1923

Diane Nemerov, the second child of Gertrude (née Russek) and David Nemerov, is born in the family apartment at 115 West 73rd Street in New York City on March 14, 1923. The Nemerovs' oldest child, Howard, is three. David Nemerov is the merchandising director of Russek's, one of the city's leading fur emporia, founded in the late 1880s by his father-in-law, Frank Russek, a Polish émigré, along with two other Russek brothers.[1]

I came into the world at 1:30 A.M. on Tuesday, March 14, 1923. I was a 9 lb. baby, very large, roly poly, blonde and blue eyed.

—1934 AUTOBIOGRAPHY, SEVENTH-GRADE CLASS ASSIGNMENT, FIELDSTON SCHOOL[2]

When I was very young I was blond and red-cheeked and round. I was cranky, always crying, yelling, screaming. I remember that we lived then mostly in warm climates (although we must have lived in New York in the winter) and I can always remember the feeling I had. I always felt as if I was very warm and tired and there was a hot sun on me and I had been asleep. I didn't want to wake up and people would try to wake me and I'd be angry at them; I'd yell at them and hate them. I think I always had a sort of haze of sleep around me then. I don't mean that in any symbolic sense—I mean really physically.

—1940 AUTOBIOGRAPHY, SENIOR CLASS ASSIGNMENT, FIELDSTON SCHOOL[3]

I remember the first dream I remember having. It was a picture of the upper right or left-hand corner of my room as I would see it from my bed. It was quite dark but vaguely lighted so that I was able to see the walls and the ceiling meeting and a ball of black wool sitting on air in the corner with one end a little untwisted.

—1940 AUTOBIOGRAPHY, SENIOR CLASS ASSIGNMENT, FIELDSTON SCHOOL

1924–1926

In September 1924, Russek's moves to its new headquarters, a McKim, Mead, and White building on the southwest corner of Fifth Avenue and 36th Street, which was originally built in 1905 for it previous occupant, the Gorham Silver Company.[4] The new location coincides with the expansion of Russek's as a department store specializing in women's fashions. David Nemerov is a key proponent of this development.

The Nemerovs move to 1133 Park Avenue at 90th Street.[5] *This house I remember quite faintly,* Diane notes in her seventh-grade autobiography. *It was here that I cut myself with a china doll.*[6] Her brother, Howard Nemerov, refers to the same incident in his memoir, *Journal of the Fictive Life,* published in 1965: *The scar on my sister's face. Did she really get that in our struggle for a doll that broke in our hands? I believe so, but this belief is not a memory, or it is a memory of having been told so.*[7]

1927

As a vice president and fashion director of Russek's, David Nemerov,

(LEFT) PORTRAIT OF LIEUTENANT DAVID IRWIN NEMEROV AND *(RIGHT)* NEWSPAPER CLIPPING OF GERTRUDE RUSSEK'S ENGAGEMENT ANNOUNCEMENT, BOTH CIRCA 1919.

(ABOVE LEFT) DETAIL OF A SNAPSHOT OF RUSSEK'S IN 1920 ON FIFTH AVENUE BETWEEN 34TH AND 35TH STREETS AND *(ABOVE RIGHT)* THE BUILDING OCCUPIED BY RUSSEK'S STARTING IN 1924 ON THE SOUTHWEST CORNER OF FIFTH AVENUE AND 36TH STREET. *(BELOW)* FORMAL PORTRAIT BY WALTER SCOTT SHINN OF DIANE NEMEROV, AGE 2.

often accompanied by his wife, Gertrude, sails to Europe regularly to attend the couture collections and assess the latest fashion trends. In 1927, the Nemerovs bring the two children with them.[8]

...we started our trip across the ocean to France. We went over on the Aquitania and came back on the same...I don't [remember] our stay at Paris except for registering at the Majestic Hotel. My parents went from Paris to Switzerland and left my six year old brother and my governess and myself in La Touquet, a summer resort in France.

—1934 AUTOBIOGRAPHY, SEVENTH-GRADE CLASS ASSIGNMENT, FIELDSTON SCHOOL

[My governess was] French and she took care of me for the first seven years of my life. She had a hard, sad, quite lovely face and I adored her. I don't think I ever talked much to her but I was very happy with her ...she always looked as if she had a very sad secret and she would never tell anyone.

—1940 AUTOBIOGRAPHY, SENIOR CLASS ASSIGNMENT, FIELDSTON SCHOOL

1928

In September, following in her brother's footsteps, she enrolls at the Ethical Culture School on 63rd Street and Central Park West, a progressive private school begun by Felix Adler, founder of the Ethical Culture Society (1878). Originally known as The Workingman's School, it emphasizes *moral education, psychological development, teacher training, and the integration of "manual arts" with academics.*[9] The academic curriculum is designed to parallel the evolution of human civilization, from tree dwellers to contemporary society. Students in each grade study their subjects through the lens of a particular time period and culture.[10]

When I was quite little I heard about mottoes and I wanted terribly to have a motto that I would keep all my life. I searched about for a long time before I found, written on pennies, "in God we trust." I thought it was wonderful and I swore I would never change it...It made me very proud to have a motto when I was so young and I wanted terribly to be faithful and constant to it. I always wanted something I could be faithful to forever. I hated fickle people.

—1940 AUTOBIOGRAPHY, SENIOR CLASS ASSIGNMENT, FIELDSTON SCHOOL

Younger sister, Renée, is born on October 13, 1928.

1929–1931

In the summer of 1929 the Nemerovs move to 1185 Park Avenue.[11]

By her own account, the stock market crash of 1929 and the Depression that follows have little direct impact on her life. One of her few memories of the period is recounted in a 1968 radio interview with Studs Terkel, portions of which are later included in his book *Hard Times: An Oral History of the Great Depression* (1970). Like many of the interviewees in the book, her recollections appear under a pseudonym. She calls herself "Daisy Singer."[12]

ON THE DECK OF *THE AQUITANIA* IN 1927: *FROM LEFT TO RIGHT* (BETWEEN TWO UNIDENTIFIED FAMILY FRIENDS) DIANE, AGE 3, SEATED AT GERTRUDE NEMEROV'S FEET; GERTRUDE'S MOTHER, ROSE RUSSEK; AND DAVID NEMEROV WITH HOWARD, AGE 6, RECLINING IN HIS LAP. THE EMBOSSED INSIGNIA OF THE SHIP IN THE LOWER LEFT CORNER LEADS ONE TO BELIEVE THAT THE PICTURE WAS TAKEN BY THE SHIP'S OFFICIAL PHOTOGRAPHER.

DIANE WALKING WITH HER MOTHER, GERTRUDE, AND BROTHER, HOWARD, IN LA TOUQUET, AN ELEGANT SEASIDE HOLIDAY RESORT ON THE COAST OF FRANCE, IN 1927. THE PHOTOGRAPH IS CAPTIONED IN RED PEN BY GERTRUDE NEMEROV.

(LEFT) DAVID AND GERTRUDE NEMEROV WITH ROSE RUSSEK AND TWO UNIDENTIFIED FAMILY FRIENDS IN ST. MARK'S PLACE, VENICE, IN 1927. ON THE BACK OF THE PHOTOGRAPH GERTRUDE HAS WRITTEN: *...THE YEAR WE BROUGHT THE CHILDREN AND LEFT THEM IN LA TOUQUET WITH MADEMOISELLE. (RIGHT)* A 1936 NEWSPAPER PHOTOGRAPH OF DAVID AND GERTRUDE NEMEROV ABOARD *THE CONTE DI SAVOIE*, ARRIVING IN NEW YORK HARBOR FROM PARIS.

HOOVERVILLE, A SHANTYTOWN IN CENTRAL PARK. IN THE BACKGROUND ARE THE SPIRES OF THE SAN REMO APARTMENT BUILDING WHERE THE NEMEROVS LIVED. PHOTOGRAPH BY NAT NORMAN, CIRCA 1932, COURTESY OF THE MUSEUM OF THE CITY OF NEW YORK.

THREE-DIMENSIONAL STANDING PORTRAIT OF HOWARD, AGE 9, AND DIANE, AGE 6, IN 1929. DIANE LATER SAID: *ONE OF THE THINGS I SUFFERED FROM AS A KID WAS I NEVER FELT ADVERSITY...AND THAT SENSE OF BEING IMMUNE WAS—LUDICROUS AS IT SEEMS—A PAINFUL ONE.*

I had a governess I really loved when I was young...I remember once going to the park to the site of the old reservoir which was at that time empty, because presumably they had put the water in the new one and there was a cavity and there was a shanty town there...the image is not really so concrete. But you know, it was for me the most palpable potent memory of the other side of the railroad tracks...you know holding the hand of one's governess and feeling...I don't mean to say I envied those people, but just to see that you couldn't get in there, you know, that you couldn't just wander down. That there was such a gulf.

—1968 RADIO INTERVIEW WITH STUDS TERKEL ON THE DEPRESSION[13]

The family fortune always seemed to me humiliating. When I had to go into that store...I would come on somebody's arm or holding somebody's hand at what must have been a fairly young age and it was like being a princess in some loathsome movie of some kind of Transylvanian obscure middle European country and the kingdom was so humiliating.

—1968 RADIO INTERVIEW WITH STUDS TERKEL ON THE DEPRESSION

I remember the special agony of walking down that center aisle, feeling like the princess of Russek's: simultaneously priveleged and doomed. The main floor was always very empty like a church and along the way were poised the leeringest manikins ever whose laps and bosoms were never capacious enough for refuge and all the live people bowed slightly and smiled like the obsequies were seasoned with mockeries. It seemed it all belonged to me and I was ashamed.

—POSTCARD TO MARVIN ISRAEL, MARCH 4, 1960[14]

1932–1933

The Nemerovs move to the San Remo, an apartment house at 146 Central Park West.[15] After the children's maternal grandparents, the Russeks, move in with them, Diane and Renée share a room: *I used to try to give my sister dreams when we shared a room. I would lean over her, the hair at the back of her neck was wet, in ringlets, and whisper "elephant, waterfall, dancing" but it never worked at all.*[16]

Once I remember my brother was robbed. This is when we lived on Central Park West...he was perhaps 12...I would have been 9...which was three years after the Crash...My brother and I were skating outside of the apartment house where we lived. We were dressed sort of young for our age. He must have looked a bit sissified although he was a good football player sometime later. Anyway, two sort of poor boys called to him and he didn't hear them. I remember feeling terrifically proud that he should be summoned by, you know, just regular [boys]. They were older. So I called to him. And he came over and I very sort of dutifully kept my distance so I wouldn't interrupt this sort of manly exchange which apparently consisted of their demanding his money. I don't remember how much they got...It was probably just a few dollars. But they made a dash for it over the low stone wall and my brother made as if to follow them but he was on roller skates. And I, like some sort of Lillian Gish in some ancient film, restrained him, saying, "Don't."

—1968 RADIO INTERVIEW WITH STUDS TERKEL ON THE DEPRESSION

1934–1935

Enters Fieldston, the Riverdale campus of the Ethical Culture School. A classmate, Stewart Stern, recalls her this way: *I idealized her so much from the time of my earliest recollection that I don't know if I remember her. She came full-blown with her mature privacy intact, and she seemed to know from the beginning of my recollection who she was and who she was going to be and what her private space consisted of.*[17]

...She could shock you with the directness of what she had to say and with...the way she looked at things...She was like a wonderful film director because when you watch them they're doing such body English to the actors they're directing when they're behind the camera...Her face did that. You could almost look at her and get the story of what she was watching unfold. It was so naked and so tender and so empathic...I think the thing I remember most is the depth of her earnestness and at the same time the flicker of amusement almost constantly. And one of the most raucous laughs. I can still hear it across the din of the dining room.[18]

Her 1940 autobiography seems preoccupied with questions of loyalty, authenticity, and courage:

We used to go into the park in the afternoons to play games and climb rocks. Whenever there was something a little dangerous or daring to do, like jumping over a wide crevice between rocks or playing a trick on the teacher or teasing one of the strong girls I would be the leader and the first one to do it. I was always considered the most daring but I am sure I was more afraid than the others.

—1940 AUTOBIOGRAPHY, SENIOR CLASS ASSIGNMENT, FIELDSTON SCHOOL

The Nemerovs' professional involvement in the fashion world coupled with their frequent travel to Europe broadens their knowledge of culture and the visual arts. David Nemerov has a particular interest in Impressionist painting. They encourage the artistic impulses of each of their children.

About this time everyone suddenly decided I was meant to be an artist and I was given art lessons and a big box of oils and encouragement and everything. I painted and drew every once in a while for about 4 yrs. with a teacher without admitting to anyone that I didn't like to paint or draw at all and I didn't know what I was doing. I used to pray and wish often to be a "great artist" and all the while I hated it and I didn't realize that I didn't want to be an artist at all. The horrible thing was that all the encouragement I got made me think that really I wanted to be an artist and made me keep pretending that I liked it and made me like it less and less until I hated it because it wasn't me that was being an artist; everybody was lifting me high up and crowning me and congratulating me and I was smiling—and really I hated it and I hadn't done one single good piece of work. It was the craziest pretense in the world but even though I was pretending I believed in it, for about four years I had visions of being a great sad artist and I turned all my energies toward it when I wasn't an artist at all.

—1940 AUTOBIOGRAPHY, SENIOR CLASS ASSIGNMENT, FIELDSTON SCHOOL

ETHICAL CULTURE SCHOOLS
CENTRAL PARK WEST AND 63RD STREET
NEW YORK CITY

From Sept. 29 '31 to Jan. 29, '32

REPORT OF Diane Nemerov

No. times tardy 0   No. days absent 7

Diane has a great deal of poise and self-control; she is sufficient unto herself, being capable of carrying on her work independently or with a group. Her academic work is of very good quality, her effort is excellent. She has many friends in the group and her quiet, well-controlled influence is very desirable. She is interested in all group activities and she contributes to them generously. She is strong and dependable.

Subject teachers' reports:

Music: Diane does excellent work; she is always helpful.

Domestic Art: Excellent work.

Natural Science: Diane seldom contributes to the nature class. She is very shy in response. She is helpful in attitude.

(ABOVE) DIANE NEMEROV REPORT CARD FROM ETHICAL CULTURE SCHOOL, SEPTEMBER 29, 1931–JANUARY 29, 1932. *(BELOW)* GROUP PHOTOGRAPH AT CAMP ACCOMAC, 1933. DIANE IS IN THE MIDDLE OF THE SECOND ROW, MARKED IN RED PEN BY GERTRUDE.

(BELOW LEFT) DIANE IN THE COUNTRY WITH HER GREAT-GRANDMOTHER, HANNA ANHOLT, AND HER GRANDMOTHER, ROSE RUSSEK, CIRCA 1934. *(BELOW RIGHT)* DRAWING MADE BY DIANE AS AN AD FOR RUSSEK'S WHICH READS: *PERSIAN LAMB LAVISHLY USED ON RUSSEKS COATS AT THE ASTOUNDING PRICE OF $98.*

NEMEROV FAMILY IN THE COUNTRY ONE SUMMER WITH THEIR COUSINS: DAVID AND GERTRUDE IN THE CENTER, WITH DIANE AT RIGHT, RENÉE AT LEFT, AND HOWARD BEHIND.

(ABOVE LEFT) AT CAMP IN ARIZONA, SUMMER, CIRCA 1937. (ABOVE RIGHT) DIANE'S PAINTING OF ALLAN FROM HER SUMMER AT CUMMINGTON, 1938. COLLECTION OF ALEX ELIOT AND JANE WINSLOW ELIOT. (BELOW) SUMMER 1939.

(BELOW) FIELDSTON ART STUDENTS AT THE MUSEUM OF MODERN ART, 1939. DIANE IS AT RIGHT. COLLECTION OF MARILEE AND STEWART STERN.

According to Stewart Stern: *When she picked up her brush for the first time she was simply not doing what anybody else did. We were all trying to be representational and she had no interest in that, except as a kind of satire.*[19]

After two summers at Camp Accomac in Maine (1933 and 1934), she vacations in the country with her family and her young cousins, where she spends most of her time alone, reading: *Although I admit I was proud of it for its own sake, I think I was really happy...I began to believe in myself.*[20]

1936–1938

Meets Allan Arbus (born 1918, New York City), who is working in the advertising department at Russek's. David Nemerov's partner, Max Weinstein, is Allan Arbus's uncle by marriage. Arbus had attended City College (1933–35) but left before graduating.[21] They begin to see each other on Saturday afternoons for walks in the park or tea. Together they attend exhibitions at The Museum of Modern Art, including *Photography 1839–1937* (1937) and *Walker Evans: American Photographs* (1938). After a while, they begin meeting in secret, as well. *In confronting the world, we were really always tremendous allies,* Allan recalls.[22]

In 1938 Diane attends Cummington, a summer school for the arts in western Massachusetts. Victor D'Amico, her art teacher at Fieldston, recommends her to the program: *She has exceptional ability and shows a definite sense of composition, color, and form in painting. Her style is highly individual and her manner of expression unique. We have tried to develop her powers without damaging her personal gifts in any way.*[23]

While at Cummington, she studies with the painter Herman Maril. She meets Alexander Eliot, who had spent a year at Black Mountain as a student of Josef Albers and is also in the Cummington painting program.[24] Eliot later comments: *Her painting was very like the photographs were going to be: extremely reverent, extremely reverent in the face of the object.*[25] But her frustration with the medium persists. The following November, she writes Eliot: *Sometimes...I feel as if I could just take anything and know it <u>my way</u> and <u>paint it</u> but it doesn't paint as well as I know it.*[26]

1939–1940

Chooses art as her major at Fieldston. D'Amico (who was named director of education at The Museum of Modern Art in 1937) is her advisor. The Museum of Modern Art, founded in 1929, opens its building on 53rd Street in May 1939. Fieldston art students visit the museum as a class excursion.[27]

She is selected for Elbert Lenrow's Senior English Seminar, along with nine or ten other students, including Stewart Stern. The students sit around a table with Lenrow at the head of it, whom Stern describes this way: *He was a big, broad-shouldered man...[who] always wore glasses...[and] a handkerchief in his breast pocket with a kind of lilac cologne on it. He taught with his eyes shut because he had problems with his eyes. The first class he said, "It's*

When I was very young, I was blond and red-cheeked and round. I was cranky, always crying, yelling, screaming. I remember that we lived then mostly in warm climates (although we must have lived in New York in the winter) and I can always remember the feeling I had. I always felt as if I was very warm and tired and there was a hot sun on me and I had been asleep and I didn't want to wake up and people would try to wake me and I'd be angry at them; I'd yell at them and hate them. I think I always had a sort of haze of sleep around me there. I don't mean that in any symbolic sense — I mean really physically. I don't remember anything else about that time except my governess. She was french and she took care of me for the first seven years of my life. She had a hard, sad, quite lovely face and I adored her. I remember that I told her I'd die if she ever went away from me and whenever she went on a vacation I would cry and try to make her not go. I don't think I ever talked much to her but I was very happy with her. She had a bun in the back of her head and she was very quiet! She loved me a lot but I don't think she kissed me much and she was very strict; she always looked as if she had a very sad secret and she would never tell anyone. We used to speak in french all the time and I liked it, but I remember that when I went to school I used to get terribly frightened that I would never be able to speak english and I would beg to be allowed to speak english at home too. I was always afraid that one day I would wake up and find I had forgotten everything! I wasn't ever very sure of things I learned. My governess taught me a french prayer and although I spoke french "fluently" I never knew what it meant. I didn't know it was french. I learned it by the sound and I just repeated it every night. It wasn't until I took french in school that I learned that the first line was: "notre père donnez-nous notre pain." I always thought of it as "nowtrepare donaynoo nowtrepain (?)"

When I was very little I heard about mottoes and I wanted terribly to have a motto that I would keep all my life. I searched about for a long time before I found, written on pennies, "In God we trust". I thought it was wonderful and I swore I'd never change it. I always repeated it at night. It made me very proud to have a motto when I was so young and I wanted terribly to be faithful and constant to it. I always wanted something I could be faithful to forever. I hated fickle people. I remember the first dream I remembered having. It was a picture of the upper right or left hand corner of my room as I would see it from my bed. It was quite dark but vaguely lighted so that I was able to see the walls and the ceiling meeting and a ball of black wool sitting on air in the corner with one end a little un-twisted.

By this time I must have been going to school. I had changed a lot. I was tall and thin with dark brown, long hair in curls. I was terribly shy. In first grade I can't remember much except that I rarely spoke to anyone much. There was a festival in the middle of the year and the first graders were supposed to come out on the stage wearing pajamas and wave to their parents or grandparents in the audience and run around and wave their arms. I wouldn't do it and they sent me to the principal and she scolded me and I remember coming back to the class with my eyes all red from crying and Mr. Black was sitting in the middle of a semi-circle telling stories and I felt awful. Some people pretended not to notice that I was crying and others stared; I was angry at them all.

In second grade I was happy I think, although I don't remember much. I remember painting pictures of giraffes which the teacher put up behind glass cabinet doors and also that the teacher used to make us "lock our mouths and put our thinking caps on". We all thought it was silly going through the motions and I remember feeling I ought to do it seriously because otherwise I might hurt the teacher's feelings. Third grade was a terribly sad year. There was a girl in my class who was

THE FIRST PAGE OF DIANE NEMEROV'S 1940 AUTOBIOGRAPHY, WRITTEN FOR ELBERT LENROW'S ENGLISH CLASS, FIELDSTON SCHOOL. LENROW, WHO HAD BEEN HOWARD NEMEROV'S TEACHER AS WELL, SENT HIM THE ORIGINAL AUTOBIOGRAPHY IN 1972. IT IS CURRENTLY HELD WITH THE HOWARD NEMEROV PAPERS AT WASHINGTON UNIVERSITY LIBRARIES, ST. LOUIS, MISSOURI.

ALLAN ARBUS AND DIANE NEMEROV IN CENTRAL PARK, SUMMER 1939. ON HER LEFT WRIST IS A BRACELET HE GAVE HER THAT HE HAD INSCRIBED ON THE INSIDE...*AND SHE WAS MY IMMUNITY.*

(ABOVE) TWO DRAWINGS BY DIANE NEMEROV FOR THE 1940 FIELDSTON YEARBOOK, *THE FIELDGLASS.* COLLECTION OF MARILEE AND STEWART STERN. *(BELOW)* A PAGE FROM THE YEARBOOK.

nothing personal. I've seen who you all are, I know you all, you're very attractive people, but I'm going to shut my eyes because I need to save them for my reading."[28]

Students in the class are required to write brief essays on each book they read. Her responses, in style as well as content, prefigure her mature sensibility.

The Bible is wonderful and beautiful. It is man's creation; like the desperate attempt of a race of men, faced with things they couldn't understand, to account for it all and be able to believe in what they had created. They were made and placed on the earth and faced with substance and space, with wet and dry, with soft and hard, with big and small, with dark and light, with pain, with unhappiness, with hunger, with desire—and they couldn't understand it. Everything was so wonderful and so horrible that they had to have something to make them know that everything would be all right. A man cannot believe in what he doesn't understand at all, a man cannot believe in nothing. A man must have a sense that there is an order behind everything, good and bad, an order which is bigger than himself but which he can at least in part understand.

—JANUARY 16, 1940, PAPER ON THE OLD TESTAMENT, SENIOR ENGLISH SEMINAR[29]

Chaucer seems to be very sure and whole and his attitude toward everything is so calm and tender because he was satisfied and glad that he was himself. The way he describes meeting the 29 pilgrims gives you a feeling of easiness; it isn't a frenzied need for companionship—it is a delight he gets in speaking and being with people...you get the feeling that he is a little bit beyond them, but that he doesn't want to seem so. The pleasure he gets from meeting them is part physical, part spiritual. He seems to love physical things, even obscene ones, and from looking at them, he gets a contact with the other person. His way of looking at everything is like that of a newborn baby; he sees things and each one seems wonderful, not for its significance in relation to other things, but simply because it is unique and because it is there. When he describes the nun's daintiness, it doesn't seem as if he thinks that that is a standard of good conduct...rather he turns separately to each one and looks on them as whole miracles not as compounds of abstract qualities, and he seems to know that each one will always be himself and he wants that.

—MARCH 5, 1940, PAPER ON CHAUCER'S *THE CANTERBURY TALES,* SENIOR ENGLISH SEMINAR

[Don Quixote] wanted to be right, I guess, but all the time you feel that he was so un-sophisticated that he could never be quite like other people. And being out of tempo with the world, he felt that he was wrong. His "madness" is a way of being himself to the limit. You feel that suddenly and deliberately he threw off his already limited awareness of the conventions of the world, and threw himself in the world's face defiantly, because he was what he was, and he felt that that was good enough.

—APRIL 16, 1940, PAPER ON CERVANTES'S *DON QUIXOTE,* SENIOR ENGLISH SEMINAR

Graduates from Fieldston in June.

For the next several months she continues taking private painting classes—arranged by her father—with Dorothy Thompson, a fashion illustrator who worked for Russek's,[30] and whom she later refers to as *probably an interesting woman.*[31]

(*ABOVE LEFT*) ALLAN'S PHOTOGRAPH OF DIANE ON THEIR HONEYMOON AND (*ABOVE RIGHT*) DIANE'S PHOTOGRAPH OF ALLAN ON THEIR HONEYMOON. (*BELOW*) THE FLYLEAF OF DIANE'S COPY OF THOMAS HARDY'S *TESS OF THE D'URBERVILLES* (SUBTITLED *A PURE WOMAN*) WITH HER NAME INSCRIBED ON IT AT VARIOUS TIMES OVER THE YEARS.

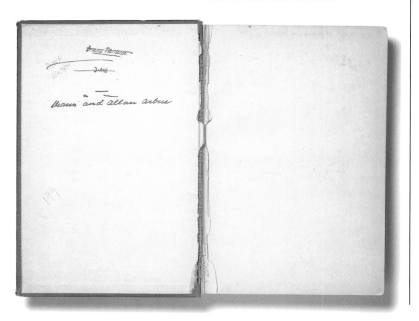

I hated painting and I quit right after high school because I was continually told how terrific I was...it made me feel shaky. I remember I hated the smell of the paint and the noise it would make when I put my brush to the paper. Sometimes I wouldn't really look but just listen to this horrible squish squish squish. I didn't want to be told I was terrific. I had the sense that if I was so terrific at it, it wasn't worth doing."

—1968 RADIO INTERVIEW WITH STUDS TERKEL ON THE DEPRESSION[32]

While at Harvard, Howard Nemerov writes a series of letters to his parents describing his plans to launch, along with five friends, a literary magazine. He expresses the hope that *Diane will contribute, since we all believe thoroughly in her drawing.*[33]

The Nemerovs move to 888 Park Avenue.[34]

1941

Marries Allan Arbus on April 10, 1941, in a small ceremony. The Reverend Dr. Israel Goldstein performs the wedding in his study at 270 West 89th Street.[35] The couple spends their three-week honeymoon on a farm in Columbia County, New York.[36]

They move into an apartment at 325 East 37th Street, where their bathroom doubles as a darkroom. Soon after, Alexander Eliot moves in across the hall with his wife, Anne.[37] Eliot describes the dynamics of their friendship this way: *I used to talk all the time, but I was inarticulate, really. I mean I couldn't think my way out of a paper bag. And Diane of course said very little. Diane was like a lodestone or a touchstone...In that sense she would be the center of things...And Allan was always very strong on the discriminating side. He could say what the experience wasn't. Always. Wonderfully well. This was a great champion to have around, to clear the air, to say, Not that, not that.*[38] When the Eliots' daughter, May, is born, Alex and Anne choose Diane to be May's godmother.

She receives a Graflex 2¼ x 3¼ camera, as a gift from Allan. Takes class with Berenice Abbott, which primarily covers technical aspects of photography, and teaches what she learns from Abbott to Allan. He proves to be an adept technician. On a vacation in Montauk, Allan takes a series of fashion photographs, using Diane as a model, which inspire David Nemerov to hire them as photographers for Russek's newspaper advertisements.[39]

They visit An American Place, Alfred Stieglitz's gallery for modernist art and photography. They meet Stieglitz and from time to time show him their work. According to Allan, the photographers who interest her most in this period, in additon to Stieglitz, are Matthew Brady, Timothy O'Sullivan, Paul Strand, Bill Brandt, and Eugène Atget.[40]

Howard Nemerov graduates from Harvard and the following autumn enlists in the Canadian Air Force, flying combat missions against German shipping in the North Sea.[41]

1942–1944

Following the entry of the United States into World War II, Allan enlists in the army and is sent to Camp Crowder in Missouri for basic training. When he is transferred to Fort Monmouth, New Jersey, Diane joins him. His subsequent reassignment to the Photography Division of the Signal Corps enables the couple to move back to Manhattan, where they rent a small midtown apartment on the east side.

Diane develops a friendship with Pati Hill, whom she meets at a party. In Hill's own words, she has come to New York from Virginia *to live a bohemian life in Greenwich Village, but by then there were no more bohemians.*[42] Hill is working as a fashion model and as a writer. Diane later describes her this way: *She is enormously complex...her thinking, doing, saying are all three always working simultaneously and fast...(but not much together except as in a dance, to meet, to merge, to bow, to entwine) in ever varying relations to each other...*[43]

When Allan is posted to India in 1944, Diane—who is now pregnant—moves into her parents' apartment at 888 Park Avenue. There is a darkroom in the basement of the building for the use of the tenants. During this period she takes photographs of family and friends, using a 5x7 Deardorff view camera David Nemerov had given them.

She also makes a series of self-portraits that chart the progress of her pregnancy (p. 15), which she prints and sends to Allan. Her letters to him include detailed descriptions of photographs she has seen, and often the photographs themselves, torn from the pages of magazines. Among these are some of Richard Avedon's first fashion pictures for *Harper's Bazaar.*[44]

In London in 1944, Howard Nemerov marries Peggy (Margaret) Russell.

1945

On April 3, daughter Doon is born. The night before, Diane slips away to New York Hospital alone, leaving behind a note for her parents (which David Nemerov saves and later shows to Allan) asking them not to visit her there: *I've gone to have my baby...since I can't have Allan I don't want anyone.*[45]

In a handwritten note dated April 8 she writes Alfred Stieglitz:

Our baby is a girl...curious and even a little funny. I simply stare at her. I expected to feel deep recognition but I don't. She isn't like either of us but lovely: very alive and with very beautiful shoulders. I love our lack of connection: that she doesn't feel anything towards me and I feel in such an odd, separate way about her.

I expected great changes (first, I expected it from pregnancy, then when it didn't come, I expected it from birth.) but I'm glad I didn't change or at least feel changed. I trust myself better as I am. It was very simple—I have forgotten most of the bad part because of the anaes-

(LEFT) Diane on her honeymoon, 1941, and *(RIGHT)* Allan in the army's Signal Corps in India, circa 1944.

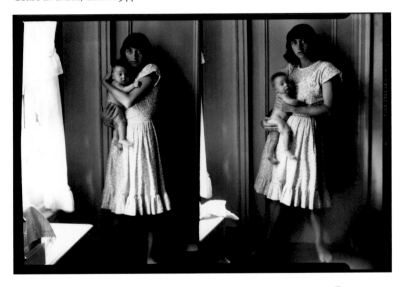

(ABOVE) Diane's 5x7 double self-portrait with her infant daughter, Doon, 1945. *(BELOW)* Allan Arbus army discharge papers, January 1946.

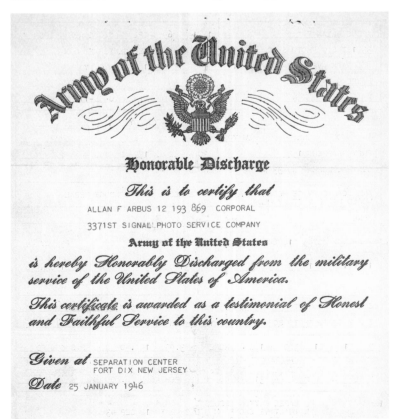

thetic—but I still know it was simple. I guess events are always simpler than people—which is good.

Born April 3, 8lbs. Her name is Doon.[46]

And to Pati Hill, whose birthday also happens to be April 3: *A girl...I know you hate them but she is quite fantastic. She reminds me of a monkey and makes me laugh...*[47]

When Walker Evans leaves *Time* to become staff photographer at *Fortune*, Alex Eliot, who has been working for the March of Time newsreel company, becomes a sportswriter for *Time* and later its arts editor.[48]

1946

On January 25 Allan is discharged from the army.[49] He returns to New York. For a few months the Arbus family continues to live with the Nemerovs at 888 Park Avenue.

Eventually, they move to an apartment on West 70th Street and, with David Nemerov's financial help, rent studio space at 108 West 54th Street and purchase equipment for their fashion photography business. They resume work on the Russek's account using the credit line "Diane & Allan Arbus."

In addition to the commercial photography of their partnership both Diane and Allan continue to make pictures individually, which they show to Nancy Newhall, Acting Curator of Photography (1943–46), at The Museum of Modern Art.[50]

They are both avid readers. The books in their library at the time, inscribed by Diane on the flyleaf "Diane and Allan Arbus," include works by Plato, Marcus Aurelius, Thomas Aquinas, Spinoza, Schopenhauer, Kierkegaard; Dostoevsky, Melville, Conrad, Gogol; Donne, Blake, Rilke, and Yeats.[51]

1947–1950

After several months, Diane and Allan gather together some of their fashion pictures and take them to Alexander Liberman at Condé Nast. Allan describes Liberman's response as *enthusiastic and very gallante*.[52] One of their first regular clients is *Glamour*. Their main contact at that magazine is Tina Fredericks, the art editor. They also work for *Vogue*, *Seventeen*, and advertising agencies.

Often dependent upon an imaginative use of props and locations, their style is the result of Diane's art direction and Allan's camera work. *They were always idea pictures*, Allan recalls. *For some reason, we couldn't work without an idea and ninety per cent of them were Diane's.*[53] They are admirers and somewhat baffled students of the work of many photographers in the fashion field: Louise Dahl-Wolfe and Martin Munkasci, as well as Paul Hoyningen-Huene, John Rawlings, Irving Penn, and Richard Avedon.[54]

ALLAN'S 8x10 PHOTOGRAPH OF THE ARBUS STUDIO AT 108 WEST 54TH STREET, CIRCA 1948.

Allan describes their experience in the business as a kind of balancing act between triumph and despair: *Each month there'd be the magazines we were just thirsting for. And if the pictures in them were good—which usually meant there was something of Dick's [Avedon]—the work would all seem possible again.*[55] Or as Diane puts it: *Every few days, after it had rained like we needed it to, or Liberman had complimented us like we wanted, and the picture was going to be used, and nobody thought it was as bad as it was, then the next day was like a miracle, gratis...*[56] Allan concludes: *And whenever we did a picture we liked, we couldn't go to sleep. We'd stay up all night looking at it. We were just two terrified, totally uninformed, wildly enthusiastic photographers.*[57]

They meet Nancy Christopherson (Bellamy), who, with some help from their friend Pati Hill, is exploring a modeling career. Nancy recalls her first encounter with Diane: *It was mysterious the way we met...Pati Hill had given me a list of fashion photographers to see and I'd been walking up and down with it and the next name on my list was Arbus. That's when I noticed this woman on the street. She looked solemn, profound, and I knew, instantly, I just knew we were destined to be great friends. I entered the studio which was very black and white, very sterile, and met a young man with enormous eyes, very nervous and thin. He interviewed me and he was very nice but my mind was still on the woman I had seen on the street. And then she walked in! I wanted to start the friendship right there...*[58]

Howard Nemerov, who has been living in New York with his wife, Peggy, since the end of the war, working as an editor of the literary periodical *Furioso*, publishes his first book of poetry, *The Image and the Law*, in 1947.[59] The same year, Renée Nemerov, recently graduated from the Dalton School, marries Roy Sparkia.[60]

The Arbus family spends summers on Martha's Vineyard (1948 and 1949) with Alex and Anne Eliot and their daughter, May, and on Lake Champlain (1950) with Nancy and Dick Bellamy and Nancy's five-year-old daughter, Poni.[61]

In 1950, Alex Eliot meets Jane Winslow and separates from his wife, Anne.[62]

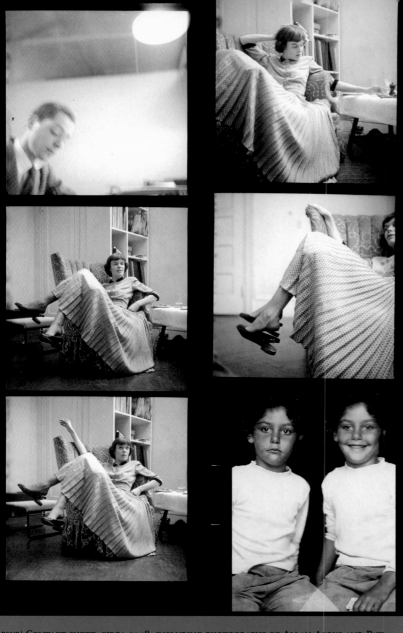

(BELOW) CONTACT STRIPS WITH ROBERT MESERVEY, DIANE, AND ALLAN IN THE ARBUS APARTMENT, CIRCA 1950. (FAR RIGHT) AN ARBUS SITTING IN CENTRAL PARK, CIRCA 1950.

(ABOVE) CONTACT SHEET, CIRCA 1948, INCLUDING PHOTOGRAPHS OF ALLAN ARBUS AND PATI HILL. THE FRAME ON THE BOTTOM RIGHT IS DIANE'S DOUBLE EXPOSURE OF DOON AS TWINS, CIRCA 1950. (BELOW LEFT) DICK BELLAMY SEATED AT A TABLE IN A CABIN, CIRCA 1950.

20

(ABOVE) DIANE ARBUS PHOTOGRAPH OF HER GRANDMOTHER, ROSE RUSSEK, AT THE DINING ROOM TABLE, CIRCA 1950. (LEFT) ANNE ELIOT AT THE BEACH AT MARTHA'S VINEYARD, CIRCA 1948, AND CONTACT SHEET SHOWING ALEXANDER ELIOT AND HIS DAUGHTER, MAY, AT MARTHA'S VINEYARD, CIRCA 1948. (ABOVE, FAR RIGHT) DIANE'S SISTER, RENÉE, WITH HUSBAND, ROY SPARKIA.

ROLLEIFLEX SELF-PORTRAIT OF ALLAN AND DIANE BY DIANE AND ALLAN ARBUS, WHICH APPEARED IN THE ARTICLE "MR. AND MRS. INC.," *GLAMOUR*, APRIL 1947.

1951

In the spring, Diane and Allan sublet their studio for a year and sail for Paris on the *Île de France* with their six-year-old daughter, Doon, and their blue Ford sedan. Alex Eliot refers to this trip as their *sabbatical venture*,[63] but according to Allan: *We were really running away.*[64] In a letter from the ship, Diane describes the transatlantic voyage:

Everyone is sleepy—a little screwed up with boredom (the weather has been cold windy rainy—gorgeous but not easy.) There are thousands of children and old people and almost everyone smiles but no one speaks more than two sentences. It's very queer—everyone is always jumping up as if they had a pressing appointment in some other part of the boat...I speak lots of french to the waiters and stewards and occasionally to the crew. They are charming—very eager to share your bad french with you. We say nothing interesting except that the effort involved on both sides is so sweet that it approaches communication.

—LETTER TO ALEX ELIOT AND JANE WINSLOW FROM *ILE DE FRANCE*, MAY 1951

They arrive in France on May 7. They spend the better part of the spring and summer in Paris with brief trips by car to Burgundy (to visit Pati Hill, who is living on a farm there, writing her first novel), to Versailles, to Brittany, and, for a few weeks in June, to Spain. Diane writes Alex

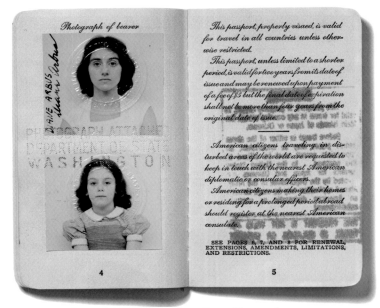

PASSPORT OF DIANE ARBUS AND DAUGHTER DOON, MARCH 28, 1951.

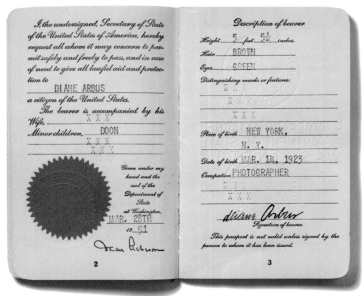

CATHOLIC NUNS AND THEIR CHARGES, FROM A DIANE ARBUS CONTACT SHEET, ITALY, 1951.

Eliot and Jane Winslow: *God what a place this is—Spain—I would rather be here than anywhere.*[65] And about Toledo:

...The atmosphere was so potent, oriental, flowering with corruption, crawling with nursing mothers, sick animals, swaggering soldiers, blind people screaming out about lottery tickets, priests hurrying about on what looked like pretend urgent business, american phonograph records (like Anchors Aweigh) whining a thousand times over behind the beaded curtains, and those birds I told you about, circling low, even into the ruined buildings (in some of which the balconies remained though the house was gone)...

—LETTER TO ALEX ELIOT AND JANE WINSLOW FROM BARCELONA, JUNE 13, 1951

Eliot reports having wangled two assignments for them from *Time*: color photographs of El Greco's Toledo and of Matisse's Chapel at Vence.[66] They investigate both possibilities, but neither comes to fruition. Diane writes:

I was, still am, obsessed by the desire to do something for...[*Time*]...but the only things that came to me were impossibly ambitious complex things which you haven't the space for...and, very likely they wouldn't work anyway...like the Greco-ish images in Toledo...one boy with a greenish face and incredible long hands, working on jewelry...one priest with small shorn head, lean nose, sharp eyes, who got bigger and bigger down to the bottom of him, under his billowing gown, huge folded hands and great massive feet...But much more...there are Goya images mostly from the drawings (so it wouldn't be color)...one we have seen several times: a blindfolded ass with ears fully a foot long walking in a hopeless circle, pulling a water wheel which is attached to him by a stick with another stick outstretched in front of him...as if tempting him but there is nothing on it...

—LETTER TO ALEX ELIOT AND JANE WINSLOW FROM BARCELONA, JUNE 13, 1951

In September, they leave Paris for Italy, eventually settling in an apartment in Florence for the month of October.

We've just moved in, just now, and I'm tired and not all unpacked, but don't feel like it so perversely decided to write you. The apartment is perfectly beautiful...large, tall, skylighted living room with a fireplace and an easel and an impressive round table with upholstered chairs whose backs come as high as my head...Our landlord, Dottor (of law) Gordigiani looked fairly unpleasant in this first encounter, raising all sorts of vague objections to our using the garden, and upturning his palm with distressing frequency, but I have hopes that his wife will be nicer.

—LETTER TO GERTRUDE AND DAVID NEMEROV FROM FLORENCE, SEPTEMBER 30, 1951

We feel very small here. At breakfast the table was so big that we had to keep pushing the butter, salt, and sugar at each other like at a bowling alley...Last night Allan and I stayed "in the living room" after Doon went to bed and talked in wee small voices like we were breaking the silence. So amazing to have a living room, but especially such an immense one, that we often say to each other, "where shall we sit?" and when anyone leaves one room, Doon asks, "where are you going?"

—LETTER TO GERTRUDE AND DAVID NEMEROV FROM FLORENCE, SEPTEMBER 30, 1951

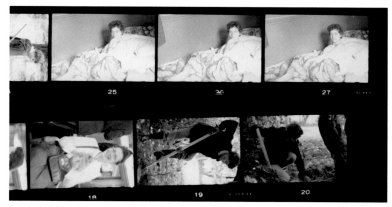

FRAGMENT OF ALLAN ARBUS CONTACT SHEET PHOTOGRAPHED IN BURGUNDY, FRANCE, WITH DIANE IN BED AND PATI HILL DIGGING ON THE FARM.

(ABOVE) TWO PHOTOGRAPHS PRINTED BY DIANE ARBUS, EUROPE, 1951–52. *(BELOW)* DIANE ARBUS, "LAUGHING GIRL, ITALY," CIRCA 1951.

...it has been such a wonderful month here. It's even lovely ending, because it makes so clear the picture of it. We lived so well, accomplished something photographing and reached a kind of peak of feeling between the three of us.

—LETTER TO GERTRUDE AND DAVID NEMEROV FROM FLORENCE, NOVEMBER 2, 1951

In December they rent a house on a farm in Frascati, outside of Rome, and make arrangements for Doon to attend the nearby Montessori School. Although the trip to Europe is intended to provide them a respite from fashion photography, it is also seen as an opportunity for each of them to pursue their own individual photography.

...Sunday we almost caused a riot going with our cameras and our great big blue Ford and the dog, into one of the nearby hill towns and walking around. What seemed liked thousands of children came scrambling out of every nook and cranny and crowded around us, jumping and laughing, so that we had to maneuver in a real complex way when we wanted to go home in order not to have thirty children riding home on the roof of the car with us...

—LETTER TO GERTRUDE AND DAVID NEMEROV FROM FRASCATI, DECEMBER 17, 1951

TWO FRAMES FROM A DIANE ARBUS CONTACT SHEET, CIRCA 1952. *(LEFT)* A HILL IN FRASCATI, ITALY,* AND *(RIGHT)* DOON GETTING OUT OF A DRESS.

1952–1954

As the prospect of their return home approaches, they begin to seek magazine assignments that may enable them to prolong their stay.

We have two assignments [for *Vogue*], one non fashion...someone's collection of paintings with the collector...the other, some evening gowns from the collections here (in color—worse luck...we have to scour Rome today for extra equipment.) This means some extra money, but more important I have several more ideas which they might use that we could do here or in Spain. This besides being a grand opportunity means we could come home as Vogue photographers instead of Glamour photographers who disappeared for a while, and also enables us to stay until we can get the studio back (May 1st) which skirts the problem of having to beg and rent studio space the first two months we are back...Also I'd love to stretch things out a bit and [would] love to go to Spain. All this IF they are interested...

—LETTER TO GERTRUDE NEMEROV AND ROSE RUSSEK FROM FRASCATI, JANUARY 27, 1952

Her method of developing a magazine project in this period, from the original idea to the proposal, research, and pursuit is consistent with the way she later approaches her own personal work.

... I think we will be going to Milan next week for Vogue, then a few days work in Rome for Vogue, then a weeny job in Florence for Glamour. Meanwhile, I have almost completed a lovely mammoth letter to a Vogue editor full of further suggestions which may or may not catch their fancy. Anyway, if we do get the Vogue pages done (it is still not absolutely definite) with some assurance that they will [be] published and paid for, we may do on our own one lovely idea which we had, because if Vogue won't use it, some other magazine probably will. It all depends on whether we can cut some of the red tape involved, which is fantastic. (It involves a certain amount of cooperation of the part of Vatican officials, and the organization of the Catholic church is too big to care, too Italian to be efficient.)

—LETTER TO GERTRUDE NEMEROV FROM FRASCATI, FEBRUARY 14, 1952

While living in Frascati, they receive from Pati Hill the completed manuscript of her first novel, *The Nine Mile Circle* (published in 1957 by the Riverside Press, Houghton Mifflin). Diane had known only what Hill had told her, that it was about *a child who killed its fantasy self for the sake of a friend*.[67] Diane responds to the manuscript:

Dear P.

The book is beautiful. It enchants so that when I stop reading it I am drunk with it. It's not circular like so many books (where the end is a prelude to the beginning)...it grows as surely as a flower does and its petals get plucked and blown away and in the end I was so sad I thought it must have died. Read it twice with interruptions, and then sometimes just picked up any part. It's very sad, not by anything in the subject of it, but like it's constructed by loss, I mean the losing of its parts, fading, forgetting...whereas most books, even the saddest, are resolved and tied up, each thread to another, so that somebody (author or reader) ends up with a package and takes it home. Really marvelous (the peoples, times, places, meshings, crossings)...and the marvelous absence of an obstreperous, omnipotent author...and the brilliant floating center of it. (I remember wondering ages ago where everything goes when you throw it away, garbage, things you lose, forget, etc and vaguely expecting they'd all turn up in some immense spiritual city dump...but it's like you followed a thousand things and found they all go different places and never stop.)

—LETTER TO PATI HILL FROM FRASCATI, FEBRUARY 16, 1952

I am in bed with a cold and Allan is getting one and every fifth person in Rome has flu. We have been "working" without doing much work. I mean we suddenly were assigned several assignments and invented several more and made all sorts of preparations and hunted for necessary equipment because it all meant we could stay longer. But suddenly, the best paying and also ghastliest assignment has been canceled. And we are relieved and horrified at the waste...(Haven't photographed in ages because of "work")...Dread going home, dread working, dread my family unreasonably. But I don't dread NY or Central Park or lots of places (which I secretly think belong to me).

—LETTER TO PATI HILL FROM FRASCATI, FEBRUARY 16, 1952

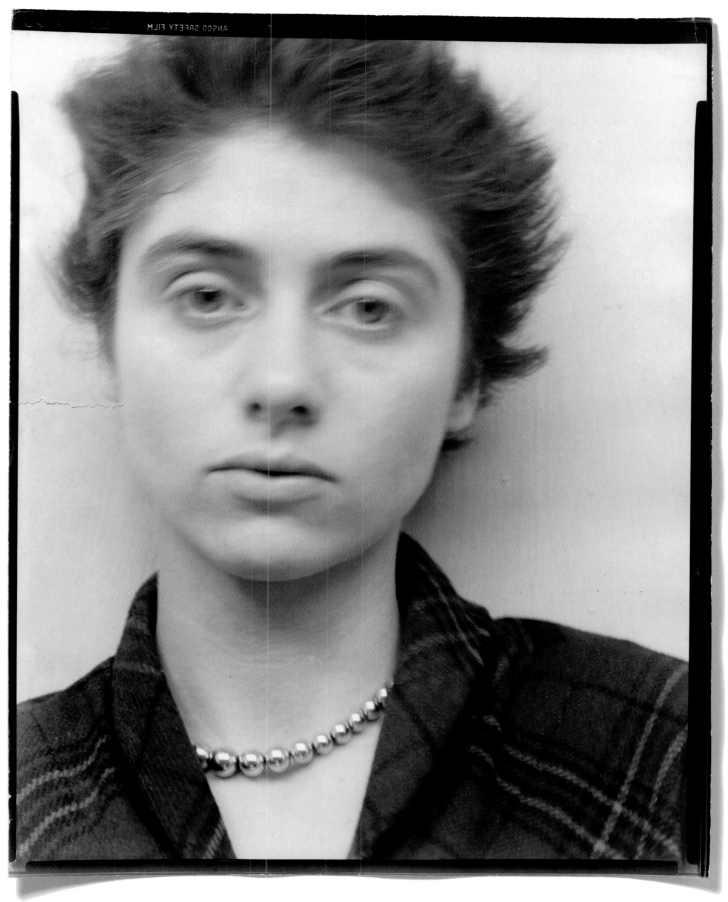

An Allan Arbus 8 x 10 film test on Diane, circa 1949.

After a number of changes in plans, they leave Italy on March 23 and sail home from France to resume their fashion photography business. They arrive in New York on April 7 in time to attend Alex Eliot and Jane Winslow's wedding.[68]

By mid-May they have rented a triplex at 319 East 72nd Street, in a building owned by the sculptor Paul Manship. The studio and darkroom are on the second floor, with a balcony overlooking a spare, white, two-story living room. Along one wall of the living room is a built-in bench with cushions and marble inset coffee tables designed by their friend Arthur Weinstein. Diane writes the Eliots, who are honeymooning in Europe: *Our house is perfectly beautiful in spite of the chaos and full of the loveliest views and the loveliest shadows at night.*[69]

...There are many simple pleasures, like our radiant bedroom, waking up in the morning with sun shining through our curtains and the tangled ivy, and cooking in our glorious big kitchen...and our lovely colored couch cushions, and the bookcase Allan built rising out of the chaos, and the general delight of finding that the choices I had felt so damned by making could materialize into such pleasant surprises...Allan is full of energy and courage and optimism, and builds and paints and wires things and fixes others with a whole assortment of unsuspected skills...

—LETTER TO ALEX AND JANE ELIOT ON THEIR HONEYMOON IN EUROPE, MAY 1952

I am full of human feeling because we don't see hardly anybody, only Nancy by appointment and I don't feel much like talking but when I see a face I think it looks wonderful, so I find myself complimenting everyone with quite a note of wonder in my voice...

—LETTER TO ALEX AND JANE ELIOT ON THEIR HONEYMOON IN EUROPE, MAY 1952

Robert Brown, an actor with whom they become friends, moves into the neighboring apartment with his wife and daughter. He recalls the Arbus home as a refuge in which he spends almost as much time as he does in his own.[70] On occasion, their studio and living room provide the setting for workshop productions in which he has a role. Through him, Diane renews her friendship with Fieldston classmate Stewart Stern, now a screenwriter living in Los Angeles and a friend of Brown's.[71]

In the autumn of 1952, the Arbuses enroll Doon in the Rudolf Steiner School, probably on the advice of the Eliots—May Eliot is a student there. A few years later Diane makes note of the following remarks by Steiner's principal, Henry Barnes, on the subject of progressive education: *In being encouraged to express themselves, the students were made to think that self-expression was the coin of life and that any bill could be paid with it. They didn't realize that experience won from life itself was necessary to cope with reality.*[72] These words appear to have struck a chord with her view of her own experience at Ethical Culture Fieldston School.

She and Nancy Christopherson, inveterate moviegoers, often take Doon and Poni with them. They see many Italian neorealist films: Vittorio De Sica's *Shoeshine* (1946), *The Bicycle Thief* (1948), *Miracle in Milan* (1951); Roberto Rossellini's *Open City* (1945); and Federico Fellini's *La Strada* (1954).

April 16, 1954, daughter Amy is born.

PHOTOGRAPHS FROM DIANE ARBUS CONTACT SHEETS OF *(LEFT)* THE ARBUSES' FRIEND ROBERT BROWN, AND *(RIGHT)* ALLAN HOLDING INFANT DAUGHTER AMY.

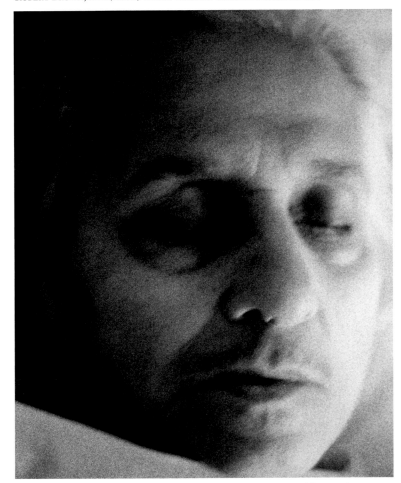

DIANE'S PHOTOGRAPH OF HER DEAD GRANDMOTHER, ROSE RUSSEK, MARCH 18, 1955.

THE MUSEUM OF MODERN ART'S 1955 CATALOG FOR *THE FAMILY OF MAN* EXHIBITION, CURATED BY EDWARD STEICHEN. THE DIANE AND ALLAN ARBUS PHOTOGRAPH OF A FATHER AND SON ON A SOFA IS AT THE BOTTOM OF THE SPREAD, SECOND FROM THE RIGHT.

1955

On March 28, Rose Russek, widowed in 1948, dies in her bedroom in the Nemerov apartment at 888 Park Avenue. Diane photographs her there. Three years earlier, in a letter to the Eliots, she had written: *My grandmother is sick…not alarmingly, but sadly ailing, sick and seventy and moving in with my parents, which is like the defeat of a proud spirit who forgot what the fight was all about.*[73]

A Diane and Allan Arbus photograph of a father and son on a sofa taken for *Vogue* is included by Edward Steichen in *The Family of Man* exhibition at The Museum of Modern Art.[74]

According to Allan, Diane's belief in herself as a photographer never wavers, in spite of the fact that she is continually plagued by uncertainty about what to photograph and constantly dissatisfied with the pictures she actually makes. She studies photography with Alexey Brodovitch, art director of *Harper's Bazaar*, at the New School for Social Research. Although she remains in contact with Brodovitch, in the ensuing years she finds the course of little help to her work.

The family moves to a triplex garden apartment with studio at 18 East 68th Street.

1956

Although she has been photographing since the early 1940s, Diane now, and apparently for the first time, starts numbering her negatives and corresponding contact sheets beginning with #1. She will maintain this system for the rest of her career. Among the first of these are a few rolls of 2¼ square negatives made with a Rolleiflex. She soon abandons this format in favor of the 35mm Nikon and only returns to it in 1962 when the square begins to become a hallmark of her mature style. During this period, she experiments with cropping both her images and her prints. Some of the prints are mounted on mat board, trimmed flush to the edges and treated as objects.

She and Allan end their photographic partnership. Her growing frustration with the business and with her role in the partnership (which she regards as essentially that of a glorified stylist) culminates one evening in the company of their friend Robert Brown when her account of a *Vogue* sitting leaves her in tears. In the end, Allan suggests she quit the business and she agrees. *I'm sure she felt like she was deserting the ship*, he says later. *But she was very glad to be out of it.*[75] She continues to do all her own printing in the studio darkroom, while her negatives are still processed and contacted by Allan's assistant under Allan's supervision.

She responds to an advertisement for a photography course taught by Lisette Model, whose work had been published by Brodovitch in *Harper's Bazaar* and exhibited at The Museum of Modern Art. *In the beginning, she*

(LEFT) ART DIRECTOR ALEXEY BRODOVITCH IN HIS OFFICE AT *HARPER'S BAZAAR*, CIRCA 1950, PHOTOGRAPH BY MAURICE TABARD. *(RIGHT)* PHOTOGRAPHER AND TEACHER LISETTE MODEL, CIRCA 1950, PHOTOGRAPH BY RAY JACOBS.

FULL FRAME OF 35MM PHOTOGRAPH OF A WOMAN IN A CROWD, N.Y.C. THE RED RECTANGLE WITHIN THE IMAGE INDICATES THE WAY THAT DIANE CROPPED AND PRINTED IT IN 1956.

TWO OF HER PHOTOGRAPHS: *(LEFT)* BOY IN A MAN'S HAT, N.Y.C. 1956; *(RIGHT)* WOMAN ON THE BOARDWALK, CONEY ISLAND, N.Y. 1956.

ALLAN ARBUS PHOTOGRAPH OF DIANE WITH DOON AND AMY IN 1956 ON SHELTER ISLAND, N.Y. IN A LETTER TO HER PARENTS THAT SUMMER, DIANE WRITES: *WHAT CHILDREN!...THEY ARE LIKE A NYMPH AND A SPRITE—ESPECIALLY WHEN THEY JUMP AND TUMBLE AROUND NAKED...AMY CAN RUN A MOST UNRELIABLE, HEADLONG, BRAVE AND BUMBLING LITTLE RUN, BUT SHE GETS THERE FAST.*

brought photographs which were nothing but grain...[76] Model recalls, a description that mirrors an account Diane later gives to her 1971 master class:

In the beginning of photographing I used to make very grainy things. I'd be fascinated by what the grain did because it would make a kind of tapestry of all these little dots and everything would be translated into this medium of dots. Skin would be the same as water would be the same as sky and you were dealing mostly in dark and light not so much in flesh and blood...It was my teacher, Lisette Model, who finally made it clear to me that the more specific you are, the more general it'll be...

— *Diane Arbus, Aperture 1972.*[77]

A number of attempts have since been made by Diane and others to account for the ensuing transformation in her work and, more significantly, in her feeling about photographing. One of several versions offered by Model goes as follows: *One day I said to her, and I think this was very crucial, I said, "Originality means coming from the source, not like Brodovitch — at any price to do it different..." And from there on, Diane was sitting there and — I've never in my life seen anybody — not listening to me but suddenly listening to herself through what was said.*[78]

In any event, as Allan recalls: *It was an absolutely magical breakthrough. After three weeks she felt totally freed and able to photograph.*[79]

1957–1958

Takes a second course with Lisette Model. According to Model, Diane frequently asks to look at her work and Model always refuses. At any rate, Diane would surely have seen the exhibition *70 Photographers Look at New York*, at The Museum of Modern Art, which includes Model's work.[80]

In a letter to her friends Lyn and Bob Meservey, who are living in New Haven while he is working on his doctorate degree in physics from Yale, Diane writes:

I am terribly behind in photographing—it's almost as if everything has to be done all the time. But at the same time I think I see how to do it. Photographing all day long, I used to get so high and dry, into a sort of a weird and rarefied air that I was not only in danger of never coming home but even of ceasing to photograph...like being in the ocean when the waves make you feel so strong you might swim to Europe...I am full of a sense of promise, like I often have, the feeling of always being at the beginning. (And I had a dream...which made perfect sense at the time and when I woke up it scattered and shattered...into something like 'Balance destroy supply under.' Bob will grin like always. Of course, he'll say, that's obvious.)

— LETTER TO BOB AND LYN MESERVEY, CIRCA 1957

For the sake of an application submitted to the Guggenheim Foundation in 1962, Diane categorizes her work of this period as follows: *children's games; sideshows; secret photos of steam bathers; photographs at the beach; movie theater interiors;* and *female impersonators.*[81] Locations

(*ABOVE LEFT*) MOVIE THEATER USHER BY THE BOX OFFICE, N.Y.C. 1956; (*ABOVE RIGHT*) CIRCUS WOMAN LEANING ON HER KNEE, N.Y.C. 1956. (*BELOW*) THE ENTRANCE TO HUBERT'S DIME MUSEUM AND FLEA CIRCUS ON 42ND STREET, 1956.

(*ABOVE LEFT*) DIANE AND ALLAN'S FRIENDS BOB AND LYN MESERVEY. (*ABOVE RIGHT*) AUDIENCE WITH PROJECTION BOOTH, N.Y.C. 1958; (*BELOW*) COUPLE EATING, N.Y.C. 1956.

DIANE ARBUS AT THE CIRCUS, CIRCA 1957. PHOTOGRAPH BY RICHARD KNAPP.

include Central Park, Times Square and its environs, Hubert's Dime Museum and Flea Circus, the Horn and Hardhart automat, Grand Central Station, the roller derby, rodeo, and circus at Madison Square Garden, Sammy's Bar on the Bowery, Coney Island's sideshows and wax museums, Woolworth's department store, Harlem dance halls, and the Carmine Street pool. She photographs traditional events such as the Macy's Thanksgiving Day Parade, the Feast of San Gennaro street festival, and Easter, Halloween, and New Year's Eve celebrations.

During this period she is also attempting—apparently without success—to find editorial work for herself as a photographer:

...once I made [for Tina Fredericks at the *Ladies' Home Journal*] and didnt never get paid for some pictures of how you shouldn't litter up the place, any place, so I spent a week sifting through cans and finding puddles with floating cigarette butts in them and squashed cellophane and orange peels and broken bottle ends and I followed flying newspapers especially comics because it was some of it color film...running like mad to keep up with dick tracy, and I ended up in the rambles part of the park, because she wanted a pastoral scene defaced with litter and it was autumn and two ducks swim there called charlie and lucy and they swam by the sort of strewn up grass very obediently and amy was with me and all of a sudden she said something in a small voice and came up out of the pond dripping with grasses and litter and tears and water like an angry inept mermaid and I had to scoop her into my arms with the camera and hobble out of the park and take her clothes off in the cab because she was shivering something fierce and carry her naked and giggling into that fancy house on 68th street, meeting one of our unspeakable neighbors on the way and dripping everything all over the lobby.

—LETTER TO MARVIN ISRAEL, SPRING 1960

The Nemerovs move to 60 Sutton Place South in 1957. The following year, David Nemerov, now retired from Russek's, moves to Palm Beach with Gertrude and devotes himself full-time to his painting.

Henry Wolf succeeds Alexey Brodovitch as art director of *Harper's Bazaar* in 1958.

1959

She begins keeping a yearly appointment book as well as a series of small working notebooks, a practice that will continue for the rest of her career.[82] The appointment books are primarily devoted to day-to-day events: scheduled meetings with friends, acquaintances, or professional colleagues; newspaper clippings or notations about upcoming events or phenomena she means to investigate; reminders of responsibilities related to home or family; ideas for photographic projects, and information about people or methods that may help her pursue them.

The notebooks are more eclectic. They include passages copied from books she is reading and observations made by her friends or happened upon by chance: *In this culture we tend each to think of ourselves as the protagonist of our own drama. There is little precedent for playing a subordinate role in someone else's* — N. (Nancy Christopherson), or *The best revenge is forgiveness.—Salada Tea*.[83] There are proposals for photographic projects and related lists; words, synonyms, conundrums, and thoughts; stories told by people she is photographing; an occasional impromptu release accompanied by a brief description of the picture. There are also the titles of books she intends to get for research purposes and names of people to track down as possible subjects or sources of ideas. From time to time, the contents mingle: a scheduled appointment may appear in a notebook or a project proposal on the page of an appointment book.

It is probably her friend Nancy Christopherson who introduces her to Zen literature and to the *I Ching*. One of the notebooks of 1959 consists in large part of excerpts from Zen literature, including Suzuki, *Zen Buddhism;* Alan Watts, *The Way of Zen;* Eugen Herrigel, *Zen in the Art of Archery;* Wei Wu Wei, *Fingers Pointing Towards the Moon;* and *Zen Flesh, Zen Bones*.[84] Much of what she jots down seems concerned with the nature, or the illusion, of time and appears in the notebooks between passages copied from Dostoevsky's *Notes from the Underground* and Bram Stoker's *Dracula*.[85]

In May, at the suggestion of *Esquire* articles editor Harold Hayes, she meets with the magazine's art director Robert Benton. The magazine is planning an issue devoted entirely to New York. She shows pictures to

TWO GIRLS ON THE BEACH, CONEY ISLAND, N.Y. 1958.

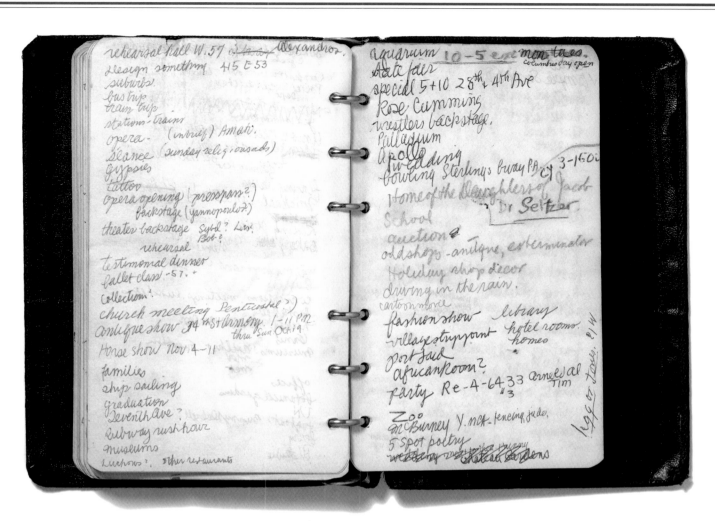

A SPREAD OF LISTS AND
A SPREAD OF QUOTATIONS FROM 1959 NOTEBOOK (NO. 1).

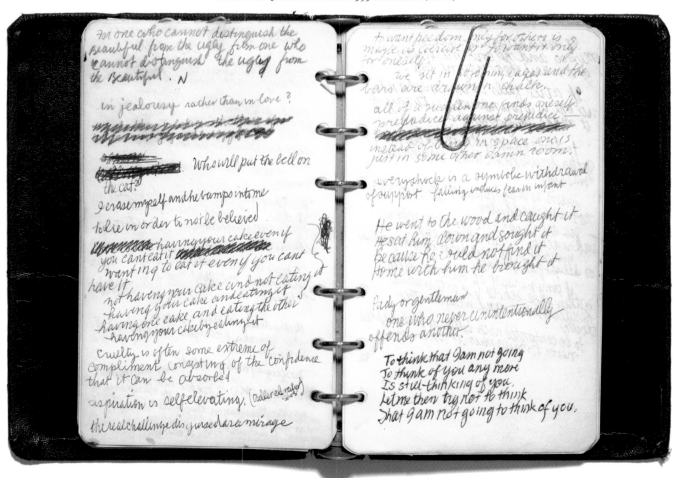

(LEFT) WOMAN AT A PUERTO RICAN DANCE, N.Y.C. 1958;* *(RIGHT)* WOMAN AND A DWARF BACKSTAGE AT THE CIRCUS, N.Y.C. 1959.

Benton, who is interested in her 35mm photographs taken inside darkened theaters. On May 7 she writes in her appointment book: *Benton wants movie pics, likes waxworks.*

Sends Benton subject ideas, as well as prints and contact sheets. She annotates some of the images with brief typewritten notes glued on verso of mounts. A picture of an eyeball from the horror movie *The Man Without a Body* is captioned: *An experiment by an eminent British doctor in keeping separate organs alive with a whole system of flashing lights and buzzing wires, dials and gauges, prior to grafting them on to people who happen to need such spare parts.* [86]

By this time she has almost entirely ceased cropping her images. With rare exceptions, she is printing the full 35mm negative as a vertical or horizontal rectangle in the center of an 11x14 sheet of photographic paper, leaving a border some 2 to 4 inches wide surrounding the image.

Moves in August with Doon and Amy from 18 East 68th Street to 131½ Charles Street, a converted carriage house adjacent to the 6th Precinct police station in Greenwich Village. Allan moves to 71 Washington Place where he establishes a studio and darkroom, and continues his work for fashion magazines, keeping the name of their former partnership, Diane and Allan Arbus. She still shares his darkroom, and the family meets regularly for long Sunday breakfasts at Charles Street. Although this is in fact a separation, they do not tell their parents until three years later. (As Diane notes in a letter to Model on September 25, 1962: *I finally told my family that Allan and I were living apart and they suffered a whole series of delayed hysterical reactions, ranging from poignant to revolting.*) [87]

In October, begins work on the New York issue for *Esquire.* The original plan to assign her all photography in the issue is soon abandoned in favor of the concept of an independent photographic essay. [88] Collaborating with Benton and Hayes, she develops a project about the city from the *posh* to the *sordid.* [89] In a letter to Benton, she elaborates:

...I have been looking in the Redbook [the Yellow Pages] under clubs. There is one called the Tough Club and the Scientific Introduction

Service and something called Ourselves, Inc. I was looking for some club that would look good for the upper in the sense of respectable reaches like Harold Hayes was talking about. Something like the D.A.R. or the W.C.T.U. or a society for the suppression of something or other like vice or sin. Maybe his secretary could find one such. Brady once photographed the D.A.R. and it was, in the French sense, formidable...I will go anywhere. The Edwardian Room and the Salvation Army.

—LETTER TO ROBERT BENTON, CIRCA OCTOBER 1959 [90]

The spectrum of photographic permissions Hayes helps her obtain during the course of the project ranges from the Grand Opera Ball at the Sheraton East Hotel to a trackman in the tunnel of the city subway system, from a children's dancing class at the Colony Club to the Greenwich Street Women's House of Detention. [91] One such request from Hayes is addressed to Walter Arm, Deputy Police Commissioner:

Dear Sir:

In connection with a special issue of Esquire on the subject of New York, we have assigned Miss Diane Arbus, 131½ Charles Street, New York 14, N.Y., to photograph various aspects of city life. For some of her work she will need a Police pass. Detective Wanderer, with whom we spoke on the telephone this morning, suggested that we write to you for this permission.

Is there any way in which she could have special permission to accompany on police calls officers working out of the Charles Street Precinct? Thank you very much for whatever you can do for us. [92]

The *Esquire* assignment crystallizes for her some of the moral issues that have traditionally haunted photography and that will continue to preoccupy her in one form or another. From the pragmatic point of view, as she writes Benton: *The releases are sometimes a problem: if people are grand enough they have learned never to sign anything and if they are degraded enough they can't.* [93] And more poignantly: *Couldn't the comment be foreborne or foregone? Tuesday I saw a man lying on the steps of a church on Lex Ave under a sign saying Open for Meditation and Prayer, with his fly open and his penis out. I couldn't ask him to sign a release, could you?* [94]

Toward the end of November, she meets Marvin Israel, a painter, graphic designer and former art director of *Seventeen* magazine (1956–58). In the early stages of an enduring friendship as lovers and colleagues, they write to each other nearly every day. [95] Both are struck by ironic parallels within their separate histories: parents in the women's clothing business, an Ethical Culture education. As she puts it a few months later in a postcard to him:

...Our bourgeois heritage seems to me glorious as any stigma, especially to see it reflected back and forth in the mirror of each other...It is magic, and magic chooses any guise and ours is just perhaps more hilarious than to have been Negro or midget. It always makes me laugh in the middle of some unbelievable instant to think how our parents would approve of each other. That is the joke we are on them and us and it. To be so Jewish and rich and middle class and from good families and to run so variously away from it that we come full circle and bump into each other. Like they say in the comics*?!!#$?Boinggg......

—POSTCARD TO MARVIN ISRAEL, JANUARY 19, 1960

A 1960 APPOINTMENT BOOK WITH A FLYER FOR THE HUMAN BLIMP.

1960

As a continuation of the *Esquire* project, she investigates and photographs bodybuilders, beauty contests, debutantes, derelicts at the Christian Herald Bowery Mission, Boy Scout meetings, youth gang meetings, a condemned hotel on Broadway and its residents, many of the performers from Hubert's Museum (including Andrew Ratoucheff, a Russian midget who does impersonations of Maurice Chevalier, and Hezekiah Trambles, known professionally as Congo the Jungle Creep, both of whom appear in the final published article), a pet crematorium, and members of the Jewel Box Revue's touring female impersonator show "Twenty-Five Men and a Girl." In the margin of a letter to Marvin Israel, she writes: *I would like to photograph everybody.*[96]

Her letters include detailed accounts of her photographic expeditions, punctuated on occasion by thoughts about the nature of being a photographer, about the power and responsibility of the enterprise:

The debutantes had to repeat over and over to each person who shook their hand on the receiving line, their name and the name of the place where they came from. There were about sixty of them. And maybe a thousand to shake their sixty hands. And those thousand mostly told the debutantes who they were too. Me and the press photographers were blessedly quiet.

—LETTER TO MARVIN ISRAEL, CIRCA JANUARY 1, 1960 [97]

I am photographing sluggishly but yesterday I found a nearby waterfront hotel whos inmates were so gracious and dippy that I photographed 5 of them and they signed releases and invited me back to see the rest...

—POSTCARD TO ALLAN ARBUS, ST. THOMAS, VIRGIN ISLANDS, CIRCA JANUARY 2, 1960

I went to the Grand Central ladies room to find your nomads but the matron said there was only that one Negro lady with the rag shoes and she hadn't seen her for a long time.

—POSTCARD TO MARVIN ISRAEL, JANUARY 4, 1960

I am not ghoulish am I? I absolutely hate to have a bad conscience, I think it is lewd...There was a lady stretched out on the ground... fallen, I think, yesterday weeping and saying to the cops please help me with

(ABOVE) MARVIN ISRAEL IN HIS STUDIO WITH HIS CAT, MOUSE, CIRCA 1964, PHOTOGRAPH BY MICHAEL FLANAGAN. (BELOW) POSTCARD FROM DIANE TO MARVIN ISRAEL, JANUARY 5, 1960.

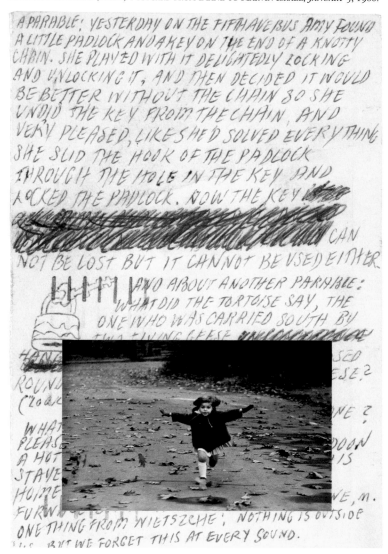

(ABOVE, SUPERIMPOSED ON THE POSTCARD) CHILD RUNNING IN THE PARK, N.Y.C. 1959. A SIMILAR PHOTOGRAPH OF AMY, AGE 5, AND THREE OTHER PHOTOGRAPHS BY DIANE, ARE PUBLISHED AS "THE AUGURIES OF INNOCENCE," *HARPER'S BAZAAR*, DECEMBER 1963.

(LEFT) Woman pointing, N.Y.C. 1960; *(RIGHT)* Boy in a cap, N.Y.C. 1960.

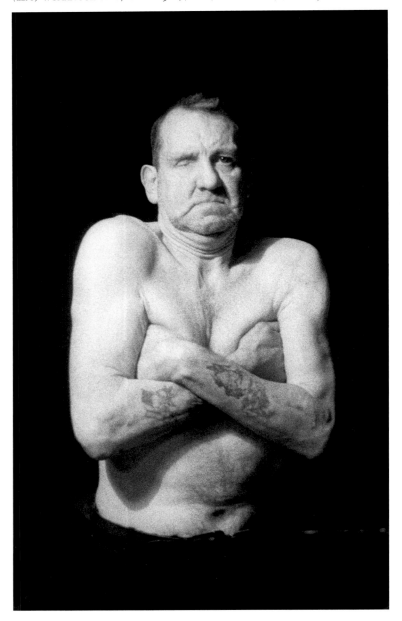

Walter Gregory, the Madman from Massachusetts, in the offices of *The Bowery News* on January 28, the night Diane first met him. As Diane later informed *Esquire*: *On the last Sunday in February, while crossing the street at Lexington and 125th on a foggy morning, 3 a.m., Gregory's coat caught on the back of a moving bus and he was killed instantly, age 63. This photograph is one of the six published in the photo essay "The Vertical Journey," Esquire, July 1960.*

one shoe off and covered with a blanket waiting for an ambulance which came, on lexington ave and 57th Street. Is everyone ghoulish? It wouldn't anyway have been better to turn away, would it?

—Postcard to Marvin Israel, January 5, 1960

I think it does, a little, hurt to be photographed. Please may I someday photograph your house, your ark, your things?

—Postcard to Marvin Israel, January 5, 1960

She makes several visits to Mother Cabrini, a disinterred saint, and reports that, according to an illuminated scroll on the wall: [She]...*had been buried in Chicago and...when she was canonized they dug her up and there was just a skeleton of her with shreds of flesh, they said luridly, clinging to it...They make it sound like a frightful faux pas on the part of god...*[98] In her current incarnation, *Mother Cabrini's bones are covered with wax so no wonder she looks like the waxworks and her coffin is crystal so no wonder she looks like snow white...*[99]

I got a terrible impulse to photograph her and I tremulously did which wasn't legal so I pretended to be praying and pregnant and once I used the long lens and that camera makes such a fearful groan and clamor that I almost was praying.

—Postcard to Marvin Israel, January 15, 1960

...A talk with the man from the Christian Herald (Harry Baronian) which runs the Bowery Mission so he could see what I was like and what my intentions were...he said the Bowery is going to be torn down and the men will move somewhere and make a new Bowery and then the Christian Herald will build a new mission for them. How indefatigable everyone is.

—Postcard to Marvin Israel, January 15, 1960

I went to the Mr. Universe Health Parlor and while I was waiting for the manager who proved to be a very sharp, bearded, flirtatious, snobbish, sculptor, pianist, ex-Mr. Universe, one man was weightlifting a bar with 325 lbs of weights on it, making heartrending grimaces and worse little series of gasps when suddenly he cried for help and stood there like Atlas in despair till two other guys rushed over to relieve him. It was uncanny because he couldn't put it down or drop it.

—Postcard to Marvin Israel, January 18, 1960

I am sitting in the meat market waiting for the heads...

—Postcard to Marvin Israel, January 19, 1960

There was a somewhat fantastic struggle between me and the pastor [Rev. Olford] of the Calvary Baptist Church over my soul...He is a real Baptist preacher who speaks like Maurice Evans, looks like a sort of David Niven and was born in Africa...There were several henchmen and they all wanted [to convert] me so badly that one of them even pushed me bodily thinking thereby to nudge my soul...I think they thought I would encourage ...[the derelicts] to follow, like the judas calf...[100]

—Letter to Marvin Israel, circa January 22, 1960

Two weeks later, Harry Baronian, acting as a kind of self-appointed impresario, arranges her first encounter with Walter Gregory, a legendary Bowery character known to neighborhood residents as the Madman from Massachusetts, whom she has been hoping to photograph:...*He has only one eye and the other is a small and pretty crescent folded absolutely shut like an eternal wink, and he is indeed quite drunk but pretending to be drunker...and his nose is folded once over sideways, like someone had tried to press him flat like people do to flowers...*[101]

...When I came in the madman looked furious and thrust his finger in my face saying who was I and lifting a bentwood chair over his head in a fine demonstration of madness he told me to say boo which I did and every time he got too mad harry would hum the stars and stripes forever and madman would drop everything and salute...and look like he was about to cry, murmuring about how he was undefeated middleweight champion of the us navy and belonged to the fbi.

—LETTER TO MARVIN ISRAEL, JANUARY 29, 1960

I don't press the shutter. The image does. And it's like being gently clobbered.

—POSTCARD TO MARVIN ISRAEL, FEBRUARY 4, 1960

Someone told me it is spring. but everyone today looked remarkable just like out of August Sander pictures, so absolute and immutable down to the last button feather tassel or stripe. all odd and splendid as freaks and nobody able to see himself, all of us victims of the especial shape we come in...[102]

—NOTE TO MARVIN ISRAEL, CIRCA SPRING 1960

The female impersonators are the real examples of playing a single role because each one forms only one kind of woman which has precious little to do with the kind of man they look like and you cant see one behind the other. It looks like a leap into a new doom....

—POSTCARD TO MARVIN ISRAEL, MARCH 17, 1960

This photographing is really the business of stealing...I feel indebted to everything for having taken it or being about to.

—POSTCARD TO MARVIN ISRAEL, CIRCA APRIL 1960

In a postcard to Israel, she suggests the following distinction between being a painter and being a photographer: *You invent what I discover.*[103] And on another occasion, makes a wry allusion to her own journalistic curiosity:

In the times yesterday there was something about a movie by Fellini [*La Dolce Vita*] about a reporter for a flossy picture magazine who in doing a story about Roman high, low and wild life falls utterly into it and is corrupted, lost, damned. Hmmm.

—LETTER TO MARVIN ISRAEL, CIRCA APRIL 20, 1960

On the April 19 page of her 1960 appointment book, apparently searching for a title for the *Esquire* article, she writes in pencil (and crosses out) the following musings on *Alice in Wonderland*: *I fell into it like Alice; Hayes and Benton were the White Rabbit;* and finally, *The journey was vertical and dizzying like Alice's.* The *Esquire* project is published in July as "The Vertical Journey: Six Movements of a Moment Within

FEMALE IMPERSONATORS IN MIRRORS, N.Y.C. 1958.

Dear Harold,

This is just to absolve ESQURE of any liability or responsibility for my safety and/or well-being while I am photographing at the Greater New York Packing Co.

See you in a month,

Thanks,

(ABOVE) WAIVER FROM DIANE IN CONNECTION WITH HER WORK AT THE MEAT MARKET. *(BELOW)* OPENING SPREAD OF "THE VERTICAL JOURNEY," *ESQUIRE*, JULY 1960; *(LEFT)* CONGO THE JUNGLE CREEP; *(RIGHT)* DAGMAR PATINO, GRAND OPERA BALL.

Schmierenschauspieler

In 1959, the Swiss magazine *Du* published a portfolio of August Sander photographs entitled "Deutsche Menschen," which included the above photograph. Marvin Israel gave Diane a copy of the portfolio. In a January 24, 1960, postcard to Marvin Israel, Diane writes, *A Schmierenschauspieler (there is a picture of one in the August Sander book the one I said looks like a magician) is a third-rate provincial actor, maybe in a traveling company. German words are wonderful the way they contain whole paragraphs.*

(left) Child teasing another, N.Y.C. 1960; *(right)* card for Professor Heckler's Trained Flea Circus at Hubert's Museum. In a postcard to Doon on July 11, 1960, Diane writes about taking Allan, who had apparently never been there before, to Hubert's Museum: *One night Pa asked me to take him to the freak show and everyone was delighted with him. Charlie said he was very handsome and that he'd always imagined him to be old and fat. Pa loved the fleas, specially the one who kicks a football. (Did you see that?) We both patted the snakes and Pa sat in the electric chair with great aplomb.*

the Heart of the City." Although she supplies detailed descriptions for the pictures in the six-page photo essay, only brief captions based on her texts are used.[104]

Even before completing "The Vertical Journey"—and months before its publication—she is exploring ideas for her next project. In late April she writes Israel: *It appears as if I can have another assignment so to speak for Esq if I can think of one, (I am to lunch with them on Monday and they sound benevolent though they may outgrow it by then.)*[105] The new project begins to evolve out of the one before like another branch of the same tree and is shaped, in part, by language:

Last week I looked up the word anomaly because I always thought it meant a fish out of water but I knew I was wrong and I was right. It means something not subject to analogy or rule, or something odd or strange or exceptional...and I saw the connection between freaks and eccentrics, the exception to every rule.

—Letter to Marvin Israel, April 20, 1960

At the suggestion of Charlie Lucas, manager of Hubert's Museum (*the great Mr. R.C. Lucas also known as Woofoo, Impresario Extraordinary, Inside Talker who's like I think that I will never see again...*),[106] she visits a number of small-town circuses, fairs, and carnivals, including Wirth's Circus in West Hempstead, Long Island; World of Mirth Carnival in Plainfield, New Jersey; Hunt's Circus in Palisades Park; and a carnival in Hagerstown, Maryland.[107]

...And backstage in the sun and mud squinting spangled mothers spank their squealing children or stuff plastic milk bottles into their mouths and I back up to get more in the frame and bump into an elephant... If in the big circus the art is to make something which has become easy look difficult again, here it is not quite to be able to do it at all.

—Letter to Marvin Israel, April 20, 1960[108]

Throughout the year she seeks and maintains contact with everyone who may help lead her to where she wants to go. There is Joe Loebenthal, *the man from the Dept of Corrections who knows about gypsies and white slave trade.*[109] There are the magicians James Randi (The Amazing Randi), who is also an expert on parapsychology,[110] and Milbourne Christopher, whose act, she says, *includes a trick of explaining a trick by a further trick, which is the supremest kind of eloquence...like a witty rejoinder in the dialogue with God...*[111] There is William Gresham, author of *Nightmare Alley*, a 1946 noir novel of carnival life;[112] Long John Nebel, host of a radio talk show whom she listens to regularly because of his unpredictable panoply of guests; and Joseph Mitchell, whose pieces in *The New Yorker* seem the work of a kindred sensibility.

Each subculture she begins to explore turns out to be, not only a territory unto itself, but a key to deciphering the rules of another, apparently unconnected, subculture so that the world, as she puts it, *seems...not so much small as done with mirrors.*[113] By the same token, what looks like a dead end often turns out to be a hidden door to an unlikely subject she hadn't thought to pursue.[114]

(ABOVE LEFT) WOMAN AT A BALL, N.Y.C. 1959; (ABOVE RIGHT) A COUPLE AT A DANCE, N.Y.C. 1960;* (BELOW LEFT) 35MM CONTACT STRIP OF RUSSIAN MIDGET ANDREW RATOUCHEFF AND HIS FRIENDS AT HOME. IN 1963 DIANE PHOTOGRAPHS RATOUCHEFF AND HIS FRIENDS AGAIN IN THE SAME LOCATION.

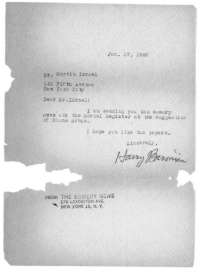

Jan. 17, 1960

Mr. Marvin Israel
141 Fifth Avenue
New York City

Dear Mr.Israel:

I am sending you the Bowery
news and the Social Register at the suggestion
of Diane Arbus.

I hope you like the papers.

Sincerely,

Harry Baronian

FROM: THE BOWERY NEWS
176 LEXINGTON AVE.
NEW YORK 16, N. Y.

(ABOVE) LETTER FROM HARRY BARONIAN, EDITOR OF *THE BOWERY NEWS*, TO MARVIN ISRAEL; (BELOW RIGHT) TATTOO PARLOR, CONEY ISLAND, N.Y. 1959; (BELOW LEFT) BUSINESS CARD FOR CHARLIE LUCAS, MANAGER OF HUBERT'S MUSEUM.

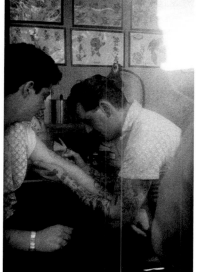

R. C. LUCAS
HUBERT'S MUSEUM

226 WEST 42ND ST.   FRI. - SAT. - SUN. - 2 TO 12 P.M.
NEW YORK 36, N. Y.   MON. TUES. WED. - 2 TO 11 P.M.

To Mrs.ⁿ Sanfelice:
100 Bono Natales

1960 APPOINTMENT BOOK, WITH CLIPPING ABOUT THE 100TH BIRTHDAY OF MRS. SANFELICE, WHOM DIANE LATER PHOTOGRAPHS.

WOOGIE WITH SNAKE, HUBERT'S MUSEUM, N.Y.C. 1959. WOOGIE WAS THE WIFE OF CHARLIE LUCAS, MANAGER OF HUBERT'S MUSEUM AND A PERFORMER THERE. IN A LETTER TO MARVIN ISRAEL, CIRCA NOVEMBER 1960, DIANE WRITES: *WOOGIE LEFT ME ALONE WITH THE RAT AND THE SNAKE SAYING DARKLY THAT I SHOULD KEEP MY HANDS WELL OUT OF THE WAY AND CALL HER AS SOON AS THE ONE HAD SWALLOWED THE OTHER. BEING ALONE WITH THEM WAS LIKE A SORT OF REVERSAL OF WHAT HAPPENED IN EDEN, WITH THE SNAKE SUCCUMBING TO ITS OWN TEMPTATION. THE RAT WAS MOSTLY WHITE WITH A PINK EYE AND ITS LEGS WERE SPLAYED WIDE APART IN COMPLETE ABANDON WHILE THE SNAKE WAS VERY KNOWING AND THE ENORMITY OF ITS MOUTH WAS A LITTLE LIKE A SMILE...IT LOOKED LIKE A SEXUAL PARADOX, A PARABLE TO BE ENACTED ON JUDGMENT DAY, IN WHICH THE FEMALE AT LAST ENTERED THE MALE. MAYBE IT IS THE GENET IN ME WHICH IS TRANSFORMING EVERYTHING.*

284 STEPPENWOLF

through this spring, sometimes on the cliffs, sometimes over the garden hedge; and when the elde—
began to bloom we gave each other the first sh—
kiss. It was little that children like us had —
give each other and our kiss lacked warmth an—

"Asexual reproduction of this plant with— our license is strictly prohibited under the provisions of the Plant Patent Act"

STEPPENWOLF 285

I was now, as I perceived, that good looking
and ardent boy whom I had seen making so
eagerly for love's door. I was living a bit of myself only—a bit that in my actual life and being
had not been expressed to a tenth or a thousandth
part, and I was living it to the full. I was watching it grow unmolested by any other part of me.
It was not perturbed by the thinker, nor tortured
by the Steppenwolf, nor dwarfed by the poet, the
visionary or the moralist. No—I was nothing
now but the lover and I breathed no other happiness and no other suffering than love. Irmgard
had already taught me to dance a—
and it was Emma first, the most bea—
all, who on an autumn evening be—
ing elm gave me her brown breasts t—
cup of passion to drink.

I lived through much in Pablo's—
and not a thousandth part can be —
All the girls I had ever loved were
gave me what she alone had to give
I gave what she alone knew how to
love, much happiness, much indulgen—
bewilderment, too, and suffering fell
All the love that I had missed in my
magically in my garden during t—
dreams. There were chaste and te—
garish ones that blazed, dark ones sw—
There were flaring lust, inward reve—

JEAN GEN[ET]
OUR LA[DY] OF THE FLO[WERS]
n° 36
THE TRAVELLER'S CO[MPANION]

(ABOVE) PHOTOGRAPH OF NANCY CHRISTOPHERSON (BELLAMY) FROM A CONTACT SHEET, CIRCA 1957,* WHOM DIANE ONCE DESCRIBED THIS WAY: *NANCY IS SOMEWHAT DOOMED TO KNOW WHAT SOMEONE IS GOING TO DO BEFORE THEY DO IT.* (RIGHT) GIRL WALKING ON A DIRT ROAD, SHELTER ISLAND, N.Y. 1955 ABOUT WHICH DIANE WROTE DOON: *I HAVE A BEAUTIFUL NEW PICTURE OF YOU THAT I GO TO LOOK AT OFTEN...ITS EVENING I THINK AND YOUR HAIR IS WILD AND YOU LOOK SO PROUD AND SWEET AND TOUGH LIKE THE PRINCESS AND THE YOUNGEST SON ALL AT THE SAME TIME.*

(ABOVE LEFT) MARVIN ISRAEL'S COPY OF HERMAN HESSE'S *STEPPENWOLF* (NEW YORK: HENRY HOLT & CO., 1957) WITH HIS WOODEN BOOKMARK. (ABOVE RIGHT) COPY OF JEAN GENET'S, *OUR LADY OF THE FLOWERS* (PARIS: THE TRAVELLER'S COMPANION SERIES, OLYMPIA PRESS, 1957) GIVEN TO DIANE BY MARVIN ISRAEL. (LEFT) DIANE'S 1960 APPOINTMENT BOOK. (RIGHT) COLLAGE POSTCARD FROM DIANE ARBUS TO MARVIN ISRAEL, NOVEMBER 1960: *WAS MENDELSSOHN BACH REINCARNATED.*

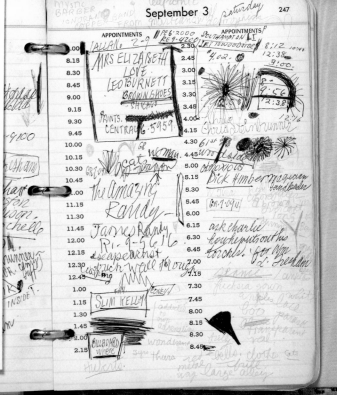

SUZY Nature's Enigma — A puzzle to the entire scientific world

BIOGRAPHY OF THE WORLD'S STRANGEST HUMAN

This young lady was born with a normal face (as you can see) but with the strangest body the world has ever known. She peels the skin on her face nightly. She is the only child of normal Swiss parents and was born in the year 1925 as the most remarkable Human Enigma. For many years doctors used her as a fit study to demonstrate a miracle to medical science, but could not help her to be the same as you.

September 3 — Saturday — 247

```
i am so joined.we are a circus.breathtaking,dazzlingand hushed.you,th
e firexix fireater,strongman,juggler.me,the tightrope walker and the
lady liontamer.we,the aerialists swinging and falling and catching fro
m our toes to our fingers.and shot from a cannon and bareback or perf
orming a trumpet duet of my country tis of thee.i am the clown who we
eps and you the one who sits rocking on a structure of precarious cha
irs.Then we tumble,form a human pyramid,somersault,bow and applaud r
if we fall we land giggling,dizzy,xxxxxxxxxx in the net.      ♡
```

(ABOVE) NOTE FROM DIANE ARBUS TO MARVIN ISRAEL, MARCH 27, 1960. (NEAR RIGHT) THE CYCLONE ROLLER COAST-
ER AT NIGHT, CONEY ISLAND, N.Y. 1959.* (FAR RIGHT) "THE ARTIST AT WORK," AN ESSAY BY ALBERT CAMUS IN HIS
BOOK *EXILE AND THE KINGDOM* (NEW YORK: KNOPF, 1958) WITH A CLIPPING (*WOMAN TORTURED BY AGONIZING ITCH*)
STUCK INSIDE AS A BOOKMARK.

"...ery tight inside a man's head."
—Céline

Yes Santa Claus there is a Virginia.
Eddie Kirkman

208   *Louis-Ferdinand Céline*

"The Minstrels," it said on their big drum . . . They went on and on . . . a roll of the drum . . . a happy landing . . . a pirouette . . . A great big enormous siren rips through the echoes . . . The crowd stops in its tracks . . . They all move down to the edge to watch the ship landing . . . I wedge myself into the staircase right next to the waves . . .

A lot of brats in little boats were whirling around in the eddies looking for the hawser . . . The launch, the big upper boiler in the middle, was bringing the papers. The launch had a tough time with the current . . . in the middle of the blackwater to come closer . . . with her . . . Finally the wise guy against an enormous bundle of . . . from the dock . . . It cracked . . . had her nose into the current, after . . . She churned against the tethered monster . . . She let loose . . . was beaten . . . all alone in the water . . . We turned back to the with the organs and the mountains . . . ill going on . . . I felt better once . . . magic . . . an entirely different . . . like a crazy picture . . . never catch me again . . . that . . . that no one would ever recognize . . . more to fear, that nobody'd . . . created myself to a ride on the merry change. I took three whole frenzies and some soldiers . . . faces like dolls, eyes like blue . . . I wanted to take another . . . how my dough . . . I went off . . . I tore open my lining, the banknote, the whole pound. And . . . frying steered me to a place . . . It was fritters . . . I could . . . on a cart with little wheels . . . with the batter . . . I can' . . . he had two teeth missing in

Mar WIN Israel
NEW YORK, TEN. N. Y.

THIS SIDE OF CARD IS FOR ADDRESS

The following behaviors are at all ages considered worse by girls than by boys: truancy, destroying school materials, lying, cheating, stealing, profanity, smoking, notewriting, interrupting, disobedience, impertinence, cruelty, tattling, contrariness, temper tantrums, impudence, domineering, being too shy, being over-critical of others, nervousness, dreaminess, slovenliness, suspiciousness.

DEATH ON THE INSTALLMENT PLAN   209

front . . . She never stopped laughing . . . She had a fringed hat with a big pile of flowers on top . . . crushed under the weight . . . a regular hanging garden . . . and long muslin veils that hung down into her kettle . . . She took them out with a sweet smile . . . She seemed very sick . . . make motions to show that I'm going to walk over by the pubs . . . to have a little fun . . . I leave her my suitcase in exchange and my blanket . . . I put them down beside her camp chair . . . I make a sign for her to watch them . . . I go back to the crowd . . .

With nothing to weigh me down, I head for the shops . . . I stroll past the piles of grub . . . But I'm full up, I can't eat anymore . . . The clock strikes eleven . . . Drunks come out in waves and stream down the esplanade . . . this way and that way, crashing against the wall of the customs house . . . tumbling, roaring, spreading out, dispersing . . . The ones that are stewed but still swag-

Healing Is Divine

s Mendelssohn GOD'S TRUTH

After The Ectoplasm cash,

Does Hanging Kill the Man?

lled Death.

n Reincarnated

EXORCISM STANDARD ALUMINUM TRUMPETS

My Psychic Observer subscription expires with the next copy. I am not renewing because I find I am not enjoying the paper as once did. ION ALL MEDIUMS

open up my unde Student Size $4.00
ut the devil the Professional Size $5.00
sure that from here HOW TO OVERCOME MEDIUMSHIP BLOCKS.
elieve in You and my knowledge of our Spirit.
ct that You ar loved ones has shown me any-
HY SUFFER? thing it is that a "Beauty Con-
ealing power test" would never interest them.

impressionist "I waited anxiously to hear the first words of Spirit. It came, in now become f Spanish! For a moment I didn't , is working th know what I could do. Then ng hankies impregnated man body. Jesus Christ is the Water of Life Paul Klee has hin is the sexual fluid that gives light and life to th ed to he has seer The sexual fluid produces blood which th ectly clear, as it

materialization
as a spirit lives s
body and not attached
body and is identical
in material world or
body, which also loo
ut spirit made. If
or had, please write to
they could as the spirit
cling to a material p
that a material person
as birds and animals al
hout spiritual envelopment.
Jesus Christ is the Water of Life

Please enclose love offering to cover cost of air
no American stamps. | 100% VIRGIN WOOL SEA
Stoles, 70x17 inches, knotted frin

The Artist at Work

to become panic. Their attentions multiplied and the child wanted for nothing.

His alleged misfortune finally won Jonas a devoted brother in the person of his friend Rateau. Rateau's parents often entertained his little schoolmate because they pitied his hapless state. Their commiserating remarks inspired their strong and athletic son with the desire to take under his protection the child whose nonchalant successes he already admired. Admiration and condescension mixed well like everyt

When ished his get into there and the leadi of the op in cultu he wor

War
and Proc
BROOKS APPLIANC
E State St., Marshall, Mich.
ble for
l War I
their hus-
ected dis-
certain in-
uildless wid-
ll qualify if

Woman Tortured by Agonizing ITCH

"I nearly itched to death for 7½ years. Then I discovered a new wonder creme. Now I am happy," writes Mrs. D. Ward of Los Angeles. Here's blessed relief from the tortures of new am

Paralyzed Wife And, Lo, She Is Cured

Toulon, France, Jan. 17 (UPI).—Julien Hauspiez, 75, tried to kill his wife to end her suffering as an incurable paralytic. He wound up by curing her, police said today.

Two years ago, his wife, Marie, now 77, became bedridden with a mysterious paralysis which doctors pronounced incurable.

Late Friday night after his wife was asleep, police said, Hauspiez slipped into her bedroom with a knife. He tried to plunge the knife into her heart but inflicted only a superficial wound on the side of her head.

She Flees Screaming

Mrs. Hauspiez woke up, leaped from the bed and ran screaming across the room. It was the first time she had used her legs in two years.

Then the husband tried to hang himself, but a neighbor arrived, cut him down and revived him.

Doctors said today that both husband and wife apparently had completely recovered.

Mob Marche On En

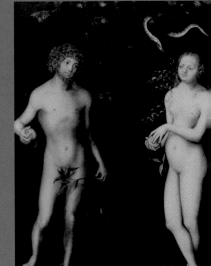

(*ABOVE*) CONEY ISLAND, N.Y. 1960 [WINDY GROUP]; (*BELOW*) CONTACT STRIPS OF THE MEXICAN DWARF LAURO MORALES, IN HIS HOTEL ROOM IN 1960. IN A LETTER TO MARVIN ISRAEL, APRIL 20, 1960, DIANE WROTE: *WHEN CHA-CHA-CHA (HIS THEATRICAL NAME) CAME CLOSER AND INCLINED HIS HEAD IN A SORT OF RAPTURE I WAS PHOTOGRAPHING IN A KIND OF AMAZE OF MY OWN...* SHE WILL PHOTOGRAPH HIM AGAIN ON A NUMBER OF OCCASIONS, INCLUDING IN HIS HOTEL ROOM IN 1970.

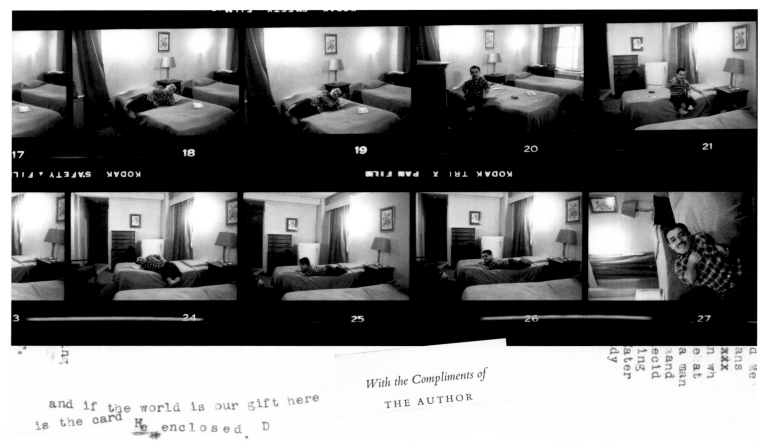

BENEATH CONTACT STRIP A TYPEWRITTEN MARGINAL NOTE ON A LETTER TO MARVIN ISRAEL, NOVEMBER 13, 1960, AND THE ENCLOSED CARD TO WHICH IT REFERS.

...I am delighted to be on the track. I am really dick tracy. only when I get on the trail it lengthens...Everything is corroboration so that although the trail lengthens it is a lot like the farther afield you go the more you are going home. as if the gods put us down with a certain arbitrary glee in the wrong place and what we seek is who we really ought to be...

—LETTER TO MARVIN ISRAEL, NOVEMBER 13, 1960

Running parallel to—and sometimes intersecting—the research and amateur detective work during the course of the year are the more aimless, yet in many ways equally significant, ventures:

Friday night...I went into a Child's—I mean the restaurant...and at a near table there was a couple and the woman was an incredible spastic, very plain and pale and middleaged like lillian gish, like an out of order mechanical doll. She was eating her custard when I came in and dancing while she was eating it, seven motions for every once the spoon got to her mouth. The man was very tall and thin, graceful fatherly agile cheerful, affable, talkative, when they got up he held her coat for her to dance into and her face didn't ever change, she looked terribly plain and dazzled, like someone seeing visions, and after she got into her coat he bent over like a tree and kissed her.

—LETTER TO MARVIN ISRAEL, CIRCA JANUARY 19, 1960

I am on the train in New Jersey, very sleepy and only roused by the barrenness of what is out the window, winter grass and, once, yellow mud and sometimes pink earth...The wedding was not very good. The bride looked like a fashion editor and this is a blind spot for me and the church was like an airplane hangar but I feel better just walking among strangers...

—POSTCARD TO MARVIN ISRAEL, APRIL 13, 1960

...I am in Coney Is. In a glorious hotel I will show you when you get back. It is like a merry-go-round in a garden, never saw such a glorious place. My room is the color of blue ice cream. Last night there was a wild storm first the surf was pale and white and wild and foggy and the wind was fierce so everyone was flapping, blowing, whirling, running and the few swimmers leaped and giggled with hair dripping like snakes across their faces, then it poured so that the streets were flooded. I walked home sloshing through a sort of lake mid calf deep, littered with garbage and swirling like mad, feeling for the place where you step down off the curb because it was too deep under to see. Today is glorious. Happy Independence Day. How is it? Independence, I mean.

—POSTCARD TO DOON ARBUS, AT CAMP INDIAN HILL, STOCKBRIDGE, MASS., JULY 4, 1960

Yesterday I went all wet and bedraggled to the preliminaries of the miss america contest where they were choosing miss new york city...The categories of judging were 1. personality in a bathing suit. 2. personality-inaneveninggown and 3. talent which counted double what the other two categories counted...It took about ten hours of interviews, sashaying and performing what they called their talent and the poor girls looked so exhausted by the effort to be themselves that they continually made the fatal mistakes which were in fact themselves...Our only

(LEFT) EDDIE CARMEL AT HUBERT'S MUSEUM AS THE WORLD'S BIGGEST COWBOY, 1960;* AND (RIGHT) AT HOME WITH HIS PARENTS.* (BELOW) FRAGMENT OF DIANE'S MAY 16TH 1960 APPOINTMENT BOOK.

WOMAN SHOUTING, CONEY ISLAND, N.Y. 1960.

hope for judgement day is that god judges us for personalityinan-eveninggown while we are in a bathing suit...

—LETTER TO MARVIN ISRAEL, JULY 15, 1960

I went to the assembling of the columbus day parade. women in long capes lined with orange silk and girls with flagpoles coming up from between their legs and ancient veterans and boys in marine battle dress and girls with SACRED HEART written on their left breast, acres of them...I have phorgotten how to photograph. Every once in a while that happens. Still its not bad.

—LETTER TO MARVIN ISRAEL, OCTOBER 13, 1960

Last night I went to a church dance on henry street for neighborhood kids some of whom are gang kids. It was terribly dark, marvelous dancing, very natty guys, everybody negro except about 4 people including me and the priests who wore their full regalia and looked very splendid sweeping through and among the dancers like cats watching mosquitoes...

—LETTER TO MARVIN ISRAEL, CIRCA NOVEMBER 1960

...I spent one fine day on 42nd st, a dark day which started to rain a lit-tle...and oh that street was wonderful, everyone winking and nudging and raising their eyebrows and running their hands through their mar-celled hair and I saw one of your seeing blind men and a man like you have told me about with the pale ruined face-that-isnt-there and a thou-sand lone conspirators...

—LETTER TO MARVIN ISRAEL, CIRCA NOVEMBER 1960

Around mid-November she appears to be on the verge of purchasing a new camera, probably another Nikon. Allan recalls her asking him to test some lenses: *I must have tested five lenses*, he says. *Nothing was sharp enough for her.*[115] The dissatisfaction with her relationship to the camera will recur at various intervals throughout her career, often signaling an impending change in her work. On this occasion, having borrowed Israel's camera in the interim,[116] she writes:

...I need my new camera badly. Meanwhile, I only use yours for which I thank you, it seems to me very fine, even intellectual and aristocratic but it is like I am pretending to photograph. I cannot believe it really is doing it. I have to keep hoping and IMAGINING which I hate, and nothing looks so wonderful that I just want to stay with my eye to the keyhole forever like with that other camera which is just a damn seduc-tive liar where you see what you're going to get but you don't get what you saw. So I am turning over a new leaf but the page is stuck.

—LETTER TO MARVIN ISRAEL, CIRCA NOVEMBER 1960[117]

Toward the end of the year, in preparing to write a proposal to *Esquire* on the subject of eccentrics, she reports: *I have been holed up in the public library with Kirbys Wonderful Museum of Remarkable Characters and Wilsons Magazine of Curious and Odd Memoirs and Anecdotes and I am agog with stories...*[118] She also sends a letter to her brother, who has been teaching at Bennington College in Vermont, in which she gives the fol-lowing description of what she hopes to do:

I am working on something now, the eccentrics I have so long thought of, or rather people who visibly believe in something everyone doubts,

and remembering a commodity of dreams [the title of Howard Nemerov's collected short stories, published by Secker & Warburg, London, 1960] I wondered if there were any such anywhere round your vicinity which would provide me the excuse and oppty for a visit...Any imposters, or people with incredibly long beards, or ones who believe in the imminent end of the world, or are reincarnations or keep lions in their living room or embalmed bodies or even skeletons or have devel-oped some especial skill like a lady in Florida who is meant to eat and sleep under water, or affect some remarkable costume or other, or collect things to the point of miserliness? Don't trouble about it, or bother to answer, unless when you look up from the page the Messiah comes wan-dering out of the woods. Anyway how are you? and what working on? I am fine except obsessed. mch lve d.

—LETTER TO HOWARD NEMEROV, CIRCA FALL 1960[119]

In response to the proposal she submits to Benton and Hayes in November, *Esquire* assigns her the story. Presumably at her request, Hayes provides her a brief To Whom It May Concern letter of accred-itation.

1961

The Eccentrics preoccupy her throughout most of the first half of the year and account for the contents of three of her notebooks (No. 4, No. 5, and No. 6). In some cases, her search is merely a matter of finding potential candidates she already knows, like Joe Allen, a contortionist from Hubert's, also known as the Backwards Man.[120] (*Joe Allen is a metaphor for human destiny—walking blind into the future with an eye on the past,*[121] she writes on a page of her appointment book, and in one of her notebooks: *The Backwards Man: the man who can see where he was...nostalgia...*[122]) In other cases, locating the people she describes as *a few of the most lyrical, mag-ical, metaphorical,*[123] requires more ingenuity.

...I found William Mack the sort of furry rasputin who is courtly and tedious and sinister, remarkably like someone who will appear in the daily news newly dead...a retired german merchant seaman and moslem convert and that sort of union square etymologist who can derive any word from any other...He is given to saying things like that moses wasn't a jew and shakespeare didn't write any plays which make me quite tired to hear and I never know what to say in reply. But he is very splendid looking, like a seer who has forgotten his own secret or an anachronism who wishes it was obsolete. proud, formidable and airless like an unprincipled martyr...the world is full of fictional characters looking for their stories.

—LETTER TO MARVIN ISRAEL, JANUARY 12, 1961

On January 19, she travels to Washington with Max Maxwell Landar, *an 80-year-old man about 4 feet high who pretends to be Uncle Sam because he thinks people would like to think he is.*[124]

He took me to Washington for the Inauguration [of John F. Kennedy], walking the entire way from one end of the train to the other, pro-

Dear Robert and Harold,
       About eccentrics.....
       Edith Sitwell says in what is the prettiest definition:
ANY DUMB BUT PREGNANT COMMENT ON LIFE,ANY CRITICISM OF THE WORLD'S
ARRANGEMENT,IF EXPRESSED BY ONLY ONE GESTURE,AND THAT OF SUFFICIENT
CONTORTION,BECOMES ECCENTRICITY.Or, if that word has too double an
edge we could use some others:the anomalies,the quixotic,the dedicat
ed,who believe in the impossible,who make their mark on themselves,
who-if-you-were-going-to-meet-them-for-the-first-time-would-ave-no-
need-of-a-carnation-in-their-buttonhole.
       Like the very irate lady who appears at night pulling a
red kiddies express wagon trimmed with bells and filled with alley
cats in fancy hats and dresses.And a man in Brooklyn called The Mystic
Barber who teleports himself to Mars and says he is dead and wears a

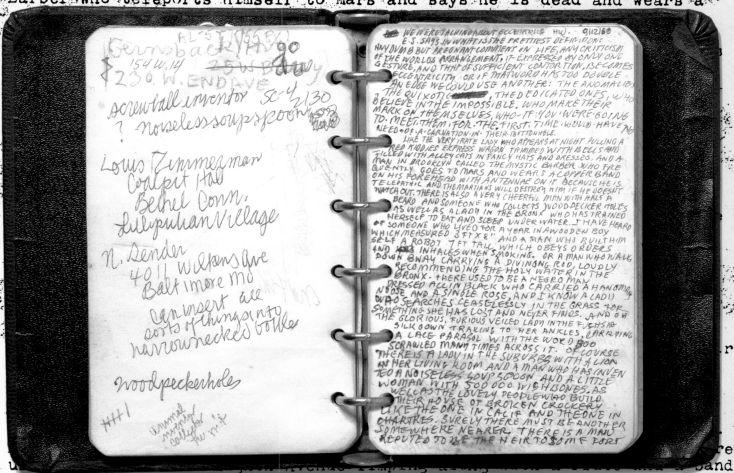

aged head,a living replica of The Spirit Of '76.And there is a man who
has 82 skeletons and 26 mummies in his basement as well as someone who
can write the Gettysburg Address on a human hair,although that might be
rather hard to see.All we need are a few of the most lyrical,magical,
metaphorical,like the man in New Jersey who has been collecting string
for 20 years,winding it in a ball which is by now 5 feet in diameter,
sitting monstrous and splendid in his living room.And I have heard of
a one-eyed lady miser who can be found in the Automat.
       These are The Characters In A Fairy Tale For Grown Ups.
       Wouldn't it be lovely?
       Yes.

Diane

FACSIMILE OF DIANE'S LETTER TO ROBERT BENTON AND HAROLD HAYES ABOUT THE ECCENTRICS PROJECT, CIRCA NOVEMBER 1960,
AND A PAGE IN HER 1960 NOTEBOOK (NO. 5) WITH AN EARLIER HANDWRITTEN DRAFT OF THE LETTER.

WILLIAM MACK IN HIS 7x8 ROOM, N.Y.C. 1961. ACCORDING TO DIANE'S TEXT, *PICKING UP BOTTLES IS WHAT HE CALLS HIS DIVERSION AND HE IS HUMOROUSLY INDULGENT WHEN PEOPLE GIVE HIM MONEY, WHICH THEY MUST SELDOM DARE TO DO BECAUSE HE IS SUCH AN AWESOME, NOBLE, ENORMOUS, POSSESSED AND LEGENDARY FIGURE. HE APPEARS TO BE THE BEARER OF AN UNDECIPHERABLE MESSAGE.*

(LEFT) AN UNPUBLISHED PHOTOGRAPH OF JACK DRACULA, THE MARKED MAN, WHO, DIANE WRITES, *IS EMBELLISHED WITH 306 TATTOOS (ESTIMATED VALUE: $6000.00). (RIGHT)* MISS STORMÉ DE LARVERIE, THE LADY WHO APPEARS TO BE A GENTLEMAN. THE TEXT PUBLISHED IN THE FEBRUARY 1962 ISSUE OF *INFINITY* READS: *STORMÉ REGARDS THE TRANS-FORMATION AS A DELICATE ART AND HAS CONSCIENTIOUSLY EXPERIMENTED TO PERFECT THE CUT, FIT, SHAPE, AND STYLE OF HER APPEARANCE AS A MAN, WITHOUT EVER TAMPERING WITH HER NATURE AS A WOMAN, OR TRYING TO BE WHAT SHE IS NOT.*

claiming his mission. The plan was for me to photograph him being the First Man To Shake The Hand of Dwight D. Eisenhower When He Was No Longer President but we couldn't get close enough. Instead we slept on benches in Union Station...and he climbed the Washington Monument in a blizzard, all 898 steps of it...solemnly delivering his oration to George Washington at the bottom, for an audience of the five guards and me.

—"THE FULL CIRCLE," *HARPER'S BAZAAR*, NOVEMBER 1961

An entire subcategory intrigues her for a while: the Spiritualists, or Psychics, or, as she puts it on one occasion, "Sensitives." She considers including in the story both Andy Sinatra (*The Mystic Barber, who teleports himself to Mars and says he is dead and wears a copper band round his fore-head with antennae on it to receive his instructions from the Martians*[125]) and Bishop Ethel Predonzan of the Cathedral of the Creator, Omnipresence, Inc. of Astoria, Queens. This prompts Harold Hayes to send her the fol-lowing cautionary note:

Dear Diane,

Two things:

We've had a legal ruling that under no circumstances are we entitled to pub-lish photographs of people under any conditions other than those represented to the subject. That is, you can't take a picture of someone for the purpose of showing him as an "eccentric" unless that person knows he is being shown in this light.

Two, all this comes up because we received a couple of calls in the office from some distressed people (most recently, Bishop Ethel Credonzan [sic] of Jamaica, Long Island) wanting to know why we are printing pictures on spiritual sub-jects...I do believe that you'd better stay exactly within the letter of the law when describing your assignment to anyone you desire to photograph.[126]

Immediately preceding or following this letter from Hayes, Diane receives a phone call from the Bishop herself:

the bishop called again to say that some man has been casting doubt on me, saying that Esquire is not a spiritual magazine and that I am just try-ing to make a fool of her but she hates this man and he is not spiritual, in fact he is a press agent and this morning the Lord told her to beware of jack bell which is his name and He talked very nice about me and He said of me, she is innocent, and the bishop prayed over the telephone for the ball of fire to be made manifest in my photographs and she wept and she blessed me and said no one could hurt us and I agreed.

—LETTER TO MARVIN ISRAEL, CIRCA 1961[127]

By the beginning of June, Diane has narrowed down the subjects for the Eccentrics story, made and printed the photographs, and is starting to write the text to deliver the project to *Esquire*.[128] In July, she sends a let-ter to Doon, who is working at a summer theater in Maine:

...I spent the weekend of the fourth holed up writing about twelve hours a day on the rest of the Odd People and taking walks and eating pickles and I finished it and they are most terrifically pleased and so am I. I am hoping to start on another assignment or two, similarly long range kinds, right away, for which I have several delicious ideas...I have been in a queer empty excited state ever since I finished the assignment, wak-ing at 4 or 5AM restless as a jumping bean and going for a walk and to the movies where I then don't want to stay and feeling alternately haunted and blessed.

—LETTER TO DOON ARBUS, CIRCA JULY 1961

The completed story, entitled "The Full Circle," includes portraits of six people with accompanying texts on each. In addition to William Mack, Sage of the Wilderness, and Uncle Sam, there is Jack Dracula, The Marked Man; Miss Cora Pratt, The Counterfeit Lady; His Serene Highness Prince Robert de Rohan Courtenay (*the rightful Hereditary claimant to the Throne of the Byzantine Eastern Roman Empire*) and Miss Stormé de Larverie, The Lady Who Appears to Be a Gentleman. (Stormé, whom Diane first encountered in 1960 in connection with her work on "The Vertical Journey," is in fact the girl in the Jewel Box Revue's female impersonator show "Twenty-Five Men and a Girl.")

When Henry Wolf becomes the first art director of Huntington Hartford's new cultural magazine *Show*, Marvin Israel replaces Wolf as art director of *Harper's Bazaar*. Israel—who had studied with Brodovitch at Yale—is both temperamentally and philosophically allied with the Brodovitch tradition. He envisions the magazine as a forum for challenging, nurturing, and celebrating the photographers and artists it publishes. He and Richard Avedon, *Bazaar*'s staff photographer since 1945, form an immediate bond as co-conspirators, committed to pushing the magazine into uncharted territory.

Esquire was wildly appreciative but...they admitted they probably plan to leave out Stormé and Cora for lack of space and I said I didn't know if I would agree to let them have it in that case.[129] Meanwhile Marvin called them to say he'd like to publish it [in *Harper's Bazaar*] if they don't which must have made them jump and which would be wonderful but unlikely so as it stands no one has bought it and everyone likes it and its fine but I'm glad to stop thinking about it because praise is very unsettling.

—LETTER TO DOON ARBUS, CIRCA JULY 1961

In late August, after notifying her that *Esquire* has decided not to publish the Eccentrics, Hayes writes asking her to *destroy or return...whichever you prefer* the letter of accreditation he had given her in connection with the project.[130] She replies: *Enclosed is the letter of accreditation which I am both destroying and returning since I couldn't decide which I preferred. Thank you for it.* And adds: *If I am to deduce that you are feeling injured or outraged or infuriated, I now challenge and dare you to lunch with me. Benton too. RSVP. Yours, Sincerely, Cordially, Truly, Frankly, Fondly, Diane.*[131]

At this juncture, ideas for new projects are beginning to fill her notebooks and appointment book. For *Show*—scheduled to debut in October—she jots down something about a quickie horror movie company, archetypical heroes and villians, as well as *theatrical children and their agents and mothers and makeup and dance lessons and auditions...and the whole world of making believe for real.*[132]

I am fine but still too excited and waking at 5AM again and again. I have a new assignment and several more pending ones for a new magazine

(*ABOVE*) A 1963 PHOTOGRAPH BY DIANE OF MOONDOG, THE LEGENDARY BLIND BEGGAR, STANDING AT HIS REGULAR POST. IN A 1961 LETTER TO MARVIN ISRAEL, DIANE WRITES, *MOONDOG'S FAITH IS OTHER THAN OURS. WE BELIEVE IN THE INVISIBLE AND WHAT HE BELIEVES IN IS THE VISIBLE.* (*BELOW*) UNCLE SAM ON THE OPENING PAGE OF "THE FULL CIRCLE," *HARPER'S BAZAAR*, NOVEMBER 1961.

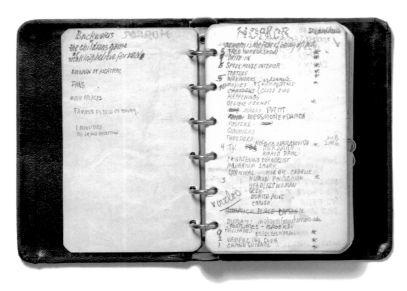

1961 NOTEBOOK (NO. 7), WITH LIST FOR THE HORROR SHOW PROJECT.

(*ABOVE LEFT*) THE HUMAN PINCUSHION, LOUIS CIERVO, MD. 1961, OF WHOM DIANE WRITES IN HER UNPUBLISHED PIECE HORROR SHOW: *LOUIS CIERVO WAS THE CHILD OF AERIALISTS, BUT WHEN THEY DIED HE FOUND HIMSELF WITHOUT A TRADE, SO A FRIEND WHO PERFORMED AS A HALF-MAN, HALF-WOMAN UNDERTOOK TO TEACH HIM TO BE A PINCUSHION. BUT HE WANTS TO QUIT AND LEARN TO READ AND WRITE AND FIND LESS DANGEROUS WORK IN THE CARNIVAL SO HE CAN MEET A NICE GIRL WHO WILL BE MORE IMPRESSED THAN APPALLED, AND THEY CAN GET MARRIED. (ABOVE RIGHT)* HEADLESS MAN, N.Y.C. 1961. IN HER CAPTION, SHE REMARKS THAT THE *SPEECH BY THE INSIDE TALKER OF AN ILLUSION SHOW...MUST ACCORDING TO STATE LAW...[BE PREFACED] WITH THE ADMISSION THAT THE WHOLE THING'S A HOAX SO THAT NO ONE WILL FEEL FAINT OR CHEATED. (BELOW)* MASKED CHILD WITH A DOLL, N.Y.C. 1961.*

called *Show*. The one I am working on first is about HORROR in films, theater, TV, waxworks, spookhouses, any kind of entertainment and although at first I was somewhat cool to the idea maybe that was because I didn't think of it myself because it has begun to...GRAB ME...

—LETTER TO DOON ARBUS, CIRCA AUGUST 1961

The new assignment is nicely different because I don't have to talk to anyone and be nice or take notes and its fun...seeing what is scary and how afraid we are to be afraid. I spent hours in the waxworks watching little kids and pregnant women staring bugeyed at the ghouls and murderers. and next week I will be able to visit the lit up interior of one of those spook rides which I have wanted to see all my life.

—LETTER TO DOON ARBUS, CIRCA AUGUST 1961

The word horror itself spawns a series of thoughts on the connection between fear and horror, as if she were in search of a definition: *anxiety is the fear of being afraid*, she writes in her appointment book on July 16, 1961; and in a notebook, *anxiety is fear looking for a cause*, and later, *if anxiety is the fear of being afraid horror is the experience of what there is no need to be afraid of*.[133] The completed assignment—which she submits to *Show* in September, and which is never published—is subtitled "These Are Nightmares to Beguile Us While We Wait." As in the case of her other magazine projects of the period, each photograph is accompanied by its own text. There is a headless man, a headless woman, a monster makeup artist modeling his own handiwork, two human pincushions, and the World in Wax Musée at Coney Island:

Still and always, in the murky half light behind chicken wire, murderers and their victims grapple silently and ambiguously for their last lasting time in the scuffed shoes and crumpled stockings and faded wallpaper of their hell where nothing ever happens or stops happening. A man cuts up his mistress, the Duke and Duchess of Windsor smile faintly, a five year old girl gives birth to a baby, a child is raped in a stone quarry and James Dean looks sheepish. The fee is 30 cents but babies are admitted free and everyone tiptoes about, nervous and rapt and polite as if they are in church.

—HORROR SHOW, UNPUBLISHED TEXT, CIRCA 1961

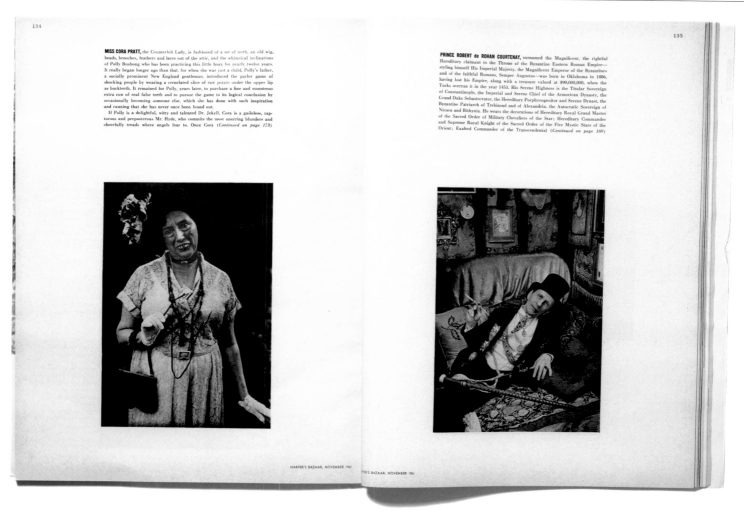

A SPREAD OF "THE FULL CIRCLE," PUBLISHED IN THE NOVEMBER 1961 ISSUE OF *HARPER'S BAZAAR*, AS DESIGNED BY MARVIN ISRAEL.

"The Full Circle"—with the exception of the portrait and text on Miss Stormé de Larverie—is published in the November 1961 issue of *Harper's Bazaar*. This omission aside, the article remains faithful to her original conception. Her introductory paragraph encapsulates her view of those portrayed in the story: *These are five singular people who appear like metaphors somewhere further out than we do, beckoned, not driven, invented by belief, author and hero of a real dream by which our own courage and cunning are tested and tried; so that we may wonder all over again what is veritable and inevitable and possible and what it is to become whoever we may be.* The portraits constitute a major stylistic departure from "The Vertical Journey" photographs. A month or so later, in response to a letter from her brother about the article, she writes:

Dear h

...I been gloomy. Publication, although very splendid, felt a little like an obituary. I have figured out what the next thing to do is but i haven't done it. I want to find something like the eccentric event; (like i have heard of a twins convention[134]...unrealized legends or archaeologists delights or american rites. We'll see. I seem to have forgotten how to proceed. If my illusion is everyone elses disillusion, as it sometime seems, why do i feel so sad? I think i think i have forgotten what wasn't necessary to remember in the first place. Don't feel obliged to answer. I don't hope to stay this way.

—LETTER TO HOWARD NEMEROV, BENNINGTON, VT., CIRCA DECEMBER 1961

1962

The record remains unclear as to exactly when she begins considering the 2¼ format as an alternative to the 35mm, or precisely what begins to drive her in that direction. A yearning for greater clarity seems to be one factor: *I wanted to see the real differences between things...between flesh and material, the densities of different kinds of things: air and water and shiny...I began to get terribly hyped on clarity.*[135] The possibility of a more direct relationship with the person she is photographing may be another factor. At any rate, the transition occupies a good portion of the year and seems at times as fraught and poignant as a romantic triangle.

I am very gloomy and scared. Maybe I have discovered that I have to use the 2¼ x 2¼ instead of the 35mm, but the only tangible result so far is that I can't photograph at all. I am inept and hopeless with the bigger [camera] and I no longer believe the language of the littler one, which I so loved...I can't see beyond my nose to tell you how everything else is.

—LETTER TO LYN AND BOB MESERVEY, CIRCA JANUARY 1962[136]

Lisette Model, with whom Diane maintains a close relationship as friend and colleague, recalls a conversation they had on the subject of this dilemma: *She came once and she said she couldn't work anymore with the Nikon and she bought herself a Rolleiflex and now she cannot work with either one of them. Which has happened to me and which is absolutely clear. And I said to her, Take both of them and take the same picture with the Rollei and with the [Nikon]. And that, I think, helped a great deal.*[137] Diane employs this suggestion in a number of instances during the year, particularly when dealing with inanimate subjects.[138] In a September 25 letter to Model, she writes: *I have learned to be happy with the rolleiflex so now I have two cameras and I am proud of that.*[139]

Meanwhile *Infinity*, the publication of the American Society of Magazine Photographers, reprints "The Full Circle" in its February 1962 issue, with William Mack on the cover and all six original portraits and texts. In a note to Marvin Israel, Diane alludes to several of the projects she is hoping to pursue next, whether it be for *Harper's Bazaar*, another magazine, or simply herself:

dear m I wanna do the children the overpriveleged ones (of tycoons and aristocrats and notables and luminaries) who are almost as toomuchblessed as freaks. (even I who was not such an heiress and jewish to boot can remember being afraid of being kidnapped as the most precious possession of someone with a lot to lose). It'll be gorgeous. I'll write what they say. (THE SILVER SPOON)...and I was so tired I cant remember what you said about doing amy [Arbus] in clothes for... [Harper's Bazaar children's fashions][140] but if I do could I do her with a series of splendid sour pets like her best friends enormous turtle or a white mouse[141]...and I am looking for the faces of places which I would rather find than anything...and if I could go to photograph the living pictures at the Laguna Beach Art Festival (do you still have the clipping in your pocket?) I would hitchhike...

—NOTE TO MARVIN ISRAEL, CIRCA APRIL 1962[142]

The notion of winners of all kinds intrigues her as well. A list that appears in her 1961 appointment book (*the utmost, the winners, the most, the first, rituals, contests, fame, immortality, Secret Rites*) is a harbinger of the more complete project statement in a 1962 Notebook (No. 8).[143] This is followed by pages of events she has researched and plans to investigate: *singer-sewing contest, soap box derby, eating or drinking (pie watermelon), diaper derby palisades, walkathon st.louis, chess champ, miss appetite, miss fluidless contact lens, yeast raised donut queen, miss peel appeal natl idaho potato wk, tooth health week queen, miss press photog, miss antifreeze, miss salt water taffy wk.*[144]

In mid-July Diane leaves on a cross-country bus trip heading for Los Angeles, where she intends to remain for about a month to work. She means to pursue, among other projects, a story on fortune-tellers to the stars for *Harper's Bazaar*.[145] The plan is for her to stay with her friends, the actor Robert Brown (who moved there in 1960, *to seek his fortune in the movies*[146]) and Bunny Sellers, who were recently married.[147] In a postcard to Allan from Tennessee, Diane reports on the cross-country trip.

I have no desire to get anywhere. It is nice to come to a town at 4AM and walk around the block. My brown suitcase is not on the same bus as me thru somebody else's error but perhaps it will find me in the

COSTUMED MAN AT THE MUMMERS' PARADE, PHILADELPHIA, PA. 1962. THIS PHOTOGRAPH AND ALL OTHERS TAKEN AT THE MUMMERS' PARADE ON NEW YEAR'S DAY WERE MADE WITH THE 2¼ ROLLEIFLEX, BUT ON SUBSEQUENT OCCASIONS SHE OPTS FOR THE NIKON INSTEAD. IN AN APRIL 15 POSTCARD TO PHOTOGRAPHER CLARENCE LAUGHLIN RESPONDING TO HIS SUGGESTION THAT THEY TRADE PRINTS, SHE WRITES: *I HAVE BEEN HAVING SERIOUS GROWING PAINS CHANGING CAMERAS AND RELEARNING TO PHOTOGRAPH AND PROGRESS HAS BEEN SO TERRIBLE SLOW THAT I HATE TO GO BACK AND PRINT OLD THINGS...*THE ORIGINAL POSTCARD IS IN THE HISTORIC NEW ORLEANS COLLECTION.

A GIRL IN A HAT AT CENTRAL PARK LAKE, N.Y.C. 1962.

end...May switch to a more devious route to see some Indians later. I sleep and wake a lot of tiny times and forget where I am so dawn this morning came as a sweet shock. Think of you a lot. D.

—POSTCARD TO ALLAN ARBUS FROM TENNESSEE, JULY 16, 1962

Bunny Sellers and Robert Brown are living in Malibu as houseguests in the home of a friend and, apparently, on the periphery of some sort of romantic melodrama. Diane describes the situation this way:

I arrived yesterday and my suitcase was not lost and I wasn't tired but it is all quite hard to believe. I seem to be living in the lap of what is surely the most unutterable luxury in a gorgeous house on the ocean built around and terracing an outdoor room furnished with bougainvillea trees. There are a thousand rooms and nooks and niceties and winding staircases and a largesse I have never seen. Bunny and Robt seem to be the mainstays of this household and there is an explosive drama transpiring of which James Mason, the real James Mason that is, plays one of the characters. They do this with more grace but less conviction than most people but it is all so handsome that one cannot care until one cares too much. Bunny and Robt seem to be paying a kind of emotional rental and we do quite considerable of tiptoeing although the freedom is enormous and the generosity so great that one cannot find a donor to thank. Parties are planned, lives are crumbling, everyone is charming...Fitzgerald should write this letter...I am a little jittery but one nice thing is that other people's problems are more crucial and I look to myself relatively little and simple like I can fit in a brown suitcase and get lost. I am frighteningly dependent in the matter of a car but I may be a help in getting Bunny and Robt out from the under they are in. I mean they are being a bit bled I think...I am at any rate well taken care of and there are a million plans for where to take me. I am just not absolutely sure my heart will follow...

—LETTER TO ALLAN ARBUS, JULY 19, 1962

...This place is so amazing. I am feverish with it. The not being able to drive is the worst. Trying to solve these things. Spent two glorious days wandering photographing around Venice and Santa Monica Pier and between and in an amusement park, overexposing and all that but free again and able to use the camera which on one black bleak day driving around with Bob [Brown] sightseeing (which is so something else from photog. that my heart was drowning) I thought I would never be able to do again...I only wish I could leave everyone alone. They need it and so do I. It's too luxurious and emotional here for me. Like a house full of children playing with matches. Triangles, scenes, flirtation, passion. Terrible. And I have lots of energy which gets wasted going to fancy restaurants or parties...

—LETTER TO ALLAN ARBUS, AUGUST 1962

With Bunny's help as driver, companion, and note-taker, she investigates the fortune-tellers—each of whom has his or her specialty, from astrology to tarot cards to crystal balls, and each his or her devoted movie stars.[148] They also go to the Laguna Beach Art Festival together but Diane is forbidden to photograph because the people enacting the living pictures are naked.[149] Her friend and former Fieldston classmate, screenwriter

IN MAY, DIANE AND WRITER THOMAS MORGAN—A REGULAR CONTRIBUTOR TO *ESQUIRE* AND, COINCIDENTALLY, HER NEW LANDLORD AND NEIGHBOR—COLLABORATE ON A STORY ABOUT THE COMMITTEE FOR NON-VIOLENT ACTION'S 700-MILE "WALK FOR PEACE" AND ITS ORGANIZER, PAUL SALSTROM. THEY JOINED THE 13-MEMBER MARCH IN ITS SEVENTH WEEK AS IT PASSED THROUGH WOODBURY, N.J. "DOOM AND PASSION ALONG RTE. 45" WAS PUBLISHED IN *ESQUIRE*'S NOVEMBER 1962 ISSUE WITH THE PHOTO ABOVE.

MARCELLO MASTROIANNI IN HIS HOTEL ROOM, *SHOW*, MARCH 1963.

A 1962 PHOTOGRAPH PUBLISHED IN *HARPER'S BAZAAR*, SEPTEMBER 1964.

(ABOVE) A ROCK IN DISNEYLAND, CAL. 1962.
(BELOW) DRAFT OF A TELEGRAM TO HAROLD HAYES AT *ESQUIRE* ON PSEUDO PLACES FROM DIANE'S 1962 NOTEBOOK (No. 10).

Stewart Stern, arranges to take her to the Universal backlot at dawn and to Forest Lawn Cemetery, Disneyland, and other Pseudo Places.

When she returns to New York near the end of August, financial pressures are weighing heavily on Allan and, as a result, on her. Amy—who had been attending The Little Red School House in Greenwich Village —enrolls that fall in third grade at Public School 41, *which fascinates her*, Diane says.[150] Diane begins to explore the possibility of obtaining a grant in photography from the Guggenheim Foundation, seeking advice and help from several former recipients, including Robert Frank and Lee Friedlander.[151] She writes Model, asking her to *sponsor me or recommend me or vouch for me or whatever it is called.*[152]

I am fine if a little precarious, I mean it all depends on how I look at it and there are bad moments when that depends much too much on the way someone else does, like a tightrope walker who might fall if somebody screamed. but mostly tightening my belt is exhilarating for me...I had to make it clear to myself that I had to at least try to become self supporting. So I am trying to work for money, even childrens fashions which is a little like an old nightmare but I got through it, and to apply for a guggenheim and to find a cheaper place to live, Sometimes these things are awful but other times they are fun. I mean I am terribly proud to make money for something I do except when I feel I would give anything not to have done it.

—LETTER TO LISETTE MODEL, SEPTEMBER 25, 1962

She contacts a number of other people in connection with the Guggenheim grant, including Edward Steichen and Grace Mayer in the photography department of The Museum of Modern Art,[153] and Walker Evans, whom she meets through Marvin Israel.[154] In late September, following an afternoon with Evans, she writes to thank him *for your generosity and the pleasures of this afternoon, for your counsel and conversation and for your worldliness* and encloses a copy of *Infinity* and caption material for the Horror pictures and the female impersonators, which she has apparently shown him.[155] In early October, shortly before the deadline, she sends Evans a copy of her Guggenheim project proposal, "American Rites, Manners and Customs" (p. 41), for his criticism or approval. Somewhat daunted by the application form, she adds in a postscript: *The application itself is going to be pretty barren or pristine because I never went to college or won an award or had a position with an organization or joined a learned or artistic society and though I speak a little French that will hardly be much help in the project.*[156]

Her Guggenheim project statement begins as follows: *I want to photograph the considerable ceremonies of our present...* Judging by the contents of her appointment books and notebooks, the topic has been brewing in her mind for more than a year. These are some notes from October 4, 1961: *the stuff of dreams, ritual, aristocracy, imposters, fame, anonymity, figments, real visions, american dreams, daily dreams, walking dreams, american hallucinations, real mirage.* And from November 22: *through the looking glass, legends of the here and now, shades of the here and now.* In accordance with the application instruction to supply a list *of the works of artistic creation you already have accomplished,*[157] she includes Psuedo

Places and Portraits in Central Park as 1962 projects and Contests, Seers (for *Harper's Bazaar*), Silver Spoon (for *Harper's Bazaar*), and Winners as ongoing ones.

John Szarkowski—who had come to The Museum of Modern Art that summer to head the photography department—also receives a letter from Diane, dated September 23: *Walker Evans and Robert Frank and Lisette Model and Lee Friedlander have each said that they would speak for me and sponsor my request for a Guggenheim Fellowship for Photography. Each of them has suggested that I show you my work because your recommendation, if you could give it, would be so significant.*[158] Due to his schedule, however—as his secretary informs her—he is unable to see her work until after the October 15 Guggenheim deadline.[159]

She has already made a number of her important early 2¼ Rolleiflex pictures by this time [notably, Child with a toy hand grenade (p. 104), Two boys smoking (p. 90), Man and boy on a bench (p. 76), A castle in Disneyland (p. 288)]. Given her standard practice, she would surely have printed them as well but there is no evidence that they are included in the portfolio she submits. Szarkowski recalls his reaction to the work he sees and to his subsequent meeting with her:

She sent in her portfolio, you know the way photographers do, and I didn't like it very much...They were a lot of the early freak pictures and the early eccentric pictures. There was one that I loved of the man and woman arguing on the walk at Coney Island [p. 238]. I didn't really like them but they were very forceful and you really felt somebody who was just enormously ambitious, really ambitious. Not in any cheap way. In the most serious way. Someone who was going to stand for no minor successes. And that feeling colored all our relationship because if you feel that it automatically sets up a kind of distance that you've got to respect no matter how well you may come to know each other.

WOMAN WITH A BRIEFCASE AND POCKETBOOK, N.Y.C. 1962.

CONTACT SHEET #1341 OF CHILD WITH A TOY HAND GRENADE IN CENTRAL PARK, N.Y.C. 1962. THE IMAGE DIANE PRINTED (#10) IS AT TOP LEFT.

There's something untouchable about that kind of ambition. You can't man-handle it...I think she wanted every word she said, every picture she took, everything she did, I think she wanted it to be just perfect — for some great revelation to come through. Terrifying.[160]

Szarkowski recalls showing her *This Was Logging*, a 1954 book of photographs by Darius Kinsey, as well as the 1929 August Sander book, *Antlitz der Zeit*.[161] *She was floored*, he reports and, based on her response, has the impression that this is the first time she has seen Sander's work. In a note dated January 2, 1963, Diane follows up on their meeting: *That was nice, that little time I saw you a couple of months ago.* She goes on to ask for the title of the Darius Kinsey book and for August Sander's address *because there is something I would like to write him about.*[162]

1963

A month or so following the Guggenheim application deadline, the Foundation requests examples of the applicant's work. There appears to be no record of the photographs Diane chooses to submit for review by the Foundation's Advisory Jury. At any rate, a few days after delivering her prints to the offices in person, she sends Model a postcard, to remind her that the sponsors' recommendations are due.[163]

Dear Lisette, the g'gg'nh'm have summoned all photos and plan to keep them only until Jan 15 so I guess now is the time when they (whoever they are) make up their collective mind. I brought them there and it's so odd: just a small series of offices like judgement day in a bad dream.

—POSTCARD TO LISETTE MODEL, JANUARY 2, 1963

Model's letter of recommendation, dated January 4, begins as follows: *Photographers can be good, bad, excellent, first rate, or tops, but there are hardly any artists among them. Here is an exception.*[164]

In the meantime, Diane has proposed her Silver Spoon project (Children of Good Fortune) to *Harper's Bazaar* editor-in-chief, Nancy White. *I want to...discover the thousand ways they inhabit their rare and marvelous habitats...in a predicament as poignant as it is pretty,* she writes.[165] White encourages her to proceed with it. In a letter to a friend Diane says, *I am beginning the work of photographing rich children and the climb upwards appears to be a very long one. I mean I think I have found a whole new hidden hierarchy within the upper class and I am determined to get to the top of it, although I think it makes me uneasier than the bottom.*[166]

She is accumulating a list of qualified parents and their children, about three dozen in all, most of whom she visits and takes notes on: *Juan Carlos...darling ears, doesn't speak much english but smiles; Cecile has short hair, cross eyes slight, piquant, whimsical, sweet; Christopher...* [with whom, according to her notebook, she has the following exchange, *I hope to see more of you. There isn't any more.*] *is kind of darling funny typical spoiled looking, english hair; Elisabeth...beautifully pale blond bangs wide jowls wondrously sour like a Shirley T ugly doll.* About Penelope Tree, the thirteen-year-old daughter of Ronald and Marietta Tree, Diane writes simply, *Wonderful.*[167]

(LEFT) IN RESPONSE TO HER FRIEND PATI HILL'S FOURTH BOOK, *ONE THING I KNOW* (CAMBRIDGE, MASS.: THE RIVERSIDE PRESS, 1962) — A FIRST-PERSON NOVEL NARRATED BY ITS SIXTEEN-YEAR-OLD HEROINE, FRANCESCA HOLLINS, AND WITH THE DEDICATION "FOR DIANE ARBUS" — DIANE WRITES: *...I AM MORE THAN EVER CONVINCED AND MAYBE SHE* [FRANCESCA] *IS TOO, THAT PEOPLE ARE BORN OLD AND THAT DISENCHANTMENT IS MORE A BEGINNING THAN AN END IN ITELF...I THINK LIFE HAS ABSOLUTELY TO BE LIVED BACKWARDS AND THERE IS NO CONVENIENT SHORTCUT LIKE FORWARDS. (RIGHT)* IN A 1962 NOTEBOOK DIANE WRITES THIS QUOTE FROM HER BROTHER'S BOOK *THE NEXT ROOM OF THE DREAM* (UNIVERSITY OF CHICAGO PRESS, 1962): *AS WITH A DREAM INTERPRETED BY ONE STILL SLEEPING / THE INTERPRETATION IS ONLY THE NEXT ROOM OF THE DREAM*, FROM THE POEM "TO CLIO, MUSE OF HISTORY," SUBTITLED "ON LEARNING THAT THE ETRUSCAN WARRIOR AT THE METROPOLITAN MUSEUM OF ART IS PROVED A MODERN FORGERY."

PENN STATION, N.Y.C. 1963.* TAKEN DURING THE DEMOLITION.

With the exception of the Silver Spoon (another project that, as it turns out, is never published), her magazine assignments in this period—for *Show, Harper's Bazaar,* and *Esquire*—consist of occasional portraits of writers, performers, directors.[168] They are of little interest to her beyond the professional challenge they present. On the other hand, many of the subjects and ideas she has been pursuing on her own are coming to fruition. These include a portrait of Andrew Ratoucheff—the Russian midget she first photographed for "The Vertical Journey"—with his friends in their living room (p. 100), the widow Betty Blanc Glassbury, National President of Composers, Authors and Artists of America (p. 44), and the 1963 winning couple of the Junior Interstate Ballroom Dance Championships (p. 40), an event she has been attending for several years.[169]

Marvin Israel is fired from *Harper's Bazaar.* Some later suggest that he deliberately engineers his own firing because he is fed up with the bureaucracy, longs to devote himself to his painting full-time, and also wants to ensure his severance pay.[170] In a sense, however, his influence on the magazine persists even in his absence. Bea Feitler, a former student of Israel's at Parsons School of Design, and Ruth Ansel—both of whom he had hired as his assistants in the art department—succeed him as co–art directors and remain in that position for almost a decade.

On April 15 Diane receives a special-delivery letter from Henry Allen Moe, president of the Guggenheim Foundation: *Dear Mrs. Arbus: I have the honor to inform you that the Foundation has awarded you the Fellowship you requested.* The grant is for "photographic studies of American rites, manners and customs" in the amount of $5,000, covering a twelve-month period that commences in June 1963. He asks her for a written acknowledgment, Diane replies: *Dear Mr. Moe, Along with my acknowledgement, my profoundest thanks.* To which he answers: *Yours is the shortest acknowledgement and there is none better.*[171]

She sends a note to Walker Evans: *Dear Walker, I called to tell you I got it (Guggenheim), and to thank you. It is dizzying and if you have further counsel I will gladly listen.*[172] And to Model: *Dear Lisette, My father told me to thank you but your eloquence is your own and your friendship is mine so I cannot.*[173]

Around this time her father is hospitalized in New York, suffering from lung cancer. The family is resigned to the fact that he is dying.[174] *He would hallucinate when he was dying,* Diane recalls. *Businessman's hallucinations. He had an imaginary pocket with imaginary papers and he would keep stashing them away in a gesture that was familiar to him.*[175] Beneath the words "my father" in one of her 1963 notebooks (No. 13) she records two statements of his, followed by a question: *this message is paid for in advance; I cant get into the ceremony without it (piece of paper, breast pocket); and who made the moon?*

It's true I didn't really adore him [but]...I was really sort of awful when he died in the way that I watched. I stood in the corner of the room almost like a creep...I was just spellbound by the whole process. The gradual diminishment was fantastic. People really get to look like nobody, or just like somebody, you know what I mean?...All his lineaments changed. And I photographed him then which was really

(LEFT) MICHAEL LERNER, THE FIVE-YEAR-OLD SON OF MICHELINE AND ALAN JAY LERNER, THE LYRICIST. THIS MONOLOGUE IS RECORDED IN HER 1962 NOTEBOOK (NO. 8): *I WANT TO BE CAPTAIN OF A SHIP AND I WANT TO BE AN ARTIST OF MUSIC AND I WILL HAVE MY PIANO ON THE TOP OF THE SHIP AND I WILL MAKE STAIRS GOING UP TO IT SO I CAN CLIMB UP AND PLAY TO THE FISHES. (RIGHT)* PENELOPE TREE IN HER LIVING ROOM, N.Y.C. 1962.*

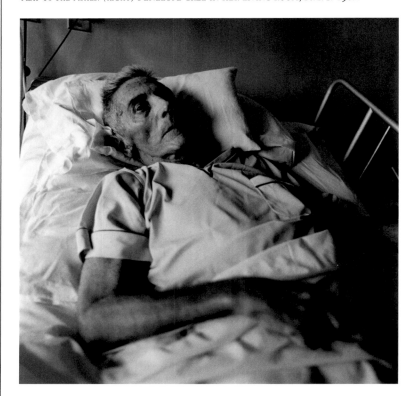

DIANE'S PHOTOGRAPH OF HER FATHER, DAVID NEMEROV, IN HIS HOSPITAL BED IN NEW YORK CITY A FEW WEEKS BEFORE HE DIED OF LUNG CANCER.*

PHOTOGRAPH OF DIANE WITH RUSSIAN MIDGETS IN THEIR 100TH STREET APARTMENT, TAKEN BY ONE OF HER HOSTS USING HER CAMERA.

tremendously cold. But I suppose there is something somewhat cold in me. Although I resent that implication.

—1968 RADIO INTERVIEW WITH STUDS TERKEL ON THE DEPRESSION

David Nemerov dies on May 23. On that date Diane writes at the top of the page in her appointment book: *Daddy's death.*

Her enthusiasm for photography frequently extends to images produced by pragmatic, unself-conscious practitioners of the medium, in which the purpose is primarily to record information. In a 1962 notebook (No. 9) under the title "Photographers—The Double Image" she makes a list: *daily news, coney is or bway, wedding, baby, family, pony, graduation, theatrical, spirit, portrait, bachrach, itinerant, amateur, chinese-spanish school, passport or taxi, machine, lineup, banquet, postcard, candid, girlie, funeral, animal, nightclub, publicity.*

It is not clear how she becomes aware of James Vanderzee, a seventy-three-year-old studio portrait photographer, whose work is virtually unknown outside of the Harlem community where he has spent his entire career.[176] She seeks him out, buys some of his photographs, and later attempts to interest Szarkowski in his work. In a 1963 notebook (No. 11) she quotes what appears to be one of Vanderzee's principles of portraiture: *full length shows your shape, half shows your character, your type.*[177]

She spends the first week of July at Sunshine Park, a family nudist camp in New Jersey.[178] *I had always wanted to go but I sort of didn't dare tell anybody,* she says later. *It was a terrific subject for me.*[179] A year or two later, in an attempt to secure an assignment from *Esquire* on the topic, she writes a text largely based on her notes from this visit. It begins: *There is not much to it, you might say. It's like walking into an hallucination without being quite sure whose it is.*[180]

Some ladies wear beach hats or sunglasses or wedgies and curlers or earrings and pocketbooks. In the cafeteria the teenage waitresses wear organdy demi-aprons. Some men have on only a wrist-watch, or shoes and socks with their cigarettes and money tucked into their socks for safekeeping. Sometimes you see someone wearing nothing but a bandaid or a pencil behind their ear or walking a dog on a leash. Nudists aren't purists. Occasionally they even feel the impulse to slip into something more comfortable.

—"NOTES ON THE NUDIST CAMP," UNPUBLISHED 1965 ARTICLE FOR *ESQUIRE*[181]

Sometimes you begin to wonder. There is an empty pop bottle or a rusty bobby pin underfoot, the lake bottom oozes mud in a particularly nasty way...some guy asks, "What kind of bees give milk?" and answers, "boobies," the outhouse smells, the woods look mangy. It is as if way back in the Garden of Eden, after the Fall, Adam and Eve had begged the Lord to forgive them; and God, in his boundless exasperation, had said, "All right, then. STAY. Stay in the Garden. Get civilized. Procreate. Muck it up." And they did.

—"NOTES ON THE NUDIST CAMP," UNPUBLISHED 1965 ARTICLE FOR *ESQUIRE*[182]

When Doon leaves to attend Reed College in Oregon, Suzanne (Sudie) Victor, a student of Howard Nemerov's and recent graduate of Hollins

CHILD SKIPPING ROPE AT THE PUERTO RICAN FESTIVAL, N.Y.C. 1963.

DEAR MR MATHIAS,
YES, I AM READY TO BEGIN MY PROJECT.
THANKYOU,
DIANE ARBUS

(ABOVE) FACSIMILE OF A NOTE TO JAMES MATHIAS, SECRETARY OF THE GUGGENHEIM FOUNDATION, MAY 1963.

HUSBAND AND WIFE WITH SHOES ON IN THEIR CABIN AT A NUDIST CAMP, N.J. 1963.

College in Virginia, moves into Doon's old room. Sudie Victor is working as a copy editor at Random House and the plan is for her to live with the family and be available when needed to take care of nine-year-old Amy.[183]

Before the end of the year, Robert Benton resigns from *Esquire*.

1964

Diane's 1964 magazine projects and her own personal projects overlap and merge and evolve into and out of one another throughout the year. For *Harper's Bazaar*, she embarks on two assignments simultaneously: photographs of "young heiresses" that will appear in a regular feature of the magazine, "Fashion Independents,"[184] and "Affinities," portraits of creative partners. In the case of the latter, the lists of possible subjects in the early pages of her 1964 appointment book are soon narrowed down to four couples: the musicians Pearl Bailey and Louis Bellson, the ballet dancers Erik Bruhn and Rudolf Nureyev, the poets W. H. Auden and Marianne Moore, and the silent film star sisters, Lillian and Dorothy Gish.[185]

Accompanied by *Harper's Bazaar* feature editor Geri Trotta, who will write the article, she meets with the Gish sisters on January 13 and photographs them in Central Park in the snow. On that day in her appointment book she records these fragments of conversation: *D: [Dorothy] Lillian's face is in every museum in the world. L: [Lillian] Dorothy is the dearest sweetest funniest creature in the world. Always sees something odd. D: Lillian and Garbo had that something-plus, I can't say what it is. L: Come Dorothy—follow in my footsteps. (snow).*[186]

In late January, she begins planning a trip to New Orleans for the February 11 Mardi Gras celebration. When she leaves on February 5 she has obtained from friends and through research the names and addresses of people to contact. She already has the address of photographer Clarence John Laughlin,[187] whose work interests her and with whom she has corresponded. It also includes—probably thanks to Lee Friedlander—the name of Lorenz (Larry) Borenstein. (It is from Borenstein and his partner, Al Rose, that Friedlander purchases the eighty-nine E. J. Bellocq glass plate negatives, which he prints and The Museum of Modern Art exhibits and publishes in 1970 as *E. J. Bellocq: Storyville Portraits*.)[188] Curiously enough, as far as Diane's own photographs are concerned, the New Orleans trip results in only one picture she chooses to print.

On her way home, she stops in Baltimore on assignment for *Esquire* to photograph Blaze Starr, known in many quarters as the Queen of Burlesque. This is her second collaboration with writer Thomas B. Morgan, whose article "Blaze Starr in Nighttown" appears in *Esquire*'s July 1964 issue accompanied by two of her pictures.[189]

Diane's relationships with many of the people she photographs continue long after the pictures have been taken. Her 1963 portrait of the Triplets in their bedroom (p. 85) is a prelude to a subsequent encounter with the family at a triplets convention in Palisades Park. She makes regular visits to Hubert's Museum and stays in touch with a number of the individual performers she has come to know, goes to a party for Prince Robert de Rohan Courtenay, or a performance by Stormé de Larverie, and keeps note of Michael Lerner's ensuing birthdays. Bishop Ethel Predonzan, whom she has been in contact with since 1960, is now living in Santa Barbara, and when Diane goes to California in August, meeting with the Bishop is one of the items on her agenda.

ERIK BRUHN AND RUDOLF NUREYEV, N.Y.C. 1964, PUBLISHED IN "AFFINITIES," *HARPER'S BAZAAR*, APRIL 1964.

LADY BARTENDER AT HOME WITH A SOUVENIR DOG, NEW ORLEANS, LA. 1964. THIS IS THE ONLY PHOTOGRAPH PRINTED BY DIANE FROM HER NEW ORLEANS TRIP.

She stays again, for at least part of the time, with Bunny Sellers and Robert Brown in their home at 14 Malibu Road. Bunny goes with her on her visit to see the Bishop and describes the experience as "heart-breaking." *This perfectly together wedgie, neon lady living in Santa Barbara. The whole question of what's sane and what's insane, what's real and what's unreal.* And yet, as Bunny observes: *Diane was very caring* [with the Bishop] *and she was also terrifically persistent because she wanted her. In a sense she wooed her in the same sense as a lover would woo...One of the glories of it was that Diane had won her by that time. They were terrifically jolly together. But that was also an extraordinary thing about Diane. It was always like she knew exactly where she was headed—to the absolute inside of the inside. I never knew if she had a plan—I don't mean a plan—a device or technique for getting there. But she always seemed to arrive.*[190]

In an earlier letter to Marvin Israel on an unrelated subject, Diane remarks on her ability to elicit from people, sometimes without even wanting to, the revelation of their own unabashed images of themselves: *I think I must have been brought up to be a sort of magic mirror who reflects what anyone wants to believe because I can't believe they believe it, like atlas holding up a bubble and groaning.*[191]

On a cliff overlooking the Pacific, in a cemetery in the sun, a small lady in damask robes with hair of phosphorescent pink holds aloft a styrofoam cross encrusted with smaller crosses and raises her eyes till they pale at the vision of Jesus Christ. She is called Bishop Ethel Predonzan of The Cathedral of the Creator, Omnipresence, Inc. Christ, she declares, has summoned her there to Santa Barbara, California, all the way from Astoria, Queens, to await His Second Coming on December 4th of this year.

— "The Bishop's Charisma," unpublished text, 1964

According to the text, the Bishop acknowledges that Christ was scheduled to come once before, in 1957, but as she goes on to explain, *Everything depends on cadence and vibration. Conditions were too negative.* And, in the words of the final sentence of the piece, *if Christ does not come this time no doubt she* [the Bishop] *will wait till He does.*[192] On the December 3rd and 4th pages of her 1964 appointment book Diane makes a note for herself: *Call the Bishop.*

An echo of the Bishop's spiritual fervor occurs in Diane's text on Mae West, a story assigned to her by *Show* editor Nicky Haslam, which she has been planning and researching for months.[193] At the appointed time Robert Brown drives her to West's home (*a fortress...almost as impregnable as Sleeping Beauty's*[194]) and by prearrangement leaves her there.[195] Diane writes of her encounter with the seventy-two-year-old "original Sex Symbol": *She is imperious, adorable, magnanimous, genteel and girlish, almost simultaneously. There is even, forgive me, a kind of innocence about her.*[196] The article, published in the January 1965 issue of the magazine along with three photographs,[197] concludes:

But the world of Mae West is not entirely physical. Her psychic eye has been opened. She has seen visions...And she has heard voices...a deep rich masculine voice in her solar plexus uttering phrases from another century like THEE and THOU. "I don't know what He was talking

Bishop on her bed, Santa Barbara, Cal. 1964.

Christ in a lobby, N.Y.C. 1964.

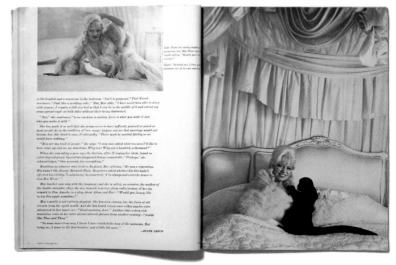

The second spread of the article on Mae West as it appeared in *Show,* January 1965, which included one of her few color photographs. Diane writes about West: *She has made it* [love] *so well that she seems never to have suffered or yearned or pined like most people do, in the tradition of the love song. She is an unmitigated optimist.*

(LEFT) HARPER'S BAZAAR ART DIRECTORS BEA FEITLER (IN MASK) AND RUTH ANSEL AT ANSEL'S HALLOWEEN COSTUME PARTY, OCTOBER 31, 1964. (RIGHT) DR. TIMOTHY LEARY AND HIS BRIDE, NENA VON SCHLEBRUGGE, AT THEIR WEDDING ON BILLY HITCHCOCK'S MILLBROOK ESTATE. MONTI ROCK III, A HAIRDRESSER TURNED POP SINGER, WHO IS SCHEDULED TO SING AT THE RECEPTION, ARRANGES FOR DIANE TO ATTEND THE WEDDING.

(ABOVE) 1964 APPOINTMENT BOOK WITH A LIST OF SOME CURRENT PROJECTS. (BELOW) GIRL IN PATTERNED STOCKINGS, N.Y.C. 1965. DIANE FIRST ENCOUNTERED THIS GIRL AT THE OCTOBER 24 ROLLING STONES CONCERT AT THE ACADEMY OF MUSIC AND LATER PHOTOGRAPHED FOR HER PROJECT ON TEENAGERS.

about," she says, but she knew who He was. "I knew that in some marvelous way I had touched the hem of the unknown. And being me, I wanted to lift that hemline a bit more."

— "MAE WEST: EMOTION IN MOTION," *SHOW*, JANUARY 1965[198]

During the month or so that she remains in California, Diane also photographs the eighty-two-year-old pioneer of modern dance, Ruth St. Denis;[199] several residents of a home for retired actors in their private rooms; and the children of movie stars, a new and far less happy incarnation of the Silver Spoon (probably for *Show*).[200] After returning to New York, she writes Stewart Stern:

...I am still stricken with good fortune and basking in it, a little frivolous, maybe a trifle smug but something like serene which is in itself therapeutic. If my cup doesn't run over it is only because I am always drinking. Autumn was here today which reminds me of when I was little...There are an awful lot of beggars around. Many of them sitting on the street and one with pink wooden legs. The city is like a terrible hallucination...You don't think, like the bishop does, that God has gone to california?

— LETTER TO STEWART STERN, CIRCA OCTOBER 1964[201]

Throughout the rest of the year, her projects continue to overlap. People and Their Pets, an idea that must have been intended originally as a magazine story, results instead in at least two photographs of carnival performers: Tattooed lady with her dog (p. 294) and Circus fat lady (p. 171).

An acquaintance with the disc jockey, Murray Kaufman (known professionally as Murray the K), organizer and emcee for the rock 'n roll shows at the Brooklyn Fox Theater, enables her to get in touch with some of the girl groups (the Orlons, the Dixie Cups, and the Ronettes). The individual portrait sessions with Estelle Bennett and Ronnie Spector of the Ronettes resemble, both in style and content, a project she has been working on—variously entitled Ethnic Beauties, Racial Pin-ups, Minority Pin-ups—which she continues to pursue for several years.[202] Her extensive notes on each of the subjects indicate she intends to write an accompanying text.

A *Harper's Bazaar* fashion assignment on underwear (never published) provides her an opportunity to photograph several women who interest her. One is her friend Carlotta Marshall (p. 171) *(My, she is pretty. Like the paintings of a certain art nouveauish period I can't remember the name of).*[203] Another is a call girl she has come to know whose comments she records in one of her notebooks (No. 15): *I'm in love with love. I love to please. I could smother someone with love.*[204]

The list that appears on the November 6th page of her appointment book under the heading Plans to Do, reiterates a list in one of the 1964 notebooks (No. 15): *racial pinups (Jill and Gina); teenagers (April, Barry and other, Betty Berry) family (Ed Carmel), gangster (Scavullo), homosexual (Monti), wedding prep. (Nick P.) whores, pimps (China Monti Ida Puente), roxcknroll group, old people's club).*[205] At various times during the year, she attempts to interest editors in one or another of these projects. In the case of *Harper's Bazaar*, sometimes she approaches Ruth Ansel with an idea,

(ABOVE) A CARNIVAL PERFORMER AND HER PET WITH A FACSIMILE OF THE HANDWRITTEN TITLE INSCRIBED BY DIANE ON THE FRONT OF THE PRINT. (BELOW) CARD FROM JAMES VANDERZEE'S PHOTO STUDIO, PASTED IN THE FRONT OF DIANE'S 1964 APPOINTMENT BOOK, ALONG WITH A NUMBER OF OTHER BUSINESS CARDS.

(BELOW) AN UNATTRIBUTED QUOTATION WRITTEN ON THE JANUARY 22ND PAGE OF DIANE'S 1964 APPOINTMENT BOOK. ON THE MAY 7TH PAGE, ALSO WITHOUT ATTRIBUTION, SHE WROTE: *IN ORDER TO BE ABLE TO DO ANYTHING ONE MUST RELINQUISH CONTROL.*

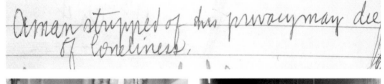

(LEFT) DIANE'S FRIEND CARLOTTA MARSHALL, PHOTOGRAPHED FOR UNPUBLISHED *HARPER'S BAZAAR* FASHION ASSIGNMENT. (RIGHT) MEMBERS OF THE RED SHIELD SENIOR CITIZENS CLUB, N.Y.C. 1964.

sometimes Bea Feitler, sometimes the two of them together.

Richard Avedon's second book, *Nothing Personal*, with a text by his former DeWitt Clinton High School classmate James Baldwin, is published by Atheneum.[206] The book, which is designed by Marvin Israel, renews his collaboration with Avedon and is the first of many photographic books Israel edits and designs.

Around mid-October, The Museum of Modern Art acquires seven Diane Arbus prints, six by purchase, one as a gift of the photographer. The MoMA records and Diane's own notes identify the following images as those selected: Child, night, Greenwich Street, Miss Venice Beach (p. 58), Child with a toy hand grenade (p. 104), A widow in her bedroom (p. 44), Two female impersonators backstage (p. 58), Retired man and his wife (p. 253), and A husband and wife in the woods (p. 118).[207] These are the first photographs of hers included in a museum collection. In the Artist's Record, dated October 5, 1964, which she fills out in connection with the acquisition, Diane describes her "Special Field of Interest in Photography" as *a kind of contemporary anthropology.*[208]

1965

Once again, commercial work dominates the first few months of the year. The *Harper's Bazaar* assignment "On Marriage" (published in the "Fashion Independents" feature in the May 1965 issue), happens to echo an idea Diane outlined five years earlier in a 1960 notebook (No. 3): *Marriage: the sort of why or wherefore of it with a text by anybody like B.Russell* [Bertrand Russell] *or MM* [Marilyn Monroe] *or Ashley Montagu or by a lot of people who do or don't believe in it, or what is becoming of it or anybody's quotes on the subj. like the inq. rep.* [the inquiring reporter] *asked people last week if they were better off married or single and pics of people who have chosen each other...*[209]

The couples she is asked to photograph for *Harper's Bazaar* constitute a less eclectic group than those she had envisioned doing earlier, but she records their observations and epigrams on the subject all the same. Elizabeth Oxenberg, married to Howard Oxenberg for five years, remarks: *mystery in a marriage helps preserve an otherwise impossible relationship;* the Gilbert Millers, married thirty-eight years, concur that *having the same interests is really the most important thing.*[210] The list of names on the March 10th page of her appointment book suggests that she photographs about twenty couples for the project. Nine portraits appear in the magazine.[211]

"Familial Colloquies," a simultaneous and somewhat parallel assignment for *Esquire* (July 1965) also consists of photographs of two people together, in this case a renowned parent with his or her adolescent child. Included are portraits of sculptor Richard Lippold and his daughter, Taina; politician Ogden Reid and his son, Stewart; sociologist Jane Jacobs and her son, Ned (p. 172); and actress Jayne Mansfield and her daughter, Jayne Marie (p. 172).[212] The four published photographs are accompanied by captions she writes, which consist almost exclusively of quotes from the parent and child portrayed.[213]

PAINTER JANE WILSON AND HER HUSBAND, WRITER JOHN GRUEN, FROM "ON MARRIAGE," *HARPER'S BAZAAR,* MAY 1965. *(BELOW)* TWO PORTRAITS FROM *ESQUIRE'S* "FAMILIAL COLLOQUIES": *(LEFT)* JAYNE MANSFIELD AND HER DAUGHTER; *(RIGHT)* JANE JACOBS AND HER SON.

TWO YOUNG MEN ON A BENCH, WASHINGTON SQUARE PARK, N.Y.C 1965.*

Her continuing fascination with self-enclosed communities, their customs and practices, leads her in a number of different directions at the same time. She investigates motorcycle rallies as well as Kerista, a free love society that occupies a commune in the East Village.[214] Many of these avenues prove to be dead ends, at least as far as her photography is concerned.

Beginning in May and throughout a good portion of the summer, she spends a lot of time working in and around Washington Square Park, photographing the people who hang out there. Curiously enough, she seems to find it one of the more intimidating and impenetrable worlds she has yet attempted to explore, although it also proves to be among the more productive.[215] Speaking of the experience several years later, she describes the park in terms of a kind of complex hierarchical social geography:

...One summer I worked a lot in Washington Square Park...The park was divided. It has these walks, sort of like a sunburst, and there were these territories staked out. There were young hippie junkies down one row. There were lesbians down another, really tough amazingly hardcore lesbians. And in the middle were winos. They were like the first echelon and the girls who came from the Bronx to become hippies would have to sleep with the winos to get to sit on the other part with the junkie hippies...I got to know a few of them. I hung around a lot. They were a lot like sculptures in a funny way. I was very keen to get close to them, so I had to ask to photograph them. You can't get that close to somebody and not say a word, although I have done that.

—DIANE ARBUS, APERTURE, 1972[216]

Two typewritten pages, dated September 20, 1965, and included in a folder of hers that contains drafts of most of her writings,[217] tell the tale of a series of chance encounters with some of the members of this impromptu community she has come to know.

I had seen Jamie once and he had said sure that he would be photographed and we had trundled off, very motley him and Dexter who looks like Mick Jagger and has probably very accurately since been described by Jamie as a mad dog, and a number of peripheral characters, one of them a blooming insistent photographer. Someone who never showed up was looking for someone's pad for me to photograph them in but someone yet else had made off with the key and Dexter was so far gone out of his head that he kept sliding unseemly to the sidewalk and everyone's interest started to wane. But not before Jamie looking...seedy and Edwardian, pimply and ardent, delicate and messianic with the uncanny blue eyes of a child who will be forgiven anything, told me he was fifteen years old and could save people. Had in fact saved an old drunk that yesterday simply by looking him in the eye or saying a few words or something but the only trouble was that then the old guy wanted to stick around and be Jamie's friend and keep right on being saved or some such thing which wasn't it at all. Well the party broke up because some other messiah I knew passed by across the street and came over to tell me a great deal of unparalleled importance for the next eleven hours.

—UNPUBLISHED TEXT, 1965[218]

Contact Sheet #4038 with photographs taken in and around Washington Square Park. The image at bottom left was printed by Diane and titled Girl with a straw bag, Washington Square Park, N.Y.C. 1965.

Then last night I was wandering around looking for Theresa with her plain pop eyes, her formidable boots and arrogant devotions. Her kiss seals a thousand small bargains like a bank presidents signature, almost the more so because she is ugly...The sort of girl who in high school would have suffered her ugliness in isolation, she had turned it to advantage and thrust her face full into the mouth of every boy and inflicted tongues mutually, or put her arms round everyone in vast tenderness and conspiracy and a sort of ready friendship which was by definition valuable.

— UNPUBLISHED TEXT, 1965

Later Andy turned up, shy as a boy at dancing class with the wrong pants on, solemn, enormous-nosed with his hair combed down in a great wave over his eye, like Barbra Streisand before anyone believed in her.

— UNPUBLISHED TEXT, 1965

Marty appeared on W. 3rd St looking odd and in a different costume from usual. He is very like a weasel and in the oddest way I find him trustworthy as if he were a REAL weasel. He was wearing an oversize apricot corduroy shirt. His eyes look hung like dark chandeliers and he appeared to be hiding something which is not unusual. He started a story about how he had got in a fight...with three guys who had jumped him but he hadn't begun the story with any urgency...so I was listening mildly when quietly...he opened his mouth not very wide but I guess he rarely opens it at all and there was a space so large it seemed as if it could accommodate 6 or 8 teeth which weren't there at all. They knocked 'em out was all he said about it...so I broke one guy's kneecap which is the worst thing you can do to anybody, he said portentously. So now the cops are looking for ME he said with heavy sarcasm, for a guy with a black t shirt and a red bandana, that's why I'm wearing this, fingering it contemptuously (the big shirt).

— UNPUBLISHED TEXT, 1965

That's the way it is, Diane writes in a kind of wistful summary about these young people midway through the piece. *You figure they are lying to you and they do indeed lie a lot and exaggerate and dramatize and allude and whatnot, but suddenly you will look into the mouth of the veritable brink they live on and it is truly the black pit you have only just ever imagined.*[219]

Since 1962 when she first adopted the 2¼ format, she has been printing her square pictures on 11x14 paper in the usual manner, with a clean, sharp edge framing the image. At some point in 1965—although it remains unclear precisely when—she makes what appears to be a radical change and begins printing her photographs with thick, irregular black borders. Whatever the genesis of this new method—whether it is conceived deliberately or happened upon initially by chance—it obviously strikes her as important. All the prints she makes of the Washington Square pictures are done this way, as are those of all the photographs that follow. For the next several years the black border continues to be a distinctive feature of the way her prints look.[220]

The Washington Square project is punctuated in early July by a trip she has been planning to Sunnyrest, a nudist camp in Pennsylvania.[221] Several months later, she sends John Szarkowski at MoMA a note asking him to refrain *just for the present* from showing one of the nudist pictures. She explains: *I am now for one thing a member of the movement and following where it leads in civilian life and I don't want any tiny blunder to betray me. This may sound nutty but I have discovered that life really is a melodrama.*[222]

The Ethnic Beauties project that she has been pursuing on her own for a few years—and for which she has already made a number of pictures—finally results in an assignment from *Esquire*. In a letter dated August 9, 1965, and signed *Sincerely, and ever your friend,* Harold Hayes writes: *For an acceptable story—hereafter referred to as "Minority Pin-ups,"—we will pay you at the rate of $250 per page, regardless of the amount of text or photography on the page...If for any reason this story fails to work out, we will pay you a spread guarantee of $400—twice the usual amount for an unsuccessful story, since you are submitting both text and photographs.* She continues to work on this project for at least the next six months, jotting down brief descriptions of prospective subjects she encounters. Several photographs appear to have come out of it, as well as the draft of a text intended to accompany one of them. As a story, however, it is never published.[223]

In accordance with arrangements made the previous spring—probably at Marvin Israel's suggestion and maybe with some help from him as well[224]—she begins teaching a photography course in the fall at Parsons School of Design on Tuesday afternoons. The class includes about twelve students and, although she has access to the Parsons darkroom for teaching purposes, it focuses primarily on photographic assignments and critiques.

The Museum of Modern Art includes two of the seven prints acquired from her the year before—Retired man and his wife at home in a nudist camp one morning, N.J. 1963 (p. 253) and Female impersonators, N.Y.C. 1961 (p. 58)—in its Fall group show, *Recent Acquisitions: Photography*.[225] In applying to the Guggenheim Foundation for a renewal of her 1963 fellowship grant, she cites this exhibition, along with an earlier group show at the University of Wisconsin,[226] in a list of work accomplished. The list cites twenty-four of her photographic subjects as well, including: *Evangelist, Faith Healer; Nudists (convention, portraits, family groups, homes); Burlesque Show (stars, strippers, comics, the performance); Masquerade (Mardi*

Sharon Goldberg, N.Y.C. 1965. Portrait of a sixteen-year-old beauty wearing her Star of David. *So the boys will know I'm Jewish.* Diane wrote a draft of a text about Goldberg but neither the portrait nor the article were published.

A VARIANT PRINTED BY DIANE OF HER PHOTOGRAPH TWO FRIENDS AT HOME, N.Y.C. 1965 (P. 75). SHE ORIGINALLY MET THESE WOMEN IN WASHINGTON SQUARE PARK AND LATER VISITED THEM AT HOME.

NUDIST LADY WITH SWAN SUNGLASSES, PA. 1965. THIS PICTURE, THE ONLY IMAGE OF THIS WOMAN THAT DIANE MADE, WAS TAKEN AT SUNNYREST, A NUDIST CAMP IN PENNSYLVANIA, IN JULY 1965 AND PRINTED BY HER THE SAME YEAR.

Gras, Beaux Arts Ball, Halloween Party); Games (Canasta, Baseball, Jump-Rope);...Parlor (rooming house, widow, midgets)...Carnival; Beggars; Rock'n Roll groups; Triplets (portraits, club, convention).[227]

As requested, she summarizes the title of her present position, current salary, marital status, and the number and ages of her children: *I am a photographer (freelance) and I have undertaken to teach photography part-time at the Parsons School of Design. Altogether I earn about $4000 a yr. I am married, but separated, and have two children, aged eleven and twenty.*

Her project is entitled The Interior Landscape and is described in the following four sentences: *The Fellowship enabled me to go far enough to find the way to go further. I have learned to get past the door, from the outside to the inside. One milieu leads to another. I want to be able to follow.* On the same page, as a footnote, she adds: *For example, to photograph: a certain group of young nihilists, a variety of menages, a retirement town in the Southwest, a new kind of Messiah, a particular Utopian cult who plan to establish themselves on a nearby island, Beauties of different ethnic groups, certain criminal types, a minority elite.*[228]

Reading her brother Howard Nemerov's memoir, *Journal of the Fictive Life* (Rutgers University Press, 1965)—a kind of tapestry composed of unfinished fiction; meditations on writing fiction or the inability to do so; recollections of his childhood and his family; dreams and his interpretations of them; puns and jokes and other fragments—elicits the following response from Diane:

hdearh I awoke with such an urgent necessity to write you not my last word about it, but it hits me with a kind of contagion, not precisely as though it were my book but I recognize so nearly everything in it, like

I am possessed...it is as if our dreams people each others and endlessly like offshoots of branches the book is multiplying in my head...[I] have also stopped photographing a week or so...[and] have believed in both the guilt and innocence of photographing (which I privately call the butterfly collection), there are these thousand things...[and] that incredible place where it says Mommy, where do images come fr...[229] I am embarrassed even to write it. I havent ever read anything I so believed...

— LETTER TO HOWARD NEMEROV, CIRCA NOVEMBER 1965[230]

Nemerov's book also contains musings on the nature of images and image-making, and a surprising number of references to photography, including this one: *My vocation as a grownup has to do with making images, but I have never much cared for photographs. The same sister [Diane] is a professional photographer, whose pictures are spectacular, shocking, dramatic, and concentrate on subjects perverse and queer (freaks, professional transvestites, strong men, tattooed men, the children of the very rich). Thou shalt make no graven image.*[231] In the same letter to him Diane replies to this as well:

The only thing that I took personally in the way of feeling sort of pointed at was the list of my photogr subject matters which read like a dirty catalogue and perhaps the temporary exemption you grant me from what you say about photography, which because it is only temporary makes a sort of hilarious sense...[well not so hilarious, she writes in the margin]... the silent dialogue we have had all our lives on these matters is the more extraordinary for what we seem to have heard.

— LETTER TO HOWARD NEMEROV, CIRCA NOVEMBER 1965[232]

She invites him to stay at her place if he can when he is in town on the 12th and adds as a postscript, *There is a great deal more to say as well as not to.*[233]

Hubert's Museum is scheduled to close its doors forever in November. For weeks prior to its last day, Diane arranges sessions with the individual performers and does a few group portraits of them in the vacant basement space. She writes a text entitled "Hubert's Obituary," which she hopes to persuade one of the magazines to publish along with some of her photographs as a kind of requiem for the establishment, but her efforts prove unsuccessful.

It used to be that if, as your mother would say, you didn't know what to do with yourself, you would do it at Hubert's Museum. You'd...descend, somewhat like Orpheus or Alice or Virgil, into the cellar which was where Hubert's Museum was...Coming into the unholy fluorescent glare of it you'd see yourself dwarfed and fattened and stretched in several distorting mirrors and all around you like flowers a thousand souvenirs of human aberrations, as if the world had quite literally stashed away down there everything it didn't need.

—"Hubert's Obituary," *Diane Arbus: Magazine Work*, 1984[234]

She goes on to describe the show, which *was circular like the seasons or the stars* and each one of the performers: Charlie, the impresario Mr. R.C. Lucas, *he of the glittering eye, who talked like a spider, so sweet and scary at once in his old fez ringed round with a beaded snake...*; and Woogie *who was really Charlie's wife as Princess Wago, the African Dancing Venus,* [who] *undulated in the awful rosy darkness under her pythons and boa constrictors;* and Albert-Alberta, *a creature half man and half woman, seductive as a nightmare, a veritable French psychological novel...flirtatiously revealing a powdered perfumed sequined female left breast with a rugged muscular hairy male right hand while our mouths fell open in disbelief;* and Estelline, *such a pleasant motherly sword-swallower who taught us how we could swallow a bent wire coat hanger if we didn't happen to have any swords around the house;* and Presto, *a magician who looked like a rabbit himself ("I don't really do this," he'd say. "It just looks like it.");* and Ramon Batiste, *a legless man...*[who] *did the twist with his torso, for that was all there was of him, poised on the bottom end of an upside down Pepsi-Cola bottle...*[235]

And naturally she also mentions Professor Heckler and His Trained Fleas; and Andy Potatochips, who is really the multilingual Russian midget Andrew Ratoucheff; and the water glass musician, Harold Smith; and, of course, Congo the Jungle Creep. *We had our awe and our shame in one gulp,* she adds. *What if we couldn't always tell a trick from a miracle? If you've ever talked to somebody with two heads you know they know something you don't.*[236]

Medical Science being what it is they don't hardly make 'em like that anymore and the laws prevent pretending or people are rich enough nowadays to hide their relatives away instead of selling them to the Carnival like they used to...If you feel like it you can go on over to Hubert's tonight, anyway...No one is there except the pictures on the walls of all the people who used to be there. As Mr. Schaefer the owner points out: prices being what they are these days, at a dime, even if you just want to go to the bathroom it's worth it.

—"Hubert's Obituary," *Diane Arbus: Magazine Work*, 1984

Portrait of some of the performers for "Hubert's Obituary." (from left to right) Congo the Jungle Creep; Woogie, Princess Wago; Woogie's husband, Charlie Lucas, seated with his arm around the Russian midget Andrew Ratoucheff; Manzini, the Strong Man (also seated); and Harold Smith, the water glass musician, crouching. In the background are two unidentified men.

1966

In connection with her pending application, she delivers fifty-five prints to the Guggenheim Foundation prior to January 10 for review by the Advisory Jury. Although many of the photographs presumably involve subjects mentioned in her list of accomplishments (*Evangelists, Nudists, Burlesque, Masquerade, Parlor, Carnival, Triplets*) there is apparently no record of the specific images she selects.[237]

She resumes teaching at Parsons on Tuesday afternoons. The first class of the semester meets at The Museum of Modern Art on February 1 and the corresponding page in her appointment book contains some reminders for the occasion: *2 monitors, new people, strictness, new assignment.*[238]

On March 16 she receives notification from James Mathias of her second Guggenheim award (in the amount of the $7,500 she requested) and asking once again for her acknowledgment. She writes: *Dear Mr. Mathias, (This is my acknowledgement). With it my joy, my thanks, a little awe and that wee small voice that says to myself be quiet and get to work.*[239]

During the early part of the year she completes two magazine assignments. For *Esquire*'s July 1966 issue, she does a portrait of Brenda Diana Duff Frazier (Mrs. Chatfield Taylor), the 1938 debutante of the year, at her home in Medfield, Massachusetts (p. 261).[240] For Clay Felker's *New York*, she photographs James Brown, "the hardest working man in show business." Two of these pictures (p. 95 and p. 178) are published in the March 20, 1966 issue of the magazine along with the article "James Brown Is Out of Sight," by her twenty-one-year-old daughter, Doon.[241]

James Brown is scheduled to appear at Madison Square Garden in March and the idea for an article about him originates with Diane, who has seen him in performance at the Apollo Theater in Harlem.[242] This is the first of four magazine pieces she collaborates on with Doon.

Her work on the Guggenheim project is postponed for the month of April by her biggest magazine assignment to date, in terms of the number of portraits published. *Harper's Bazaar* co–art director Ruth Ansel is probably responsible, at least in part, for the assignment "The American Art Scene," which concerns an area of special interest to Ansel. Diane appears to have some degree of input in choosing the subjects for the piece. In the ensuing weeks she photographs the following artists: James Rosenquist; Charles Hinman; Larry Bell; Agnes Martin; Tom Wesselmann; Frank Stella; Roy Lichtenstein; Lucas Samaras;[243] Richard Lindner; Claes Oldenburg; Kenneth Noland; Lee Bontecou; and Marvin Israel (whose first New York exhibition of paintings opened at Cordier & Ekstrom Gallery on March 1).[244]

On the weekend of April 22, she joins Doon at Billy Hitchcock's Millbrook estate, the home of Dr. Timothy Leary's League for Spiritual Discovery (LSD). Doon has been there for about a week working on an article about Leary for Clay Felker's *New York* and Diane is assigned to do the photographs. The article is delayed and finally abandoned after G. Gordon Liddy, Assistant District Attorney of Dutchess County, organizes a drug raid on the mansion that results in the arrest of a number of residents and guests (including Leary, his future wife, Rosemary Woodruff, his eighteen-year-old daughter, Susan, and his colleague Dr. Ralph Metzner).[245]

In addition to her continuing interest in twins and triplets—especially adult twins or elderly twins, who seem more difficult to find than the children—she is pursuing another project. Her appointment book reflects a number of attempts to investigate the science of sexual research. She contacts the Institute for Sex Research at Indiana University, which was founded by Kinsey in 1947. She makes some phone calls about Dr. Hans Lehfeldt, an influential German doctor living in New York, who is an early advocate of birth control, founder of the *Journal of Sexual Research*, and a member of the Society for the Scientific Study of Sex.[246] She gets in touch with Dr. Albert Ellis, author of *Sex Without Guilt*, and his Institute for Rational Living.

But the subject does not merely interest her as *a kind of contemporary anthropology*. It is one of the *Secret Rites* she hopes to photograph. She goes in search of willing couples among her friends and acquaintances.[247] (Ruth Ansel recalls being asked—and declining—to pose naked with her husband, sculptor Paolo Buggiani. *Too uncomfortable with my body*, Ansel later explains.[248]) She photographs orgies in which she is a participant and some of her own individual sex partners posing naked in the aftermath. The challenge of rendering in a photograph something akin to the experience of being there intrigues her. Although she prints a number of these pictures, she regards the majority of them as failures in the terms she prescribes herself, for what she perceives as their lack of eroticism and authenticity.[249]

James Brown backstage, N.Y.C. 1966, one of the two photographs (p. 95) published in the March 20, 1966, issue of Clay Felker's *New York*, the Sunday magazine of *The World Journal Tribune*, in connection with the article "James Brown Is Out of Sight," by Doon Arbus.

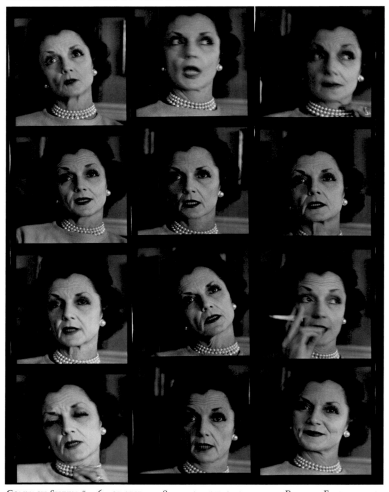

Contact sheet #4265 of the 1938 debutante of the year Brenda Frazier photographed by Diane at her home in Medfield, Massachusetts. The image Diane printed (p. 261) was published in *Esquire*'s July 1966 issue in conjunction with an article by Bernard Weinraub.

Among her acquaintances within the community of documentary photographers of her era, in addition to Walker Evans, Robert Frank, and Lee Friedlander, are Garry Winogrand, Bruce Davidson, Larry Fink, Ben Fernandez, Danny Lyon, Duane Michaels, and Joel Meyerowitz.[250] Although she is not part of a community—and there may in fact be no community to be a part of—she often attends a colleague's exhibition, visits a class or workshop as a guest, or meets up with one of them while roaming the streets or attending public events in which they happen to share an interest. Meyerowitz's description of his encounters with her may be typical: *We would meet on these infrequent occasions by chance and then spend an hour or two with each other just drifting, until she had had enough or until she found something she wanted to do...A few times we all went down to her house to see work. But that was it.*[251]

Her bed at the Charles Street carriage house occupies a far corner of the living room and is separated from the rest of the room by a screen of irregular weather-beaten wooden planks hinged together. Pinned to both sides of the screen are clippings, postcards, and a number of her own, mostly recent, rough prints on torn curling sheets of photographic paper. Other prints are stored in boxes in the adjacent closet under a staircase. On those occasions when she shows someone her work, she usually does so here.

THREE PORTRAITS PUBLISHED IN THE JULY 1966 ISSUE OF *HARPER'S BAZAAR* AS PART OF "THE AMERICAN ART SCENE": *(ABOVE)* MARVIN ISRAEL ON HIS ROOF; *(BELOW LEFT)* LUCAS SAMARAS; *(BELOW RIGHT)* AGNES MARTIN.

John Szarkowski is in the process of planning an exhibition, scheduled for February of the following year, which will be called *New Documents*. *In the past decade a new generation of photographers has directed the documentary approach toward more personal ends*, he writes in the exhibition brochure. *Their aim has been not to reform life, but to know it.*[252] He has selected three photographers as independent manifestations of this development: Lee Friedlander, Garry Winogrand, and Diane Arbus. During the next several months Szarkowski works individually with each of the three photographers, selecting the pictures to be included in the show.

Szarkowski later summarizes the nature of his friendship and working relationship with Diane. *I did not really know...[her] well, although she was a cherished friend for...years. There was a large area of private thought and feeling that our friendship did not attempt to enter, except perhaps occasionally through jokes or other elliptical codes. She had about her an almost ceremonial sensitivity to roles—not only her own role, but the roles of others, defined according to her own subtly demanding intuitions. This made friendship with her rather like a measured dance at a masked ball—more exciting and more challenging and less spontaneous, than real life. This careful self-discipline, with its suggestion of reticence, was I think required by her work. She had assigned herself the task of photographing mysteries so shy, fugitive, and terrific that they, or she, might have been frightened off, had the issues been openly stated.*[253]

A letter from Diane to James Mathias dated June 9, 1966, reports that she plans to begin her Guggenheim project on July 1, requests a To Whom It May Concern letter, confirms payment arrangements, and refers in a postscript to the enclosed doctor's *good word*: a note from Theodore J. Edlich, M.D., dated June 7, stating that he has examined

DIANE'S 1966 PHOTOGRAPH OF MEMBERS OF THE LEAGUE FOR SPIRITUAL DISCOVERY ON THE LAWN OF THEIR MILLBROOK HEADQUARTERS. DR. TIMOTHY LEARY IS CROUCHING IN THE CENTER BETWEEN HIS SON, JOHN *(LEFT)*, AND ROSEMARY WOODRUFF *(RIGHT)*. LEARY'S COLLEAGUE DR. RALPH METZNER IS CROUCHING SECOND FROM THE RIGHT. THE PRINT GIVEN BY DIANE TO METZNER IS CURRENTLY IN THE COLLECTION OF SFMOMA.

CONTACT SHEET #4457 OF A COUPLE ON A COUCH. IN THE FRAME SECOND FROM
THE TOP OF THE CENTER STRIP DIANE IS LYING ACROSS THE MAN'S LAP IN PLACE OF THE WOMAN.

Diane Arbus and has found her to be *in good physical and mental health and free from communicable disease.* A subsequent notation at the bottom of the letter, probably written by Mathias, records the fact that *Diane Arbus called today 6-13-66 to say she has hepatitis.*[254]

On July 5, almost a month later, Diane writes to Mathias again: *I am considerably better and though it means proceeding more slowly than I would have liked I think I know some ways and means of doing that. So would you go ahead in accordance with my letter of ~~several weeks~~ a month ago.*[255] Mathias replies the following day: *Dear Diane: It's no go! And I won't budge until I get a release from your doctor. I am about to have my own check-up and intend to ask mine whether I can come to see you.*[256]

It is not until July 29 that she is able to satisfy his medical requirement. Mathias writes: *I am delighted to know that you are up and about and that your doctor has given his o.k...* The date for the commencement of her project is officially given as July 15, probably in order to facilitate the desired schedule of payments.[257] Judging by the scant entries in her appointment book for July and August, she seems in fact to have spent almost the entire three months recuperating. As she later summarizes the experience in a note to Stewart Stern: *I was horribly sick with hepatitis last summer which reduced me to despair for three months but when I found myself I was so happy to be happy I could hardly contain myself.*[258]

After resuming work in the fall, she encounters someone she comes to know *pretty well* and whom she photographs several times during the course of the next few years (p. 250, p. 291):[259]

...I just saw her on the street one day. I was riding my bicycle on Third Avenue and she was with a friend of hers.[260] They were enormous, both of them, almost six feet tall, and fat. I thought they were big lesbians. They went into a diner and I followed them and asked if I could photograph them. They said, "Yes, tomorrow morning." Subsequently they were apparently arrested and spent the night in jail being booked. So the next morning I got to their house around eleven and they were just coming up the stairs after me. The first thing they said was, "I think we should tell you"—I don't know why they felt so obligated—"we're men."

—*DIANE ARBUS, APERTURE, 1972*[261]

Obtaining releases from the people she photographs has always been an issue—*sometimes I've gotten a release without even taking a picture*, she says on one occasion[262]—but the prospect of the exhibition makes it more pressing. She visits many of the people she has photographed in the past to tell them about the show and the possible inclusion of their portrait. In a letter to Stewart Stern she writes: *Saw Shirley* [Fingerhood, a lawyer, friend, and former Fieldston classmate] *who has given me legal advice because my photographs are becoming more and more questionable...*[263] On another occasion she writes Szarkowski: *I forgot to get back from you the release for the nudist couple you were going to xerox. Would you keep it for me or send it to me because it begins to strike me as having a value of its own.*[264]

By early November she and Szarkowski seem to have made an initial selection of pictures to include in the show, but she is having second thoughts:

TWO CONSECUTIVE FRAMES OF A 35MM ROLL OF FILM (CONTACT SHEET #4375A): A COUPLE IN BED, AND ARTIST JAMES ROSENQUIST AT WORK.

(ABOVE) THE MAY 15 PAGE OF DIANE'S APPOINTMENT BOOK RECORDS HER VISIT TO THE BRONX HOME OF A YOUNG BROOKLYN FAMILY (P. 8), WHERE SHE TAKES THIS PICTURE. *THEY WERE UNDENIABLY CLOSE IN A PAINFUL SORT OF WAY*, SHE RECALLS IN A 1968 LETTER. *(BELOW)* SEATED TRANSVESTITE WITH CROSSED ANKLES, N.Y.C. 1966.*

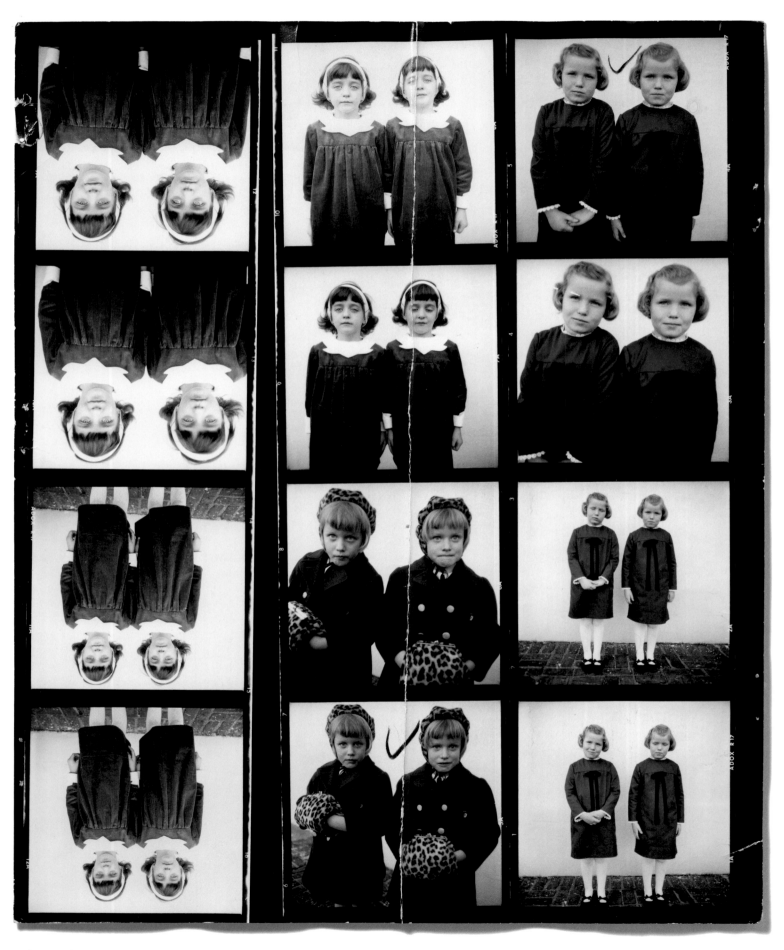

CONTACT SHEET #4539 OF THREE DIFFERENT SETS OF IDENTICAL TWINS. THE CHECK MARKS ON THE BOTTOM CENTER FRAME AND TOP RIGHT FRAME WERE PROBABLY MADE BY DIANE IN CONTEMPLATION OF GIVING A PRINT TO THE SUBJECTS, ALTHOUGH IT IS NOT CLEAR WHETHER SHE DID SO. THE IMAGE SHE PRINTED OF *IDENTICAL TWINS*, ROSELLE, N.J., #14, IS UPSIDE DOWN, SECOND FROM THE BOTTOM AT LEFT. ON THE DECEMBER 11 PAGE OF HER APPOINTMENT BOOK, SHE WRITES: *GREAT GIRL TWINS. REN EYES* [A REFER-ENCE TO HER SISTER, RENÉE] AND IN A NOTEBOOK (NO. 26) ON THE SAME SUBJECT, *WONDERFUL RENÉE TWINS*.

Dear John I looked in the box and maybe I was still sick that first time or something but I don't like a lot of the pictures so...[could we meet] please for dinner (or breakfast or lunch) so we can come to an understanding. I am in no particular hurry though because I fancy that what I am doing now is better than most of what I have done but it's true I haven't even seen it yet.

—POSTCARD TO JOHN SZARKOWSKI, NOVEMBER 8, 1966

In spite of her apparent dissatisfaction with some of the choices for the show at this stage, she has already begun printing. For the first time, she is making 16x20 prints of some of the photographs—the largest she has yet attempted—probably in consideration of the effect she wants the images to have when they are seen on the exhibition wall.[265]

She makes several references to her eagerness to give Szarkowski a print as a present. In a postcard about his book *The Photographer's Eye* (The Museum of Modern Art, 1966), she refers to his essay as not only *lucid but encouraging too* and adds *while I am printing, anything you want an extra of, just tell me*.[266] In another instance, she writes: *It would please me to give you a photograph so if you think of one you'd like or perhaps you should see some of the more recent ones you haven't seen or you might like to wait for one of the ones I haven't made yet. Tell me.*[267]

Her progress on the exhibition is briefly interrupted by an assignment that takes her to Kingston, Jamaica. On December 28, she and Amy leave with *New York Times* editor Patricia Peterson and Peterson's son, Jan, to work on the newspaper's upcoming spring children's fashion supplement. The goal is to use the children they happen to find there as models. The four of them spend the next several days or so traveling around in a rented car filled with clothes, on the lookout for potential subjects.[268] "Children in the Sun" is published the following spring and consists of the magazine cover and eleven color and black-and-white photographs by Diane Arbus.[269]

1967

She has recently learned to drive, has a license and has purchased a 1962 Renault for $200, which she describes to a friend as *famous for being no good but it is fine for me to learn bklyn and N.J.*[270] Responding to an inquiry from her brother as to whether she has a picture that might serve as the cover of his next book of poems (*The Blue Swallows*, Chicago University Press, 1967), she offers this incidental description of her photographs:

Dear H. Cannot think what I have. It is all so specific. The only landscape is one of a photomural of a landscape with an electric socket in it [p. 78]. Is that too something or other? Anyway its got no swallows but it might have. Can you wait and look when you are here but no—I can't see what else there is that is lyrical or allusive or elusive. It's all people who are right there...

—POSTCARD TO HOWARD NEMEROV, CIRCA JANUARY 1967[271]

She notes on the January 27 page of her appointment book that this is the day Szarkowski is framing the 16x20 prints for the show. There are

WHAT A GOOD TIME I HAD...THANK JILL FOR THE GRACIOUS EXTRA PLACE AT YOUR TABLE, SHE WRITES JOHN SZARKOWSKI FOLLOWING AN IMPROMPTU DINNER AT HIS HOME WITH HIS WIFE, JILL. THIS PHOTOGRAPH OF SZARKOWSKI PLAYING THE CLARINET AND JILL AT THE PIANO WAS PROBABLY MADE THAT EVENING AND LATER PRINTED BY DIANE AND GIVEN TO HIM.

four out of the thirty images involved: Puerto Rican woman (p. 84), Young man in curlers (p. 46), A family one evening (p. 295), and Identical twins (p. 265). All her prints are framed unmatted in Kulicke plastic boxes the same size as the prints themselves.[272]

The exhibition space designated for *New Documents* is on the ground floor of the museum and consists of one discrete room and a contiguous long hall that opens onto a second room about twice the size of the first. Early on it is decided that Diane's work will occupy the first room, while Lee Friedlander's and Garry Winogrand's photographs are to be hung in separate areas of the larger one.

According to Szarkowski, this decision is partially a response to the difference in format, style, and subject matter of Diane's work, which would look strange paired with the work of either Friedlander or Winogrand.[273] There may also be a desire to exhibit her photographs in the more sequestered of the two available spaces. Szarkowski recalls a mild, subtly expressed, but persistent disagreement he has with the director of the museum, Rene d'Harnoncourt, on the subject of the hanging of Diane's pictures: *We walked through the gallery and Rene said, "I've never liked that gallery. It's always been such an unsatisfactory space. Wouldn't it make the space more interesting if we put up a wall here." He knew that I knew what he was trying to say: Segregate the transvestites in a nook of their own. And I said, "No, Rene, it's impossible. You can't divide these people up according to your private standard of morality because if you do, there are always those people who are going to fall between chairs. You have to put the respectable suburban matron right next to the transvestite..." But he wasn't altogether persuaded. He'd pretend he was persuaded and then he'd go at it again in some other round-*

INSTALLATION PHOTOGRAPH OF THE FIRST ROOM OF *NEW DOCUMENTS*. THE PHOTOGRAPHS INCLUDE *(FROM LEFT TO RIGHT)* PUERTO RICAN WOMAN WITH A BEAUTY MARK (P. 84); A WIDOW IN HER BEDROOM (P. 44); TRANSVESTITE SHOWING CLEAVAGE (P. 82); MISS VENICE BEACH BEAUTY CONTEST (P. 58); A YOUNG MAN IN CURLERS (P. 46); RUSSIAN MIDGET FRIENDS (P. 100); CHILD WITH A TOY HAND GRENADE (P. 104); TRANSVESTITE WITH TORN STOCKING (P. 291); AND THE JUNIOR INTERSTATE BALLROOM DANCE CHAMPIONS (P. 40).

about Viennese way. So finally I said, "Look, Diane is coming in and why don't the two of you get together."[274]

The meeting between them takes place at the museum on February 23, less than a week before the opening. Szarkowski describes it this way: [Rene] *was about six feet eight, this mountain of a man with a Viennese ceremony every bit as formidable as Diane's was...They met here in the office and it was one of the best confrontations I ever saw. I stood in the corner, smiling, and watched them. Absolutely polite. Absolutely gracious on both sides. Absolutely smiling. Both of them really understood and respected each other but finally Rene with great graciousness just gave up and bowed and retreated from the field.*[275]

Diane remains a little torn about the prospect of showing her photographs. As she puts it in an interview on the subject with *Newsweek*'s Ann Ray Martin after the fact: *I always thought I'd wait until I'm ninety to have a show or...[do] a book because I figured I was good for only one shot — that I wanted to wait until I had it all done.*[276] Her ambivalence is not lost on Szarkowski who later suggests some additional reasons for her hesitation. *Diane was not at all eager to exhibit her work...When [the pictures] were exhibited or published she wanted to be certain that it was at the right time and in the right way and under the right circumstances, so that the pictures were not in violation of her personal, moral commitment. In addition to that, she was conscious of the fact that what she was doing was quite differ-*

ent from what other photographers were doing, and she wanted a chance to complete it...before getting it out in public.[277] On the other hand, he believes that *what was there* [in the *New Documents* show] *I think she found very satisfactory.*[278]

In anticipation of the opening, Diane supplies Szarkowski's secretary, Pat Walker, with a handwritten list on lined legal size yellow paper bearing the names and addresses of people she hopes will be invited on her behalf. This is followed soon after by a two-page typewritten list with additional names accompanied by marginal notes on some of the prospective guests. She includes the names and addresses of three editors *who have asked me about doing a book of photographs* and then adds in the margin *No, let's not invite them...more colorful people are more fun.* As she notes in conclusion: *I'm not greedy. I just want it to be a good party.*[279]

She makes uncharacteristically elaborate preparations for the evening: gets her hair cut, permed, and set at Vidal Sassoon, buys a new dress, and arranges for a friend to do her makeup especially for the occasion.[280] Szarkowski recalls her entrance the night of the opening: *Diane came in. Very fashionably late. Very elegant like a movie queen from the thirties. And Dick [Avedon] was there with a great big bouquet of yellow roses. She was very radiant. But studied...she did have split feelings about those kinds of public displays. She couldn't just come and have a good time. Like Lee or Garry.*[281]

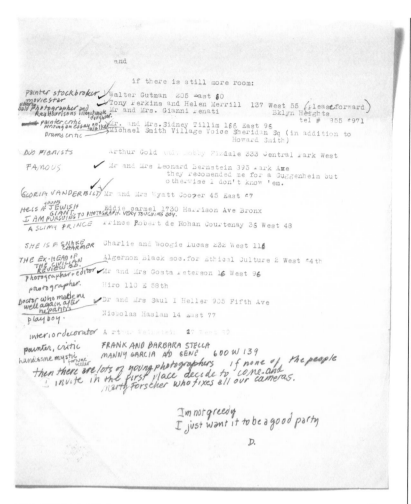

THE SECOND PAGE OF A TWO-PAGE INVITATION LIST FOR THE OPENING OF *NEW DOCUMENTS* SENT BY DIANE TO SZARKOWSKI'S SECRETARY, PAT WALKER. IT BEGINS: *AND IF THERE IS STILL MORE ROOM…*

OPENING NIGHT OF *NEW DOCUMENTS*: ALLAN ARBUS AND ACTRESS MARICLARE COSTELLO IN CONVERSATION WITH HOWARD NEMEROV; DIANE IS IN THE BACKGROUND. PHOTOGRAPH BY GEORGE CSERNA, COLLECTION OF THE MUSEUM OF MODERN ART.

NOTEBOOK (NO. 26) WITH DIALOGUE DIANE OVERHEARD AT THE EXHIBITION.

Richard Avedon and Marvin Israel have organized a photographic workshop together that takes place once a week at Avedon's studio on East 58th Street. Among the young photographers participating in the class are Peter Hujar, Deborah Turbeville, and Chris von Wangenheim. Diane attends one of the sessions as a guest following the opening of *New Documents*.[282]

She makes her photograph of the twins into a postcard (inscribed on the back in pen *Identical twins Diane Arbus Postcard*) and sends it to a number of friends as an announcement. To Stewart Stern on March 5 she writes: *From now till June 7* [the show actually ends May 7 so this date is probably a misprint] *there's one third of a show of my photographs at the museum of modern art. I wish you could see it. It's just much more beautiful than I had ever seen it at home.*[283] And to the Meserveys: *Everything here is too overwhelming. The show I mean. I go from laughter to tears. I bought a $200 car and have braces on my teeth for four months.*[284] And to her friend the peace activist Paul Salstrom, who is living in Berkeley:

Now there is a show…30 of my photographs at the modern museum. I long for you to see it. It is so beautiful, all in a splendid room and people stare into them, hundreds of strangers as if they were reading. I stand there for hours watching people watch the pictures and listening to what they say.

—POSTCARD TO PAUL SALSTROM, MARCH 5, 1967[285]

WOMAN WITH PEARL NECKLACE AND EARRINGS, N.Y.C. 1967. AS DIANE WRITES HER FRIEND CARLOTTA MARSHALL: *THE PICTURES ARE GETTING BIGGER. SOME ARE LIFESIZE OR MORE.*

The reviews of her portion of the exhibition—both positive and negative—focus almost exclusively on the issue of her subject matter. "Showing It Like It Is," John Gruen's review in *New York* [*The World Journal Tribune Sunday Magazine*] says: *Diane Arbus is the most shockingly alert to a human stratum most of us have little contact with...Her photographs are brutal, daring and revealing because she not only succeeded in invading closed territories, but obviously gained the confidence of subjects living on the peripheries of the accepted.*[286] In *The New York Times* review entitled "People Seen as Curiosity," Jacob Deschin writes: [*She*] *seems to respond to the grotesque in life...there is occasionally a subtle suggestion of pathos, now and then diluted slightly with a vague sense of humor. Sometimes it must be added, the picture borders close to poor taste.*[287] And in the March 20, 1967, issue of *Newsweek,* Ann Ray Martin—who interviewed Diane on March 6 at the museum—summarizes her work this way: *With the sharp crystal-clear generous vision of a poet, Mrs. Arbus turns her lens on the margins of society.*[288]

By the end of March, she is planning a trip to Florida that she seems to regard at least in part as an escape from the heady atmosphere engendered by the show. She responds to a letter from Stewart Stern:

You sound edgy and wild and miserable and I don't know but you made me feel good...I am going to Florida for 10 days to Ft. Lauderdale and Miami and I dunno wherever the travel brochures tell me. Just to photograph. With the Guggenheim money. The show was splendid but too many calls and letters and people thinking I am an expert or incredibly lovable. I need to be forlorn and anonymous in order to be truly happy. Get edgier yet and try to visit NY. It's a nice place to visit.

— POSTCARD TO STEWART STERN, CIRCA MARCH 1967[289]

She leaves for Ft. Lauderdale on March 25 and sends Marvin Israel a postcard from Miami recounting in brief her failed attempt to meet with *the World's Greatest Female Pinup Photographer,* Bunny Yaeger,[290] who fascinates her but who when they spoke *was wary if not downright hostile and very snobbish. Just because I have heard of her it does not follow that she has heard of me.* She concludes with this summary of the place, *Ionesco would be pleased here but my hotel is for Beckett* and then adds as an afterthought, *It cannot be anti-Semitism but they do not accept me here.*[291]

A few days later she sends him a second postcard, this time with one of Yaeger's photographs on it that bears the credit line *color by Bunny Yaeger.* She writes underneath *blk & wht by Diane.*

There is kind of a bad smell here like God cooking chicken soup in the sky. And the language is full of money. There is a word called condominium something to do with real estate. It is written everywhere. And high-rise means skyscraper. When my mother says she realized [something] she doesn't mean an insight she means profit on an investment. Ask me about Oedipus when I come home because I think I realized something...There is a law here against miniskirts but they are too embarrassed to invoke it...It is as if I am a bottomless waitress...How will we be when we are old? A thousand times D.

— POSTCARD TO MARVIN ISRAEL, CIRCA MARCH 1967[292]

Ruth Ansel gets a postcard from Florida, too: *...I'm in the land of our ancestors. They look at me very oddly...It is like a dream. (My car is a turquoise air conditioned nightmare Mustang). yours till retirement.*[293] Ansel recalls several conversations with Diane about *photographing the Fontainbleau Hotel in all its Miami glory,*[294] an assignment that Ansel, Bea Feitler, and Diane continue to hope will be forthcoming from *Harper's Bazaar.* But as Ansel later explains, *It was too "downmarket unglamorous" for the editors. A real loss.*[295]

Following Diane's return to New York in early April, her interests as a photographer prompt her to attend an unusual number of public events, both political and social.[296] These include the Rouge et Noir Ball at the New York Hilton, the Heart Association Ball at the Waldorf Hotel, the Spring Mobilization to End the War in Vietnam on April 15, the march to "Support Our Men in Vietnam" on May 13, and a Human Be-In in Central Park's Sheep's Meadow in June.[297] She begins considering a trip to San Francisco and asks Paul Salstrom's advice.

Dear Paul, would it be a good thing if I was to come to San F. in the beginning of July? I would come in no official capacity. Are there too many photographers. Could you be my guide...

— POSTCARD TO PAUL SALSTROM, CIRCA JUNE 1967[298]

RICHARD AVEDON AND MARVIN ISRAEL'S PHOTOGRAPHIC WORKSHOP AT AVEDON'S STUDIO, 110 EAST 58TH STREET, ON FEBRUARY 28, 1967. *(FAR LEFT)* RICHARD AVEDON, MARVIN ISRAEL (BARELY VISIBLE BEHIND AVEDON), THE PHOTOGRAPHER HIRO (SEATED ON A LEDGE), AND DIANE; *(CENTER)* MARVIN ISRAEL POINTING; *(RIGHT)* DIANE WITH A CIGARETTE. PHOTOGRAPHS BY GIDEON LEWIN.

Apparently his response persuades her. She travels on American Airlines, arriving July 6 as scheduled. She stays in a house at 591 Waller Street in the Haight-Ashbury, where Salstrom is living with a group of war resisters. She finds San Francisco—with its glut of hippies, tourists, and journalists—oppressive. In a letter to her brother she confesses: *California...made me queasy and repudiated. Probably I took it personally.* She blames her failure to meet with writer Kay Boyle—a friend of Nemerov's whom she knows and who is a resident of San Francisco—on the fact that she *couldn't bear to see anyone who felt comfortable being there.*[299]

She and Salstrom leave the city and drive to Southern California together, then head back East. They part in Oklahoma City, where Salstrom decides to stay a while. After her return to New York, Diane writes him about the rest of her trip:

...The bus began to hearten me and I read McLuhan [*Understanding Media* (New York: Mentor/Penguin, 1964)] and lots of sh. Stories. But on the last lap the stench and filth and tragic aspect of all those abandoned sleeping creatures was nearly too much. Arrived at 5:00 A.M. and walked N.Y. all day, exhausted, refreshed, elated. Even met a gypsy who asked me (unprecedented!) to photograph her. I will not apologize or thank you. It is all too mysterious. Diane.

—POSTCARD TO PAUL SALSTROM, JULY 28, 1967[300]

She gives Amy, who is away at camp in upstate New York, this account of the summer's progress:

dear amy I have been strange as anything, curioser and curioser as alice said. Last night I dreamed you had taken all the pictures off my wall "because you needed the tape" (!)...today it seems to have turned blessedly cool...The other night I went to Times Sq and suddenly there is a parking lot smack in the middle of Broadway a Whole Block Sq. I guess it is where the Astor Hotel used to be. It looked the way it would if someone you knew awfully well but hadn't seen very recently had lost two front teeth...We miss you. You are somehow the backbone or the lifeblood of this house. It is oddly random without you. I hope the people look promising. I hope you have enough pants. I love you beloved (Amy)...your ma.

—LETTER TO AMY ARBUS, SUMMER 1967

On August 16 she goes to Palisades Amusement Park in New Jersey for the 30th annual Diaper Derby contest to photograph the event as well as the winner and losers. The experience seems connected in her mind to some incipient change she believes is occurring in the pictures. She writes her brother in the fall about her recent photographic projects: *The subjects are terribly odd—dogs and babies—but that pleases me. It is like starting over again.*[301] And in a letter to her friend Carlotta Marshall: *I have been photographing babies which is odd and absorbing. Also the pictures are getting bigger. Some are lifesize or more. That is fun. Like making people instead of photographs.*[302] To Amy she puts it this way: *I suddenly realized that when I photograph people I don't anymore want them to look at me. (I used nearly always to wait for them to look me in the eye but now its as if I think I will see them more clearly if they are not watching me watching them.*[303])

TWO PHOTOGRAPHS FROM CONTACT SHEETS: *(ABOVE)* THE DIAPER DERBY WINNER'S CIRCLE PHOTOGRAPHED BY DIANE ON AUGUST 16, 1967; *(BELOW)* A CRASH PAD IN NEW YORK CITY.

(BELOW LEFT) A WOMAN IN FLORIDA FROM A CONTACT SHEET. *(BELOW RIGHT)* ACTOR MICHAEL J. POLLARD PHOTOGRAPHED FOR AN ARTICLE IN *CHEETAH* BY DOON ARBUS.

CONTACT SHEET #5027 OF PHOTOGRAPHS MADE AT THE PRO-WAR PARADE IN NEW YORK ON MAY 13, 1967. DIANE PRINTS THREE OF THESE IMAGES: #1 AT BOTTOM LEFT, BOY WITH A STRAW HAT (P. 87), LATER INCLUDED IN HER PORTFOLIO *A BOX OF TEN PHOTOGRAPHS*; #2, SECOND FROM BOTTOM LEFT, BOY IN A REVOLUTIONARY WAR UNIFORM; AND #11, TOP CENTER, MAN IN AN INDIAN HEADRESS.

The magazine assignments she works on in 1967 are not published until the following year. These include a portrait of Gloria Vanderbilt and Wyatt Cooper's infant son, Anderson, for *Harper's Bazaar* (p. 69);[304] folk singer/prophet Mel Lyman for *Esquire;*[305] and a project of her own on a camp for overweight girls.[306] She also has several assignments from a new magazine, *Cheetah.*[307]

Stewart Stern has written the screenplay for *Rachel, Rachel*, a movie that marks Paul Newman's directorial debut, with his wife, Joanne Woodward, in the lead. Stern, a friend of the Newmans', introduces the notion of hiring Diane as the still photographer on the set, which is seriously considered for a while. By September, however, to Stern's chagrin, the prospect has fallen through, probably for financial reasons.[308] She writes to him at the Danbury Motor Inn in Connecticut where the movie is being shot.

I don't know quite how it happened that I'm not doing it. I miss you and would have liked just doing it for you. I may have asked too much money...Dunno. I am working on two marvelous assignments. Feel much stronger. One is on prophets.[309] Don't bother to answer. I know you are at the grindstone. Will see you afterwards. Try to save an evening...Till then...

—LETTER TO STEWART STERN, SEPTEMBER 27, 1967

Following publication of his book *The Blue Swallows,* Howard Nemerov inquires as to whether Diane was paid for the use of her picture on the cover. She answers: *Yes yes I got pd. And when I saw it I didn't feel any sort of twinge. It is an odd red but I didn't take it personally.* She goes on:

I've been jumpy. Going in fits and starts since the show...But suddenly I have a lot of work, an odd combination of public and private work and probably that will be good.

—LETTER TO HOWARD NEMEROV, CIRCA OCTOBER 1967[310]

Responding to news of the recent birth of Carlotta Marshall's first child (a son named Jamie, born October 18) Diane writes to her in Holland where she has been living with her husband, Louis Berger. *Dear Carlotta we are so glad to picture it. your parenthood. tell us more than we can picture.* She adds:

The first breath of cold frightened me into staying home today to write you as I ought to have long ago. My popularity or success or whatever it was has ebbed somewhat which has its compensations and now it is time to get back to a sort of obscurity and see what I come up with...I have wangled a weekly ride in a radio car with a press photographer. This is more adventure than photography but perhaps eventually some of it will become photographable. I would like to make a sort of news photographs.

—LETTER TO CARLOTTA MARSHALL, CIRCA NOVEMBER 1967[311]

During the summer, Diane has been in touch with two editors from *The London Sunday Times Magazine,* Michael Rand and Peter Crookston, and with one of the magazine's writers, Pauline Peters. In late October, when Crookston comes to New York, she meets with him several times and invites him to Charles Street to see her work.[312] Among the pictures she shows him are Widow in her bedroom (p. 44) and a number of images from the Diaper Derby (both of which inspire stories written by Pauline Peters and published in the magazine the following year accompanied by Diane's photographs).[313] On November 30 she writes Crookston a follow-up letter consisting of eleven short, hand-numbered paragraphs with asterisks indicating those items that *require answers or actions.*

(1)YES I will send the photographs of the lady poet tomorrow (friday) evening. Must print the new ones first. They amaze me.[314] (2) *Would you give me a special Big Credit Line because I really love that photograph...saying PHOTOGRAPHED BY DIANE ARBUS... thanks (3) I will also send the Diaper Derby photographs and the ones you chose of women for possible use. Some of the prints are crude and not for reproduction but I will send what you want when you do. (4) *Please when you have finished with the ones you do not need would you send them back and the stats you borrowed as well. Thanks... (7) *If you have any sort of press credentials that look nice and professional would you send them. (8) *If there is some way of getting me some money for these three stories we worked on please do Either by paying me a daily rate or some sort of arrangement for the ideas...

—LETTER TO PETER CROOKSTON, NOVEMBER 30, 1967[315]

She says she expects to be coming to London around January 5—*The man I spoke about* [a reference to Marvin Israel] *has asked me to go with him*—and suggests Crookston think of something she might photograph for the magazine while there. She concludes with this:

I am so happy and the strangest things have been happening as if someone had turned my life around for me and showed it to me in a whole different light. It makes me giddy. If all goes well I will see you soon how truly nice diane.

—LETTER TO PETER CROOKSTON, NOVEMBER 30, 1967

The imminent expiration of her lease at Charles Street and the threat of a substantial rent increase as a result compel her to look for another place to live. A couple of weeks later, in answer to what she describes as *a happy headlong letter* from Crookston, she writes him again:

It is raining endlessly and I have been apt [apartment] hunting ceaselessly so I have developed a cold and a dislike for all dwelling places and a sort of blankness about christmas which even surpasses my normal scroogeness. Thanks for your painstaking replies and reactions to every one of my queries and requests. I could not be in better hands...We never mention... London, marvin and me, (the man who asked me to go). partly out of superstition or discretion or prudence or the plain old sense that so much has to be cleaned out of the Augean stables first that one had best not speak of it at all so that it will come in the nature of a surprise if it comes and not a disappointment if...oh well we'll see...

—LETTER TO PETER CROOKSTON, DECEMBER 12, 1967[316]

On December 15 Allan goes with her to look at an apartment she is considering renting at 120 East 10th Street between Second and Third avenues in the East Village.[317] *Might have found an apt*, she says when she writes Crookston a few days later to let him know that she won't be coming to London after all.

I'm not disappointed really. I couldn't have taken more in. The changes I've embarked on like moving and some odd new thing I think I see ahead in the photographs are either necessary or exciting and I must do one thing at a time...I want to make order and begin again.

—LETTER TO PETER CROOKSTON, DECEMBER 19, 1967[318]

A PEACE MARCH GATHERING IN CENTRAL PARK'S SHEEP'S MEADOW ON APRIL 15, 1967. DIANE IS CARRYING HER MAMIYAFLEX WITH ITS STROBE ATTACHMENT. PHOTOGRAPH BY GARRY WINOGRAND.

1968

The apartment at 120 East 10th Street is actually two separate apartments on the top floors of a five-story brownstone walk-up, connected to one another only by the building's public staircase. The apartment on the lower floor consists of three small bedrooms (for Diane, Doon, and Amy), an entrance hall, and bathroom; the one on the upper floor is a living room, open kitchen, and second bathroom. In early January, just before the move, Diane sends Crookston some prints she had promised him for the magazine, accompanied by a note:

I am in the midst of cleaning and packing and moving—haven't worked for so long it makes me queasy and strange to myself. But it is fun. I have thrown out and given away more than I have kept it seems. I am pure housewife and I hate that it is so barren and obsessive but I look forward to the new beginning like a bride.

—NOTE TO PETER CROOKSTON, CIRCA JANUARY 1968[319]

The move takes place on January 15. *Fell into a terrible funk, moving. The old house fell apart and the new won't fall in. My incompetence looms like a middle name*, she reports a few weeks later in responding to a proposed assignment from Crookston to photograph the Republican presidential hopefuls. *Yes Ive wanted to do those baroque Republicans. Can someone make all arrangements for me? Or would I go with a writer.*[320] The January 29 page of her appointment book includes a list of names (*Reagan, Rockefeller, Nixon, Percy, Romney*) but the magazine's attempts to organize this project apparently fail.[321]

On February 14 she travels to South Carolina for several days on assignment for *Esquire* to accompany crusading country doctor Donald Gatch on his rounds and photograph him and his patients.[322] Dr. Gatch is in the midst of a campaign to call attention to widespread malnutrition and discriminatory medical practice in poverty-stricken rural Beaufort County. Diane describes the experience to Studs Terkel a few months later when he interviews her about the Great Depression of the 1930s: *I never saw poverty like that. I have never been in homes like that. There was one family with fourteen children. One of the children had one eye. One was a hydrocephalic...The doctor...told me an incredible story of a mother with an illegitimate mentally defective boy who, because she couldn't get welfare, had to go to work and since she had no one to take care of the boy she chained him to the bed for her eight hours of working.*[323] Bynum Shaw's article "Let Us Now Praise Dr. Gatch," accompanied by three Diane Arbus photographs, is published in *Esquire* in June.

Of the six previous 1968 magazine pieces in which her pictures appear, three are published by *The London Sunday Times Magazine*, all using photographs she made independently the year before or earlier: "Pauline Peters on People: Dr. Glassbury's Widow" (January 7, 1968); "Pauline Peters on People: How to Train a Derby Winner" (March 21, 1968); and "Please Don't Feed Me," by Hunter Davies, about a camp for overweight girls (April 14, 1968).[324] The only new assignment she receives in this period is from *New York* magazine, recently inaugurated as an independent entity following the demise of its parent newspaper, *The World Journal Tribune*.[325] In March editor Clay Felker assigns her to photograph the underground movie actress Viva, star of several Andy Warhol films including *Blue Movie, aka Fuck*. Diane visits Viva on several occasions and describes the results to Crookston following publication of the April 29 issue: *The article* [by Barbara Goldsmith] *is harsh and humorless, but there are lots of fascinating pictures. It was something of a cause celebre, much mail and cancelled subscriptions and pro and con phone calls and whatnot, even a threatened lawsuit.*[326]

She continues to research and explore possible photographic projects for *Esquire, New York, Harper's Bazaar, The London Sunday Times*, and for herself. On the March 5 page of her appointment book, under the heading *Dandies*, are five names of possible subjects and some additional topics—*chic beauties* and *generation gap*—apparently as suggestions for *New York*. The May 17 page reiterates these ideas and adds others: *activist youth leaders abbie H.* [Abbie Hoffman], *richest and poorest, pot proliferation, and heroes of the underground: Marcuse, Taylor Mead, Abbie* [Hoffman, again]. She gives Crookston this summary of things:

My new apartment is cozier than I had imagined. Work goes along oddly and obsessively...Lots is happening here and I live two blocks away from St. Marks Pl which has become one of the great corners in the city where just standing still you feel in the heart of the maelstrom. The underground has a whole bunch of new heroes. There are some amazing flamboyant bewigged and empurpled whores who hang out on one particular place on Broadway...I am also trying to do something on criminals, and maybe on returned runaways.

—LETTER TO PETER CROOKSTON, MAY 18, 1968

The project on criminals leads her to the books of Dr. Frederick Wertham: *Dark Legend: A Study in Murder, Show of Violence*, and *A Sign for Cain: An Exploration of Human Violence*.[327] She also obtains Wertham's phone number,[328] although it is possible that the two never actually speak. She is anything but single-minded, however, about what she intends to pursue. Around the same time, in a message written sequentially on two separate postcards, she adds this:

One more thing, perhaps too exotic...I know a Jewish giant who lives in Washington Heights or the Bronx with his little parents. He is tragic with a curious bitter somewhat stupid wit. The parents are orthodox and repressive and classic and disapprove of his carnival career...Once many years ago I photographed them but I don't know where it is[329]...They are a truly metaphorical family...Also. I know an incredible set of triplets. And an association of twins in New Jersey some of whom are identical...

—POSTCARD TO PETER CROOKSTON, CIRCA MAY 1968

The same communication goes on to mention *the largest family* and *an association who pick the mother of the yr*, and concludes, *You can see I've got suddenly more energy than I can use. I need a dam...I hope I can really do something, not just feel elated.*[330] In response to a subsequent suggestion by Crookston that she come to London to work on an issue the magazine is planning to devote exclusively to the subject of the family, she responds:

AN UNPUBLISHED PHOTOGRAPH OF SOME OF DR. DONALD GATCH'S PATIENTS IN RURAL BEAUFORT COUNTY, SOUTH CAROLINA, INTENDED FOR THE ARTICLE "LET US NOW PRAISE DR. GATCH," BY BYNUM SHAW, THAT WAS PUBLISHED IN THE JUNE 1968 ISSUE OF *ESQUIRE*. THE ARTICLE INCLUDED THREE OTHER PHOTOGRAPHS OF DR. GATCH AND HIS PATIENTS.

CONTACT SHEET #5604 OF PHOTOGRAPHS MADE IN THE SPRING OF 1968. ABBIE HOFFMAN IS IN THE FRAME AT RIGHT, SECOND FROM THE TOP. IN A MAY 1968 LETTER TO *LONDON SUNDAY TIMES* EDITOR PETER CROOKSTON, DIANE WRITES: *I HAVEN'T BEEN TO THE COUNTRY NOT EVEN CONEY ISLAND BUT THE PARKS HAVE TURNED SO PRETTY. FOR WEEKS I WANDERED IN THEM JUST PHOTOGRAPHING BABIES LIKE I WAS EVERYBODY'S MOTHER.*

I have been wanting to do families. I stopped two elderly sisters the other day and three generations of jewish women from Bklyn whom I am to visit soon...the youngest is pregnant. And especially there is a woman I stopped in a Bookstore[331] who lives in Westchester which is Upper Suburbia. She is about 35 with terribly blonde hair and enormously eyelashed and booted and probably married to a dress manufacturer or restaurateur and I said I wanted to photograph her with husband and children so she suggested I wait till warm weather so I can do it around the pool!...They are a fascinating family. I think all families are creepy in a way.

—LETTER TO PETER CROOKSTON, CIRCA JUNE 1968[332]

In the same letter she notes, not altogether parenthetically: *(my mother [widowed since 1963] is getting married again this month!!!! I have only a photograph of her fiance. It is so odd. He looks like a dentist...[333])* She details the financial and logistical impracticality of her making a trip to London for this purpose, suggesting Crookston *think about American Families I might provide you with at this end,* and adding, *I don't think I can come unless I can make a little money to bring home. I am so behind in work. Reams to print.[334]* She is also reluctant to leave home because of her own pending photographic projects:

Someone is getting me permission they swear, from someone at the head of the New Jersey prisons and mental hospitals to photograph in them, just for me.[335] Meanwhile I still have the opportunity to ride in a radio car for crimes in the long hot summer nights...I havent done returned Runaways, only thought of it as part of my Families...Of all these possibilities two thirds will fall through. (there is also sex clubs still and country clubs and vigilante women but these are only notions.)

—LETTER TO PETER CROOKSTON, CIRCA JUNE 1968

In a marginal note scrawled in pen at the end of this two-page letter which she refers to as *all in haste, like a waterfall,* she returns once more to the word family:

The working title if you can call it that for my book which I keep postponing is Family Album. I mean I am not working on it except to photograph like I would anyway so all I have is a title and a publisher[336] and a sort of sweet lust for things I want in it like picking flowers or Noah's Ark. I can hardly bear to leave any animal out...

—LETTER TO PETER CROOKSTON, CIRCA JUNE 1968

Running parallel to the torrent of ideas that constitute the bulk of her correspondence with Crookston is an equally persistent series of pleas and complaints about payments from the magazine. On May 18, following publication of the three Diaper Derby photographs, she writes: *I've received an unaccountable check for $166.93 for the How to train a Derby winner photos. I haven't cashed it because it isn't at all the right amount...*She proceeds to defend her arithmetic for this story *(Even figured at the ASMP minimum daily rate which is $150 per day that comes to $750)* and for the other two stories she has worked on and delivered, all of which, as she points out, were her suggestions. *I think the fee...should come to $900. Let me know how to bill it and what to do with the check I received which doesn't seem to signify anything at all.[337]*

A SPREAD FROM A 1968 NOTEBOOK (NO. 35) LABELED "NOVEMBER 1968" LISTING A NUMBER OF ONGOING PROJECTS. AT THE BOTTOM OF THE RIGHT-HAND PAGE DIANE HAS WRITTEN: *THE PRINCIPLE OF PHOTOGRAPHY, WHAT AMAZES, SECRETS NO ONE KNOWS.*

THREE UNPUBLISHED PHOTOGRAPHS FROM CAMP LAKECREST, SPRING 1967: *(ABOVE LEFT)* CAMPERS IN LINE;* *(ABOVE RIGHT)* CAMPERS AS TREES;* AND *(BELOW)* GIRL IN THE GRASS. *THE LONDON SUNDAY TIMES* PUBLISHED "PLEASE DON'T FEED ME" ON APRIL 14, 1968, WITH TWO DIANE ARBUS PHOTOS, UNCREDITED AS SHE REQUESTED.

IN 1968 LISETTE MODEL GAVE DIANE A PRINT OF HER PHOTOGRAPH CONEY ISLAND BATHER, 1941, IN RESPONSE TO WHICH DIANE SENT HER THE FOLLOWING NOTE: *DEAR LISETTE, I HAVE BEEN STARING AND STARING AT IT. MAKES ME FEEL GOOD. I WANT TO GIVE YOU ONE TOO.*

This letter is followed soon after by one that begins *I don't mean to quibble but I will*, in which—responding to a cable from Crookston—she rehashes earlier discussions about the $150 page rate she agreed upon with the magazine. *We all seemed satisfied with this arrangement for the fat girls*, she notes in the margin, *and I assumed it was the precedent for all future assignments with the possible exception of a future alteration upwards rather than down...I don't see why it has to suddenly dip down to $120 like it says in your cable. or the mysterious dribbly payments on the diaper derby.* Then, somewhat apologetically, she adds near the end: *Thirty dollars is unimportant but multiplied by the real and happy possibilities of our working together as much as we might it shld be considered...I like to work for you because you are daring dashing fair decisive formidable and even rather wise but those are the Financial Expectations Michael [Rand] himself had led me to. are they too Great? (my enthusiasm alone should be worth it.)*[338] A subsequent letter from her offers this explanation:

If I sounded sharp or irate it was only trying to get into a sort of efficiency about my financial state which is confusingly and delightfully wed to my husbands and he seems to be perhaps planning to marry a very nice girl [actress Mariclare Costello] although I may be over anticipating. Anyway I just wanted to gather everything together because part of my snobbery is to act excessively casual about money as if I didn't care if I ever got any and if I am to be supporting my small self soon I should know something about how much I make.

—LETTER TO PETER CROOKSTON, CIRCA JUNE 1968[339]

The matter remains unresolved and in a letter dated July 4 she writes: *please lets settle this because I do not want to feel that I am impractical and imprudent to the point of idiocy and since I have only so far recd 300 actual dollars for working for you, I might easily feel that.* The letter also contains, buried amid a slew of proposed ideas, the following casually prophetic sentence: *I seem to be undergoing some subterranean revolution in which the surface hardly stirs but I sleep and dream a lot and once in a while signs erupt that seem portentous to me at least.*[340]

A week or so later she writes to Amy at camp, apologizing for her failure to be as prolific a correspondent as she'd intended to be and explaining what happened: *I told you I had been feeling lousy and I went to a doctor and he said there wasnt anything wrong but altho that was nice I still felt rotten and he just looked at me like I was imagining things...*[341] She later gives Carlotta Marshall the following, somewhat more detailed, account:

For months...doctors kept reassuring me I didn't have hepatitis all over again like I kept thinking and that it was purely psychosomatic or menopausal or just old age itself which scared the shit out of me and theyd prescribe some little bunch of pills and I would 'plunge myself into my work' feeling lousier and lousier till it got so that I couldn't walk up the stairs to my own apartment without resting halfway up and collapsing onto my bed for 15 minutes at the top. Finally these symptoms erupted into whatever sort of reality...is the opposite of psychosomatic and I crawled into the hospital.

—LETTER TO CARLOTTA MARSHALL, AUGUST 4 OR 5, 1968

The Thursday July 18 page of her appointment book records in Allan's handwriting: *into hospital period began.* Other than childbirth, this is her first experience as a hospitalized patient.

I am having a terrific time in the hospital where I have gone to get all sorts of tests made on my liver and all the rest of my inner workings. It is really fun. They give me enemas and take my temperature and blood pressure and give me marvelous baths in bed. I have a marvelous room with an air conditioner and a TV which I work with a pushbutton from my bed and every time I pee or shit they ask me to save a sample of it. I am starting to feel much better...

—LETTER TO AMY ARBUS, CIRCA JULY 1968[342]

In a typewritten letter on Doctors Hospital stationery, Diane responds to Carlotta—who at this point is unaware of their parallel circumstances—and to Carlotta's news that she has been hospitalized in Holland with some mysterious and as yet undiagnosed disease of her own: *I was so touched and saddened by your letter. The only good thing is that I have been undergoing some of that myself and have come through the other side and the difference between sickness and health is so extraordinary and absorbing I must just see if I can shed any light at all for you.*[343] She recounts a few of her recent comically nightmarish adventures in the land of medical care:

One day the Dr would come in and say I was progressing just fine and the next day he would explain squeamishly that...they might have to remove my gall bladder or see if I had TB and it wasn't that they suspected cancer...etc etc. and I would start to cry partly out of the snobbish feeling that I shouldn't be a sick person...So they took out a piece of my liver...It was a strange Dr. and to show him I wasn't scared I said brightly what is the liver for? well, he answered let's put it this way: you couldn't liver without it...Then I couldn't move for a day and had to be fed by an aide who stuffed such big pieces sideways into my mouth that the gravy or remains would dribble down my chin. I was a 45 yr old infant and angry to boot.

—LETTER TO CARLOTTA MARSHALL, AUGUST 4 OR 5, 1968

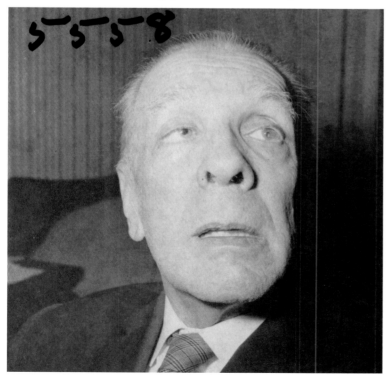

DOCTORS HOSPITAL
EAST END AVENUE AT 87TH STREET
NEW YORK 28, N. Y.

Aug 4 or 5

Dear dear Carlotta I was so touched and saddened
by your letter.The only good thing is that I have
been undergoing some of that myself and I have come
through the other side and the difference between
sickness and health is so extraordinary and absorb
ing I must just see if I can shed any light at all
for you.(Of course our experiences are not identic
al but I figured out quite a lot of things in the
three weeks I have been here and gone through so many
changes and there are Some advantages to being 45
because I have learned to see that no state of being
is intrinsic or autormous.Oneself is dispensable
and so are a whole bunch of ones most precious att
ributes... but they come back when you can afford
the luxury of them again.When I was most sick and scai
red I was no longer a photographer (I still am not
and something about realizing that I dont Have
to Photograph was terribly good for me) or a
mother and I lost my curiosity,and most of what
humor I've got, but I learned that is OK. An enor
mous gulf separates you from the well people.They
just used to look scared when they looked at me
and it got so that I didnt want to be visited even
by the people I love best. And I learned to say
so.In fact in lots of ways I came to trust my own in
stincts for survival more than I ever had before.
To explain: for months I had been suffering
gnawing distressing symptoms like incredible fatigue
and mild nausea and recurrent stomach aches but
doctors kept reassurring me I didnt have hepatitis
all over again like I kept thinking and that it
was purely psychosomatic or menopausal or just oldage
it self which scared the shit out of me and theyd
prescribe some little bunch of pills and I would'plung
e myself into my work' feeling lousier and lousier
till it got so that I couldnt walk up the stairs
to my own apartment without resting halfway up
and collapsing onto my bed for 15 minutes at the top
Fine!

(ABOVE) First page of a four-page letter to Carlotta Marshall on which Carlotta spilled something she was drinking while reading it. *(BELOW)* Picture from a contact sheet of Argentine writer Jorge Luis Borges,* whom Diane photographed for the March 1969 issue of *Harper's Bazaar*.

5-5-5-8

But she is primarily intent on describing to Carlotta some of what she believes she has figured out during her three-week hospital stay, while going through so many changes:

...I have learned to see that no state of being is intrinsic or autonomous. Oneself is dispensable and so are a whole bunch of one's most precious attributes...but they come back when you can afford the luxury of them again. When I was most sick and scared I was no longer a photographer (I still am not and something about realizing that I don't Have to Photograph was terribly good for me) or a mother and I lost my curiosity and most of what humor I've got, but I learned that is OK....Life continually gets better and worse and better. Demand your share.

—Letter to Carlotta Marshall, August 4 or 5, 1968

She says she is *scheduled to go home the following day and then to the country to recuperate and I am not allowed to do too much or to have any responsibilities which is just dandy as far as I'm concerned.*[344] From her friend Tina Fredericks's home in East Hampton, a frequent place of refuge, she writes to Amy, attempting to provide some reassurance about things: *I have to eat a pound of red meat a day and take endless vitamins...but I am quite OK and apparently if I...do just as I am told I will be better than new in a few months.*[345] At the same time, however, she is obliged to break the news of the recent death of their seven-year-old cat, Ishmael, whom Allan had discovered to be seriously ill on the day before Diane's release from the hospital.[346] *Pa felt you should know now so you wouldn't come home and suddenly find out and feel we had been lying to you,*[347] she writes. This is how she describes her recuperation to Carlotta:

It is so pretty and calm here. Rabbits and pheasants and chipmunks alternately appear and disappear on the lawn in front of me and I am learning such serenity ...Once in a while I feel a vague anxiety about what is happening around where I am supposed to be but then I remember that I am 'not supposed to have any responsibilities.' So I look once more out upon the lawn and see who is chasing whom and hope for the best.

—Letter to Carlotta Marshall, circa mid-August 1968

Shortly before her return to New York, she learns from her hostess, Tina Fredericks—and relays to Marvin Israel—that Rene d'Harnoncourt, former director of The Museum of Modern Art, *died OUT HERE last week, run over while crossing the street, reading the morning paper.*[348] That night she has a dream which she recounts to Israel the following day in a detailed four-page handwritten letter:

I dreamed that Rene d'Harnoncourt was my doctor...looking for all the world like Bela Lugosi...He was 9 ft tall. I could never reach him. I summoned the courage to face him, saying unequivocally in a ringing voice... "Please Doctor tell me what is wrong with me and how you propose to cure it," but he affected not to hear me and strode off...looking elated like a mad scientist who has discovered a cure that kills people... I pursued him to Times Square...even though he kept outdistancing me because I was sick and not supposed to EXERCISE...He was starting to change (metamorphose) to elude me...growing absolutely flat (2 dimensional) and utterly black like a silhouette and then at 45th St...as he was

stepping off the curb…he suddenly split into lots of silhouetted little men scurrying off in different directions so there was no way of knowing whom to pursue and I realized you are dead when you ask the doctor why you are sick and he doesn't hear you…This morning I am quiet and nice again like Mr. Hyde but tired because I have been exorcised all night and the doctor said not to, (Dr. Jekyll I presume.) Smile when you meet me at Max's [referring to Max's Kansas City, one of their regular Manhattan hangouts]. Love, D.

—LETTER TO MARVIN ISRAEL, CIRCA MID-AUGUST 1968

On August 25, about a week after her return to New York, she attends a screening of the Stewart Stern, Paul Newman, Joanne Woodward movie *Rachel, Rachel* but doesn't stay for the event that follows. In a letter to Stern she explains: *I wouldn't have left so fast except it was hepatitis that I had, a sort of relapse and it was my first public event since. I lost energy quite suddenly which left me feeling very shy. But illness is terrific for taking you back to the beginning like bankruptcy. I think its better to start from scratch than anywhere.* About the movie she adds: *I'm glad about Rachel. I'd know you in it anywhere…You left none of your old stones unturned.*[349]

In response to Carlotta's latest news of her progress, medical and otherwise—which includes an operation on her brain that has left her bald with two holes in her head and temporarily seeing double—Diane writes: *Dear Carlotta, Wow, you really do things gloriously. My illness looks positively anemic beside yours…and my romance with death ludicruously onesided.*[350] Of her own recovery she has this to say:

Convalescence is rather extraordinary…I think it seemed to me for a while as if I had the option of being any of a number of things and I couldn't bear to be merely me but now I am glad to have somewhere to begin…some history, some attitudes because I am back in the city and

here it's hard being as faceless as I felt. I dread work a little and sometimes pretend I am an imposter but last week I put the camera around my neck although I didn't use it and I was grateful just to wear it.

—LETTER TO CARLOTTA MARSHALL, CIRCA LATE AUGUST 1968

A week or so later she writes to Crookston:

I have started to work. In a way I miss being sick but during convalescence a strange rage developed in me. It especially appears every night around 4AM like a werewolf. I don't know if it can be made to make something but it feels like raw wild power. I don't yet know how to make it energy.

—LETTER TO PETER CROOKSTON, CIRCA SEPTEMBER 1968

Somewhat reluctantly she begins to teach again at Cooper Union.[351] *They called me one day before the Semester and we are too poor for me to have refused,* she tells Carlotta.[352] Around the same time she receives a tantalizing offer that will require her to spend several months away from home, in California, Mexico, and Rome. She later describes it to her brother this way:

…I have been asked, via Mike Nichols who will direct it, to photograph stills on the set of Catch 22 which films for 5 mos, mostly in Mexico and a little in Rome. It all started out terribly grandiose with long distance calls from Hllywd and considerable insertions of flattering words like genius and I could bring my child along and come and go as I pleased. Meanwhile on the best advice (Avedon) I asked for 3000 dollars a wk, which they found rather high and so did I but I wd easily dwindle. They just havent given me a chance. I alternately think whatthehelldoiwant-todo thatfor and then realize we are so flat broke that there is simply no question but that I must and then think it would be fun and amazing to

(LEFT) CONTACT SHEET #5639 FRAME #12 (MAN SEATED ON HIS BED) AND *(RIGHT)* CONTACT SHEET #5643 FRAME #2 (THE SAME MAN ON A PARK BENCH). THE IMAGE DIANE PRINTED FROM THIS SERIES, A NAKED MAN BEING A WOMAN, N.Y.C. 1968 (P. 98), APPEARS ON CONTACT SHEET #5639 (THE SAME ROLL AS THE TWO CENTER IMAGES).

see a million Hollywood people at work and play and at least in the original offer there were to be no restrictions or demands on What I shd photograph...just anything I want. Occasionally I feel enormous zest for it and also know it is a much more intelligent way to make money that will let me do what I want for a yr or so than my current way of dashing off everywhere for $100 at a time which leaves me a little frazzled altho the variety is nice.[353]

—LETTER TO HOWARD NEMEROV, NOVEMBER 10, 1968

The London Sunday Times Magazine's upcoming issue on the family is still on her mind. She has already sent Crookston her 1966 photograph of A young Brooklyn family (p. 8) and provided what information she could about them based on her notes at the time. *(They live in the Bronx. I think he was a garage mechanic. Their first child was born when she was sixteen...[354])* She follows up with another newly discovered possibility.

If your material on The Family is not utterly signed and sealed, I have one of the upper middle class suburban family on their lawn [p. 329], just two parents and a child [adds in the margin, the ones I told you I would do and was going back] which I did before I was sick[355] and just printed and its so odd, nearly like Pinter but not quite, it might just serve to introduce the whole thing along with that quotation you sent me of...("the family with its narrow somethingorother and its etc etc might be the source of all our woes"...I've forgotten it, but in the picture the parents seem to be dreaming the child and the child seems to be inventing them, Maybe its more like Charles Addams.) Anyway I have a print so if you could use it you could get it fast.

—LETTER TO PETER CROOKSTON, CIRCA SEPTEMBER 1968

She has a couple of assignments from *Harper's Bazaar* in this period, including a trip to Atlanta to photograph the widow of Dr.

Martin Luther King, Jr. *(awful photos, but glorious fun hanging around and peering at everything. I have decided photography is a sort of private sin of mine. As a virtue I find it really hard to sustain.[356])* *Esquire* sends her to do a portrait of Democratic presidential nominee Eugene McCarthy on election eve,[357] an adventure she later recounts to her brother, who turns out to have been unwittingly instrumental in the success of it.

The night before Sudie [Trazoff, nee Victor] told me that he read poetry and wrote some etc. and that he would know and care about you. Well the minute I was ushered into the office and introduced in a mumble by the press secretary...McCarthy looked as pained as if I was a dentist and began that curious gesture of looking like he was about to give me his face to photograph managing all the while to avoid inhabiting it. Well right then and there I knew I would have to stoop to it and I did... said my schoolgirl piece about my brother the Howard Nemerov and the whole climate changed...Finally by the end of the day when he came to sit in the chair in front of me he was terribly open and curiously willing, although in the photograph he looks haunted. Anyway I'd never have been able to do it without you. I needed that kind of attention from him and he gave it on the assumption that any sister of yours must be an artist instead of a reporter.

—LETTER TO HOWARD NEMEROV, NOVEMBER 10, 1968[358]

She is also assigned by *Esquire* to photograph Tokyo Rose in Chicago,[359] and by *The London Sunday Times Magazine* to photograph a Weight Watcher's success story, Alice Madeiros, the heroine of an article written by Doon which Crookston plans to republish.[360] These jobs, however, appear to provide her little reassurance about either money or work. She makes the following observation about her situation:

...Editors appear to be putting me off...It is partly that my reputation has gotten enormous and...somehow people decide either that I am too big for my britches or temperamental or simply that I need taking down a peg. It is a terribly familiar syndrome...I am not as good a photographer as people think except sometimes and in my head. And somehow they don't like it that I am no good or too good. I will never be just right.

—LETTER TO CARLOTTA MARSHALL, CIRCA NOVEMBER 1968

A few weeks after the opening of a Brassaï exhibition at The Museum of Modern Art, she attends an event that takes place there in honor of the photographer. (About his work and its impact on her she later says: *He taught me something terrific about obscurity, that obscurity could be as thrilling as clarity, which for a long time I didn't realize because I had been moving more and more towards clarity for years.*)[361] The event itself however turns out to be something of a disappointment.

I've been meaning to say I'm sorry I (or we for as much as I can speak for the others) flubbed the Brassai occasion. My essential question seemed to me by turns banal, vulgar, vague or simply unanswerable, like how do you do it Monsieur? And some of the people who took the bull by the horns made it seem more than ever that we were in a china shop. But it would be really nice to have a robust dialogue, a bit less frantically polite or sycophantish.

—LETTER TO JOHN SZARKOWSKI, CIRCA MID-NOVEMBER 1968

On November 10 *The London Sunday Times Magazine* publishes its special issue on the family which includes, under the title "Two American Families," the Diane Arbus photographs Family on their lawn one Sunday in Westchester, N.Y. 1968 (p. 329) and A young Brooklyn family going for a Sunday outing, N.Y.C. 1966 (p. 8). The pictures are

accompanied by extended captions credited to Diane but actually fashioned by the editors from the contents of her letters about them. The publication prompts this reply from her to Crookston: *The family on the lawn looked good I think but let me next time write it so it makes more sense. Wish I had photographed more. Would love to have done a family tree.*[362]

She is still pursuing her attempts to obtain permission to photograph at institutions and has received considerable help from Carlotta's friend Adrian Condon and Condon's cousin by marriage, Mary Stevens Baird, who is a member of the New Jersey State Board of Control of Institutions and Agencies. She writes Crookston:

I would like to photograph mentally retarded people, idiots, imbeciles and morons (morons are the smartest of the three). especially the cheerful ones. And I am looking for elderly twins. I have heard of a source. And there is an old retired actors home in NJ I want to visit if I can get permission. And I wonder about plastic surgery and Beauty Queens.

—LETTER TO PETER CROOKSTON, CIRCA DECEMBER 1968

She is also preoccupied with the idea of another project she has so far been wary of pursuing: *I begin to think about a book or rather about a book I might do with someone before I get to doing The Book which I know Im not ready for although some people refuse to believe that,* she says in a letter to Carlotta.[363] And to Crookston: *I think I am going to do a book, not The Book but a book of all new things, a book About something.*[364] A few weeks before Christmas—when she leaves with Amy for two weeks in St. Croix to work on her second job for *The New York Times Magazine Children's Fashions* supplement with Patricia Peterson[365]—she sends Paul Salstrom a letter in response to his request that she do the illustrations for his new book of poetry.

...I must begin at whatever pace is possible, to work on the book of my own that i vaguely keep assuming lies at the end of the rainbow. It is after all my rainbow and if I don't do it no one else will. So I musn't photograph with/for your poems or with or for anyone else except when it is absolutely necessary to make a living at...Survival is the secret so you really can't afford to doubt yourself for long because you are all you've got. The only thing to do is to go the limit with it. Exceed. thats whats nice. We go in different directions...godspeed...Diane

—LETTER TO PAUL SALSTROM, DECEMBER 5, 1968[366]

1969

She returns from St. Croix with Amy around January 10. Museums are beginning to evidence a growing interest in acquiring and exhibiting her photographs which—encouraging as it may be—requires her spending more time than usual in the darkroom. (*I have taken to printing 16x20 which somehow takes lots more time than doing smaller prints*, she notes in response to the request of one curator.[367]) Meanwhile, many of the projects she is most eager to pursue for herself entail a lot of red tape, both official and personal. The result is that she keeps encountering obstacles that stand between her and the work she wants to be doing.

In February Peter Crookston is appointed editor of the British magazine *Nova*, and in his new capacity suggests she come to London for a few weeks to work on some assignments for the magazine, including the Wives of Famous Men and a portrait of the rock group The Who.[368] *Of course I'll come over*, she replies in a letter congratulating him on the new job and proposing a few other possible notions:

In August there are two National Baton Twirling competitions in the south which sound marvelous. I am checking on it. Enclosed is a Terry Southern story about one of the schools. It is an enormous Passion and they absolutely Have to retire at the age of 21.

—LETTER TO PETER CROOKSTON, CIRCA FEBRUARY 1969

And in a follow-up letter that includes a number of additional ideas[369] as well as a drawing of a *Nova* press pass she hopes he can provide her with, she adds:

...Ive been reading R. D. Laing (The divided Self [London: Tavistock, 1961] and I forget the name of the other more recent more popular one [*Sanity, Madness and the Family* (London: Tavistock, 1964)] I read a while ago). He seems so extraordinary in his empathy for madness that it suddenly seemed he would be the most terrific guide.

—LETTER TO PETER CROOKSTON, CIRCA LATE FEBRUARY 1969

There is something to be done about Singles (here) but I don't yet see how to do it. In the Catskills there are entire weekends devoted to the procurement of people for people...For later [in the year]...there are extraordinary motels in the midwest, veritable oases like miamibeach in a desert or snowstorm.

—LETTER TO PETER CROOKSTON, CIRCA LATE FEBRUARY 1969

There is another thing which I dont remember whether I mentioned. Drs. Phyllis and Eberhard Kronhausen are sexologists and they edit collections of erotic art and promote sex causes and make movies and money and meanwhile have private patients whom they analyze by a technique of living in their homes and spending 24 hours at a time with them. They were very eager to be photographed by me...and to talk about everything and although they may well be self appointed apostles of sex they certainly have a lot of authentic information and an eagerness to divulge it. They love publicity but are also...quite straight.[370]

—LETTER TO PETER CROOKSTON, CIRCA LATE FEBRUARY 1969

Near the end of the letter she reneges on this last suggestion: *...I don't think I am really eager to do the Kronhausens after all. Its too verbal and it gives me a funny eerie sense of mutual exploitation which I don't like.*[371] She expresses her impatience and uneasiness about journalism (*the prospect that...[it] might expose its own privacy*) and reiterates a little wistfully: *I want to do something unfathomable like the family.*[372]

In a later report on the progress of an assignment for *Nova* to photograph defense attorney F. Lee Bailey (a portrait the magazine doesn't publish in the end)[373] and on the plans for her approaching trip to London, she updates Crookston on other news:

The main thing that has happened to me is that Allan is going to close the studio and move to California to become an actor in earnest. It is terrific for him and wildly adventurous. At moments though I feel like Little Orphan Annie. I must find a darkroom of my own and learn a thousand things I don't know. But I am not really abandoned and he will set me up and his ex assistant [Howard Harrison] will probably share the dkrm with me etc.

—LETTER TO PETER CROOKSTON, CIRCA LATE MARCH 1969

I have a bit of nasty advertising to do. but the money is too much to say no to. It is supposed to be a photograph of a camera by 'one of the greatest photographers in the world...' the others are avedon, penn, Bruce [Davidson] and I dunno who. it really gives me nightmares. Dick

DIANE WITH A CIGARETTE SEATED IN HER BEDROOM AT 120 EAST 10TH STREET IN 1968. THE COLLAGE WALL TO HER RIGHT, WHICH IS DIRECTLY OPPOSITE HER BED, INCLUDES ROUGH PRINTS OF TWO OF HER PHOTOGRAPHS, SUPERSTAR AT HOME (P. 286) AND LOSER AT A DIAPER DERBY (P. 117).

TRANSVESTITE AND HER BIRTHDAY CAKE, N.Y.C. 1969. THIS PICTURE OF DIANE'S FRIEND VICKI, WHOM SHE FIRST MET IN 1966 AND PHOTOGRAPHED ON MANY OCCASIONS (P. 250 AND P. 291), WAS TAKEN ON MARCH 29, WHICH TURNED OUT TO BE THE LAST TIME THEY SAW EACH OTHER. AS DIANE LATER DESCRIBED THE EVENT TO HER STUDENTS: *SHE CALLED ME UP AND SAID IT WAS HER BIRTHDAY AND WOULD I COME AND I SAID, "HOW TERRIFIC." ...THE BIRTHDAY PARTY WAS ME AND HER, A WHORE FRIEND OF HERS AND HER PIMP, AND THE CAKE.*

[Avedon] got me into it which was good of him but I keep wishing it was all a bad dream. The Agency man gave me carte blanche…you can even, he said brightly, photograph it (the camera) on the point of a knife to show how sharp it is…we want your interpretation, something creative and totally honest.[374]

— LETTER TO PETER CROOKSTON, CIRCA LATE MARCH 1969

Her reaction to jobs of this sort—and in fact to any assignment she doesn't actually originate—strikes her on occasion as a bit perverse. *I have never understood whether it is a certain intransigence in my nature that makes me inwardly partly sabotage anything anyone else wants me to do*, she muses in a letter to her goddaughter May Eliot. *It must be more complicated than that. But because I am so little rebellious I think it manifests unwittingly.*[375]

On April 2 she sends Crookston the following account of her itinerary in the weeks prior to her departure for London: *Going to Texas tomorrow to photograph a terrible Texan who owns the Astrodome.*[376] *Then to New Jersey [to the April 7 Easter parade at one of the state's residential institutions for the mentally retarded[377]] and then to you.*[378]

She arrives in London as scheduled on April 17 and begins work on a story she had proposed, "People Who Think They Look Like Other People."[379] *Nova* places the following ad in *The Times* and *The Evening Standard* which generates a tremendous response from prospective candidates:[380] *Have you ever been told you look the double of someone famous? Like Elizabeth Taylor…Twiggy, The Queen, Mick Jagger, Sir Winston*

Churchill? If you think you are the double of someone famous you could be famous too.[381]

In connection with what might be considered a related theme—people or things that appear to be what they are not (a theme she has been exploring for years in all sorts of manifestations, from twins to transvestites)—she gains access to Madame Tussaud's Wax Museum on behalf of the magazine. *I got permission to go there at night when it was empty. I touched some of them,* she confesses in a letter to Amy.[382] But the *Nova* assignment that appears to provide her the greatest satisfaction is photographing the Rockers, a teenage motorcycle gang in Brighton. A month or so later when she sends Crookston the pictures she writes, *I thought of the rockers as a sort of family album,*[383] and comments after seeing the story in the magazine, *I liked the way the rockers looked. Really more than any published thing in a long time.*[384]

On the other hand, the city of London itself (which she had once written Crookston she imagined as having *the dirtiest secrets in the world*[385]) she finds eerily antiseptic. In a postcard to Ruth Ansel, she observes: *Nobody seems miserable, drunk, crippled, mad, or desperate. I finally found a few vulgar things in the suburbs, but nothing sordid yet. Where have they hidden it?*[386] And in a postcard to Richard Avedon: *Its nice here but I think I'd have been a Pilgrim.*[387]

About a week after her return to New York on May 5 and a few days before Allan's scheduled departure *to someplace just across the mexican border to get our divorce which is so amicable that we cannot even divide the monies so we arent going to,*[388] she writes:

Things are in a state of flux, more subterranean than overt, well both I guess. Allan moved the darkroom and has taken over the hideous task of getting carpenter plumber etc to do what must be done…but he has designed it beautifully…all the film from England is undeveloped which makes me feel constipated and anxious as if there might be nothing there (did I leave the lens cap on or forget to adjust the whatchamacallit?) But Allan has gotten someone to do all 175 rolls in the specially mixed formula so I will know soon.

— LETTER TO MAY ELIOT, CIRCA MID-MAY 1969

TWO OF THE EIGHT PORTRAITS OF "PEOPLE WHO THINK THEY LOOK LIKE OTHER PEOPLE," PUBLISHED IN THE OCTOBER 1969 ISSUE OF *NOVA* WITH TEXT BY PAULINE PETERS AND MARGARET PRINGLE. THE PORTRAIT OF QUEEN ELIZABETH'S DOUBLE *(LEFT)* WAS HAND TINTED BY MAXINE KRAVITZ, A FRIEND OF MARVIN ISRAEL'S, AT DIANE'S REQUEST. *(RIGHT)* SIR WINSTON CHURCHILL'S DOUBLE. THERE WERE MANY ELIZABETH TAYLORS AND SOPHIA LORENS.

She reports to Crookston around the same time: *I am marvelously exhausted by the trip...the splendid and the sleazy of it. My darkroom is heavenly...through an alley with its own anonymous door, like a secret house. It will be in working order soon I hope.*[389] Her next job is for the Social Security Administration's Office of Public Affairs. The Agency has hired several photographers, including Duane Michaels and William Gedney, to take pictures of selected beneficiaries. Diane's assignment entails a trip to St. Petersburg, Florida, to photograph retirees and nursing home residents.[390] Among her subjects are Andrew Ratoucheff, the Russian midget she first photographed for *Esquire* in 1960, and his friend Al Krauze. A 1969 notebook—which dutifully records each of her Florida encounters in anticipation of the need to write them for the Agency—contains the following account of her visit with Ratoucheff and Krauze in their Tampa home:

Andrew Ratoucheff and Al Krauze were at home in their little house at 6319 Little River Dr. They have a new Evinrude outboard motor for their rowboat on the brackish creek out back and rifles for shooting rats. Andy says he is an inch and a half shorter than Al but Al says he is only an inch taller. They own the house together and have been friends since 1939...After that we went to the El Sol Retirement Motel to meet Mr. Maloney who is the oldest living softball player in the world...

—1969 NOTEBOOK (NO. 37)[391]

In retrospect the whole experience—as she describes it to former *Glamour* editor Marguerite Lamkin (now married to Mark Littman and living in London)—strikes her as *a little grim because everyone seemed to be the same age and they were so pink, so powdery so well behaved except a little petulant...I did the oldest living softball player in the World and the oldest Dance instructors in America and a lot of firsts or rather lasts like that.*[392] She adds this summary of her personal situation:

Allan has gone to California and we are divorced although I don't have any papers to prove it. Arent you supposed to have divorce papers. I've always heard of them and they sounded like the best part of it. Doon and I saw a psychiatrist on television saying that divorce is terribly good for everybody especially the children but that amicable divorce is no good...there should be total severance he said, using some image which had to do with surgery.

—LETTER TO MARGUERITE LAMKIN LITTMAN, CIRCA EARLY JUNE 1969

During the same trip she also goes to Palm Beach to photograph the bodybuilder Charles Atlas for *The London Sunday Times* (p. 64)[393] and to Gainesville to give a speech.[394] *My speech in Gainesville was lousy*, she says in a letter to Allan in early June, *but they gave me the 400 bucks anyway and I ran feeling I had done something fraudulent. Feels so good to be back. My next speech is to nuns.*[395] She is not looking forward to her immediate prospects with much enthusiasm:

My mother is taking measures to Save Her Marriage [measures which soon prove unsuccessful]. The London Times wants me to go to LA to do a middleaged super fag Joan Crawford fan which would only be a day

MOURNERS GATHERED OUTSIDE FRANK E. CAMPBELL FUNERAL HOME ON JUNE 27 FOR THE FUNERAL OF JUDY GARLAND. IN A LETTER TO AMY, DIANE WRITES: *I HAD A DUMB TRIP TO THE CEMETERY WHERE JUDY GARLAND IS BURIED. THE MOST AMAZING THING HAD NOTHING TO DO WITH HER. THEY WERE LITTLE ROOMS WHERE PEOPLE WERE BURIED WITH A FRAMED PHOTOGRAPH OF THE PERSON AND A VASE OF FLOWERS LIKE A HOTEL ROOM FOR THE DEAD. THE REST WAS LIKE A BANK VAULT OF BODIES.*

PHOTOGRAPHS MADE ON ASSIGNMENT FOR THE SOCIAL SECURITY ADMINISTRATION. *(ABOVE)* ANDREW RATOUCHEFF *(LEFT)* AND HIS FRIEND AL KRAUZE *(RIGHT)*. *(BELOW)* THE OLDEST LIVING DANCE INSTRUCTORS IN AMERICA.*

or two.[396] I put it off because I am really tired of travelling, but if I do it I will see you next month I guess. Meanwhile I have four pages to do for them on the Women's Liberation Movement which I have begun.[397] These vary from Revolutionaries to real nuts who think men are totally dispensable even for sex and reproduction. I do not feel in the mood for them but I guess a little sleep will change all that.

—TYPEWRITTEN LETTER TO ALLAN ARBUS, CIRCA EARLY JUNE 1969

I miss you. and this isnt exactly total divorce, she writes on one occasion. *I'll be OK. So will you.*[398] A subsequent letter the same month offers the following amendment: *If you want more total divorce lemme know.*[399] Their correspondence in this period consists largely of professional issues, both technical and strategic, punctuated by news about Doon and Amy, and about Mariclare Costello—who frequently joins them for Sunday breakfast, as she and Allan used to do when he was living in New York— and by domestic anecdotes: *The laundry has been losing all our clothes and giving us back other peoples clothes marked ARBUS and staunchly maintaining it is a sinister plot on our part to pretend they arent ours or that there is another arbus sneaking in his shirts. I don't get mad till I leave.*[400]

There is also, on both sides, a good deal of anxiety about money.[401] *I guess most of this panic is transitional,* she volunteers. *The rest is traditional.*[402] When he responds to her anxiety by sending her a check at one point, she answers: *Thanks for your response to my hysteria but I didn't mean it that way. You know me by now. I've torn up your check.*[403] A month or so later she tells him, *I have nearly 4000 if you need any.*[404] These acts of generosity on both sides continue with some regularity but it is not clear whether they result in any cash from their joint bank account actually changing hands.[405]

In the meantime, although the prospects of exhibitions and museum acquisitions persist, they hold out little hope of providing any financial solace. In January, prompted by Henry Geldzahler, curator of contemporary art, and by John McKendry, curator of prints and photography, The Metropolitan Museum of Art purchases three of her photographs.[406] In late June, however, having failed to pay for them as yet, the museum revisits the subject, asking *if it could buy Two Prints instead of the three they had bought because they were short of the money ($75!). So I guess being broke is no disgrace,* she remarks to Allan.[407] The Smithsonian Institution's Division of Graphic Arts and Photography selects five prints for purchase at a total of $125.[408] Her work appears in a show called *Thirteeen Photographers* at the Pratt Institute [409] and in *Human Concern/Personal Torment: The Grotesque in American Art,* organized by Robert Doty for the Whitney Museum.[410] Ten of her photographs are included in The Museum of Modern Art's traveling exhibition *New Photography U.S.A.*[411] She is approached by Irving Blum, director of an eponymous Los Angeles gallery, about purchasing twenty prints on behalf of an anonymous collector who intends to donate them to the Pasadena Museum of Art. (*He* [Blum] *just called and wanted to do a show. I said no, not for a year or so, but when he came I said I needed money to work and somehow we arrived at this.*[412]) In spite of all this activity—or more precisely, because of it—she writes in a moment of exasperation:

I feel paranoid and besieged…Partly it is the goddam honors and people wanting to see me and show me pictures just like mine and museums wanting prints for no money. (I had a letter from the Bibliotheque Nationale de France asking for 20 prints.[413]) It all means I cant photograph. And most of what Ive been doing is such junk…I hate the world

(LEFT) A PHOTOGRAPH MADE IN 1968 DURING THE FILMING OF A PORNOGRAPHIC MOVIE.* IN A LETTER TO CROOKSTON IN OCTOBER 1969, DIANE WRITES: *I AM TRYING TO GET PERMISSION TO PHOTOGRAPH THE FILMING OF A DIRTY MOVIE. OR RATHER I HAD PERMISSION BUT THEY REVOKED IT. THEY SHOOT 3 AT ONCE. THE SET ALONE IS REMARKABLE. SO SEEDY. AND THE MEN WHO MAKE IT ARE ALWAYS LOOKING OVER THEIR SHOULDER, FURTIVE AND TURTLENECKED AND WHEN THEY TALK TO ME AND I TRY TO ASSURE THEM OF MY UNIMPEACHABLE REPUTATION AND THAT I WILL NOT SIC THE COPS ON EM THEIR EYES WANDER IDLY, UNCONTROLLABLY UP AND DOWN MY ANATOMY LIKE BERSERK BALLS ON A PINBALL MACHINE. (RIGHT)* JACQUELINE SUSANN AND HER HUSBAND IRVING MANSFIELD, LOS ANGELES, CAL. 1969. THE PHOTOGRAPH WAS ORIGINALLY MADE FOR *HARPER'S* MAGAZINE OCTOBER 1969 ISSUE AND RESOLD SEVERAL TIMES.

of photography and photographers. Everyone is turning to Rolleis and Portriga [the photographic paper she uses] and printing with borders.

—LETTER TO ALLAN ARBUS, CIRCA MID-JUNE 1969

In reflecting on what he describes as her *great sense of privacy… and…pride of ownership about her work,* and on the changes that begin to take place in her photographs over the next couple of years, John Szarkowski later observes: *I'm sure in a lot of this last work she was intentionally reformulating so she could get out from under all those people she felt she was carrying on her back.*[414] She alludes to her restlessness and her desire to give up the 2¼ twin lens reflex and find herself a different camera in the following remark to Allan: *I think I am about to abandon the square* [format] *too. Which seems a great leap to me.*[415]

A series of ideas that began taking shape the previous year in the form of a list (p. 191) now reappear, clustered around the heading *stigma.* *Stigma: Notes on the Management of Spoiled Identity* (New York: Prentice Hall, 1963) is the title of a book by sociologist Erving Goffman that intrigues her.[416] In her own lexicon the word has a very broad reach. (Earlier in the year, for example, she suggests a story to Crookston on The Stigma of Beauty. *Think of this: That Beauty is itself an aberration, a burden, a mystery, even to itself.*[417]) The subjects listed in her current notebooks in connection with this heading include: *Beauty Queens, hypnosis, leper colony, little people of America…Stigma* [Daughters of] *Bilitis, x alcoholics, x follies…old, nude, Blind, Handicapped, clubs, S&M, Stratoliners* [the club for tall people]…*masks, shame…narrative photograph.*[418] (There is also a persistent and somewhat incongruous reminder: *GO TO NIAGARA FALLS IN JUNE*—which she doesn't do.) Among the other books she investigates in this period are

Encyclopedia of Aberrations, a 1953 psychiatric handbook, and Joanne Greenberg's fictionalized autobiographical account, *I Never Promised You a Rose Garden* (New York: Holt, Rinehart & Winston, 1964), about an adolescent confined to a mental institution, from which she copies out this passage:

One had to choose or be chosen as a partner at camp, a seatmate at school, the member (in a certain order of importance) in all kinds of cliques and groups and classes…Deborah had found that she could meet the demands of this membership only with the tainted, the very poor, the crippled, the disfigured, the strange, the going-insane. These pairings off weren't planned or thought out, even secretly; they came about as naturally as the attraction of magnet and metal, yet many of the fragments which had been drawn together thus knew why in their hearts and hated themselves and their companions.

—FROM *I NEVER PROMISED YOU A ROSE GARDEN* (P. 143), 1969 NOTEBOOK (NO. 36)

In August she spends three days at a baton twirling contest in Syracuse, New York, a project she had proposed to Crookston earlier in the year to which he seems not to have responded. The following text on the subject is written in her notebook:

Twirling is the only they say American art form…It is Icathian [meaning, like Icarus] in its extremity, its uselessness and the way that uselessness has been put to use creating minor industries, major sinecures, passions and tragedies, legends and at the least a kind of frenetic belief in itself… "Don't bend both knees at the same time or pump body up and down while marching. Dress tastefully. Be a doll."…The amazing thing about a roomful of them practicing is the frenetic movement which seems like it doubles back on itself and the smiles…Its like a

(*LEFT*) PORTRAIT OF A JOAN CRAWFORD FAN AND HIS COLLECTION OF MEMORABILIA MADE FOR *THE LONDON SUNDAY TIMES MAGAZINE* BUT NEVER PUBLISHED UNTIL IT APPEARED POSTHUMOUSLY IN *DIANE ARBUS MAGAZINE WORK* (NEW YORK: APERTURE, 1984). (*RIGHT*) THE RED STOCKINGS, A RADICAL FEMINIST GROUP IN BOSTON, APPEARED IN *THE LONDON SUNDAY TIMES MAGAZINE* ALONG WITH NINE PORTRAITS OF FEMINIST LEADERS IN THE SEPTEMBER 14, 1969, ISSUE ACCOMPANYING AN ARTICLE ENTITLED "MAKE WAR NOT LOVE!" BY IRMA KURTZ. A COUPLE OF MONTHS LATER IN A LETTER TO ALLAN, DIANE REPORTS: *LOOK* [MAGAZINE] *WANTS TO SEE THE FEMINISTS WHICH IN THE BOTTOM OF MY DEPRESSION I DESTROYED ALL OF THE NEGATIVES OF. BUT I HAVE ASKED THE TIMES IF THEY STILL HAVE PRINTS TO SEND THEM.* THE NEGATIVE OF THIS PICTURE WAS APPARENTLY NOT DESTROYED AFTER ALL.

most ascetic mystic moral discipline in the bobbysox and blond flip hairdo and sequins and feathers and diadems of middle class dreams. The parents and teachers seem strict and nostalgic because they can instruct what they can no longer do and because the childrens eminence is to be so short-lived, like raising butterflies, or training fleas.

— 1969 NOTEBOOK (No. 38)

In a curious way the above account echoes her response to a project she has been looking forward to with great anticipation for months. (*Something wonderful has happened in the way of a private project for some of the summer*, she says without further explanation in a letter to Crookston in late March. And on another occasion in equally opaque terms: *I am going to be working on a marvelous project in NJ sometime this summer when I can.*[419]) She has managed to secure the necessary permission to photograph at several state institutions—but other than attending a dance at one of them in March and an Easter parade at another in April, she is unable to really begin working on the project until the end of July.

darling amy, I went to New Jersey, to the retarded school. Some of the ladies are my age and look like they are 12. I will show you in the pictures. Others look older than they are. Some of them are perfectly rational, but simple and tend to repeat things. One lady said, "Oh God," every time she saw me. "You're cute," she'd say. "You're too much." ...She Could say more but those are the things she kept wanting to say over and over. And many of them just love to hug. Some of them are so small that their shoulder would fit right under my arm and I would pat them and their head would fall on my chest. They are the strangest combination of grownup and child I have ever seen...One lady kept saying over and over "I'm sorry, I'm sorry." After a while one of the staff said "That's all right but don't do it again" and she quieted down...I think youd like them. Some of them are perturbed and miserable. One of them says over and over very earnestly, "Was I the only one born?"

— LETTER TO AMY ARBUS, CIRCA EARLY AUGUST 1969

Her record of the experience—which precedes the baton twirling contest in time, but follows it in her notebook—goes on for five pages and is marked by the following sorts of individual observations: *Pearl. Like Lennie* [in John Steinbeck's *Of Mice and Men*] *benign and violent. Could lift anyone as if they were a doll. Carried Kitty...Is Joanie the breathless one in the pale swimsuit...Rosalie has saucer eyes and the body of a doll you cant tumble. and humility...Phyllis is the one with glasses and large lips. Solemn intelligent mongoloid...Barbara is sweet and bright and modest. When I did her in her flowered nightgown she lowered her eyes before raising them...Their pocketbooks seem to keep them alive.*[420] And this:

Marlene Woodruff posed in the rose garden. I've got a boyfriend. He says I'm beautiful. I told him you haven't seen the pretty parts... Around her neck on a string was a key. Her girlfriend gave it to her before she died. It's good to remember people who die.

— 1969 NOTEBOOK (No. 38)

In a letter to Allan she describes the photographs made on this occasion with a mixture of exhilaration and bafflement, as if hovering on the verge of something new:

DIANE AT WORK NEAR THE FOUNTAIN IN CENTRAL PARK WITH HER MAMIYAFLEX AND ITS FLASH ATTACHMENT. IN A LETTER TO PETER CROOKSTON IN MAY, AFTER RETURNING FROM HER TRIP TO LONDON FOR *NOVA*, SHE WRITES ABOUT BEING HOME IN NEW YORK AND HOW THE CITY IS CHANGING: *I WENT UP TO THE PARK TO THE FOUNTAIN WHERE PEOPLE CONGREGATE...TO DEVOUR EACH OTHER WITH THEIR EYES. LOTS OF SUDDEN CROWDS KNOTTED AROUND MUSIC MAKERS OR PEOPLE HARANGUING EACH OTHER. ONE GIRL HAD AN EPILEPTIC FIT AND PEOPLE WERE STANDING, PEERING, CLIMBING, CRANING TO SEE.* MINOX PHOTOGRAPHS BY FRED GURNER.

Some of the…pictures are exciting but I must go back a lot. I am plagued by mysterious technical problems, like trying to make my sharp pictures blurred but not too much so. Having great trouble balancing strobe and daylight when used together especially on gray days but sometimes this nutty method seems just beautiful to me. And very different. It is a little agonous. a thousand misses but when it all of a sudden works I recognize it is what I wanted without precisely knowing I wanted anything. I am like someone who gets excellent glasses because of a slight defect in eyesight and puts vaseline on them to make it look more like he normally sees. It doesn't Seem sensible. But somehow I think it will be right.[421]

—LETTER TO ALLAN ARBUS, CIRCA MID-AUGUST 1969

Although she has been making all her own prints for well over a decade, processing the negatives has remained a task left to Allan's assistants, one which she is only now attempting to master. Her gradual progress toward technical independence in the darkroom is a source of pride:

I have been in the darkroom all week. Learning to do negatives. Have done two batches with Howard {Harrison, Allan's former assistant who is currently sharing the darkroom with her.} He was very nice and patient. We will do another together. And then I'll be on my own…Its arduous but good to be learning. I feel like I am making my own shoes. Dunno how anyone ever became a photographer with having to do all this. Dunno how people can bear to do other peoples. Dunno how you did it. But I see I Can. and that's a great relief.

—LETTER TO ALLAN ARBUS, CIRCA MID-AUGUST 1969

In late November she reports on her achievement in this area: *I really like doing negatives. I mean its kind of nice and quiet and pleasant and lonely going there. and it's the only darkroom activity that when I go I know I will be done in roughly an hour and a half…I really like having the darkroom to myself.*[422] The same five-page letter contains the following account of another visit to one of the New Jersey institutions that has fueled her enthusiasm for the project:

…I took the most terrific pictures. the ones at Halloween in NJ of the retarded women. Somehow and I don't understand it at all, I mean I don't know if the strobe didn't fire or did or if it was just like a fill in but they are very blurred and variable, but some are gorgeous. FINALLY what I've been searching for. and I seem to have discovered sunlight, late afternoon early winter sun light. its just marvelous. In general I seem to have perverted your brilliant technique all the way round, bending it over backwards you might say till its JUST like snapshots but better. I think its going to be marvelous. (Doon says they look like if you blew on them they'd disappear. Like made of smoke. And Amy likes the retarded photos more than anything Ive ever done.)…They are so lyric and tender and pretty…I have developed this terrific method which is to proof hundreds of them on the machine instead of making rough 16x20s.[423] Gradually I will go backwards proofing to see what I turn up. I think about doing a book on the retarded. And maybe a folio of other prints. marvin suggested that.[424]

—LETTER TO ALLAN ARBUS, NOVEMBER 28, 1969

After several digressions, she returns to the subject once more in the same letter:

The book about the retarded ladies excites me. I could do it in a year…[425] it's the first time Ive encountered a subject where the multiplicity is the thing. I mean I am not just looking for the BEST picture of them. I want to do lots…And I ought to be able to write it because I really adore them.

—LETTER TO ALLAN ARBUS, NOVEMBER 28, 1969

She has secured another job with Patricia Peterson for *The New York Times Magazine Children's Fashions* supplement that entails a trip to Barbados over Christmas. *I THINK it'll be like last year, I mean that much work and money which is a godsend (5000).*[426] John Szarkowski has asked her to research and edit an exhibition of news photography he is planning to mount at MoMA, and after thinking it over for a while she replies: *I think Id really like to do that news photography show. February, March and April seems a good time because the weather is so rotten mostly then. (forgive me.)*[427] To Allan on the same topic she writes: *…sounds good to me. I love the subject and I'll get paid, not enormously but regularly*[428] *and I think it'll be fun and surely better than teaching.*[429] Her sense of independence is at least momentarily almost intoxicating. *I did my first job all by myself this week, negatives too. For NY, which I got by calling on a flimsy excuse. Dumb. Santa Claus. but its fine and I was wondrous calm.*[430] All of which in summary prompts her to say the following:

But look, try to get calmer about money. I have a feeling I can be making it more easily and I Want to do it and it makes sense for you to feel the leeway to let me do most of it for a while. You did it for me for years

UNTITLED (10) 1970–71. THIS PHOTOGRAPH, LIKE MANY OF THE UNTITLED PHOTOGRAPHS, WAS ACTUALLY TAKEN IN THE SUMMER OF 1969 WHEN DIANE BEGAN MAKING MANY OF HER ROUGH PRINTS FROM THE SERIES. IT WAS TITLED POSTHUMOUSLY IN 1972 BY THE ESTATE OF DIANE ARBUS.

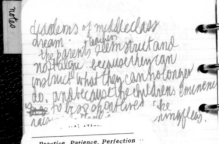

11/69 6749

diadems of middleclass dream ... the parents seem struck and nostalgic because they can instruct what they can no longer do, and because the childrens eminent ... to trap open lives ... raise ...

29 30 31

Vineland 7/69. residents. age.

twins alice + ketty alice is fatter more ade... smiles like Laurel. They're on a diet. and ketty still but alice didnt point alices belly.

alberta pearshaped ju... ran in place.

92 Joanie the breathless in the pale swimsuit.

there was a trio, Barbara the middle who had to be ... to hold her head up marlene and cathleen I think.

they formed a circle for... in place and Simon Say... their heads a... bellies.

someone vomited in the ...

Practice, Patience, Perfection
by Marilyn DeGroot
Roseville, Mich.

Twirling, spinning, turning,
Baton always whirling,
Hands and feet sometimes burning,
Wonder if I'll meet my yearning.

Why must I suffer so,
And always feel so awfully low?
With mother always saying "No"
Please make your performance glow.

But then I must remember,
Patience, practice go together,
To meet my goal I won't surrender
To be perfect even if it takes forever.

APRIL 1969

Phyllis is the one with glasses and large lips. Solemn intelligent mongoloid.

Pond Barbara is sweet and bright and modest. when I did her in bed in her flowered nightgown she lowered her eyes before arranging them.

I think Johanna is the one with the cowboy hat.

At night they sat on their beds and said prayers in unison. Hail Mary full of grace. Forgive us this day our trespasses... If I should die before I wake I pray the lord my soul to take.

I want to run away from here but I dont know how to run. I dont like the girls in my class they boss me, call me low grade. no one comes to visit me. you're letter of dead.

marlene woodruff posed in the rose garden. I've got a boyfriend. He says Im beautiful. I told him you havent seen the pretty parts. Eddie 45 going to go to school. around her neck on a string was a key ... her girlfriend gave to her before she died it good to remember people who die. their pocketbooks seem to keep them alive.

nancy is the slightly bearded one who lay in bed like an odalisque against the wall in Pond.

Sally is blind in a wheelchair. Laughing (25) 'reading' her name. red hair.

Carmela is fat. Julia is her blondfriend and crosseyed

one lady said, Am I the only one born? whats wrong with her, pointing to me Tell me why is there so much sorrow

(LEFT) LETTER FROM DIANE ARBUS TO AMY ARBUS, CIRCA EARLY AUGUST 1969. (BELOW) UNTITLED (45).

darling amy,

I went to New Jersey ,to the retarded school.Some of the ladies are my age and look like they are 12. I will show you in the pictures. Others xxx look older than they are. Some of them are perfectly rational ,but simple and tend to repeat things.One lady said "Oh God," every time she saw me. "You're cute" she'd say. "Youre too much" " Go ahead ,dear." She Could say more but those are tue things she kept wanting to say over and over.And many of them just love to hug.Some of them are so small that their shoulder would fit right under my arm and I would pat them and their head would fall on my chest.

They are the strangest combination of grownup and child I have ever seen.One day we went on a picnic and they were allowed to buy things.Sunglasses,candy, pennants,funny hats, pi wheels.They can cry over things like when their pinwheel stops turning.One lady who was about 50 years old,her name was Nellie and she was very angry because xx she hadn't been allowed to hold her money in her own hand and she knew she could and had done it before,so she was pouting and muttering really mad. She had a friend named Susie who looked to be about 12 and Susie couldn't talk and Nellie always had her arm around her and helped her with everything.Suddenly Susie burst into tears because Nellie was angry.Finally the teacher gave Nellie her 50 cents and everything seemed all right. One lady kept saying over and over "I'm sorry",I'm sorry" After a while one of the staff said "Thats all right but dont do t again" and she quieted down. There is a song written on the wall of the recreation room which says Hello Hello Hello Hello What shall we do today? Hello Today." Thats it.One of the best times was when they played Simon Says in a field.Its real a very serious game for them because when Simon Says Raise you hands high,some can some cant ,some only just put their hands on their head. And when Simon says run in place the ones that c do it as if it was nearly impossible. Lots of them are pearsha

once during Simon says there was a pause and one girl sat down. Everyone knew it was important.She bent her head to her knees and with an odd shiver somehow the rest of her rollowed in what looked like the first somersault. I think youd like them.Some of them are perturbed and miserable. One of them says over and over, ver earnestly "Was I the only one born?"

Doon is very happy in her job. She and dick get along wonde n and he seems to trust her enormously. She is ver ng hours.

you though. Your bed is made and waiting. I have to the plants.Pa's picture is in Time magazine this e section, a still from the movie he's in. It does e looks terrific.I have saved it for you in case old better? I began to wish I had a bike again.Are or used to it? I have a million questions but it w

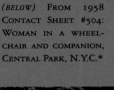

*(BELOW) FROM 1958 CONTACT SHEET #504: WOMAN IN A WHEELCHAIR AND COMPANION, CENTRAL PARK, N.Y.C.**

(ABOVE) 1969 CONTACT SHEET #7050 FROM HALLOWEEN WITH UNTITLED (52) SECOND FROM BOTTOM CENTER.

*(LEFT) FROM 1958 CONTACT SHEET #584: CROWD OF CHILDREN AT HALLOWEEN.**
(ABOVE) UNTITLED (14):

*(ABOVE) FROM 1957 CONTACT SHEET #201: GIRLS IN LINE, N.Y.C.**
*(RIGHT) FROM UNNUMBERED CONTACT SHEET CIRCA 1955, YOUNG WOMEN SEATED ON THE GRASS IN CENTRAL PARK, N.Y.C.**

and I sense that I am in shape to do it for you. I have a hunch that this sense of form I feel is going to partly translate into a freedom to make money more easily with less fuss and guilt. I don't mean fortunes but enough to sustain us. We Do have a partnership and its my turn to do that part.

—LETTER TO ALLAN ARBUS, NOVEMBER 28, 1969

Even before the move to 10th Street she had investigated the possibility of applying for an apartment in Westbeth, the former Bell Laboratory building in the West Village, which was then in the process of being converted into living and working spaces for visual, performing, and literary artists.[431] The requirements for admission are stringent and complex and subject to the approval and annual review of the Federal Housing Administration. At times during the application process she despairs of being able to meet the qualifications, which among other things restrict her maximum income to $8,400. As she says to Allan at one point: *I feel a bit boxed in between not making enough and making too much.*[432] In the end, the fact that she and Allan maintain a partnership reduces her income enough to satisfy the financial requirements. *At any rate,* she writes, *I've decided it's all worth the risk. The people in the building look terrific and I know quite a lot of them.*[433] The move is scheduled to take place shortly after the end of the year. In a letter to Carlotta she reflects on things:

I suppose freedom is a bit eerie. Its what I want but something in me tries to pretend I can't. And there is so much work to working that there are moments, moments, where I stop and look around and it seems too arduous to go on. It isnt of course. But that is why people have jobs and pay checks...it helps keep you from unanswerable questions.

—LETTER TO CARLOTTA MARSHALL, CIRCA NOVEMBER 1969

COUPLE WALKING IN CENTRAL PARK, N.Y.C. 1969. *I USED TO HAVE A THEORY ABOUT PHO-TOGRAPHING. IT WAS A SENSE OF GETTING BETWEEN TWO ACTIONS, OR IN BETWEEN ACTION AND REPOSE...IT WAS JUST LIKE AN EXPRESSION I DIDN'T SEE OR WOULDN'T HAVE SEEN.*

1970

In the course of the ten days she spends in Barbados with Patricia Peterson working on *The New York Times Magazine Children's Fashions* supplement,[434] she sends Marvin Israel this description of her stay:

Birds fly indoors in these hotels, feasting on leftovers. I have been dreaming endlessly, domestic dreams in which I am a child or a mother. Its a very pretty island, rich, pastoral, rolling, wild, flat, by turns. Tiny houses with cotton curtains printed with fruits or roses and inside a glimpse of a Christmas tree and a chair, and hardly room for more...each one like a house in the woods where Snow White or Hansel and Gretel lived...We go blithely (sort of) from one hotel to another, no one questions us, Pat [Peterson] corners children and their parents and I am often free to idly photograph ladies on the beach or corners of lobbies...I really don't like the children. I long to be with you.[435]

—LETTER TO MARVIN ISRAEL, CIRCA EARLY JANUARY 1970

Although the account she gives Allan a few weeks later of the photographs themselves sounds relatively unperturbed, it reflects no enthusiasm for the results:

The [*New York*] Times pics were rather lousy and there was a bit of trouble, Pat said it was because the cover photo was of a black girl and a white boy about 4 years old, holding hands. Pat has been incredibly sweet. They wanted a retake which I think she has effectively blocked...I am pretty calm about the whole thing. She was full of appreciation for the most minor virtues of the photos. and believe me they were minor...[436] and as for the miscegenation, junior style, it may end up being regarded as a major civil rights breakthrough, if they finally let it pass.[437]

—LETTER TO ALLAN ARBUS, JANUARY 16, 1970

She, Amy, and Doon (who is searching, so far unsuccessfully, for her own place) move to the new apartment in Westbeth on January 22. A number of people Diane knows are—or are about to become—residents of the building, including the photographer Evelyn Hofer, writers Marion Magid and Edward Hoagland, and artist Mary Frank.[438] She promptly indulges in a binge of decorating. *I have discovered the joys of spray paint in silver and gold although not much skill at it yet*, she says in a letter to Allan.[439] And to Crookston, after what has apparently been a couple of months of silence between them:

I was away on a job and then moved, marvelously to...[she supplies her new address and phone] where there is a panorama out my window... and a blessed lot of sky. Best place I ever had. I have been buying somewhat insanely. An ant farm so I can watch them working when I am not...a desk made entirely of chrome, so shiny it is well nigh invisible. marvelous toys I have always wanted...fake worms, lady shaped ice cubes, a transparent plastic lady with all her organs and bones ready for a clever child to insert but it seems too difficult so I have left her as empty as she is naked....the plants which died in the moving because it was terribly cold have been reborn, and I suddenly like to cook.

—LETTER TO PETER CROOKSTON, CIRCA LATE JANUARY 1970

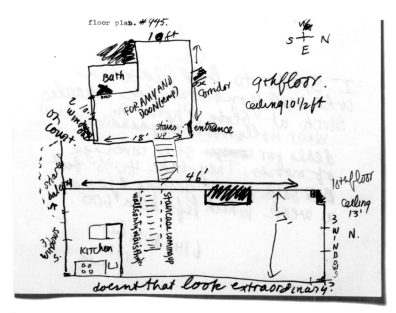

FLOOR PLAN OF HER APARTMENT AT WESTBETH (#945) DRAWN FOR ALLAN AT THE BOTTOM OF ONE OF HER LETTERS TO HIM. ON JANUARY 16, SHE WRITES: *SNUCK UP AND SAW MY APT TODAY (MOVE ON THURS, 22ND), AND IT IS MARVELOUS. WHAT A VIEW, THE RIVER WITH ICE AND TUGBOATS AND BIRDS, THE WESTSIDE HIGHWAY, BEAUTIFUL SMOKESTACKS AND SMALL INDUSTRIAL BUILDINGS STRETCHING NORTHWARD. AND AS SHE LATER REMARKS TO CARLOTTA MARSHALL, ABSOLUTELY NO ONE IN THE WHOLE VIEW CLOSE ENOUGH TO BE STARING BACK AT ME, I DON'T THINK.*

In anticipation of the stipend for researching the news photography show which has helped make her new home a reality, she writes Szarkowski to thank him and express her eagerness to begin: *This is a palace you got for me. even the fishermans wife would be pleased. I have never felt such homely bliss. Should we have lunch or something to talk over plans for our show? Come visit me and see what you have wrought...*[440]

A memorandum from John Szarkowski to Inez Garson dated January 19 regarding a proposed MoMA research fellowship for the projected exhibition tentatively titled *The Iconography of the Daily News,* reads as follows: *The exhibition is conceived as an investigation of the content and form of news photographs, with special attention to their traditional and ritualized nature. The project is based on the premise that much of what is in fact newsworthy is not photographable, and that what is photographable is generally concerned less with news than with the vicarious sharing of a few basic and constant human experiences...The force of many of these pictures on a visual and psychological level—as experience rather than information—is attested to by their affect on painters such as Francis Bacon, as well as on the awareness of other photographers.*[441]

Szarkowski requests a research stipend of $4,000 on Diane's behalf and an additional $2,000 for study prints and other documentation expenses. He adds: *I consider Diane Arbus to be an ideal person to do this work. Though she is an artist rather than a scholar, she has demonstrated through her own work a profound understanding of the central qualities of the news photography tradition. She is in addition a person of acute intelligence, and an excellent writer.*[442] The fact that the proposal does not receive final approval and funding until June delays commencement of the research.

The list of books in the front of her 1970 appointment book exemplifies the breadth of her current preoccupations. The list includes: *Prints and Visual Communication* by William Ivins (Cambridge: Harvard University Press, 1953; Boston: MIT Press, 1969) (related to her

upcoming MoMA project); *Mental Deficiency of Different Origins: A Pictorial Survey* by Hans Forssman and Hans Olof Akesson (Copenhagen: Det Berlingske Bogtrykkeri, 1964); *Ghost Hunter: True Stories of Psychic Phenomena* by Hans Holzer (New York: Bobbs Merrill Co., 1963); *On Death and Dying* by Elisabeth Kübler-Ross (New York: Macmillan, 1969) (probably connected to an assignment for *Esquire* about dying people she is supposed to work on in Chicago in July,[443] which never actually takes place); *An Essay on the Causes of the Variety of Complexion and Figure in the Human Species* (1787; Cambridge: Harvard University Press, 1965); *Further Confessions of Zeno* (Berkeley: University of California Press, 1969), the sequel to a novel by Italo Svevo she describes as *funny and marvelous and heartening*[444] and recommends to a number of friends; and a book by Lancelot Law Whyte which she refers to as *something about the nature of man* (*The Next Development of Mankind,* London: The Cresset Press, 1944), apparently suggested by her psychiatrist Dr. Helen Boigon, whom she has been seeing on a regular basis since the previous September.[445]

Although she sounds a little dubious about Dr. Boigon in the summary she initially gives Allan of the first several sessions (*I still don't move but I begin to guess Dr. B may be OK. She threatens to make me work, I get mad.*[446]), her more recent accounts of their exchanges suggest an improvement.

Dr. B said a terrific thing to me...something like that human beings are obsessed with the question WHY which is really a very gratuitous meaningless question which attempts to remove or erase the subject of

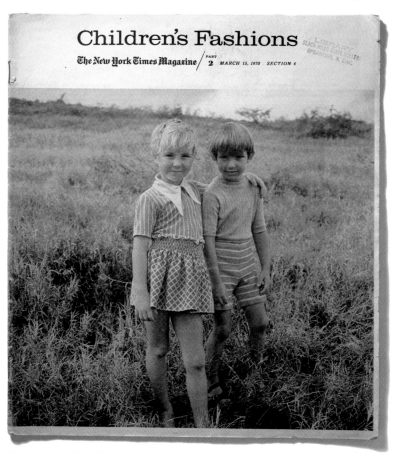

THE COVER OF *THE NEW YORK TIMES MAGAZINE CHILDREN'S FASHIONS* SUPPLEMENT, MARCH 15, 1970. THE PHOTOGRAPH DIANE REFERS TO AS HAVING BEEN INTENDED FOR THE COVER (*A BLACK GIRL AND A WHITE BOY ABOUT FOUR YEARS OLD HOLDING HANDS*) DOES NOT APPEAR ANYWHERE IN THE ISSUE AT ALL.

itself and the whole point (this is a graceless paraphrase) is in the experience of the Way It Is which WHY seeks to evade.[447] Anyway, she is endless fun, although I begin to get restless for the end to come in sight simply because it seems it could go on forever, and I feel slightly mollycoddled. I am learning something and her mind is fascinating. She translates my thoughts into her language and its terrific. She has put up the photo of the twins which I gave her and told me several stories of the reactions of patients.

—LETTER TO ALLAN ARBUS, JANUARY 16, 1970

Mariclare Costello, who is planning to leave New York later in the year and move to Los Angeles to join Allan, arranges for Doon to take over her studio apartment on West 68th Street in April. Diane has been working on the design (with Marvin Israel) and content of her limited edition portfolio and seeking advice on ways to market it.[448] A single 20x24 sheet of vellum is entirely covered with her practice handwritten titles and commentary: *what is this? a box of photographs...not a book...by me. and who pray tell are you?...how many? ten. how much? 1000...marvin israel. gosh...this isnt half bad.* It indicates several alternate images (such as A family one evening in a nudist camp, p. 295) originally under consideration. Of the ten images ultimately included in the portfolio, three are made in the spring of 1970: Lauro Morales (aka Cha Cha) the Mexican dwarf in his hotel room in March (p. 66); Eddie Carmel, the Jewish giant at home with his parents in the Bronx in April (p. 300); and The King and Queen of a Senior Citizens' Dance in May (p. 247).[449]

Her production of the portfolio is plagued by technical difficulties, even down to some basic issues like ensuring that the prints dry flat. Allan apparently volunteers some suggestions, to which she replies: *Thanks about the 16x20s. Tried it on a print which had been dried already. better. will try it again on a fresh one. Its edge ripples I get.*[450] A few months later she reports success in addressing this problem:

Thanks again about the blotter roll. Ive done a dozen each of two prints. They look terrific.Very flat and fine. Ive eliminated the black borders, left an uneven edge. Nice I think. Ive worked it out so it only takes 3½—

4 hours so I am going in to dkrm at 6AM as often as I can so it will be done by mid July roughly.

—LETTER TO ALLAN ARBUS AND MARICLARE COSTELLO, CIRCA JUNE 1970

Amy leaves for the summer on a youth hostel trip through Europe at the end of June. *A bit of an inauspicious beginning for Amy,* Diane says in describing the scene of departure to Allan and Mariclare. *The kids looked rather frightful...The girls very lipsticked or eye shadowed and prissy and suburban—like they were off to the beach...The boys very misfit and bemused...She must have been appalled.*[451] She writes to Amy the next morning:

Its weird without you. So far very virtuous. I got up at 5:30 to the darkroom by 6:15 so Ive finished printing for the day already and Im just eating breakfast in a diner. Then to the newspaper library next door where I'll look at random Daily Newses of ancient vintage.

—LETTER TO AMY ARBUS, CIRCA LATE JUNE 1970

Between her acquaintances at United Press International, Associated Press, and other photo sources, and her investigation of the files of the *Daily News,* she constructs a list entitled *Subjects (mostly 1920–1955)* that has a curious resemblance to some of her own lists. It includes the following: *accident, grief, pain...death of pet animals; murder victims, murderers...corruption, people hiding [their] faces...kidnapping, execution, lynching; suicides, before, during, after...heroes, posthumous and otherwise, mouth to mouth resuscitation; revolution (Hungarian), riots, strikes...cyclone, tornado, overturned houses, flood, fire, dust storms; depression, breadlines, apples, hoovervilles...; child abuse, closeted children...people dying of mysterious disease; photographers being shot.* And further down the page, as if on the other, upbeat side of the ledger: *Contests, Winners, crying or otherwise, Beauty, Losers, Pieeating...Queens (Beauty, Publicity, as Donut Queen, etc.), pinups, starlets; Ceremonies, ribbon cutting, contract signing...Harmless nuts, Collectors, fads, cults, New Year Babies, child brides, May-Dec Marriages, Weddings of old people, mother of the year (lots of children), feats of strength, daredevils...Dance marathons.*[452]

I have been both lazy and industrious, she says in a letter to Crookston, after another lengthy silence. *(don't lets get guilty. Its been long but that's the way it is.)* She expresses some regret at having turned down a *Nova* assignment on political groupies. *I was deep in the midst of something and it seemed I'd have to give up one thing for the other and at that moment all my enthusiasm for that notion* [the political groupies] *had utterly left me.* She reports that *Harold* [Hayes at *Esquire*] *has given me a nice page rate increase and two assignments I suggested,*[453] and describes her progress on the portfolio[454] and on the show of news photographs for MoMA.[455]

She leaves on June 29 to attend the July 2 opening of Richard Avedon's retrospective exhibition at the Minneapolis Institute of Art. Marvin Israel has designed the show as well as the catalogue and is overseeing the installation.[456] Doon—who has been working with Avedon (at Israel's suggestion) since the summer of 1969 on a long-term project of his—is there for the event too.[457] Everyone coming for the opening stays at the Ambassador Resort Motor Hotel. *Dick's show is terrific. And life is full of room service,* Diane says in a letter to Amy on hotel stationery. *The*

In a letter to Peter Crookston on June 28, Diane writes: *I went back and did a picture I had wanted to do a few years ago for your family issue. Marvelous.* She is referring to the photograph above of the giant with his parents. The image she prints and includes in her portfolio appears at the bottom of the center strip on the original Contact Sheet #6882, frame #1.

[Handwritten on photo collage:] it was a bit on the transparent side so marvin loaned me a T shirt. which I wear with my underpants!

[Labels on photos:] the saunas · view · Doon wore one of her dresses. oh amy. amy · miniature golf · is Europe different? who'd you talk most too? · the sunlanijos · me · our room · this is just what its like, I love you, ma

THE SECOND PAGE OF DIANE'S JULY 2 LETTER TO AMY ON AMBASSADOR STATIONERY. SHE HAS WRITTEN: *YOU WERE RIGHT MY NEW WHITE LEOTARD BATHING SUIT WAS A BIT ON THE TRANSPARENT SIDE SO MARVIN LOANED ME A T SHIRT WHICH I WEAR WITH MY UNDERPANTS.*

THE NIGHT OF AVEDON'S MINNEAPOLIS OPENING. MARVIN ISRAEL RECLINES ON THE BED IN THE ARMS OF AN UNIDENTIFIED WOMAN. *SEATED FROM LEFT TO RIGHT:* HAIRDRESSER ARA GALLANT IN A CAP, PETER WALDMAN, AVEDON'S WIFE, EVELYN, HENRY ARONSON, DOON ARBUS, GINNY HEYMAN, UNIDENTIFIED MAN WITH MUSTACHE. *STANDING FROM LEFT TO RIGHT:* UNIDENTIFIED MAN, HIRO; *(BACK ROW)* RICHARD AVEDON IN AVEDON T-SHIRT, LAURA KANELOUS, HARRY MATTISON, RUTH ANSEL; *(BACK ROW)* LARRY HALES, UNIDENTIFIED WOMAN, MIKE MINDLIN, HENRY WOLF, KANELOUS'S DAUGHTER HELEN AND HUSBAND JOHN, GIDEON LEWLYN.

party is tonight. There are Avedon sheets and balloons and T-shirts and ash trays but Dick doesn't know at all I don't think.[458] Her subsequent account of the event goes like this:

Minneapolis was so much fun. I loved the show and doing little tasks for it so that Doon and I felt very part of it, not just audience and Marvin was funny and splendid. Everyone felt it…The Party was a bit much at moments. The preparations were great, all the secrecy and conspiracy and everything Looked fantastic. The masks were unbelievable, a thousand Richard Avedons, the cake was Black and white with his face drawn on in icing, so good I couldnt believe it, in fact I didn't eat any. I mostly blew up 144 balloons of all colors with Dicks face on them and Doon and Marvin and Ginny [Heyman, Avedon's secretary] tied them to chairs and tables around the pool. But when Dick walked in the first moment, and there were these multiple imposters facing him and advancing towards him, he looked really shocked, "Oh no," he gasped faintly like someone in a nightmare. Then Marvin appeared in the old persons mask and then people began to take them off and Dick recovered and jumped in the pool with all his clothes on and we all swam a lot. Then lots of rowdy people, strangers, kids appeared and started cutting up a bit, swimming with clothes and taking all their clothes off. So marvin and me left for the nearby delicatessen and when we got back, mysteriously, all the strangers had dispersed, having been warned of a 10 o'clock curfew. And the rest were in Laura's [Kanelous, Avedon's agent] room and Dick was reading aloud the [phoney] telegrams and the little book [of his sayings]. He really loved it all. Then the greatest thing was that after it was all over and we were quietly swimming in little groups or some people were going to bed, there was this sudden enormous awesome thunderstorm like a benediction. It rained so hard that plastic dome leaked. so we swam under the clatter and crash. beautiful.

—LETTER TO AMY ARBUS, CIRCA EARLY JULY 1970

She returns home a little reluctantly. *The portriga* [photographic paper] *I ordered hasn't shown up which is enraging because I could have finished the box this week,* she says in a letter to Allan and Mariclare. *Anyway it'll be done in July and Dick said he'd buy the first one. and if nothing else they are flat.*[459] But, as she goes on to admit, the aftermath of Minneapolis leaves her wistful.

I'm a bit sad to be back. The show was beautiful and I loved working at menial tasks to get things done. The people were lovely and marvin was radiant and working at a fever pitch…In minneapolis the prints were enormous (some of them) BEAUTIFUL. One room had just maybe nine huge heads. Like presences. The pictures never looked so good. love. take care of each other.

—LETTER TO ALLAN ARBUS AND MARICLARE COSTELLO, CIRCA EARLY JULY 1970

At the end of July she heads for Hagerstown, Maryland, on an assignment she secured from *Esquire* to photograph at a carnival there. *A little dubious about it,* she says in a letter to Amy. *I am supposed to photograph girl shows for Esquire and I dunno how much of that they have.*[460] In spite of the fact that she turns out to be right about the girl shows—there don't appear to have been any—the trip proves very productive. She prints about six of the photographs—among them, *Albino sword swallower* (p. 304), which she considers including in the portfolio—and *Esquire* plans to publish several of them as a feature story on carnivals.[461] A week later she sends Amy the following note from Florida:

Dearest Amy I came to see <u>my</u> mama. felt sort of lousy and NY was making even me scream. Like a crowded stuck elevator. Then our phone kept breaking so I'd go to call someone and couldn't or else if they called me they'd hear it ring but I wouldn't. And work felt like day old cereal every time I'd do something it'd get undone or have to be done over. Here its quiet and insulated. Marvin and Doon call…Mom's been sweet. Lets me drive half the time although I know she much prefers to do it herself.

—NOTE TO AMY ARBUS, AUGUST 11, 1970

Within a day or two of her return to New York from visiting her mother in Florida,[462] she escapes the city again on August 15—this time with Doon as a companion—for a long weekend at Avedon's summer house in Fire Island, which is temporarily unoccupied.[463]

For some time Amy has been unhappy—both socially and academically—at Elisabeth Irwin High School. With Sudie [Victor] Trazoff's help and advice and with Diane's somewhat cautious encouragement,[464] she is investigating alternative, "liberated" schools for her junior year commencing in the fall. After sifting through the options she chooses the Study, Travel, Community School in Maine, which Diane later refers to as *totally not a school*[465] and on another occasion as *a euphemism* for a school.[466] On August 29, Amy, Diane, and Doon go to Brattleboro, Vermont, to meet with the man who runs the program. In a hasty note to Allan just before the trip, Diane writes: *It's been bad…I hope this works this school. I fall apart so easy. I think its important to get Amy away.*[467] (She reports that her regular medical doctor *has taken lots of blood tests. Wants*

ROOM WITH A PLASTIC COUCH, N.Y.C. 1970.

to give me an anti depressant but Dr. B doesn't believe in em. Don't know how I'll resolve that conflict.[468]) Almost as an afterthought she adds: *The first box is done. Dick is giving it to Mike Nichols. It looks good. He was very moved.*[469]

Her first job for *The London Sunday Times Magazine* since June of 1969 takes her to Los Angeles near the end of September. Her assignment is to photograph two separate California leisure communities: the South Bay Singles Club near Marina del Ray and the Sun City Retirement Community,[470] a project somewhat akin to an idea she proposed to Crookston for *Nova* the previous year. During the trip she has a brief visit with Allan and returns home by way of Detroit, where she stops off to do a portrait of Reverend Albert B. Cleage, Jr., pastor of The Shrine of the Black Madonna, for *Essence*, an experience she refers to as *a nightmare.*[471] About a week later she writes Allan:

You took such incredible care of me. I was very moved…Your generosity to me had some effect, some enormous reassurance I cant explain. I don't think we are good for each other in the sense that we tend to remind each other of our own sadness, but there will always be something you do for me that nobody else in the world can. thanks forever, d.

—LETTER TO ALLAN ARBUS, CIRCA EARLY OCTOBER 1970

She acknowledges—almost as if it were an embarrassment—receiving something called The Robert Leavitt Award from the American Society of Magazine Photographers, which is recorded in the September 1970 issue of *Infinity*, the ASMP's magazine, in the following terms: *for her revelation of truth in the "found" individual, who might not be noticed, otherwise, by the less observant.*[472] The ceremony takes place on October 5 and, with considerable reluctance, she attends.

I got some award from the ASMP, and I didn't want to have to go through the acceptance or make a dumb speech, it just depressed me so. And then it turned out that Bruce [Davidson] got a better award, he is the Photographer of the year, and Gene Smith got on the Honor Roll[473] *which is better too, so mine was a little like the Booby Prize, so I couldn't afford not to go because it wouldve looked unsportsmanlike. I told everyone not to come like Lisette [Model] and Dick [Avedon] and I didn't tell Marvin when it was going to be…I hadnt prepared a speech at all. I simply couldn't think of what to say and those finky others all said Oh no they werent making speeches, so up they get and talk for ten minutes…I said that I guessed I had my bunch of people that it wouldn't have been possible without but I had told them not to come and anyway what was most fun about it was that you had to do it all by yourself in the end. Then I kept working the slide machine wrong but it didn't distress me in the slightest and everyone was roaring with laughter and I talked about each picture, told funny stories (bruce had insisted on total silence: "the pictures should speak for themselves").*

—LETTER TO ALLAN ARBUS, CIRCA EARLY OCTOBER 1970

Her triumph over this dreaded event appears to have buoyed her spirits. The same letter to Allan begins with this pronouncement: *things seem better, lots better. I just feel good. I have an odd hunch you helped.*[474] She is full of news. About the status of the portfolio: *Bea* [Feitler] *is buying*

ALBINO SWORD SWALLOWER AND HER SISTER, HAGERSTOWN, MD. 1970. THIS PHOTOGRAPH IS AMONG A HALF DOZEN DIANE PRINTED FROM HER JULY 31 TRIP TO THE CARNIVAL IN MARYLAND. OTHERS INCLUDE ALBINO SWORD SWALLOWER AT A CARNIVAL (P. 304); TATTOOED MAN AT A CARNIVAL (P. 231); AND GIRL IN HER CIRCUS COSTUME (P. 243). THE LATTER APPEARS ON THE SAME ROLL (#6919) AS THE IMAGE ABOVE.

a box too (and that's just Dick's public relations...I haven't begun to hussle them...in fact they still aren't done. the manufacturer made them wrong for about the fourth time.)[475] (This goes on for months, prompting her to say at one point: *god youd think I wanted a glass house people could throw stones at.*[476]) And about her work on the MoMA show she reports: *John Szarkowski and I went over the photos I had chosen from the [Daily] News and it went smashingly, really fun, we narrowed those down to 200 (of which maybe 40 will be in the show) and we were both delighted with the way its going.*[477] About a week later the MoMA project leads her to a discovery that excites her even more.

The best thing this past week was the discovery of ALL Weegee's work in the house of an old lady he lived with, a charming lady...She is a social worker, cultivated, midwestern, sterling, thoroughly his opposite, plain looking, even a bit prim, fascinating...We went through about 8000 prints of which I chose 383, some for the news show, some for a Weegee show which seems inevitable to me. He was SO good when he was good. Extraordinary! I came across a photograph of Lisette at about my age. Wish you could see 'em. Such wild dynamics make everybody [else] look like an academician. People pushing, shoving, screaming, bits of extraneous events thrust into the main one. When he was bad he was pretty terrible, but I borrowed some of the distortions too, and a few of his utterly vulgar ones...There are among everything about 1500 photos of himself.

—LETTER TO ALLAN ARBUS AND MARICLARE COSTELLO, CIRCA LATE OCTOBER 1970

This is followed immediately by a sentence that seems a complete non sequitur: *What if I am no longer a photographer.* She says she is due to leave in a few days to be with her mother who is about to go into the

hospital for an operation. *Its for removal of something in the colon. I don't mind [going]. I seem to feel grim when I am free to do anything I want and less so when I am obliged to do something I don't. (!)*[478] Just before her scheduled departure on this mission, she sends Allan another brief letter that ends with a description of the advent of winter.

It is getting colder and that weird 4 oclock evening is setting in, people look so sad and hurry home in the bleakest light imaginable, but I guess it is a change that I feel sad for them.

—LETTER TO ALLAN ARBUS, CIRCA EARLY NOVEMBER 1970

It has been months since her last reply to Carlotta Marshall's letters. *Dear Carlotta, I have been perfectly terrible, not answering over and over. I fell into a most terrible funk from which I have emerged into a funny limbo, a bit frivolous, pleasant, lazy and somewhat apprehensive. But not bad.*[479] She volunteers this summary to make up for the silence:

I am going to a woman doctor who seems to be teaching me a lot. I am really learning to live alone...I guess it was oddly enough the finality of Allans leaving (for Calif) that so shook me. He had been gone somewhat for a hundred years but suddenly it was no more pretending. This was it...I am learning all over again it seems how to live, how to make a living how to do what I want and what I don't, all sorts of common sensical things I have tended to make a big deal about. Partly it seems a matter of severing connections in my head. Like if I do this that will happen, because sometimes it does and sometimes it doesn't and I have spent a lot of energy exercising non-existent magical controls.

—LETTER TO CARLOTTA MARSHALL, CIRCA NOVEMBER 1970

In answer to Carlotta's inquiry, she also adds the following account of what has been going on with Amy:

Amy is in Maine in a school which is totally not a school, I mean they have spent all fall digging a well, building a kitchen and bath and communal building and now she is building her own dwelling place [a yurt] BY HERSELF. She sounds happier than in years. There isnt a book in sight just woods and sky and of course it must be damn cold but she seems to be a lot closer to what she wants. She has guts.

—LETTER TO CARLOTTA MARSHALL, CIRCA NOVEMBER 1970

Since the summer of 1969 and her work on the Untitled series (which continues in the form of visits to one of the institutions every couple of months for special events) she has been in turmoil over something she is searching for—and remains uncertain how to achieve—in the quality of her photographs. This yearning for an alternative approach is exacerbated by persistent technical problems. *My strobe broke and I discovered it was the gun part so I got a new one, but I begin to suspect I am sick of strobe,*[480] she reports to Allan in November. And again a few weeks later: *Im a bit sick of the strobe outdoors. Suddenly started to look at the real light and its so various and pretty.*[481]

At the same time there is film trouble: *Avedons asst. says they use panatomic x and some faster film, either plus or tri, I will try em both because it looks like Eastman [Kodak] is squeezing out all competition. I hope Portriga [paper] doesn't go too.*[482] And subsequent frustrations about it: *I still have film trouble, hate plusx. trying panatomic. Would a cold light head on the enlarger help? Hiro has a very nice assistant* [Neil Selkirk] *who has suggested some things. There is an Ilford film I can try but so far its out of stock.*[483] At one point she writes, as if it shouldn't be too much to ask: *I just want less grain, more speed. softness, roundness.*[484]

By early December, she has narrowed this complex dilemma down to a single primary issue:

…Have gotten obsessed with buying a new camera. Utterly smitten with the new 6x7 pentax. (2¼ x 2¾). Its just like a big Nikon, which is what Ive always wanted, but there are problems…what speed short of a 250th can it be hand held at? and it only synchs at a 30th…I am borrowing Hiro's and must try all sorts of things, mainly sharpness at slow speeds. It makes an enormous difference in the pictures, Of course they arent very good. Its hard to get used to a new shape. It looks like a greater degree of reality and I havent yet learned How to use that. A little like when I switched from Nikon to Rollei. I wake at night with the excitement of it, or alternately with dread and confusion and worry and abhorrence…At some moments I have wanted it so bad and felt so positive that I thought, hell I'd give a class to pay for it, no problem. Then the next day I think, do I real-

ly want it, maybe its dumb and frivolous, maybe it wont work, maybe its just pretentious, maybe I'll never learn to take as good pictures with it as with the Mamiya. Then I think, Gamble. Then: what with? and again: Why?

—LETTER TO ALLAN ARBUS AND MARICLARE COSTELLO, DECEMBER 6, 1970

At this point she writes in the margin, *One day I nearly went in and just BOUGHT it,* and continues her account of the internal argument:

What it could do is make the pictures more narrative and temporal, less fixed and single and complete and isolated, more dynamics, more things happening. Id like that. The difference knocks me out. Of course it's not to the good, not yet anyway, and probably it wouldn't be so apparent to anybody else, I mean nobody else gives a shit, but that's OK…The pentax has such a Gorgeous ground glass. This marvelous shape (exactly 11x14, 8x10 proportions) and clarity, focusing is fun. And turning it for horizontal or vertical is delightful, like any 35, just heavier.

—LETTER TO ALLAN ARBUS AND MARICLARE COSTELLO, DECEMBER 6, 1970

Even after she seals the envelope she can't stop thinking about it. She scrawls on the outside before mailing it: *This camera controversy in my head is like the mini and the midi.* A subsequent letter to Allan and Mariclare in mid-December begins: *its pretty good here. I mean I just feel*

DIANE SEATED IN FRONT OF HER COLLAGE WALL IN HER WESTBETH APARTMENT. AMONG THE MANY PHOTOGRAPHS TORN FROM NEWSPAPERS AND MAGAZINES ARE *(FROM LEFT TO RIGHT ABOVE)* A FRAMED PRINT OF THE ATGET PHOTOGRAPH *PROSTITUTE, RUE ASSELIN* (1921), A LARTIGUE PHOTOGRAPH OF TWO WOMEN, AND A FRAMED PRINT OF DIANE'S PHOTOGRAPH *UNTITLED* (6). THERE ARE ALSO A COUPLE OF ROUGH PRINTS FROM THE *UNTITLED* SERIES AND ONE OF A WOMAN AND CHILD IN THE PARK. PHOTOGRAPH BY SAUL LEITER.

good. She sounds undaunted—possibly even elated—in her litany of what has failed to come to pass:

I didn't win the Life contest, not even the booby prize, although I must say I'm glad not to have got one of the 25 or so Honorable Mentions which yielded some Encyclopedia as a prize. I also didn't get the [*New York*] Times [children's fashions] job. So something must be done...I think I'll give a course from home (or try to borrow some space in this bldg once a week so as not to have students in snooping and hanging about like they're fond of doing but at any rate I'll give it myself. That'll give me some money and I'll get to keep it all and it need only be 6 or 8 weeks long in the middle of winter, so nothing much will be lost. Also will apply for a grant...Mainly the damn boxes had better get done and I had better peddle them in real earnest.

—LETTER TO ALLAN ARBUS AND MARICLARE COSTELLO, CIRCA MID-DECEMBER, 1970

She makes a flyer to send out for the portfolio that includes two strips of 35mm copy contacts of each of the ten prints pinned on a sheet of paper beside the following typewritten text: *...there is a portfolio of ten photographs by Diane Arbus dating from nineteen sixty-two to nineteen seventy in an edition of fifty, printed, signed, numbered, annotated by the photographer, sixteen by twenty inches in a nearly invisible box which is also a frame, designed by Marvin Israel. Available from Diane Arbus, four sixty-three West Street, New York City, for one thousand dollars.*

She responds to a series of questions from a Georgia State University student she has never met expressing interest in her and her work. She

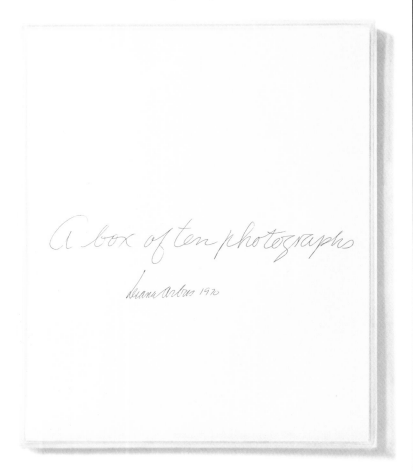

writes: *Dear Gail, yes, a lecture would be fine. I don't have a show, but I could talk and show things and look at things if the Dept has funds for that. I like doing that, talking to strangers, I mean...And it'll all come out in the talking, all the rest...never used a view camera except a couple of times about the first pictures I ever took* [p. 15, 19]*...I'd like to see Georgia and there is a camera I want which costs more than I've got so try to arrange it.*[485]

In the midst of a series of postscripts at the conclusion of a December letter to Allan and Mariclare, she reiterates almost verbatim something she said to Carlotta the month before: *I have so much to learn about how to live...what have I been doing lo these 47 years.*[486]

1971

She places an ad in the newspaper for the class she has decided to teach, posts a notice about it on the bulletin board of The Museum of Modern Art, and mentions the prospect to friends and acquaintances. Among those interested in joining the class are several people she already knows. They include Neil Selkirk, Paul Corlett (both assistants of Hiro's), Susan Brockman (a filmmaker she originally met more than ten years earlier through Robert Brown), Ann Tucker (a New York State Council for the Arts curatorial intern in the photography department at MoMA), Cosmos Savage (a photographer living at Westbeth), and Deborah Turbeville (a former *Harper's Bazaar* fashion editor—who quits after the first class). The afternoon of January 7 is set aside for interviewing prospective students in a vacant room in the Southeast Gallery at Westbeth. Almost two dozen applicants show up, more than twice as many as she had originally anticipated or intended to accept.

...I did the class interviews last thurs. a bit grim. it had been a lousy day waiting for the telephone co. to fix my fone and I felt frazzled and like Not Talking so one after another would parade into this empty room like as if I was a burlesque producer or a pimp or sumpn. I just felt confused. their pictures mostly bored me and I had a slight feeling like I didn't know what was wrong with 'em, they werent after all so wildly different from Good pictures, except there was that mysterious thing...I didn't want to look at them, as if it might be catching and I would end up learning from the students how to take just such boring pix as those. Then there was how to choose between em. it all seemed so arbitrary. this one I didn't like the way she talked, that one seemed funny, another sad etc. so I decided to take em all. let it be 22 or 3 or 4. more money for the same amount of singing and dancing on my part...

—LETTER TO ALLAN ARBUS AND MARICLARE COSTELLO, JANUARY 11, 1971

The class takes place in a vacant room at Westbeth on Thursday evenings, starting January 14 and continuing—with an occasional interruption—for ten sessions. She appears to find the teaching alternately exhilarating and draining. After a few sessions she reports to Crookston: *I am swimmingly. Giving a class. piles of students. 28 at last count. sometimes its fun. last week was a dud.*[487] In general, she is distressed by her inability to remain sufficiently interested in the photographs the students are producing.

An empty movie theater, N.Y.C. 1971.* Her 1971 appointment book suggests this is the Elgin Theater (January 5). The picture was made with the Pentax 6x7 camera she originally borrowed from Hiro. She later taught her 1971 master class at Westbeth so she could afford to purchase one of her own.

I've been jittery. waking at 4 AM which is damned annoying talking to myself endlessly (because of the class, I all of a sudden find I hardly stop talking…exhausting.) The third class was pretty good but its like a performance, and with no script. I all but sing and dance…29 students at last count. The main trouble is I don't really know, understand, care about each ones work enough. And I work too hard at it. after each class I think, whew…but that's a hard act to follow.

—Letter to Allan Arbus and Mariclare Costello, circa late January 1971

Although she has been unenthusiastic about the photographs she made the previous September for *The London Sunday Times Magazine* on "The Affluent Ghetto," she likes them better when published than she had anticipated. She acknowledges as much in a letter to Crookston: *Several people called about the pictures. It did look rather endearing, specially the schoolteacher on the bed in the bikini, What do you do about sending copies to them. I think both Ann* [Leslie, author of the accompanying article] *and I rather promised they wd see themselves become famous.*[488] The same letter refers in glowing terms to her new Pentax camera, even though she doesn't have it yet:

Its coming from Japan. Borrowed one from Hiro for several weeks and I adore it. It will change things. I am awkward with it at first. But its very thrilling. Nobody understands but me what a difference it might make. It looks hilarious like an Enormous Alice in Wonderland 35mm, a little fake as if a bird might pop out instead of a picture.

—Letter to Peter Crookston, January 25, 1971

The job that has been occupying most of her attention for more than a month is an assignment for Time-Life Books, *which doesn't pay all that much, only $500,* she tells Allan and Mariclare, *but…its more than worth it.*[489] This is the way she describes it to Crookston:

I've been working on an assignment which has opened a lot of doors I wanted open and has got me going at a great old pace. (a little like your Family assignment.) Its dumber…Its about LOVE and its for Time-Life

bks so nearly nobody says no. I have found some 60 yr old twins who have always lived together and dress alike, a lady in NJ with a pet monkey who wears a snow suit and a bonnet, an incredible heart-stopping handicapped couple. He is retarded and terribly tall and thin and she is radiant, maybe three and a half feet tall with curly red hair like Maureen O'Hara (and tiny limbs and crutches). I saw them dancing at a dance for handicapped people. Never saw anything like that. I danced with a 60 yr old man who was very shy and spoke like a 9 yr old. He sells good humors in the summer.[490] There were people dancing who could only move their arms. There is also a lady with a houseful of 150 cats I think…havent seen her yet but I will soon…Every day nearly there is a fresh delight.

—Letter to Peter Crookston, January 25, 1971

I will be working on things I have found in the course of it long after it is forgotten,[491] she adds in a letter to Allan and Mariclare after recounting the following momentarily appalling discovery which nonetheless appears to have left her undaunted.

I was at a gallery opning and met a photog I know who said in the usual way, what areyouworkinon? I was vague in my usual way and he said eagerly, "I've got this assignmt from TimeLife Bks, a stupid assgnmt, but its gotten me going again, to photograph LOVE"…(I turned white)…" and I've been photographing blind couples and deaf ones and all the most terrific things." I was so mad at this tricky game [on the part of Time-Life Books]. But oh well…I'm off to do a blind couple in Wantagh [p. 286].

—Letter to Allan Arbus and Mariclare Costello, circa late January 1971

The *LOVE* assignment is not her sole preoccupation. In addition to a number of earlier projects she continues to pursue, including the Untitled series, new prospects are on the horizon. Among those she mentions to Crookston is this:

I met a man who is one of the leading figures of the local sado-masochistic community.[492] He has one arm only (lost in an auto accident not masochistically he assured me) although he said most people suspect otherwise and it lends him a certain glamour. It is also, he explained a potent phallic symbol (the stump that is). He is terribly articulate and described his year in jail marvelously, and is going to inquire of his friends about my photographing one of his parties. So, so far it is a good winter. and you?

—Letter to Peter Crookston, January 25, 1971

On January 26, a Walker Evans retrospective exhibition opens at The Museum of Modern Art, followed by a dinner in his honor. Earlier in the week Diane has a meeting with Davis Pratt, curator of photography at Harvard University's Fogg Art Museum, to select a group of her prints for inclusion in his upcoming spring show, *Contemporary Photographs I.* They are both present at the dinner for Evans, although apparently seated at separate tables with little opportunity to speak to one another. A few days later, when Pratt writes to identify the photographs he has chosen, he says: *Marvelous to see you the other night. Your dress was really swing-*

ing![493] To which she replies: *You looked very good, too. At one of the most painful of the dinner moments I looked across the room at you and was cheered.*[494] (Pratt later volunteers, *We were both bored by the endless words of praise for Walker.*[495])

Diane's response to the Evans retrospective—which she returns to see on several occasions—leaves her somewhat baffled, as she attempts to describe both to her class[496] and in a letter to Allan and Mariclare: *First I was totally whammied by it. Like THERE is a photographer, it was so endless and pristine. Then by the third time I saw it I realized how it really bores me. Cant bear most of what he photographs. Cant explain that confusion.*[497] Her admiration for Evans—whom she describes as *a fantastically honest photographer*[498] compared to those whose work moves her much more, like Brandt or Brassaï or Lartigue—is tempered by a kind of indifference to both his subject matter and something about his approach to it, ironically the very quality she admires in him.[499] Evans has produced a portfolio as well.[500] Not surprisingly, this confronts her with further evidence of the gulf between their respective sensibilities.

He has done a box too, and this (I quote from the prospectus) just gave me the willies: 'the prints were made on bla bla bla polycontrast F paper. Glycine developer was used to give desired print color and long (8-10) min developing times so that large groups of prints bla bla. Fresh developer was used for each batch of prints to minimize any variations. to insure minimum carry over of developer in to the first hypo, prints remained for two minutes in the stop bath, which was mixed fresh for each batch etc Three baths were used, the first with hardener, the second two plain. then on and on about the selenium toning and the air drying and godknows what all.' I read it in a cold sweat, with images of those people buying my box and calling me up in a year to ask about the brown spots.

—LETTER TO ALLAN ARBUS AND MARICLARE COSTELLO, JANUARY 31, 1971

She finds her progress stalled, both on the portfolio and in other areas. *I still don't have either the boxes Or the camera Hiro sent to Japan for…All this month I thought I was working so hard and don't have anything hardly to show for it. I can make such lousy pictures.*[501] Even the film problem remains an unresolved dilemma: *Panatomic Is so hideously hard. just makes me sick… isopan is no longer made…The panatomic x doesn't look like it has anywhere near enough details in the blacks.* She has been hoarding Adox, which has been discontinued and is the only film she knows that really suits her needs. At this point she has only two rolls of it left. *I can tell just by the contacts which is adox,* she reports wistfully. *It looks so gentle.*[502] As a kind of comic relief after this litany of woes, she concludes by recounting an incident between her and Dr. Boigon that amounts to a classic tale of psychiatrist and patient noncommunication:

Had a hilarious, ridiculous fight with Boigon. Went yesterday morning. My Saturday appt is annoyingly early (8:30) which means leaving home about 7:40. Ive asked her to change it but she cant yet. well that's OK…When I arrived her door was locked (rare but not totally unprecedented) so I rang and her son opened it. He is a funny fat boy about 10 yrs old and he sat down to talk to me, more than he ever has. It was

great fun…and [then] he went off somewhere. I noted it was 9 and thought in a joke that Boigon might be testing me to see if I would get mad…A few minutes later Boigon appeared in deshabille, a robe, nightgown, no makeup, saying, "Who let you in?" I told her Seth had and she disappeared again…[then] came back into the office and started SCOLDING ME FOR NOT HAVING KNOCKED ON HER DOOR OR ASKED SETH TO MAKE SURE SHE KNEW I WAS HERE, for in short so failing to take care of my own interests, quite as if her understandable oversleeping was a symptom of MY illness. I was so furious. I burst into tears. Couldn't make her understand. SHE NEVER APOLOGIZED, not even a little. and what little time there was was taken up with that stupid controversy in the light of what it showed about ME. Everything is really fine though.

—LETTER TO ALLAN ARBUS AND MARICLARE COSTELLO, JANUARY 31, 1971

And in fact within days of the letter above, several of the nagging issues cited in it have either evaporated or been successfully addressed. A long overdue check for a thousand dollars she has been unable to extract from *Essence* arrives in the mail thanks to Jay Gold, a lawyer and a friend of hers and of Marvin Israel's, who intercedes with the magazine on her

behalf. Her new Pentax camera finally arrives at Hiro's studio from Japan. She receives two summer teaching job offers for one week each, both in New England with room and board and cars available. (*What a racket,* she remarks.[503]) And she finishes *the LOVE thing* [for Time-Life Books,] *which was very good, and has left me lots to follow up with. They are using one of a lady with a baby monkey in her lap all dressed up in a bonnet and shirt and panties. She looks very grave.*[504] Around the same time she mentions the unanticipated prospect of a new, even more ambitious, assignment she had almost inadvertently initiated.

Just got a call from Eng (London Times) I had written complaining about being paid too little and to make the letter sound better suggested a few ideas—one about the LOSS OF POWER. They are all breathless about it. Want to send me to do Kruschev, Eden, de Gaulle, Nkrumah, Truman, Johnson!!! a spread on each. They will arrange it all. I said I'd do it in July so I don't have to leave Amy.

— LETTER TO ALLAN ARBUS, CIRCA FEBRUARY 1971

She is eager to start on the prints she needs to make for the Fogg Museum exhibition in hopes of finishing them before the end of February when she expects to be away for about a week. She writes to Davis Pratt for clarification of one item—identified by him merely as *Vicki (version 1?)* in the list of seven images he sent her[505] —and offers this description of the two transvestite pictures in question:

Which picture of Vicki? One is pretty close up, very rounded, nearly classical, with a torn stocking, her cleavage line showing, something in her face both dire and delicate [p. 291, which turns out to be the one Pratt has chosen]. The other shows more of her room, funny oblique angle, two nails somewhere on the wall, a coffee table with her magazines and comic books on it, she lies there, sort of wanton and childish and terrible. remember? [p. 251]…Let me know soon so I can get to work on it.

— LETTER TO DAVIS PRATT, FEBRUARY 4, 1971

She sends the prints off on February 22: *Here they are. Seven prints. Titles and dates on back of each. value: $150 ea.* Pratt has indicated the Fogg Museum would like to buy them for its collection should funds become available, and in that event she tells him she intends to reprint three of the images. *The other four are good, archival prints. Just made 'em specially for you.*[506]

Her anticipated absence at the end of February entails a trip to Germany with Marvin Israel, which she has been looking forward to since January with mixed feelings. He is having a show of his paintings at Brusberg Gallery in Hannover and has asked her to come with him. *So I got a tiny assignment.(Schmeling.)gosh,* she says in a letter to Allan and Mariclare.[507] The approaching date of departure does nothing to alleviate her ambivalence about going. *Nearly have cold feet,* she writes.[508] And then: *Well it looks like we are going. wednesday evening* [meaning the 24th, although they do not actually leave until the 27th] *to Germany. Gulp. feel all jittery.* The Schmeling assignment has fallen through at this point and for a while she considers not even bringing a camera, *but yesterday I felt suddenly that maybe I wanted to do at least one little thing, so I called around and I think Günter Grass for the Bzah is it.*[509]

WOMAN WITH HER BABY MONKEY, N.J. 1971. THIS PHOTOGRAPH, PUBLISHED IN TIME-LIFE BOOKS' PHOTOGRAPHY SERIES, WAS ONE OF MANY MADE BY DIANE IN RESPONSE TO THE ASSIGNMENT, "LOVE." THE CAPTION SHE WROTE FOR THE PICTURE READS AS FOLLOWS: *THIS IS MRS. GLADYS ("MITZI") ULRICH…WITH SAM, THE BABY, A STUMP-TAILED MACAQUE MONKEY…THE ORIGINAL SAM HUNG HIMSELF BY ACCIDENT. IT WAS HARD FOR HER TO TELL ABOUT IT…"IT'S GOD'S WILL. IF YOU'RE DESERVING, YOU'LL FIND WHAT YOU'VE LOST. I'VE HAD A WONDERFUL LIFE AND A LOT OF LOVE. I CAN'T SAY I'VE MISSED OUT ON LOVE."*

As it turns out, a sitting with Günter Grass doesn't take place either. Instead, while she and Israel are in Berlin, she is assigned to do a portrait of Bertolt Brecht's widow, Helene Weigel, director of the Berlin Ensemble, for the magazine. Following their return home on March 8 Israel sends her a handmade postcard of one of the works from his exhibition with this message: *Dear Diane— It sure sounds like you had a terrific time in Germany. Boy, are you lucky. It is difficult not to be extremely envious of you. As ever, Marvin.*[510] The Westbeth class resumes on March 8 as well and continues through March 25. *The class is pretty good, exhausting. will give them a party at the end,* she writes in a letter to Allan and Mariclare. *I'll be glad.*[511]

Immediately before her departure for Germany she had dutifully applied for a grant from the Ingram Merrill Foundation (*a little grant. only one I know of at the moment*[512]) and requested recommendations from a few people, including Henry Geldzahler and John Szarkowski. In a note to the latter, she says: *I would rather have you speak for me than anyone. If that's okay and if you know me well enough to just write…The description of the project is enclosed. There is lots to do and I really want to do it.*[513]

Szarkowski's ensuing letter of recommendation reads as follows: *Dear Sir, Mrs. Arbus has asked me to send a reference for her application for an Ingram Merrill Fellowship. I have known Diane Arbus professionally for ten years and I consider her a photographer of exceptional talent and achievement…She is in addition a person with a very high sense of responsibility, and I am confident that she would complete her project in a way that would be creditable to herself and the Foundation. I recommend her without reservation for the Fellowship.*[514]

DIANE'S SLEEPING ALCOVE ON THE TOP FLOOR OF THE WESTBETH APARTMENT WITH
THE BLACKBOARD ON WHICH SHE KEPT LISTS OF ONGOING PROJECTS, A COKE CRATE
FOR PAPERS, AND A PHOTOGRAPHER TROPHY DOON GAVE HER ONE CHRISTMAS. THE
BEDSPREAD IS SOMETHING DIANE MADE HERSELF OUT OF SCRAPS OF FUR. SHE
DESCRIBED THE ORIGINAL BEDSPREAD, A 1970 CHRISTMAS PRESENT FOR DOON, IN A
LETTER TO ALLAN AND MARICLARE: *IT IS A MULTIFOLD PATCHWORK OF EVERY SORT OF
FUR, REPLETE WITH LITTLE FOX'S HEADS NESTLED AMONG PERSIAN LAMB AND OTTER, BAD-
GER OPOSSUM MINK FITCH ERMINE SEAL CARACUL WOLF CIVET CAT OCELOT RACCOON,
SWIRLING, CURLING TWINING ALTOGETHER. DOONS EVEN HAS A POCKET IN IT. I HAVE NEVER
DONE ANYTHING QUITE SO WELL.*

HELENE WEIGEL, BERTOLT BRECHT'S WIDOW AND DIRECTOR OF THE BERLIN ENSEMBLE,
WHOM DIANE PHOTOGRAPHED IN GERMANY FOR *HARPER'S BAZAAR* DURING HER TRIP
THERE WITH MARVIN ISRAEL IN FEBRUARY 1971. ORIGINALLY SHE HAD BEEN ASSIGNED
TO DO A PORTRAIT OF GÜNTER GRASS FOR THE MAGAZINE BUT THIS APPARENTLY FELL
THROUGH. THE PHOTOGRAPH OF WEIGEL WAS NOT PUBLISHED AND THE MAGAZINE INI-
TIALLY REFUSED TO PAY THE $165 IN EXPENSES FOR IT, UNTIL MARVIN ISRAEL INTER-
VENED WITH ART DIRECTOR RUTH ANSEL ON DIANE'S BEHALF.

Geldzahler's recommendation is brief and to the point: *To me Diane
Arbus' photographs are as sensitively original and heartbreaking as anything
in the field. I highly recommend her to your attention. Her work speaks for
itself. I know she needs the assistance.*[515]

What she writes about her intended Ingram Merrill project—entitled
"The Quiet Minorities"[516]—seems to have been inspired at least in part
by three quotations that appear on a single typewritten sheet of paper in
one of her binders next to the draft project statement. They consist of
these lines from Gerard Manley Hopkins' poem "Pied Beauty": *All
things counter, original, spare, strange; Whatever is fickle, freckled (who
knows how?)*; an unattributed statement: *Only minorities effect change*; and
a paragraph from Norman Mailer that begins: *I refuse resolutely to lump
them all together. I think that's the beginning of totalitarianism. The essence of
totalitarianism is that all people are alike.*[517] Her project description itself
reads as follows:

The sign of a minority is The Difference. Those of birth, accident,
choice, belief, predilection, inertia. (Some are irrevocable: people are
fat, freckled, handicapped, ethnic, of a certain age, class, attitude, pro-
fession, enthusiasm.) Every Difference is a Likeness too. There are asso-
ciations, groups, clubs, alliances, milieus for every one of them. And
each milieu is a small world, a subculture with a slightly other set of
rules for the game. Not to ignore them, not to lump them all together, but to watch them, to take notice, to pay attention…towards a
book of photographs.

—"THE QUIET MINORITIES," INGRAM MERRILL FOUNDATION PROJECT DESCRIPTION, 1971

She is not awarded the grant. Since around 1969, she has been in contact with Lee Witkin of the Witkin Gallery, one of the first successful
photography galleries, and on occasion he has purchased prints from her
for clients or for the gallery. From time to time she has also sold prints
through other dealers as well and through The Museum of Modern Art's
Lending Service. For the most part, however, sales of her prints have
been dependent upon her direct contact with museum curators, friends,
or private collectors.[518] Now that the first dozen sets of the portfolio are
nearing completion and the problem with the manufacture of the boxes
appears to be solved, she is looking for ways to promote it in addition to
the flyer she is sending out.

The box looks very good I guess, it'll be in Art forum in May and New
York will do two pps I think. Liberman [editor of *Vogue,* whom she and
Allan used to work for years ago] nearly did something on it but I
played my cards wrong. no matter. Fun to see him. He just looks like
Dracula has been at him. a little grayer, not really old, just brittle. And
he is just the same. Same unbelievable enthusiasm and gallantry. Could
I work for Vogue? Was I under contract to the Bazaar? It was really fun.
because it was just a sentimental journey and I knew I had nothing to
lose and even less to gain.

—LETTER TO ALLAN ARBUS AND MARICLARE COSTELLO, CIRCA LATE APRIL 1971

She concludes with a report of plans and bits of news, delivered in
uncharacteristically short staccato sentences, as if in haste. *I'm going*

up to visit Amy in a week or two, and photograph the yurts[519]...I bought a new strobe. very good. the [Pentax] camera is somewhat difficult. but absorbing. look for Art Forum. Bea is buying a box. They are at Dick's studio. havent seen em. Doon says they look good...Spring is not very pretty here yet. lots of rain and denseness. And finally: one fascinating thing I am beginning to get through my thick head from Boigon is that it doesn't matter what you do...except to yourself. I am always answering to someone who isnt even asking.[520]

The photograph, Boy with a straw hat waiting to march in a pro-war parade, N.Y.C. 1967 (p. 87), appears on the cover of *Artforum*'s May 1971 issue. In addition, five of the remaining nine images from the portfolio are reproduced, one per page, in the magazine under the title "Five Photographs by Diane Arbus,"[521] accompanied by a brief text she writes for the occasion.

Once I dreamed I was on a gorgeous ocean liner, all pale, gilded, cupid-encrusted, rococo as a wedding cake. There was smoke in the air, people were drinking and gambling. I knew the ship was on fire and we were sinking, slowly. They knew it too, but they were very gay, dancing and singing and kissing, a little delirious. There was no hope. I was terribly elated. I could photograph anything I wanted to.

Nothing is ever the same as they said it was. It's what I've never seen before that I recognize.

There is an old joke about a man who goes into a bar and he sees that the bartender has a banana in his ear so he says, *Hey, you have a banana in your ear;* and the bartender says, *Speak louder please, I can't hear you because I've got a banana in my ear.*[522]

Nothing is ever alike. The best thing is the difference. I get to keep what nobody needs.

A photograph is a secret about a secret. The more it tells you the less you know.

—"Five Photographs by Diane Arbus," *Artforum*, May 1971

The opening paragraph of this text is the retelling of a dream she had in 1959 that is first recorded in one of her notebooks (No. 1) (p. 17). This recent version is apparently recounted from memory since, although the essential features remain intact, several significant details have been altered or omitted: the original *ornate white gorgeous hotel* has become a sinking ship, the obstacles to photographing have vanished. *Artforum* had initially agreed to run an announcement about the sale of the portfolio along with the piece but, having inadvertently failed to do so, the magazine agrees to publish a separate announcement for it in the June issue.

In answer to a very enthusiastic response from Allan about the *Artforum* piece she writes: *what a good note (about artforum) yesterday on the heels of all sorts of small and nasty things...Im really glad you liked the writing. I sweated and Doon was a help and suddenly it fell into place.* About the future promotional prospects for the portfolio she adds: *It'll be in NY mag next week reduced from two pps to one with a terribly dumb interview (a girl called and said 'I don't know the first thing about you I must confess; tell me what you've done. 'uggh.)*[523]

COPY OF A DIPTYCH BY MARVIN ISRAEL FROM HIS *INTERVIEW* SERIES THAT HE MADE INTO A POSTCARD TO DIANE. WELCOMING HER HOME FROM THEIR TRIP TO GERMANY: *DEAR DIANE...I HEARD YOU WERE ABROAD...I HOPE TO SEE YOU SOON SINCERELY MARVIN.*

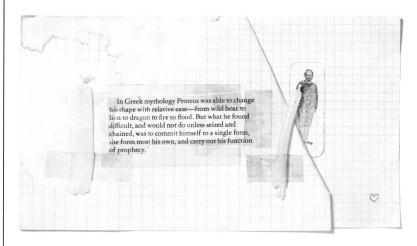

TWO PAGES FROM AN EIGHT-PAGE BIRTHDAY CARD TO DIANE FROM MARVIN ISRAEL, MARCH 14, 1971. THE MESSAGE PASTED BETWEEN THE TWO SQUASHED CANDLES READS: *IN GREEK MYTHOLOGY PROTEUS WAS ABLE TO CHANGE HIS SHAPE WITH RELATIVE EASE—FROM WILD BOAR TO LION TO DRAGON TO FIRE TO FLOOD. BUT WHAT HE FOUND DIFFICULT, AND WOULD NOT DO UNLESS SEIZED AND CHAINED, WAS TO COMMIT HIMSELF TO A SINGLE FORM, THE FORM MOST HIS OWN, AND CARRY OUT HIS FUNCTION OF PROPHECY.* THE FIGURE ON THE SECOND PAGE IS A STAMP ISRAEL MADE OF HIMSELF FROM ONE OF DIANE'S 1966 PHOTOGRAPHS.

(LEFT) DIANE WAS HOPING TO ACQUIRE A PRINT OF THIS JACQUES-HENRI LARTIGUE PHOTOGRAPH WHICH APPEARED IN HIS BOOK *DIARY OF A CENTURY*, EDITED BY RICHARD AVEDON, DESIGNED BY BEA FEITLER, AND PUBLISHED BY VIKING IN 1970. *(RIGHT)* RICHARD AVEDON'S 1964 PORTRAIT OF DWIGHT DAVID EISENHOWER, ONE OF THE PICTURES IN THE ROOM AT MINNEAPOLIS OF *HUGE HEADS, LIKE PRESENCES*. A FRAMED PRINT OF IT, GIVEN TO HER BY AVEDON, HUNG IN HER APARTMENT AT WESTBETH.

DIANE PURCHASED FROM THE MUSEUM OF THE CITY OF NEW YORK A PRINT OF THIS PHOTOGRAPH BY JACOB A. RIIS ENTITLED *SWEEPING BACK THE OCEAN*, WHICH HUNG IN HER WESTBETH APARTMENT.

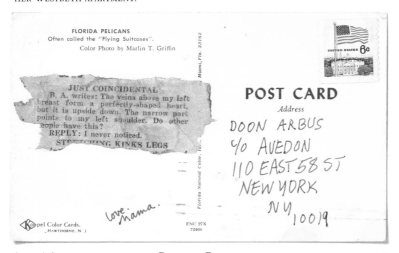

(*ABOVE*) A 1971 POSTCARD FROM DIANE TO DOON WITH A CLIPPING THAT READS: *THE VEINS ABOVE MY LEFT BREAST FORM A PERFECTLY SHAPED HEART BUT IT IS UPSIDE DOWN...DO OTHER PEOPLE HAVE THIS? REPLY: I NEVER NOTICED.* (*BELOW*) DIANE SEATED IN FRONT OF HER COLLAGE WALL IN 1971. PHOTOGRAPH BY EVA RUBINSTEIN.

The *small and nasty things* she enumerates include the fact that *Harper's Bazaar* is refusing to pay her expenses in Germany for the Helene Weigel photograph she was assigned to do *meaning that for a $200 photo I was to have spent 165+film etc. I was so mad and in tears and they were all polite...Ruth disavowing all knowledge and responsibility, clucking sympathetically about how rotten they are but refusing any real help and at one moment having the gall to say Geri* [Trotta, editor] *had given me the assignment as a favor!* This last allegation which Diane confides to Marvin Israel so outrages him that he promptly intercedes with Ruth Ansel about the matter.[524] The paucity of the sum involved only seems to make the whole thing worse. *I have a hunch I'll get the money. Ill go to Nancy White* [editor in chief] *if necessary, there is absolutely nothing to lose. I don't even ever work for them.* She also mentions, with a certain equanimity, doing *a lousy page for a terrible new magazine called NEWWOMAN, of Germaine Greer* [author of *The Female Eunuch* (London: MacGibbon and Kee, 1970)] *who was fun and is terrific looking but I managed to make otherwise.*[525]

Still, it isn't all bad, not by any means. The same letter contains this: *Spoke to Amy who is superb with a million plans for the summer, none of them fixed, but with a totally instructive sense of no worry and rich possibilities...She is so freewheeling but practical and she has developed so many means of being self determining and has access to this vast network of her generation, so that she literally doesn't feel alone in an alien world the way we always have.*[526] As she once said of Amy with a mixture of admiration and relief: *she seems so capable and so clear that it is Her responsibility and mine is mine.*[527]

There is also, to her apparent delight, interest in the portfolio from an unexpected, unsolicited source. *I had a call from some art dealer to say that jasper johns wanted a box. how terrific. first one who doesn't know me.* She adds this note in the margin: *four are sold, 2½ pd for. the owners are out of who's who. my confidence is absurdly on a roller coaster.* And trails off at the end of the letter with a summary, not unlike some observations she has made before: *There is so much to learn. mainly it is never as good as you hope or as bad as you dread.*[528]

The disposition of the completed portfolios, each with its own individually handwritten cover and title sheets accompanying the ten annotated, signed prints appears to be as follows: The first in the edition of fifty is purchased by Richard Avedon as a present for his friend Mike Nichols. The second—on which the number *ten* in the title *A box of ten photographs* is crossed out and replaced by *eleven** with a note that says **especially for RA*—is also purchased by Avedon and includes an additional print she made for him, Masked woman in a wheelchair (p. 91). The portfolio purchased by Bea Feitler is numbered 5/50 and also includes an additional print, Woman with her baby monkey (p. 217). The portfolio purchased by Jasper Johns is numbered 6/50. Each of these four portfolios, including the one for Johns is delivered by her to the purchaser in person. Evidence suggests that these are the only editions of the portfolio distributed during her lifetime.[529]

Another letter to Allan, written around the same time as the previous one quoted above, makes it clear how pervasive and haunting the issue

TWO PHOTOGRAPHS MADE WITH THE PENTAX 6X7 CAMERA: YOUNG MAN IN A TRENCH COAT, N.Y.C. 1971, AND BLONDE GIRL WITH A HOT DOG IN THE PARK, N.Y.C. 1971.

of money continues to be for her, even as she readily acknowledges that her assessment of her financial situation may be somewhat inaccurate.

Sudden money panic and as you say I always do this…will probably have to borrow and get work. The London Times job [on loss of power] looks dubious. They don't seem to have been able to round up enough heavyweights…I owe 1800 not counting normal next month bills and taxes…This is the point at which I usually get sick but I wont this time… [in a handwritten note at the bottom of the page she adds] I overreact both ways. A month ago I thought I was on easy street and today I think I am one of the neediest cases. love from the middle of the road, d

—LETTER TO ALLAN ARBUS, CIRCA MID-MAY 1971[530]

On May 21 Davis Pratt returns the eight prints[531] she had loaned to the Fogg Museum for the *Contemporary Photographs I* exhibition, noting that one of them, Boy in a straw hat waiting to march in a pro-war parade—which he refers to as *Bomb Hanoi*—was damaged. He confirms that a claim for $150 will be paid and goes on to say: *We still do not have news of the grant we have applied for so we cannot buy these prints…thanks for your brochure about your portfolio. I still hope we may buy individual prints that we particularly want.*[532]

Meanwhile, the unfulfilled *London Times* assignment on loss of power is soon replaced by another equally unlikely one that takes her to Washington, D.C., in the middle of June. The magazine sends her to cover the White House wedding of President Richard Nixon's younger daughter, Tricia—whom she describes as *very pretty really but something*

like a paper doll[533]—to fiancé, Edward Cox. Immediately following her return home, Diane sends Peter Crookston this detailed account of her experience at the event:

It is funnier in retrospect. I don't know what you and Michael [Rand, *London Sunday Times Magazine* editor] pictured but what flitted through my head was quite different from what was. I had thought to myself that mobility was the key. That I was to infiltrate at the Arrival, The Departure, The Descent into The Rose Garden. I had thought that Billy Graham might whisper something to J. Edgar Hoover and there I'd be, amid all the clothes rustling and the eyelashes flitting. Miss Wilson told me to come down friday so I weasled out of a picture of (mafia) Joe Columbo for Harpers which didn't matter to me. As soon as I arrived and Miss W showed me the Maps and Lists, like battle plans, I began to realize how remote it was going to be. There were lists of positions, all taken by newsmen and wire services. I acted irate, but nobody cared. All the positions had been filled on Wednesday…Well then saturday morning after being searched by the FBI which was great fun because you knew you were innocent, there we were in the press tent, rubbery, soggy, humid, like a shower stall the size of an airplane hangar, several hundreds of us, more than the wedding guests, and ladies, minor press attaches, would step to the microphone to explain, while a thousand reporters scribbled notes, that Tricia had risen at 8:02 and breakfasted with the President and Mrs N on orange juice and cereal. What kind of cereal, some enterprising reporter queried. Hot, she said, cream of wheat it turned out to be. And endless reports of what Ron Ziegler said the president

THE 20X24 SHEET OF VELLUM DIANE USED IN ORDER TO PRACTICE THE CONTENT AND STYLE OF HER HANDWRITTEN TITLES FOR THE PORTFOLIO, *A BOX OF TEN PHOTOGRAPHS*.

said as well as explanations of what that meant and why it was funny…Finally (no food all day) it was near arrival time and we were taken to the East Gate in the rain. The real old time newsmen who knew the score were working in teams with lenses the length of my arm and great enormous tripods and a kind of general unfriendliness which only meant that if they had to slit your throat later they didn't want to pal around too much in advance. They had ponchos and sandwiches and entrenched themselves in pre-marked positions, like assassins. We were roped in and every time you wandered off so much as a foot, the FBI or whoever they were pushed you back. So every time you clicked your shutter you heard a hundred or so other clicks and sometimes when you didn't. Meanwhile the reporters and the photographers were bickering because every time a guest ran the gauntlet, the society reporters would call them by name and ask what their dress was made of so they would turn their heads away from the photographers at the crucial moment. There was only one crucial moment because you couldn't move out of this position you'd wangled, even though someone's elbow and someone else's umbrella were poking at you, because if you moved your space would get swallowed up and the radio people were droning on about how lovely it was and what a shame about the rain…Then back to the Tent for more reports about Billy Grahams witticism about trying to stop the rain. What felt best was the end, THE DEPARTURE, I was up on a kind of column, where only a few photographers were, and there were the front steps of the White House. Inside you could see guests and lights and something going on and suddenly they piled out, guests like movie extras, and a man with a trumpet and maybe bits more of a band and fifty of the photographers straining against the ropes and Secret Service and the Pres and the Mrs and the Cox family, incredibly hometown looking and cozy…illuminated sort of unearthly by the TV lights. (Why Did Tricia Leave In Her Wedding Gown?) anyway she did and each one kissed all the others, like a midwestern small town celebration scene in the movies, endearing, exaggerated with everyone playing their part with enthusiasm. and that black limousine waiting for them.[534]

—LETTER TO PETER CROOKSTON, CIRCA MID-JUNE 1971

She encloses a bill for the expenses and requests an advance for the upcoming Twins Convention assignment which, in her own words, *sounds better and better. There will be Kings and Queens, four of em and Double Twins…(Twins who've married Twins)* [an idea she originally proposed to Crookston in 1968] *so at last we will get that story, and yes I'll do captions, twin lore, twin jokes, whatnot. Looking forward a lot.*[535]

It is not clear when the Twins Convention she is referring to is scheduled to take place, especially since she has recently returned from one held in Grand Rapids, Michigan, on June 4, 5, and 6. She photographed there and spoke with many sets of twins, whose stories appear, somewhat hastily transcribed, in her 1971 Notebook (No. 39). Among these is the first-person account by an unnamed identical twin of a shopping expedition she went on with her twin sister Martha. As

DIANE AT HAMPSHIRE COLLEGE IN AMHERST, MASSACHUSETTS, WHERE SHE TAUGHT FOR A WEEK AT THE END OF JUNE 1971. PHOTOGRAPH BY W. T. GRAHAM.

they were trying things on, *Martha wandered away.* Moments later the narrator looked up, thought Martha was there and asked her whether or not she liked the dress but it wasn't Martha she was talking to, *It was me in the mirror.*[536]

Diane spends the last week of June at Hampshire College in Amherst, Massachusetts, on a teaching assignment—one of the two summer teaching jobs she'd been offered and accepted earlier in the year—organized by the program's director, Jerry Liebling.[537] Amy is nearby attending Woolman Hill, a former Quaker Center in Deerfield, which is now functioning as a "free" school, and she comes to Hampshire College briefly for a visit. Some time after her return home, Diane goes to see Lisette Model, who later describes her on this occasion as *so beautiful and so strong coming from the beach. She looked like I've never seen her before in my life. Not one wrinkle. Brown. Young-looking.*[538] All the same, she says she is dreading her next teaching stint and refers to the Hampshire College experience as *horrible.*[539]

She remains in regular contact with many of the people and places she has photographed in the past, including Eddie Carmel, several sets of adult twins, and the homes for the retarded she continues to visit. A letter from one such state facility, dated June 14 and sent by mistake to her former East 10th Street address, thanks her for the camera she arranged to give them as a gift: *Just a note to let you know we received either the repaired camera or a new camera from Willoughby's today and it seems to be operating well. Again, we appreciate your thoughtfulness in donating the cam-*

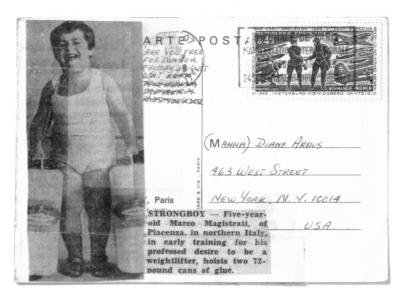

AUTOPSY

Case No. M 71-6414

Approximate Age 48   Approximate Weight 100 lbs.

Height 5'6½"

Identified by   HAROLD RUSSEK   Residence 575 PARK AVE., MAN.

Stenographer   BOC   Residence BELT 2588

I hereby certify that I   DR. YONG-MYUN RHO   have performed an autopsy on

the body of DIANE ARBUS   at 520 FIRST AVE., N.Y.C.   on the

29TH   day of JULY   1971   hours after the death,

and said autopsy revealed

Died at 463 West St.

EXTERNAL EXAMINATION

The body is that of a white adult female appearing the stated age
of 48 years, well-developed, well-nourished, measuring 5'6½" in
length and weighing 100 lbs. Rigidity is absent. Dark greenish
post-mortem discoloration is present over the face, the left side
of trunk and anterior aspects of lower legs.

The epidermis of the skin of the face has been sloughed off, due
to decomposition. Hair can be pulled out readily.

Networks of vascular markings can be visualized on these greenish
discoloration areas. The anterior aspects of the right and left
wrists have been cut transversely. There are three such cuts on
the left side and two cuts on the right side. These cuts are deep
and have severed many tendons of the muscular insertion. The
radial arteries and veins on both sides, however, are intact.
The hands are covered by a large amount of dried blood and the
anterior aspects of the lower legs, below the knees, are also
covered by a large amount of dried blood. There is no other evidence of external violence to the body surface.

HEAD & NECK

The head is symmetrical and is covered by abundant dark brown long
hair. The conjunctivi are congested; the cornea cloudy. Pupils
are round. Irides are brown. Sclerae are decomposed. The external ears and nose are not remarkable. Natural teeth are present.
The neck is symmetrical.

CHEST AND ABDOMEN WALLS

Not remarkable.

GENITALIA

The external genitalia show no evidence of external violence.

EXTREMITIES

APART from the cuts on both wrists, the extremities are not remarkable.

Back is natural.

FIRST PAGE OF A COPY OF THE AUTOPSY FOR CASE NO. M-71-6414 PERFORMED BY DR.
YONG-MYUN RHO ON THE BODY OF DIANE ARBUS, JULY 29, 1971.

THIS CARD TO DIANE ARBUS FROM DOON ARBUS WAS MAILED IN PARIS AND IS POST-
MARKED JULY 26, 1971. THE MESSAGE WRITTEN IN PEN INQUIRES: *ARE YOU FREE FOR
DINNER FRIDAY AUGUST 6TH?* THE CLIPPING IS OF A FIVE-YEAR-OLD BOY PRACTICING HIS
WEIGHTLIFTING SKILLS BY HOISTING TWO 72-POUND CANS OF GLUE.

*era and the Recreation Division will be able to take snapshots which they were
not able to do before your donation.* [540]

An announcement and reservation form for the Federation of the
Handicapped annual picnic is stapled to the July 10 page of her
appointment book. *Dear Member, Summer is just around the corner and it
won't be long before everyone's mind will be turning to thoughts of the Great
Outdoors, picnics and picnicking. With this thought in our minds, we cordially invite you to attend the 1971 Annual Picnic sponsored by the
Entertainment Committee of the Federation of the Handicapped.* She is
among those in attendance and she brings her camera along and takes
pictures at the event. [541]

For some of June and the first half of July, Carlotta is in town on one of
her regular trips back to New York and they see each other on several occasions during this period. On the evening of July 16, just before Carlotta's
scheduled departure, Diane arrives on her bicycle for a visit and the two of
them spend a long time talking in much the same way and about many of
the same subjects as they have so often in the past. [542] This is the way Diane
once described to Carlotta the unpredictable fluctuations in her state of
mind between exhilaration and gloom.

I go up and down a lot. Maybe Ive always been like that. Partly what
happens though is I get filled with energy and joy and I begin lots of
things or think about what I want to do and get all breathless with
excitement and then quite suddenly either through tiredness or a disappointment or something more mysterious the energy vanishes, leaving
me harassed, swamped, distraught, frightened by the very things I
thought I was so eager for! I'm sure this is quite classic.

—LETTER TO CARLOTTA MARSHALL, CIRCA NOVEMBER 1968

Or, as she wrote on another occasion, *the worst is I am literally <u>scared</u> of
getting depressed…And it is so goddamn chemical, Im convinced. Energy, some
special kind of energy, just leaks out and I am left lacking the confidence even
to cross the street.* [543]

Carlotta Marshall leaves on July 17 to return to Holland. Amy Arbus is
in summer school at Woolman Hill in Deerfield, Massachusetts. Doon
Arbus is in Paris completing the text of an upcoming book, *Alice in
Wonderland: The Forming of a Company and the Making of a Play.* Marvin
Israel and his wife, Margie, are spending a long weekend at Richard
Avedon's house on Fire Island. Allan Arbus is in Santa Fe filming the
Robert Downey movie *Greaser's Palace,* in which he plays a zoot-suited
aspiring singer-dancer-actor-Christ-figure in the Old West. Diane
Arbus is home.

I used to think consciousness itself was a virtue, so I tried to keep it
all in my head at the same time, past, future etc. tried even to feel
the bad when I felt good and vice versa as if any unawareness was a
marie-antoinette sort of sin. its like throwing ballast overboard to
only do what there is to do NOW. a kind of confidence that later will
bring its own now…It makes Sunday more Sunday and even Monday
is better…

—LETTER TO ALLAN ARBUS AND MARICLARE COSTELLO, JANUARY 11, 1971

Her suicide seems neither inevitable nor spontaneous, neither perplexing nor intelligible. On the evening of July 28, having been unable to reach her by phone for two days, Marvin Israel lets himself into the apartment where, according to the medical investigator's subsequent report, he *found her dead...crunched up in bath tub, on left side...wearing red shirt, blue denim shorts, no socks.* Israel gets in touch with three friends, Larry Shainberg, Jay Gold, and Richard Avedon. They each come to help in whatever way they can. The police are notified. The medical investigator arrives on the scene at 9:45 P.M., about two and a half hours after official notification, and leaves at 10:15 P.M. The body is removed to the mortuary of the Office of the Chief Medical Examiner of the City of New York. Three items are listed in the investigator's report as having been submitted separately for study: *Razor blade, "Last Supper" note, medications.*

The item referred to as *"Last Supper" note* is actually an entry on the July 26 page of her 1971 appointment book, but this page (along with those of July 27 and July 28) have since been meticulously excised from the appointment book, presumably by the medical investigator or by someone else in authority. The appointment book appears perfectly intact, but the pages in question are no longer in it and have never been recovered.

Diane's uncle, Harold Russek, Gertrude Nemerov's younger brother, assumes the responsibility of making the official identification of the body at the Medical Examiner's Office and states that his niece had *a history of depression.* As required by law under the circumstances, an autopsy is performed. The medical examiner is Dr. Yong-Myun Rho and the complete report of his findings, dated July 29, 1971, reads as follows:

EXTERNAL EXAMINATION
The body is that of a white adult female appearing the stated age of 48 years, well-developed, well-nourished, measuring 5'6 1/2" in length and weighing 100 lbs. Rigidity is absent. Dark greenish post-mortem discoloration is present over the face, the left side of trunk and anterior aspects of the lower legs. The epidermis of the skin of the face has been sloughed off, due to decomposition. Hair can be pulled out readily.

Networks of vascular markings can be visualized on these greenish discoloration areas. The anterior aspects of the right and left wrists have been cut transversely. There are three such cuts on the left side and two cuts on the right side. These cuts are deep and have severed many tendons of the muscular insertion. The radial arteries and veins on both sides, however, are intact. The hands are covered by a large amount of dried blood and the anterior aspects of the lower legs, below the knees, are also covered by a large amount of dried blood. There is no other evidence of external violence to the body surface.

HEAD & NECK: The head is symmetrical and is covered by abundant dark brown long hair. The conjunctivi are congested; the cornea are cloudy. Pupils are round. Irides are brown. Sclerae are decomposed. The external ears and nose are not remarkable. Natural teeth are present. The neck is symmetrical.

CHEST AND ABDOMEN WALLS: Not remarkable.

GENITALIA: The external genitalia show no evidence of external violence.

EXTREMITIES: APART from the cuts on both wrists, the extremities are not remarkable. Back is natural.

INTERNAL EXAMINATION
PRIMARY INCISION: The body is opened by a Y-shaped incision.

BODY CAVITIES: A small amount of blood-stained liquid is present in both pleural cavities and the peritoneal cavity. This is presumably due to post-mortem decomposition. There are no adhesions in the body cavities.

NECK ORGANS: There is no evidence of trauma or obstruction to the neck organs.

CARDIOVASCULAR SYSTEM: The heart lies within the sac and weighs 320 grams. The coronary arteries are widely patent. The mural endocardium, valves, and myocardium are not remarkable. The aorta and its major branches are not remarkable.

RESPIRATORY TRACT: The trachea and the large bronchi contain a moderate amount of reddish mucus. The lungs are not remarkable and they together weigh 600 grams. The pulmonary vessels are patent.

LIVER: The liver weighs 1400 grams. It is congested.

SPLEEN: Weighs 110 grams. Not remarkable.

URINARY TRACT: Each kidney weighs 125 grams. They are not remarkable. Urinary bladder is empty. The bladder wall is not remarkable.

GENITALIA: The vagina is not remarkable. The cervix is not remarkable. The uterine cavity contains a whitish plastic twisted contraceptive device. The mucosal surface of the uterus is not remarkable. The tubes and ovaries are not remarkable.

ADRENALS: Not remarkable.

PANCREAS: Not remarkable.

GASTROINTESTINAL TRACT: The esophagus is patent. The stomach contains approximately 100 cc. of greenish-brown liquid material. No unusual material can be detected, in the stomach. The gastric wall is not remarkable. Small intestine, appendix and large intestine are not remarkable.

HEAD: The scalp is incised by an intermastoid incision. A segment of calvarium is removed and dura incised. There is no evidence of trauma. The brain weighs 1380 grams. The leptomeninges are slightly congested. On serial section the brain shows nothing remarkable. The pituitary is not remarkable.

OSSEOUS SYSTEM: Not remarkable.

ANATOMICAL DIAGNOSES:
1. Post-mortem decomposition of body.

2. Deep scars on anterior aspects of both wrists.

3. External hemorrhage.

4. Congestion of organs.

5. Diary suggestive of suicidal intent, taken on July 26th, noted.

6. History of depresssion, given by deceased's uncle.

LABORATORY FINDINGS: Brain: Amobarbital present, Secobarbitol: present; Liver: Barbiturates present 3.45 mg %

Final cause of death (9/14/71)
Incised wounds of wrists with external hemorrhage. Acute barbiturate poisoning. Suicidal.

They are the proof that something was there and no longer is.

Like a stain. And the stillness of them is boggling.

You can turn away but when you come back they'll still be there looking at you.

—FROM A LETTER TO DAVIS PRATT, FOGG MUSEUM, CAMBRIDGE, MARCH 15, 1971,

IN RESPONSE TO REQUEST FOR A BRIEF STATEMENT ABOUT PHOTOGRAPHS

Inadvertent double exposure of a self-portrait
and images from Times Square, N.Y.C. 1957

KODAK TRI X FILM

227

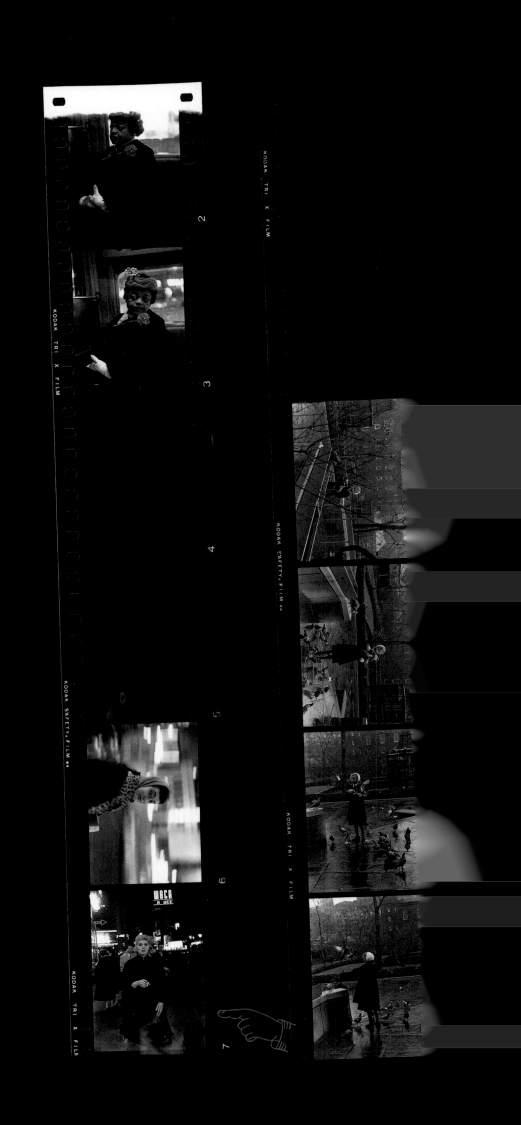

1957 Contact Sheet #376:
inadvertent double exposures,
frame 7 (bottom left) and frame 8
(top, fourth strip from left),
self-portrait and Times Square.
The pointing finger stamp was
given to Diane by Marvin Israel
and used in this book to indicate
the frames in question.

Woman carrying a child in Central Park, N.Y.C. 1956

Tattooed man at a carnival, Md. 1970

Valentino look-alike at an audition, N.Y.C. 1963

The Man Who Swallows Razor Blades, Hagerstown, Md. 1961

Girl sitting on her bed with her shirt off, N.Y.C. 1968

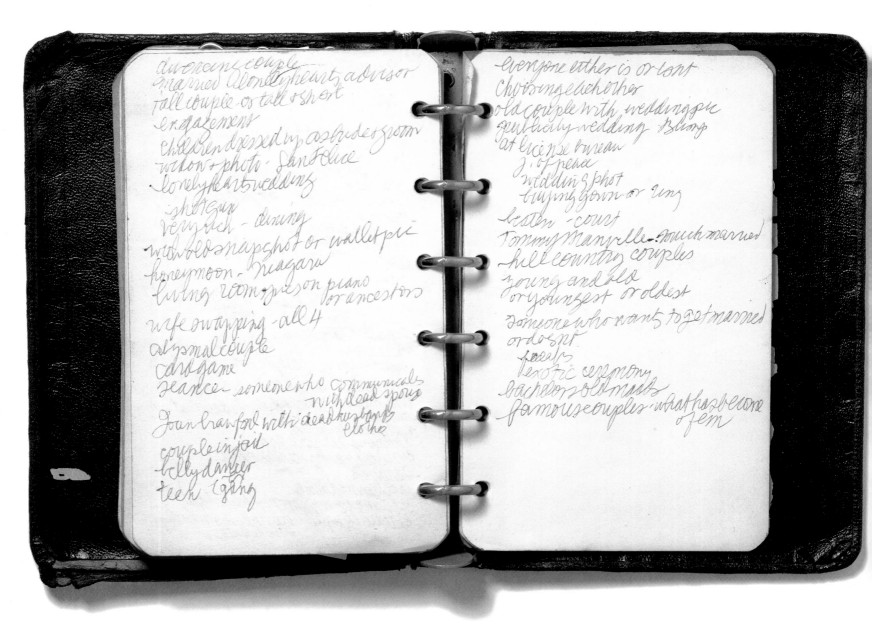

1960 Notebook (No. 3): Two of the six pages of lists following a proposal
for a project On Marriage: *...the sort of why or wherefore of it...*

1965 Contact Sheet #4106: A couple on a couch

Couple arguing, Coney Island, N.Y. 1960

Girl sitting in bed with her boyfriend, N.Y.C. 1966

Four people at a gallery opening, N.Y.C. 1968

An empty room, N.Y.C. 1968

Girl in her circus costume, Md. 1970

243

Woman with eyeliner, N.Y.C. 1964*

Groom kissing his bride, N.Y.C. 1965*

If as it is often said, you can't win,

it is perhaps because when you do you have so much to lose.

The Queen of the Kumquat festival has her season,

Mr. Universe is only as famous as he is anonymous. Miss No-Cal will get fatter

and the Olympic record will be surpassed. The Sweepstakes Winner is everybody's mark,

the Top Box Office attraction becomes less so,

the Freckle King grows up and the champion gets to be the fall guy.

To put it a little gloomily, winning could be called the mark of Abel.

It would be beautiful to photograph the winners of everything from Nobel to booby prize,

clutching trophy, or money or certificate, solemn or smiling or tear stained or bloody,

on the precarious pinnacle of the human landscape.

—1962 NOTEBOOK (NO. 8): TEXT FOR A PROJECT ON WINNERS

The King and Queen of a Senior Citizens' Dance, N.Y.C. 1970

Rocks on wheels,
Disneyland, Cal. 1962

Transvestite on a couch, N.Y.C. 1966

Nothing is ever the same as they said it was.
It's what I've never seen before that I recognize.

—Diane Arbus, "Five Photographs by Diane Arbus,"

Artforum, May 1971

Retired man and his wife at home in a nudist camp one morning, N.J. 1963

Headless woman, N.Y.C. 1961

Masked boy with friends, Coney Island, N.Y. 1956

Veteran with a flag, N.Y.C. 1971*

Topless dancer in her dressing room, San Francisco, Cal. 1968

Elderly couple on a park bench, N.Y.C. 1969

Child selling plastic orchids at night, N.Y.C. 1963

Muscle man in his dressing room with trophy, Brooklyn, N.Y. 1962

The 1938 Debutante of the Year at home, Boston, Mass. 1966

Woman on the street with parcels, N.Y.C. 1956

Untitled (8) 1970–71

What's left after what one isn't is taken away is what one is.

— 1959 NOTEBOOK (NO. 1)

Identical twins, Roselle, N.J. 1967

The handwriting on the label reads:

DIANE ARBUS.
TECHNICAL DATA.

BLUE BINDER OF FORMULAE AND OTHER TECHNICAL INFORMATION COMPILED BY ALLAN FOR DIANE IN 1969, WHICH SHE LABELED AND KEPT IN HER DARKROOM.

IN THE DARKROOM

———

BY NEIL SELKIRK

Diane's darkroom was in the West Village at 29 Charles Street, just off Seventh Avenue South, in the basement of an old apartment building. It was approached by going through an opening in the front wall, down a flight of steps from the sidewalk, and through a tunnel that ran the depth of the building. Emerging into a courtyard, you turned sharp left and there was a battered black door.

If the room was the right-hand page of a book, one entered on the bottom edge, by the page number. The room itself was perhaps twenty feet long and fourteen feet wide. On the right as you entered were shelves filled with two-hundred-and-fifty-sheet, 11x14 Dupont paper boxes. They were mostly red, but some were green. In these boxes, apparently in the order in which they had been shot, were all of Diane's more than seven thousand rolls of film, the negative sleeves stapled to matching contact sheets. In the center of the room was a long table, perhaps twenty-four inches wide, at the far end of which sat a very dilapidated flatbed print dryer. Along the left wall there was first a table on which stood a late 1940s Omega "D" enlarger, and then a resin-coated wooden sink long enough to hold four or five 16x20 developing trays. Another sink, lower, shorter, and of stainless steel, sat across the end wall. On the right, beyond the shelves of negative boxes, against the wall

and abutting the stainless steel sink, was a narrow table with three plastic five-gallon drums for storing chemicals.

One is always an intruder in someone else's darkroom. As the lights are turned on, one is blinded; then, when the eyes and mind accommodate each other, the effect is merely garish and unkind. Light itself is an intrusion, harsh and unwelcome.

No matter how fresh and pristine they may be when first built, all darkrooms soon acquire a tired and careworn quality. While obvious to a visitor, this shabbiness is invisible or irrelevant to the owner, for whom the room has become a very personal and intimate place, never intended to be scrutinized by strangers. This darkroom was no exception; it was very much Diane's space. The month was November 1971. In this recently dead, private person's private place, my task was to figure out, using only her materials and equipment, how to duplicate Diane's prints.

I had arrived in New York in the spring of 1970 to work as an assistant for Hiro, a Japanese photographer, who at that time occupied a studio adjoining Richard Avedon's. Marvin Israel, an artist, art director, and Avedon's friend and colleague, was a frequent visitor to the studio, usually at lunchtime. Diane was an occasional visitor, who dropped

in sometimes with Marvin, and sometimes alone to seek technical advice from Hiro or one of us assistants. She arranged with Hiro to borrow his new Pentax 6x7, a camera she was considering buying and wanted to try out. She had suggested that she was restless with her twin-lens Mamiyaflex, and in the case of the big Pentax was intrigued by the prospect of working again with the 35mm-like eye-level viewfinder. She was troubled, however, by the camera's limited capacity for taking flash pictures outdoors. I showed her how to load the camera and operate it, we put a strap on it, and, with almost childlike enthusiasm, she rushed off to try it out.

Later, having decided that she wanted to purchase the camera, Diane undertook to pay for it by offering a series of private classes to be held at Westbeth, a subsidized artists' housing complex, where she lived in Greenwich Village. She rounded up a group of interested neighbors and acquaintances, including myself, and advertised for more students in *The New York Times*. In the end, approximately twenty-four people came in to be interviewed. While Diane was unexcited by many of the applicants, she despaired of a means of fairly eliminating any individual, and, needing the cash, she accepted them all. The class met once a week in a public room at Westbeth and ended in the spring of 1971.

I left Hiro's in June, and shortly thereafter went to Europe; Diane had called a few times for technical advice, but I did not see her again. She committed suicide in July 1971. On hearing of her death, and assuming that her work would be memorialized in some way, I wrote to Marvin Israel, offering my services to help however I could.

By late fall of 1971 plans were under way for a book—to be edited and designed by Marvin with Diane's eldest daughter, Doon—and a retrospective show at The Museum of Modern Art in New York, curated by John Szarkowski. Although Diane had made exhibition prints of most of the images to be included in the book, they were judged to be too rare to be subjected to the rigors of the reproduction process. In the case of the show, Szarkowski made his selection, not only from Diane's exhibition prints, but also from images of hers for which only a damaged or rough print existed. Marvin and Szarkowski concurred that new prints were going to be needed for each of these projects.[*]

*Out of 112 prints in the 1972 MoMA retrospective, 40 were new prints made by me especially for the show. All of the images in the monograph were reproduced from prints I made for the book.

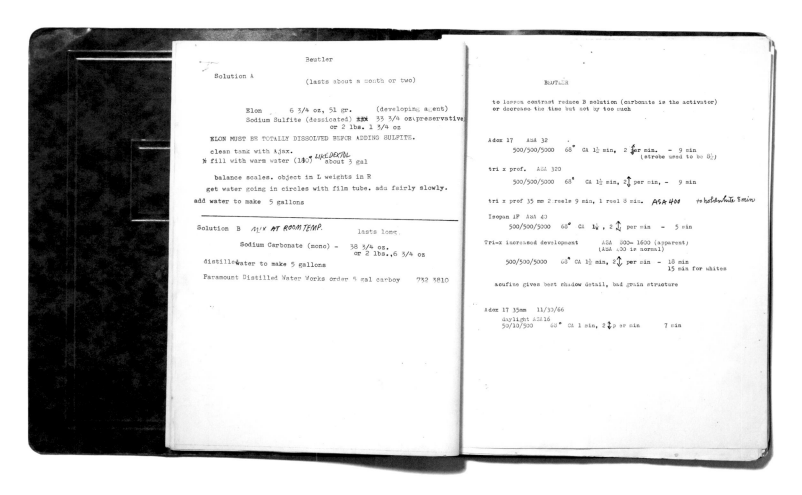

PAGES IN DIANE'S BLUE BINDER WITH BEUTLER FORMULAE.

I returned from Europe in November, and being otherwise unemployed and eager to help, was put straight to work, looking for negatives.

The process went as follows:

At the time of her death, prints of several hundred of Diane's images were found, mostly stored in boxes in a closet in her Westbeth apartment. These ranged in quality from flawless exhibition prints to scraps of torn images that had once been pinned to a wall somewhere. The existing prints were gathered together and one example of each different image that had been found was re-photographed. I was presented with the results: fifty-two, twelve-exposure proof sheets of these copies, which constituted a visual inventory of all images then known to have been printed by Diane.

There was no clue as to the location of the negative for any given photograph. Each negative sleeve was stapled to its corresponding (contact) proof sheet, numbered, and filed sequentially, but there was only very rarely any indication of date or subject. The process of locating the negatives for the images we wanted to print thus consisted of my memorizing all of her photographs on the new copy proofs, and then searching for each image from amongst the more than seven thousand filed contact sheets in Diane's darkroom.

It took all winter to repeatedly go through Diane's original contact sheets. With the exception of three images that stubbornly refused to reveal themselves until much later, we eventually located the negatives for all the photographs we were seeking. (Subsequently, prints of another five hundred, mostly early photographs, were found and added to the inventory of images that she had printed.)

We have never found any indication as to how Diane located her own negatives when she wanted to make a print. She must have either retained in her memory just where all those pictures were, or she must have spent a lot of time looking for them.

In the spring of 1972 I started to print, trying to match the exhibition prints that Diane had made from the same negatives. Each time I began to print a negative I had Diane's corresponding exhibition print sitting on the long thin table, beguiling and taunting me to match it identically. There were no notes, no clues as to how the prints were actually made, just a thin blue binder containing instructions and formulae for the developers that Allan Arbus had left for her.

Two prints of Identical twins, Roselle, N.J. 1967. At left, a print reflecting the way Diane originally printed her square format photographs; at right, the way Diane began printing her photographs with black borders in 1965.

A routine soon developed whereby I would print one negative in various ways until I was satisfied that I had made a sufficient range of prints so that one would be bound to come close. I would then stick the prints in Diane's old blotter rolls and crawl home, somewhere between two and four in the morning. I would meet Marvin Israel back in the darkroom each morning at 8:00 A.M. to go over the results.

Between 1961 and 1963 Marvin had been the art director of *Harper's Bazaar* while it was still very much a cultural icon. In addition to Richard Avedon, he had published Bill Brandt, Walker Evans, Lee Friedlander, and Diane. He had meanwhile become her friend, ally, and most discerning and committed critic. Although since 1963 he had been pursuing a career as a painter he remained very close to photography and to the photographers he admired.

In the darkroom, as Marvin led me through the differences between Diane's prints and mine, he was pointing out the same visual elements, their relationships and their consequences, that he must in turn originally have discovered with her. The language he used when explaining the differences between prints was never in terms of color, density, or contrast, but rather of aesthetic function. This was often a revelation. In the case of the line of trees in the back of Westchester family on their lawn, he said the trees needed to look *like a theatrical backdrop that might at any moment roll forward across the lawn.*

It was apparent that Diane had only made prints as she needed them, and as a consequence, virtually no two were exactly alike. The most obvious issue was the borders. Marvin had decided that the images in the book should uniformly reflect the way that Diane had made her most recent prints sit on the photographic paper. While exhibition prints existed of most of the images selected for the book, their borders were not consistent.

Starting around 1956, Diane began to print her pictures, which were shot on 35mm film, on 11x14 paper. These prints had broad white borders and hard edges to the image, which were created by the blades of the masking frame that held the paper flat underneath the enlarger. In 1962 she started to shoot some pictures on 120 film, which she also printed on 11x14 paper, with wide borders and hard-edged images. By 1963, she had stopped shooting 35mm altogether and was taking square pictures with a

wide-angle Rolleiflex and a twin-lens Mamiyaflex, and, around 1965, had begun to surround her square images with broad, irregular black borders.

The negative carrier for the Omega "D" enlarger consists of two pieces of aluminum with a rectangular hole cut out of them, which lock together, sandwiching the negative between them. As provided by the enlarger manufacturer, the carrier had an opening that was smaller than the image area of the negative, and consequently cropped part of the image. To overcome this, the aluminum negative carrier of Diane's enlarger had been crudely filed out to increase the size of its opening. This allowed the entire image area to be printed. It also left an uneven band of clear film, which printed black, between the edge of the image and the white paper border of the print. Since the actual size of the image on the film varied depending on whether the picture had been made using the Rolleiflex or the Mamiya, which lens was used, and the focusing distance, each image came with its own unique border.

Diane printed with these bold black borders until around 1969. Then, when she began to print her limited-edition portfolio—first offered for sale in late 1970—she reduced the black borders to a vestigial condition. *Everyone is using black borders now* she told us in her Westbeth class, as an explanation for what had driven her to make the change. Traces of the old borders still occurred in the prints however, sometimes to define the edge of the picture area, sometimes not. But the new borders were scarcely borders at all.

Simply placing the negative in the filed-out carrier and exposing and developing the paper inevitably resulted in a print with the old thick borders. The newer edges with their soft, unpredictable characteristics meant that the carrier must have been masked down to dimensions much closer to the size of the negatives themselves. But how?

To match the most recent existing prints, I reckoned that I would have to try taping strips of cardboard to the carrier to constrict the opening. Then, as soon as I had figured out what they should look like, I saw them! Dangling from the enlarger columns, little scraps of cardboard about two and a half inches long by a quarter to five sixteenths of an inch wide, with a little tab of masking tape on one or both ends.

The nature and thickness of the vestigial border was dictated by the precise position of the cardboard pieces, the length

The 1940s Omega "D" enlarger in Diane's darkroom. On the pipe at left, a torn test piece of the photograph A family one evening in a nudist camp, Pa. 1965. Detail of a photograph by Cosmos Savage, 1972.

of the exposure, and the enlarging lens aperture. The bits of cardboard were taped to the top surface of the aluminum carrier, slightly intruding over the edges of the rectangular hole, and thereby masking and reducing the area of clear film that had formerly created the black border. The thickness of the aluminum (about that of a kitchen match) made a space between the cardboard strips and the negative. This meant that the edges of the cardboard—which were creating the transition on the print from image to white paper—were out of focus. The quantity of light that squeezed between the out-of-focus cardboard and the sharp negative dictated the breadth and nature of the softening process.

The uncoated cardboard strips deteriorated quickly with handling. Replacing them with better-quality cardboard made it impossible to duplicate the prints. Further exploration in Diane's darkroom revealed that the source of the right cardboard was the cheap boxes containing the negative sleeves. When the boxes were cut up and the cardboard trimmed to the correct size the edges became hairy, but when the hairs were suppressed with a saliva-wetted finger, the resulting slightly uneven edge was perfect!

By employing this method to mask the negative carrier, Diane had created on each occasion a unique controlled accident at the edges of her photographs. Trying to precisely replicate that accident was a near-absurd exercise that often took me several hours and a lot of paper.

Diane had very little technical knowledge, but she had a very strong sense of what she wanted and was relentless about getting it. A key element in the unique look and feel of her photographs lay in her choice of film. She had tried all the film types available in the United States, and had made it very clear to me that she disliked them relative to the films of two German manufacturers. Since the Adox company had gone out of business, she had switched to Agfa films, but the very slow, grain-free types she preferred had ceased to be available in the States. She resorted to pressing friends and acquaintances into buying Agfa IF for her in Germany and bringing it back with them.

She developed this 50 ASA Agfa film in a two-solution developer called Beutler. She painstakingly mixed the two elements from raw chemicals and stored them separately until just before use. The compensating nature of the Beutler (which allows shadow detail to increase without harming highlights), combined with the slow, silver-heavy Agfa films, produced negatives with a huge tonal range and great detail, which was a good thing, since Diane's exposures tended to be erratic. Nonetheless, when printed on pre-cadmium-purged Agfa Portriga Rapid paper developed in Beers (also a two-solution developer mixed from raw chemicals), her negatives produced prints with deep blacks and everything else she wanted.

Her technique originated with her former husband and partner, Allan Arbus. Allan and Diane ran a commercial photography studio together from 1946 until Diane quit the business to go her own way in 1956. She continued to share a darkroom with Allan until 1969, when he moved to the West Coast. Prior to leaving, he designed and equipped the Charles Street darkroom for her. Diane had always done her own printing but up to that time an assistant of Allan's had processed her film. From late 1969 Diane did all her own darkroom work using as a reference the blue binder containing neatly typed formulae and instructions that Allan had prepared for her.

Allan had introduced her to the process of mixing the proprietary Kodak print developers Dektol and Selectol-Soft in differing proportions in order to control contrast. At some point, she may have switched to the similar, more thoroughly controllable but time-consuming Beers developer.*

As the process of my trying to precisely match her prints proceeded, the most unexpected fact emerged, namely that she apparently never dodged or burned a print. The sole quality that she chose to exercise control over was contrast. Using contrast-controlling developer, all of Diane's prints sat happily on either Portriga 3 or 4 (which were subsequently renamed 2 and 3 to align them with other manufacturers). Fully developing Portriga took at least two minutes, but in some extreme cases prints that needed reduced contrast and were pulled from the developer after as little as forty-five seconds still had a beautiful black. Out of the eighty prints made for the monograph, only one needed a burn for it to match Diane's previous version.

The process of establishing the right contrast for the print was lengthy. A developer mix was first guessed at, then a gallon was prepared by combining the two developer solutions and water in precise proportions. Test strips were then made at various exposures. Once an approximate exposure had been ascertained, a range of full-size prints was made, washed, and dried on the ancient print dryer. These were then compared to a print that Diane had made. Once the new print that most closely matched Diane's print for density had been established, it was compared for contrast. A decision was then made to either increase or decrease the contrast of the developer. The first developer then went down the drain, and the next one was

---

* At the time of my arrival at the darkroom in late 1971, there were labeled containers and chemicals for the making of Beers print developer, but nothing suggesting the presence of Dektol and Selectol-Soft. The binder containing the formulae, however, made no reference to Beers. The constituent chemicals for Beers and Beutler—which Diane used for developing film—are, however, exactly the same, so it would be easy to make Beers if one was stocked to make Beutler. Beers developer is stored as "A&B" solutions, which are mixed in infinitely variable proportions, "A" for low contrast and "B" for high contrast. Using either Beers or Dektol/Selectol-Soft, there is more or less a full paper grade difference between the softest (least contrasty) and hardest (most contrasty) mixture.

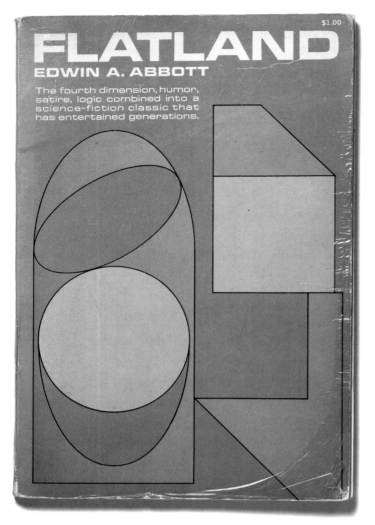

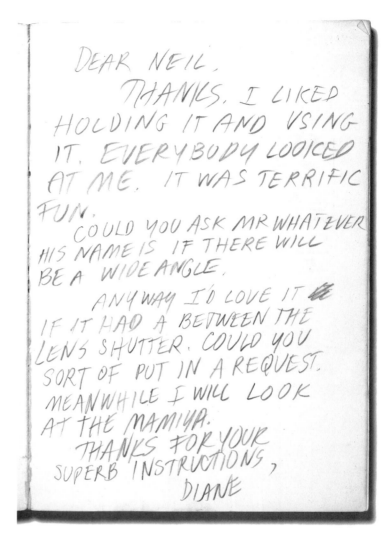

DEAR NEIL,
THANKS. I LIKED HOLDING IT AND USING IT. EVERYBODY LOOKED AT ME. IT WAS TERRIFIC FUN.
COULD YOU ASK MR WHATEVER HIS NAME IS IF THERE WILL BE A WIDE ANGLE.
ANYWAY I'D LOVE IT IF IT HAD A BETWEEN THE LENS SHUTTER. COULD YOU SORT OF PUT IN A REQUEST. MEANWHILE I WILL LOOK AT THE MAMIYA.
THANKS FOR YOUR SUPERB INSTRUCTIONS,
DIANE

Cover and flyleaf of the copy of Edwin A. Abbott's *Flatland: A romance of many dimensions*, given by Diane to Neil in 1971, who was then an assistant to Hiro, after she borrowed Hiro's Pentax 6x7 camera.

tried in its place. Each cycle took at least two hours and there were rarely fewer than four cycles before the closest match was achieved. Thus between getting both the borders and the contrast right on one print it was easy to spend twelve hours just fiddling.

Again and again Diane's technique would enable me to effortlessly generate a print that would have won accolades from the academic printing establishment, only to have her comparison print command me to dilute the richness of the result. On the other hand, she would often print far harder than would optimize the rendering of the information in the negative. In Man at a parade (p. 303), the first image to appear during development is of a man who turns out to be inside a storefront. He rapidly darkens and is replaced by a second man standing against a building. This man in turn darkens as a third man—the man standing beside the garbage container, who came to watch the parade and whom Diane wanted us to see—finally materializes. In the fully developed print, the first figure to appear has become invisible.

The easiest misjudgment for me to make related to washing time, which substantially affected both color and density. A test print washed briefly and then dried in the dryer emerged both warmer and darker than its twin, conceived identically, but washed fully and dried in a blotter roll. Judging this phenomenon blind was a tricky call. It was not unusual to arrive in the morning to meet Marvin and unroll the blotters only to find that I had simply missed and had to start again. I always approached this moment of disclosure with trepidation. Still, I never found reason to question Diane's certainty (expressed to her Westbeth class) that her technique, tedious as it was, enabled her to make better prints than those of her peers.

After several months of printing, I had worked down the pile of existing prints to the few images that we needed for which only a rough print existed. To make these I worked with whatever intrinsic qualities there were in the negative and Diane's existing rough print along with the principles I had absorbed from the process of learning to match the prints we knew she prized.

Diane's prints do actually look different from the prints of other photographers. The reason, of course, is both radiant and opaque. It lies in what she didn't do that everyone else did. The complete lack of dodging and burning, to lighten or darken specific areas of the printed image, is extraordinary in the field of black-and-white documentary photography. If she ever had the urge or the knowledge to make the print beautiful in a conventional sense, she resisted it. The unique quality of Diane's prints seems a direct response to what is required if one is extremely curious and utterly dispassionate.

The pictures look raw. The way she achieved this lay in the way she used only moderate contrast and density control (neither of which trigger notions of manipulation in the viewer) to suppress information she didn't want, or emphasize that which she did. By otherwise leaving the photograph alone, she compels the viewer to believe what he's looking at.

Beautiful as they are, the prints are only about what the lens projected onto the film, not about the philosophy of the technique or dogma about the process, or about the skill of the print maker, be she the photographer or her surrogate. Diane's aesthetic roots were based in her instinctual responses to everyday images, rather than to conventional academic ideals of print excellence, about which she cared little. Her intent may have been to make the final image owe something to the limited range of the snapshot or the newspaper photograph, perhaps to borrow from their inherent credibility. Her use of film unavailable in the United States and fussy, time-consuming developers was a deeply sophisticated response to her need to make prints that conveyed the authenticity of the moment without getting in the way of the picture.

Over the last thirty years, most of the materials Diane used have either changed or simply disappeared, but my task remains the same as it was the day I first entered her darkroom. It has been to discover the essence through pursuit of the surface, and whenever necessary, to reinvent the process in order to remain true to the essence: that no one doubts a Diane Arbus photograph.

Untitled (4) 1970–71

A photograph is a secret about a secret. The more it tells you the less you know.

—DIANE ARBUS, "FIVE PHOTOGRAPHS BY DIANE ARBUS,"

ARTFORUM, MAY 1971

Seated man in bra and stockings, N.Y.C. 1967

Blind couple in their bedroom, Queens, N.Y. 1971

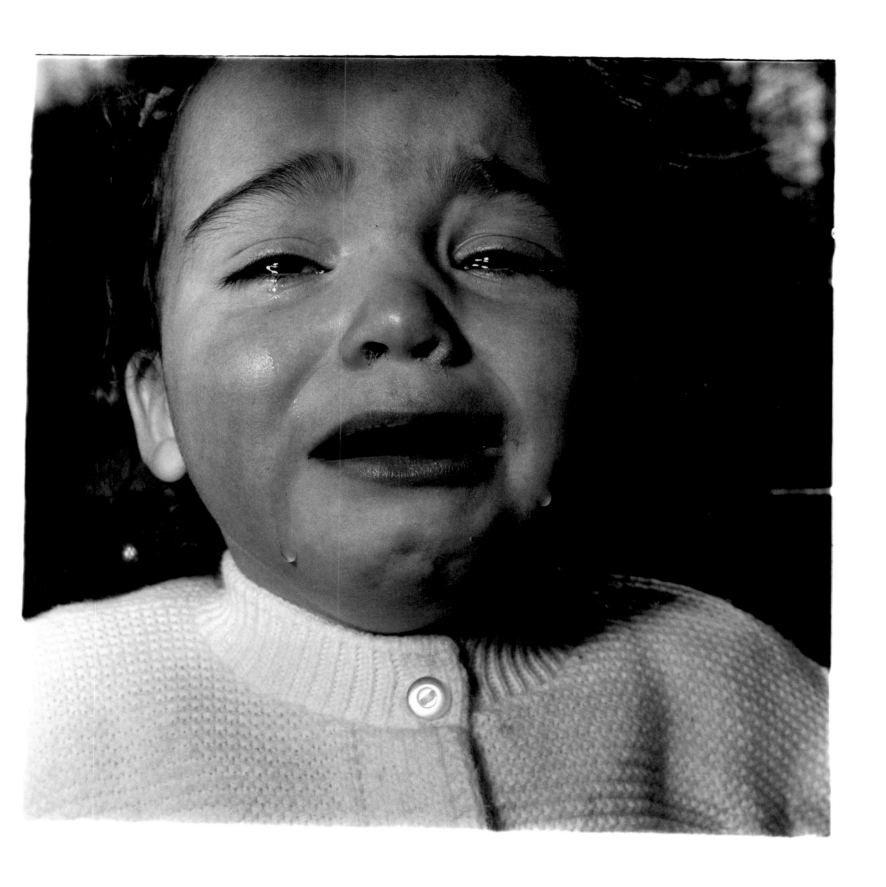

A child crying, N.J. 1967

Untitled (42) 1970–71

Jorge Luis Borges in Central Park, N.Y.C. 1969

Boy above a crowd, N.Y.C. 1956

Woman at a counter smoking, N.Y.C. 1962*

Superstar at home, N.Y.C. 1968

Boxer with a punching bag, N.Y.C. 1964*

When you try very hard to do something by the time you can do it
it is easy to do, so effort is maybe a kind of prayer.

—FROM A LETTER TO MARVIN ISRAEL, CIRCA NOVEMBER 1960

A castle in Disneyland, Cal. 1962

Untitled (7) 1970–1971

Transvestite with a torn stocking, N.Y.C. 1966

Five children in a common room, N.J. 1969

Tattooed lady with dog, Philadelphia, Pa. 1964

A family one evening in a nudist camp, Pa. 1965

A flower girl at a wedding, Conn. 1964

AFTERWORD

BY DOON ARBUS

When Diane Arbus died she had no will and, because she was divorced, my younger sister Amy and I, as her children, were deemed to be, according to law, her only heirs. Amy, then seventeen, was still legally a minor, so on October 12, 1971, I was appointed administrator of the estate. This left me officially in charge and, subsequent organizational changes notwithstanding, I essentially remain so. Aside from the intrinsic power of the photographs themselves, much of what has happened to the work of Diane Arbus in the thirty-two years since her death—including this book and the accompanying exhibition—has been contingent upon decisions I have made. While I have had a lot of help, advice, prodding, both from individuals and from circumstances beyond my control, the primary responsibility fell to me and, without precisely envisioning what it might entail, I accepted it. The result has been a long, challenging, quarrelsome, passionate, complicated, exhilarating, comical, obsessive, one-sided relationship with an absentee.

In the early stages, before the 1972 posthumous retrospective at The Museum of Modern Art, the task seemed straightforward enough: to do what was necessary to make the work as widely available as possible. After that, things changed. She was turning into a phenomenon and that phenomenon, while posing no threat to her, began endangering the pictures. She had achieved a form of immunity but the photographs had not. The photographs needed me. Well, they needed someone. Someone to keep track of them, to safeguard them—however unsuccessfully—from an onslaught of theory and interpretation, as if translating images into words were the only way to make them visible. More to the point, there were often people in the pictures, people who had certainly volunteered to be in them but who, in doing so, had not bargained on getting diagnosed by strangers as mere symptoms of someone else's hypothetical state of mind. I felt a responsibility, not exactly to the people themselves, whom I do not pretend to know, but to the aspects of them that continue to exist in the pictures.

The three previous books of her work, although hardly wordless, were informed by the stubborn conviction that the photographs were eloquent enough to require no explanations, no set of instructions on how to read them, no bits of biography to prop them up. The relevant things about her were in them anyway. Besides, in her absence, the person she was seemed best left to the vagaries of our private mis-recollections, and of little use to anyone in encountering the pictures. *Diane Arbus*, *Diane Arbus: Magazine Work*, and *Untitled* were each addressed to something left unfinished by what came before. This book is no exception.

Each successive project, each new attempt at organization, functioned inadvertently as a kind of archeology, unearthing that which had as yet remained unnoticed. Unearthing a little whetted the appetite for unearthing more. As it turns out, we kept an awful lot of stuff, partly out of diligence, or superstition, partly out of reverence for the kind of history that survives more or less intact in objects, but primarily to avoid the decisions entailed in doing otherwise. The accumulation of all this evidence, the revelations lurking there, seemed to demand a forum, a safe place for anyone who cares to wander around at will and play detective, to peer into dark corners, to touch things, or circle back, to invent a path without the interference of the tour guide, making independent discoveries, because making discoveries in that way lies at the core of what it's really all about.

This book and exhibition, by integrating her photographs and her words with a chronology that amounts to a kind of autobiography, do not signal a change of heart, but one of strategy, and a willingness to embrace the paradox: that this surfeit of information and opinion would finally render the scrim of words invisible so that anyone encountering the photographs could meet them in the eloquence of their silence.

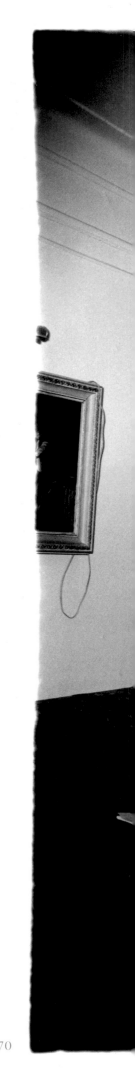

A Jewish giant at home with his parents in the Bronx, N.Y. 1970

Feminist in her hotel room, N.Y.C. 1971*

Man at a parade on Fifth Avenue, N.Y.C. 1969

Albino sword swallower at a carnival, Md. 1970

BIOGRAPHIES

BY JEFF L. ROSENHEIM

BERENICE ABBOTT (1898–1991) is equally known for her advocacy of the French photographer Eugène Atget, and for her comprehensive, Depression-era documentary project *Changing New York*, an extended photographic portrait of the city's nineteenth-century tenements, early-twentieth-century skyscrapers, and their common ground. With historical captions by art critic Elizabeth McCausland, *Changing New York: Photography by Berenice Abbott* (1939) transformed how subsequent artists and publications have portrayed the urban experience in the United States.

Born in Springfield, Ohio, and raised in Cleveland, Abbott attended Ohio State University (Columbus) for a year, then moved to New York City to pursue writing, which she soon abandoned to open a sculpture studio. In 1921 she moved to Paris where, from 1923 to 1925, she worked as a darkroom assistant to the American artist, Man Ray, who had established a fashion and portrait studio. In 1925, she left Man Ray and opened her own business on the rue du Bac.

Abbott had her first one-person show in 1926 at the gallery Au Sacre du Printemps in Paris and exhibited her photographs in numerous group shows, including the influential 1928 international exhibition, *Film + Foto*, in Stuttgart, Germany. In 1927 she met and photographed Eugène Atget, and after the artist's death in October 1928, purchased his archive of prints and negatives. She coordinated the first book on the artist, *Atget, Photographe de Paris* (1930) and organized his first New York show in 1930. Abbott regularly printed Atget's negatives, and in 1956 published *Eugène Atget Portfolio: Twenty Photographic Prints from His Original Glass Negatives*. She is also the author of *The World of Atget* (1964). Until 1968 when The Museum of Modern Art acquired the Atget archive from Abbott, she promoted the French documentarian's work through articles, exhibitions, and books.

Abbott returned to live in New York in 1929 and began to photograph the city as Atget had Paris. She participated in important shows in the early 1930s, and, in 1934, with Henry-Russell Hitchcock, the era's premier historian of modern architecture, produced an exhibition entitled *American Cities Before the Civil War: The Urban Vernacular of the Thirties, Forties and Fifties*. Her photographic project on New York, known as *Changing New York,* was sponsored by the New Deal's Federal Art Project. The exhibition opened in 1937 at The Museum of the City of New York, where the original negatives are still preserved.

In 1939 MoMA included Abbott as one of seven American photographers (including Man Ray and Walker Evans) in *Art in Our Time*, its tenth anniversary exhibition, and the first at its new building on 53rd Street. Arbus briefly studied technique with Abbott around 1946 at the New School for Social Research where she taught photography from 1935 to 1958.

Abbott had numerous retrospective exhibitions at, among other institutions, MoMA (1970) and The New York Public Library (1989), and beginning in 1976 published the first of several portfolios of her photographs. She was awarded many honorary degrees and citations, including the French government's Officer in the Legion of Arts and Letters (1988), and membership in the American Academy and Institute of Arts and Letters (1983).

RUTH ANSEL (B. 1936) graduated from Alfred University with a B.F.A. in ceramic design in 1957 and began her professional design career at *Harper's Bazaar* in 1961 working alongside Bea Feitler as an assistant to art director Marvin Israel. Two years later she and Feitler succeeded Israel as co–art directors of the magazine, a position Ansel kept until 1971. Ansel gave work to many of the era's most progressive artists, including Andy Warhol, James Rosenquist, Robert Rauschenberg, Bob Richardson, and Arbus. From 1974 to 1982 she was art director for *The New York Times Magazine* and eventually went on to art direct at numerous Condé Nast publications: *House & Garden* (1982–83); *Vanity Fair* (1983–88); *Vogue* (1988–89); and *HG* (1989–91).

In 1992 Ansel founded Ruth Ansel Design Studio and has designed numerous magazines, advertising campaigns, and books, including Richard Avedon and Doon Arbus's *The Sixties* (1999).

ALLAN ARBUS (B. 1918) was born and raised in New York City. He attended DeWitt Clinton High School and entered City College of New York at the age of fifteen. A year and a half later he left and went to work at Russek's, a women's specialty shop that was owned by Max Weinstein and David Nemerov, Diane's father. Allan met Diane Nemerov at Russek's when she was thirteen and he was eighteen. They were married in 1941. During a vacation in Montauk, Long Island, he photographed her in the fashion picture idiom and when these pictures were shown to David Nemerov, a pioneer in the use of pho-

tography in advertising, he encouraged them to pursue fashion photography. They were soon given what turned out to be successful assignments by the Russek's advertising department. When the United States entered World War II, Arbus became a Signal Corps photographer. While he was in Burma, the Arbuses' first child, Doon, was born in New York City. In 1946 Arbus was discharged and the couple established a studio on West 54th Street using the by-line "Diane & Allan Arbus." Condé Nast placed them under contract and their work appeared regularly in *Glamour* and *Vogue*. In 1954 their second child, Amy, was born.

The Arbuses continued to collaborate until 1956 when Diane left the business to pursue her own work. Allan continued the studio operation while simultaneously beginning a career as an actor. On the recommendation of a friend he began training with Mira Rostova, who had coached many prominent actors, including Montgomery Clift and Geraldine Page. He remained Rostova's student for eleven years, during which time he performed in Off-Off Broadway productions and appeared in his first movie, *Hey Let's Twist* (1961).

In 1958, while remaining close, Diane and Allan Arbus separated, and eventually divorced in 1969, when he moved to California to pursue his acting career. In 1976 he married Mariclare Costello, a fellow acting student. A year later their daughter Arin was born.

Allan Arbus is most widely known for his recurring television role as the psychiatrist Major Sidney Freedman on *M*A*S*H* (1972–83). He recently played the role of Gregory Solomon in a 2001 stage production of Arthur Miller's *The Price* at the Laguna Playhouse in Los Angeles. Arbus and Mariclare Costello live in California.

AMY ARBUS (B. 1954) is the second daughter of Diane and Allan Arbus. She is a professional photographer whose work has appeared in *The New Yorker*, *Egoïste*, *Vanity Fair*, *Rolling Stone*, and *The New York Times Magazine*, among other publications.

After attending high school in New York City, she eventually spent a year at Goddard College in Vermont, then studied arranging and composition for two years at the Berklee College of Music in Boston. She soon left music for the visual arts, studying photography for a year at the School of the Museum of

Fine Arts, Boston. In 1978 she returned to New York City to work as an assistant to the fashion photographer Jean Pagliuso. Two years later she began to freelance. Her monthly style feature for *The Village Voice*, "On the Street," ran from 1980 to 1991 and focused on street chic and the New York art and music scene in Soho and the East Village.

Amy Arbus has published two books of photography: *No Place Like Home* (1986), an examination of people and their unusual dwellings; and *The Inconvenience of Being Born* (1999), a portrait series on infants. Her work is in the permanent collections of The Museum of Modern Art, the Columbus Museum of Art, and the Spencer Museum of Art in Lawrence, Kansas, and she has exhibited her photographs in numerous group shows in the United States and abroad. She teaches portrait workshops at the Toscana Photographic Workshop in Italy, the Santa Fe Photographic Workshop, and the International Center of Photography in New York.

DOON ARBUS (B. 1945) is the first daughter of Diane and Allan Arbus. Since her mother's death she has managed The Estate of Diane Arbus. With the late Marvin Israel, she co-edited two posthumous books of her mother's work: *Diane Arbus: An Aperture Monograph* (1972), and *Diane Arbus: Magazine Work* (1984). She also edited and designed a third volume with the designer Yolanda Cuomo, *Diane Arbus: Untitled* (1995), for which she wrote the Afterword.

After spending a year at Reed College she returned to New York in 1964, and in addition to other freelance writing assignments, she collaborated with her mother on several magazine articles, contributing the text to "James Brown Is Out of Sight," *Herald Tribune Magazine* (New York), March 20, 1966; and "How Fat Alice Lost 12 Stone (Yes 12 Stone—The Weight of an Average Man!) and Found Happiness, God, and the Chance of a Husband," *The London Sunday Times Magazine*, January 19, 1969. In 1969, at the suggestion of Marvin Israel, she began working with Richard Avedon on his new project, 8x10 photographic portraits of artists, and political and social activists. Thirty years later her recorded interviews of the portrait subjects became the text of *The Sixties* (1999), a coauthored publication of photographs and monologues focusing on the civil rights movement, Vietnam, the antiwar movement, space exploration, and the arts.

In 1973 she and Avedon produced a book based on her tape recordings and his photographs entitled *Alice in Wonderland: The Forming of a Company, and the Making of a Play* (1973), a chronicle of André Gregory's Obie award–winning (1969–70) production. In the mid-1970s she and Avedon collaborated on a series of commercial television and print advertising campaigns that relied on a similar approach. These included Catherine Deneuve for Chanel and Brooke Shields for Calvin Klein jeans.

In addition to her productive association with Avedon, she has also worked independently, contributing essays and criticism to *Rolling Stone* and *The Nation* on artists ranging from Peter Beard to Walker Evans. Her play, *Third Floor, Second Door on the Right*, was produced in New York by the International Fringe Festival in 2003. She is currently writing a work of fiction.

RICHARD AVEDON (B. 1923) is known for his portraits of Buster Keaton, Marian Anderson, Marilyn Monroe, Ezra Pound, Isak Dinesen, Dwight D. Eisenhower, Andy Warhol, and the Chicago Seven. He has had numerous one-person museum exhibitions at, among others, the Minneapolis Institute of Arts (1970); the Whitney Museum of American Art (1994); and two shows at The Metropolitan Museum

of Art: *Avedon: Photographs 1947–1977*, a retrospective of his fashion work in 1977, and *Richard Avedon: Portraits*, in 2002.

Avedon was born in New York City and attended DeWitt Clinton High School in the Bronx. He served as editor in chief of *Magpie*, his school's literary and arts magazine. Avedon's classmate and lifelong friend James Baldwin was the magazine's literary editor. In 1942 Avedon joined the U.S. Merchant Marine where he became photographer's mate second class. After World War II he returned to New York and attended Alexey Brodovitch's Design Laboratory at the New School for Social Research. He was chief photographer for *Harper's Bazaar* from the late 1940s to 1965, and for *Vogue* from 1966 to 1988.

In 1959, Avedon completed his first book, *Observations*, a volume of portraits designed by Brodovitch with text by Truman Capote. In 1964 he and James Baldwin completed *Nothing Personal* (1964), a work about the civil rights movement designed by his frequent collaborator Marvin Israel. Avedon met Arbus in the 1950s and eventually purchased the first two sets of her portfolio designed by Israel, *A box of ten photographs* (1970).

Avedon discovered the work of Jacques-Henri Lartigue and later edited *Diary of a Century: Jacques Henri Lartigue* (1970). The book and exhibition at The Museum of Modern Art helped launch the reputation of the then-unknown photographer of the Belle Epoque. In the late 1960s and early '70s, Avedon photographed American antiwar protesters, politicians, and military leaders. He was assisted by Doon Arbus, who made documentary tape recordings of all the subjects. After almost thirty years, Avedon and Arbus edited selections of these photographs and recordings as *The Sixties* (1999).

In 1979 the Amon Carter Museum in Fort Worth, Texas, commissioned Avedon to produce his largest series of portraits, a study of working-class American citizens. He worked for five years and photographed 752 people in seventeen Western states. The show *In the American West, 1979–1984* opened in 1985 at the Amon Carter Museum, and the accompanying publication was designed by Marvin Israel. To date, Avedon has published two visual memoirs, *Evidence: 1944–1994* (1994), a book that accompanied his exhibition at the Whitney Museum of American Art, and *Richard Avedon: An Autobiography* (1993). From 1985 to 1992, Avedon's editorial work appeared exclusively in *Egoïste*, the French literary and arts magazine. In 1992, under the editorship of Tina Brown, *The New Yorker* named Avedon its first staff photographer in the history of the magazine.

RICHARD BELLAMY (1927–98) was born in Cincinnati, Ohio, the only child of two physicians. In the early 1950s, after a year of college, he moved to the East Coast and eventually settled in New York City having met Hans Hofmann and the artists in his school in Provincetown, Massachusetts. As director of the cooperative Hansa Gallery (1955–59), then later Green Gallery (1960–65), he emerged as one of the leading gallerists in America. Bellamy championed and represented many of the most important pop and minimalist artists of the era, including James Rosenquist, Donald Judd, Claes Oldenburg, and Dan Flavin.

When Arbus met Nancy Christopherson and Bellamy in the early 1950s their circle included abstract painters Willem de Kooning, Miles and Barbara Forst, and Alfred Leslie, as well as the photographer Robert Frank and his Beat friends Allen Ginsberg and Jack Kerouac. Between 1965 and 1974 Bellamy worked from an office in the Noah Goldowsky Gallery presenting exhibitions of Jo Baer, Richard

Artschwager, Mark di Suvero, and Richard Serra, among many others. After managing a private gallery in the late 1970s, he opened the Oil & Steel Gallery in 1980. In his final decade of work Bellamy managed almost exclusively the installation and exhibition of di Suvero's large-scale sculptures. His correspondence, gallery records, and artists' files are in the archives of the collection of The Museum of Modern Art.

ERNEST J. BELLOCQ (1873–1949) was born into an aristocratic Creole family in New Orleans, Louisiana. After enrolling in classical courses at the College of the Immaculate Conception, he devoted his efforts to amateur photography. By 1898 Bellocq had become a prominent member of the New Orleans Camera Club, and by World War I he was working as a professional photographer specializing in shipbuilding. Bellocq's international renown, however, was established by a series of intimate, mildly erotic portraits of prostitutes working in Storyville, the city's infamous tenderloin district.

In 1966, photographer Lee Friedlander purchased eighty-nine Bellocq glass-plate negatives from a New Orleans antiques dealer. Four years later when The Museum of Modern Art presented an exhibition of Friedlander's modern prints of these photographs, Bellocq was immediately recognized as a master of the modern, psychological portrait—an ancestor for a whole generation of contemporary artists, including Arbus, who acquired a few prints for her personal collection. Friedlander continues to print Bellocq's work and has published two editions of *E. J. Bellocq: Storyville Portraits, Photographs from the New Orleans Red-Light District, Circa 1912* (1970, 1996).

ROBERT BENTON (B. 1932) was born in Waxahachie, Texas, and is known for directing and/or writing such Academy Award–winning films as *Kramer vs. Kramer* (1979), *Places in the Heart* (1984), and *Nobody's Fool* (1994). After graduating from the University of Texas, he moved to New York City, worked on a master's degree in art and art history at Columbia University, then in 1954 took an editorial position in the art department at *Esquire* magazine. First as an assistant art director to Henry Wolf, then as his replacement in 1957, Benton contributed to the transformation of *Esquire* from a men's magazine to a graphically more sophisticated monthly featuring contemporary fiction, nonfiction, and photography. Benton met Arbus at *Esquire* in late 1959 and soon became one of the artist's most devoted advocates. Beginning with their seminal feature on New York's denizens of the night, "The Vertical Journey: Six Movements of a Moment Within the Heart of the City" (*Esquire*, July 1960), Benton provided Arbus with regular assignments through 1963 when he left the magazine.

Benton began writing screenplays while at *Esquire* in the early 1960s. His first effort (co-written with fellow editor David Newman) was *Bonnie and Clyde* (1967), a film directed by Arthur Penn that won him an Academy Award for best story and best original screenplay. Benton made his directorial debut with the revisionist Western *Bad Company* (1972). His most recent films are *A Great Day in Harlem* (1995), *Twilight* (1998), *Double Jeopardy* (1999), and *The Human Stain* (2003), based on a novel by Philip Roth.

PAUL BIANCHINI (1928–2000) was a gallerist and art publisher born outside of Paris whose eponymous New York gallery (1958–67) presented avant-garde European and American pop and minimal art. For his infamous 1964 exhibition, *The American Supermarket*, Bianchini transformed his gallery into a supermarket of fake food created by Jasper Johns, Claes Oldenburg, Andy Warhol, and others.

From 1967 to 1973 Bianchini worked as a private dealer and publisher of art books. Under his imprint, "A Paul Bianchini Book," he produced in the United States and Europe a series of books on artists, including Roy Lichtenstein, Alberto Giacometti, Willem de Kooning, Sol LeWitt, and Richard Lindner. He also published print portfolios and artists' books.

In 1960 Bianchini married the American author and visual artist Pati Hill, and together they raised their daughter, Paola, now a photographer. After he closed his New York business in 1973, the Bianchinis moved back to France where, in 1982, Bianchini assisted James B. Sherwood (then president of Sea Containers Ltd.) in restoring and launching the new Venice-Simplon-Orient-Express (VSOE). Returning to his primary passion, Bianchini opened in 1990 Galerie Toner in Paris, and then Galerie Jules Verne, in the town of Sens, both of which promoted artists working with toner, and then laser prints.

ALEXEY BRODOVITCH (1898–1971) was the art director of *Harper's Bazaar* for twenty-five years. He was also a professor of graphic design and one of the first to teach design as a professional discipline in America. Born in Russia, he moved to Paris in 1920 and began his career painting stage sets for Sergei Diaghilev and the Ballets Russes. Before moving to the United States in 1930, he worked as an art director for the famous French department store Aux Trois Quartiers, and designed street posters for Martini Vermouth, Le Printemps, and Au Bon Marché. In 1930 Brodovitch began what came to be called, three years later, the Design Laboratory. This workshop was conducted for more than two decades at various schools and private locations, including Yale University, the New School for Social Research, and the Corcoran Museum of Art. Brodovitch's philosophy of design influenced several generations of photographers and art directors, including Richard Avedon, Irving Penn, Garry Winogrand, and Marvin Israel.

As art director from 1934 until 1958 at *Harper's Bazaar*, Brodovitch incorporated the tenets of surrealism, abstract expressionism, and finally minimalism into the fabric of the magazine. He is credited for introducing Americans to European avant-garde artists. Between 1949 and 1951 Brodovitch and fellow editor Frank Zachary produced three issues of *Portfolio*, a journal of the graphic arts that is often cited as the most innovative visual experiment of the era. Brodovitch designed many books, most notably Richard Avedon and Truman Capote's *Observations* (1959).

ROBERT BROWN (B. 1926) was born in New Jersey, spent his childhood in the Bronx, New York, and is a stage, television, and screen actor best known for his television role as Jason Bolt, the oldest of three brothers in *Here Come the Brides* (ABC, 1968–70). He established his credentials as a stage actor in New York City in the 1940s and '50s where he studied alongside Walter Matthau and Rod Steiger at Erwin Piscator's dramatic workshop at the New School for Social Research. His first Broadway casting was in Lee Strasberg's *Skipper Next to God* (1948). Brown performed in Carson McCullers's *A Member of the Wedding* (1950) and in Maxwell Anderson's *Barefoot in Athens* (1951) and, in 1958, played Stephen Dedalus opposite Zero Mostel's Leopold Bloom in *Ulysses in Nighttown*. After moving to Los Angeles in 1959 Brown starred as Father Riccardo Fontana in the original Los Angeles production (and the national tour) of Rolf Hochhuth's *The Deputy* (1963).

Early in his New York stage career Brown lived in a small apartment adjoining Diane and Allan Arbus's on East 72nd Street, and later encouraged Allan to begin his training with the Russian acting coach Mira Rostova. Now retired from the theater, Brown does voice-overs for television and radio commercials, and is at work on an autobiography.

NANCY CHRISTOPHERSON (B. 1924) has worked as a model, dancer, painter, and costume designer. Born in Cleveland, Ohio, she attended Cleveland College, Case Western Reserve University, then in the mid-1940s moved to New York City where she lives today. She was briefly married to New York art dealer Richard Bellamy. Christopherson worked as a John Robert Powers model and posed for Diane and Allan Arbus. The Arbuses' daughter Doon, and Christopherson's daughter, Poni, were the same age and became close friends. Christopherson was interested in metaphysical disciplines, and long before it became popular in America, she introduced the Arbus family to the *I Ching, or Book of Changes*, the ancient Chinese (Taoist) wisdom and divination manual.

Soon after Christopherson moved to New York, she met Maya Deren, the Russian-born American avant-garde filmmaker and film theorist, who included her as a dancer in *Ritual in Transfixed Time* (1945–46), a celebrated short, silent film that features dance performances by Rita Christiani and Frank Westbrook, as well as Anaïs Nin. From the 1950s to the '70s, she designed costumes for several Off-Off-Broadway productions, including Al Carmines's show at the Judson Dance Theater.

MARICLARE COSTELLO was born in Peoria, Illinois, and is an actress, director, and teacher. She graduated from Clarke College in Dubuque, Iowa, attended the University of Vienna in Austria, and received a master's degree in theater from Catholic University of America. She worked as an actress Off-Broadway in a number of productions, most notably *The Hostage*. In 1962 she became a member of the original Lincoln Center Repertory Company, headed by Elia Kazan, Robert Lewis, and Robert Whitehead, where she trained and performed for four years. In its initial season she originated the role of Louise in Arthur Miller's *After the Fall* (1964). She appeared in a number of Broadway plays and began a long association with the renowned acting coach Mira Rostova. For two years she worked with Jerome Robbins in his experimental company, American Theatre Lab. She is a member of The Actors Studio, and studied improvisation with Viola Spolin.

Costello met Allan Arbus in 1965. Through him she met and subsequently developed independent relationships with Diane Arbus and the two Arbus daughters, Doon and Amy. In 1969 shortly after Allan Arbus moved to Los Angeles, California, Costello joined him there. They married in 1976. A year later their daughter, Arin, was born.

Costello's acting career broadened to include television and film. She acted in more than twenty movies, including *Ordinary People* (1980) and *Indecent Proposal* (1993). She has taught and directed children's theater and is currently a member of the theatre arts faculty at Loyola Marymount University in Los Angeles, for which she directed *The Skin of Our Teeth* by Thornton Wilder in October 2002. In February 2003 she directed another Wilder play, *Our Town*, for The Interact Theatre Company in North Hollywood.

PETER CROOKSTON (B. 1936) has been a journalist for more than forty years. He first worked as a reporter and copy editor on newspapers in his hometown of Newcastle upon Tyne, then moved to London where he wrote for the *Daily Express*. From 1961 to 1964 Crookston was picture editor for David Astor's *The Observer*, Great Britain's oldest Sunday newspaper.

In his subsequent positions as assistant, then deputy editor at *The London Sunday Times Magazine* (1964–69), he came into contact with Arbus, whose photographs he soon featured.

Crookston published "Two American Families" (*The London Sunday Times Magazine*, November 10, 1968). As editor of *Nova* magazine (1969–71), a protofeminist women's monthly, he printed, among other series, Arbus's portraits of famous-people look-alikes: "People Who Think They Look Like Other People" (*Nova*, October 1969). With his former colleagues at *The London Sunday Times Magazine*, Crookston co-sponsored Arbus's productive April 1969 trip to England which resulted in three *Nova* articles and a series of portraits of wax figures in Madame Tussaud's Wax Museum that were published posthumously in *Diane Arbus: Magazine Work* (1984).

In 1973 Crookston rejoined *The Observer* and four years later became editor of *The Observer Magazine*, a post he held until 1982. He then went on to edit many other international publications. Since 1998 he has worked as a freelance writer for several newspapers, including *The Observer* and the *Daily Mail*. Crookston is the author of *Villian: The Biography of a Criminal* (1967). He is also the editor of a series of histories of England. Crookston is currently researching a book on the Durham (Derbyshire, North Wales) coal miner and composer Robert Saint.

VICTOR D'AMICO (1904–87) was founding director of education at The Museum of Modern Art (MoMA) from 1937 to 1969. D'Amico met Arbus early in his career while teaching at the Fieldston School in Riverdale, New York.

In 1960 d'Amico and his wife, Mabel (1909–98), a high school art teacher, founded the Victor d'Amico Institute of Art, also known as The Art Barge, a summer art school built on a refurbished World War I navy barge beached along Napeague Harbor at the eastern end of Long Island. In addition to his museum and institute programs, d'Amico was also the author of numerous books on art education, including *Creative Teaching in Art* (1942, 1953); and with Arlette Buchman, *Assemblage: A New Dimension in Creative Teaching in Action* (1972). His lectures, correspondence, audio and video tapes, and teaching slides are preserved at Columbia University in the Model School Library at Teachers College.

RENE D'HARNONCOURT (1901–68) was the director of The Museum of Modern Art (MoMA), New York, from 1949 to 1967. Born in Vienna, he was schooled first in Graz, Austria, then at the university in Vienna. D'Harnoncourt studied philosophy and chemistry and was an amateur painter. In 1925 he moved to Mexico City and amassed an important collection of Mexican art. Dwight W. Morrow, then United States Ambassador to Mexico, convinced d'Harnoncourt to build a special collection of indigenous Mexican art to be shown in the United States. *The Exhibition of Mexican Arts* opened at The Metropolitan Museum of Art in 1930 and included 1,200 works of early and contemporary fine and decorative arts from the time of Spain's conquest of Mexico to the 1920s. It was the first major show on the origin and development of Mexican civilization through its arts.

Mexican Arts and its national tour circulated by the Carnegie Institute and the American Federation of Arts established d'Harnoncourt's reputation as a collector, curator, and impresario. A specialist in the art of indigenous peoples, d'Harnoncourt became a member of the Indian Arts and Crafts Board of the Department of Interior in 1936. In 1944 he joined the staff of MoMA and after five years succeeded Alfred Barr as the institution's second director.

Indian Art of the United States (1941), an exhibition catalog for a show at MoMA, was the author's first major academic publication. As director of MoMA, d'Harnoncourt provided introductions or was the coauthor of numerous museum publications including such standard texts as *Art of the South Seas* (1946) and *Ancient Art of the Andes* (1954). His last publication, *d'Hoodles* (1966), is a witty compilation of scribblings made by d'Harnoncourt during meetings at MoMA. D'Harnoncourt was killed by a drunk driver on Long Island, New York, a year after his retirement from the museum.

ALEXANDER ELIOT (B. 1919) is an art critic, novelist, and essayist who established his reputation with the book *Three Hundred Years of American Painting* (1957). After graduating from the Loomis School in Windsor, Connecticut, he went to Black Mountain College in North Carolina where he spent two years (1936–38) studying art with Josef Albers and stage studies with Xanti Schawinsky. Eliot moved to New York City in the early 1940s and worked at the Associated American Artists Gallery, then for the March of Time Newsreel Service. From 1945 to 1960 he was a sportswriter, then art editor, at *Time* magazine where he wrote features about Pablo Picasso, Henri Matisse, and Diego Rivera, among other modern masters.

Among Eliot's more than twenty publications are *Proud Youth* (1953), a novel for which Diane and Allan Arbus provided an author's photograph; *Sight and Insight* (1959); *The Horizon Concise History of Greece* (1972); and *The Universal Myths: Heroes, Gods, Tricksters and Others* (1990).

In 1938, when he was nineteen, Eliot met Arbus, a fifteen-year-old fellow summer student at the Cummington School of the Arts near Northampton, Massachusetts. Eliot and Arbus remained friends for the next three decades. Arbus served as godmother to Eliot's daughter, May, from his first marriage to Anne Dick. For most of the 1960s and early '70s, Eliot, his second wife, Jane Winslow Eliot, and their two children lived abroad and collaborated on books about the myths of ancient civilizations. After returning to the United States in 1976, the Eliots spent a decade in Northampton, Massachusetts, then moved to Venice, California, where they live today.

WALKER EVANS (1903–75) is regarded as the progenitor of the documentary tradition in American photography. His 1938 publication and exhibition at The Museum of Modern Art depicted the daily lives of ordinary citizens.

Evans was born in St. Louis and raised in the Chicago suburb of Kenilworth. After a year at Williams College he moved to New York to pursue writing. By 1928 he had taken up the camera, and small selections of his photographs soon appeared in literary and arts magazines of the late 1920s and early '30s.

Like his Greenwich Village roommate Ben Shahn, Evans found employment in Franklin Delano Roosevelt's New Deal. From 1935 to 1937 he worked primarily in the American South as a photographer for the government's Resettlement (later called the Farm Security) Administration. Evans collaborated with the poet and writer James Agee to create a written and photographic portrait of three tenant farm families in Alabama, which eventually became *Let Us Now Praise Famous Men* (1941).

In 1938 Evans began a new project on subway passengers. Art director Marvin Israel published some of the images as "Walker Evans: The Unposed Portrait" in *Harper's Bazaar* in 1962, four years before they appeared in a book, with an essay by James Agee, entitled *Many Are Called* (1966).

From 1945 to 1965, Evans worked at *Fortune* magazine as special photographic editor and produced some forty portfolios. Evans served as a long-term member of the John Simon Guggenheim Memorial Foundation arts selection committee, and in this capacity encouraged numerous artists from Robert Frank (1955) to Arbus (1963) to apply for fellowships. He met Arbus in late 1961 and included her in his chapter survey of the eighteen most important artists in the history of photography in *Quality: Its Image in the Arts* (1969), edited by Louis Kronenberger. He taught photography at Yale University and produced his last photographs in 1973–74 with an SX-70 Polaroid. In 1994, twenty years after Evans's death, his complete personal archive of negatives, transparencies, papers, and collections was acquired by The Metropolitan Museum of Art.

BEA FEITLER (1938–82) was born in Rio de Janeiro but moved to New York to study design. A student of Marvin Israel's at Parsons School of Design, she was hired by Israel in 1961 as his assistant art director at *Harper's Bazaar*. After Israel was fired two years later, Feitler and another assistant, Ruth Ansel, jointly succeeded him. The collaboration of Feitler and Ansel defined 1960s magazine design.

Feitler co–art directed *Harper's Bazaar* for ten years until she left in May 1972 to design and launch *Ms.* magazine with Gloria Steinem. Six years later she became a consulting art director for Condé Nast Publications where she developed the graphic image for *Self* magazine. From 1975 to 1981 Feitler was art director of *Rolling Stone*, which she redesigned in 1977 and again in 1981. She taught design from 1974 until 1980 at the School of Visual Arts. When in 1970 Arbus produced her only portfolio, *A box of ten photographs*, Feitler purchased one of the few sets known to have been sold. It is now in the collection of the Smithsonian American Art Museum, Washington, D.C.

In addition to her magazine work, Feitler also designed album covers, books and their jackets, and even theatrical costumes, including the cover of *Black and Blue* for the Rolling Stones (1976) and Richard Avedon's *Diary of a Century: Jacques Henri Lartigue* (1970). She also designed *Cole* (1971), a massive volume of Cole Porter's lyrics, photographs, and discography. Her final magazine project was the redesign of *Vanity Fair*; the premier issue came out after her death of cancer. Feitler's personal archive of artwork, magazines, correspondence, and photographs is housed in the Adam & Sophie Gimbel Design Library at Parsons School of Design.

CLAY FELKER (B. 1928) is director of the Felker Magazine Center, University of California at Berkeley, Graduate School of Journalism. A 1951 graduate of Duke University, Felker began his journalism career covering sports for *Life* magazine, then in 1954 worked with Henry Luce and others on the development of *Sports Illustrated*. By 1957 he was features editor at *Esquire* and, along with Harold Hayes, Robert Benton, and David Newman, transformed Arnold Gingrich's men's monthly into a more sophisticated venue featuring contemporary writers and artists such as Vladimir Nabokov, Andy Warhol, and Arbus.

One of the architects of the literary movement known as New Journalism, his influential Sunday supplement to the *New York Herald Tribune* helped introduce the work of Gloria Steinem and Tom Wolfe into the pages of American magazines. He published Wolfe's two-part evisceration of William Shawn and *The New Yorker*, "Tiny Mummies! The True Story of the Ruler of 43rd Street's Land of the Walking Dead!"

and "Lost in the Whichy Thickets: *The New Yorker*" (1965). In 1968 he became the founding editor of *New York* magazine. He served as editor of, among other magazines, *The Village Voice*. He is the author of *Casey Stengel's Secret* (1961) and served as editor of *The Best American Magazine Writing* 2000 (2000).

SHIRLEY FINGERHOOD (B. 1923) was born in New York City and is an attorney in private practice. She graduated from Fieldston School in 1940 in the same class as Arbus and their mutual friend Stewart Stern, the screenwriter. After graduating from Vassar in 1944, Fingerhood returned to the city where she renewed her friendship with Arbus. Fingerhood graduated from Yale Law School in 1951 and moved for a year to Washington, D.C.

In 1952 Fingerhood returned to New York and established a legal practice specializing in literary and First Amendment cases. In the course of her fifty-year career Fingerhood has represented a wide range of clients in the fields of entertainment, the arts, and literature, including Arbus and three Pulitzer Prize winners. In 1978 she became a judge and sat on the Supreme Court of the State of New York from 1986 to 1994.

Arbus frequently consulted Fingerhood on legal matters from the mid-1950s until her death. Fingerhood, who remains in private practice and serves on the boards of several charitable organizations, is a director of the Lawyers' Committee on Nuclear Policy (LCNP), a national nonprofit educational association founded in 1981 that uses national and international law to promote peace and disarmament.

MICHAEL FLANAGAN (B. 1943) was born in Buffalo, New York, and is a painter, graphic designer, and author. While studying painting at Parsons School of Design (1963–66), he met art director Marvin Israel through whom he was introduced to many artists, including Robert Frank and Arbus. Flanagan was greatly influenced by Arbus's first class at Parsons in the fall of 1965.

After his graduation and before he enrolled in Yale University's graduate painting program, he worked in the summer of 1966 for Allan Arbus as a darkroom assistant and processed and contact-printed Diane Arbus's negatives. In 1969, after a year studying minimalist painting at Yale, Flanagan taught himself the art of book jacket design. With Marvin Israel he designed several notable photography books, including Clark Worswick and Ainslie Embree's *The Last Empire: Photography in British India, 1855–1911* (1976), and *Unseen Versailles* (1981) by Deborah Turbeville.

By 1981 Flanagan had his first one-person exhibition at Cordier and Ekstrom Gallery, New York. Numerous solo and group shows followed, as well as fellowships in painting from Yaddo (1988), the artists' community in Saratoga Springs, New York, and from the New York Foundation for the Arts (1986, 1987, 1992). Despite his success as a painter, however, Flanagan is probably best known for the critically lauded *Stations: An Imaginary Journey* (1994), a hybrid novel that integrates his artwork and original writing.

MARY FRANK (B. 1933) is known for her gestural, figurative sculptures, drawings, paintings, and monoprints. She is the recipient of two John Simon Guggenheim Memorial Foundation Fellowships (1973, 1983) and was elected to the American Academy and Institute of Arts and Letters in 1984. She has work in numerous public collections, including the Hirshhorn Museum and Sculpture Garden,

The Metropolitan Museum of Art, The Museum of Modern Art, and the Whitney Museum of American Art. She is the subject of two major monographic essays: Hayden Herrara's *Mary Frank* (1990) and Linda Nochlin's *Mary Frank: Encounters* (2000), an exhibition catalog that accompanied a large painting retrospective at the Neuberger Museum of Art.

Born in London, Mary Frank came to the United States when she was seven years old and settled in Brooklyn with her mother, the American-born painter Eleanore Lockspeiser. While in high school she studied modern dance with Hanya Holm, then later with Martha Graham and José Limón in the first year of the summer dance program (later the American Dance Festival) at Connecticut College in New London. In 1950 she studied drawing and painting with Max Beckmann at the American Art School, and took life drawing classes with Hans Hofmann. That same year she married the Swiss photographer Robert Frank, with whom she had two children, Pablo and Andrea. Without any formal training, Mary Frank began to make sculpture in wood and plaster, then ultimately in clay, incorporating into her art her dance training and its reliance on gesture and movement. Mary Frank met Arbus in the mid-1950s through the art dealer Richard Bellamy who lived near the Franks on 10th Street.

Mary Frank first exhibited her sculpture in the 1950s at the Tanager Gallery in New York, and had her first one-person show at the Stephen Radich Gallery in 1961. From 1965 to 1970 she taught drawing at the New School for Social Research. In 1972 the Solomon R. Guggenheim Museum included her work in *10 Independents*, her first museum exhibition. Since 1968 she has had regular shows at the Zabriskie Gallery, and, since 1996, the DC Moore Gallery, both in New York City. Mary Frank separated from Robert Frank in 1969 and after her divorce married Leo Treitler, a musicologist and pianist. She is an active antiwar protester and contributes her time and art to the cause.

ROBERT FRANK (B. 1924) is a photographer and filmmaker best known for his book of black-and-white photographs *The Americans* (1959), first published in Paris as *Les Américains* (1958). A compilation of two years of picture making across the United States courtesy of an extended fellowship (1955–56) from the John Simon Guggenheim Memorial Foundation, the volume includes an introduction by Jack Kerouac. The book presents a lyrical yet unvarnished look at even the most prosaic aspects of America from gas stations and barrooms to elevator operators and conventioneers. Subsequently published in several revised editions, *The Americans* endures as one of the post–World War II era's most influential monographs. Frank is also the author of numerous other books, including *New York Is* (1959), *The Lines of My Hand* (1972), and *Flower Is...* (1987). His archive is preserved in The Robert Frank Collection at the National Gallery of Art.

Frank was born in Zurich, Switzerland, and at the age of seventeen apprenticed himself to a local photographer, Hermann Segesser. In 1947 he showed the designer Alexey Brodovitch a small handmade book of his original photographs, *40 Fotos*, and was immediately hired by Brodovitch to work for *Harper's Bazaar*. Frank would soon provide fashion and editorial photographs for hundreds of articles in *Harper's Bazaar*, as well as in *Junior Bazaar*, *Life*, *Look*, *McCall's*, and *Fortune* magazines, and *The New York Times*.

In December 1949 *Camera* magazine published "Robert Frank," the artist's first important portfolio. The following year Frank appeared in *51 American Photographers*, curated by Edward Steichen at The

Museum of Modern Art (MoMA). Subsequently he would be included in such important MoMA exhibitions as *Post-War European Photography* (1953) and *The Family of Man* (1955). In 1961 the Art Institute of Chicago organized a retrospective exhibition, *Robert Frank, Photographer*. Other major museum shows would follow, including *Robert Frank: New York to Nova Scotia*, Museum of Fine Arts, Houston (1986); *Robert Frank: Moving Out*, National Gallery of Art, Washington, D.C. (1994); and *Robert Frank: Hold Still-Keep Going*, Museum Folkwang, Essen, Germany (2000).

Frank met Diane and Allan Arbus in the late 1950s when he was switching from still photography to motion pictures. His first film, *Pull My Daisy* (1959), a groundbreaking adaptation of Kerouac's play *The Beat Generation*, was followed by *The Sin of Jesus* (1960), and *Me and My Brother* (1965–68). Among his many films and videos is *Home Improvements* (1985) and full-length features like *Cocksucker Blues* (1972), a ninety-minute cinema verité film about the Rolling Stones's 1972 North American tour.

In August 2002 Frank received the Edward MacDowell Medal from the MacDowell Colony. His most recent film is *Paper Route* (2002) and his latest photography exhibition, *Robert Frank: London/Wales*, opened in May 2003 at the Corcoran Gallery of Art, Washington, D.C.

TINA FREDERICKS (B. 1922) began her career as a magazine art director and is now head of the eponymously titled real estate firm in East Hampton, Long Island. As a *Glamour* magazine editor she gave Andy Warhol his first editorial assignment in August 1949. Born in Berlin, Germany, Fredericks is the daughter of the general manager of Ulstein Publishing, still one of Germany's largest publishers. After Hitler came to power, her family emigrated to the United States where her father took a job in 1934 at Hearst Publications. Fredericks attended Bennington College, but after winning a summer scholarship from *Mademoiselle* to work on the August "college" issue, she left school and moved to New York City. She began to sell fashion layout ideas to *Glamour* as a freelancer, and in 1943 Alexander Liberman hired her as assistant art editor under C. P. Penelis.

In 1947 Fredericks became art director of *Glamour* and gave many emerging artists their first jobs, including the illustrator Maurice Sendak, and Diane and Allan Arbus, whose first editorial photographs appeared in "The New Sweater Story Is a Long Story" (*Glamour*, May 1947). The previous month *Glamour* had featured the Arbuses among six other couples in "Mr. and Mrs. Inc." The Arbuses submitted their own portrait for the story. Known as a rebellious editor who appreciated new ideas, Fredericks left Condé Nast in 1953 to become picture editor at *Ladies' Home Journal*. After her first marriage ended, she moved to East Hampton, New York, where she lives today.

LEE FRIEDLANDER (B. 1934) is the author of more than twenty books of photographs, including *The American Monument* (1976); *Like a One-Eyed Cat: Photographs by Lee Friedlander, 1956–1987* (1989); and *American Musicians* (1998). His first book, *Self Portrait* (1970), depicts the American social landscape in snapshots—many in which the artist appears only as a shadow on his generally unsuspecting subjects—of everyday life on city streets. A fellow of the American Academy of Arts and Sciences since 1999, Friedlander has received, among many other awards, three National Endowment for the Arts fellowships (1960, 1962, 1977), the Medal of the City of Paris (1981), the Edward MacDowell Medal for Lifetime

Achievement in the Arts (1986), and a John D. and Catherine T. MacArthur Foundation Award (1990).

Born in Aberdeen, Washington, Friedlander took up photography in high school, and after graduation moved to California to enroll in the Los Angeles Art Center School. He met fellow jazz enthusiast Nesuhi Ertegun, a founder of Atlantic Records, who hired him to photograph music legends, from John Coltrane to Aretha Franklin. Friedlander would soon make record-cover portraits for Columbia, RCA, and Atlantic Records.

After moving to New York City in 1956, Friedlander began to work for *Seventeen*, *Esquire*, *McCall's*, and *Collier's* magazines. Through art director Marvin Israel he met and became friends with Walker Evans, Garry Winogrand, and Arbus. Evans wrote about Friedlander's photographs of television sets broadcasting to otherwise empty motel rooms in a short essay entitled "The Little Screens" (*Harper's Bazaar*, February 1963); and ten years later provided an introduction to Friedlander's first portfolio, "Lee Friedlander: Fifteen Photographs" (1973). The following year Friedlander edited and arranged the publication of Evans's second portfolio, "Walker Evans: Selected Photographs" (1974).

In the late 1950s Friedlander discovered and later acquired and preserved the photographic negatives of Ernest J. Bellocq, the documentarian of New Orleans's red-light district known as Storyville. He printed, exhibited, and published the images in *E. J. Bellocq: Storyville Portraits, Photographs from the New Orleans Red-Light District, Circa 1912* (1970, 1996). Arbus acquired a few of Friedlander's prints of Bellocq's negatives and was among the first of his friends to appreciate their historical importance and psychological complexity.

Friedlander has had many exhibitions, beginning in 1963 with a solo show at the George Eastman House in Rochester, New York, and including *New Documents*, a group show with Garry Winogrand and Arbus that John Szarkowski organized in 1967 for The Museum of Modern Art. His next large show will be a retrospective at MoMA in 2005.

HAROLD HAYES (1926–89) was the editor of *Esquire* from 1962 to 1973. One of the architects of the literary movement known as New Journalism, he commissioned articles from Tom Wolfe, Norman Mailer, Gay Talese, Terry Southern, and Raymond Carver. While working as a features editor for an issue on New York City, primarily written by Talese, Hayes sent the still-untried Arbus into the streets with a press pass and letters of introduction from the magazine. The resulting article, "The Vertical Journey: Six Movements of a Moment Within the Heart of the City" (July 1960), complete with Arbus's own captions, served as the catalyst for her work of the 1960s.

Born in Elkin, West Virginia, the son of a Southern Baptist minister, and reared in Winston-Salem, North Carolina, Hayes graduated in 1948 from Wake Forest University. After two years in the marines, he landed a job as an editor at *Pageant*, a competitor to *Reader's Digest*. In 1956 he moved to *Esquire* where he worked with Clay Felker and Robert Benton under Arnold Gingrich, the founding editor of the magazine. As managing editor, Hayes promoted many of the era's most creative talents—from George Lois to Michael Herr. While with *Esquire*, Hayes edited a selection of essays by his writers entitled *Smiling Through the Apocalypse: Esquire's History of the Sixties* (1969).

In the early 1970s Hayes moved to California where he took over the editorship of *California* magazine. He ended his career writing books on Africa, including *The Last Place on Earth* (1977) and the posthumous *The Dark Romance of Dian Fossey* (1990).

His November 1986 essay on Fossey for *Life* magazine served as the basis for the film *Gorillas in the Mist* (1988). Hayes's papers are in the Z. Smith Reynolds Library at Wake Forest University.

PATI HILL (B. 1921) is a writer and visual artist whose novels include *The Nine Mile Circle* (1957), *Prosper* (1960), and *One Thing I Know* (1962), which she dedicated to Arbus. The two met in New York City in the early 1940s when Hill was beginning her career as a fashion model. She and Arbus remained friends for thirty years.

In the late 1930s Hill left George Washington University for New York City and became a John Robert Powers fashion model, often seen in the pages of *Harper's Bazaar*. She also began her literary career, producing a monthly advice column for *Seventeen* magazine during its early years, and short stories for *Mademoiselle*. Hill first married Jack Long, an editor at *Collier's*, then in 1947 Robert Meservey, a photographer (later physicist). By 1950 she had appeared in advertisements by Diane and Allan Arbus for Russek's, divorced her first two husbands, and moved to Paris to model for Molyneux and other couturiers. She contributed short fiction to *The Paris Review* from 1953 to 1978 and completed her first published book, *The Pit and the Century Plant* (1955).

Hill moved back to the United States in the late 1950s and lived in New York and in Stonington, Connecticut, where she met the poet James Merrill, and Truman Capote, with whom she published "The Art of Fiction XVII" (*The Paris Review*, spring-summer 1957), an interview that anticipated the publication of *Breakfast at Tiffany's*. In 1960 she married the French gallerist and art publisher Paul Bianchini, and had a daughter, Paola (1962). In 1973, at the request of Doon Arbus, Hill translated, with Alain de la Falaise, the original text of *Diane Arbus* for the French publisher Editions du Chêne.

Hill began to work as an artist in 1975 and had three exhibitions at the Jill Kornblee Gallery in New York City. One of the pioneers of "copy art," she is recognized for her advocacy of xerography and for the quality that she demonstrated could be obtained through the use of toner as a print medium. She produced several artist's books with Kornblee, including *Slave Days: 29 Poems, 31 Photocopied Objects* (1975). The Versailles project, her chef d'oeuvre, is an ongoing work that is the subject of several published commentaries, including F. de Merdieu's *Pati Hill, or the Catalogue of Magical Objects* (Art Press, France, #76, December 1983). Hill's most recent exhibition was in 2000 at the Bayly Art Museum, University of Virginia, Charlottesville. The show, entitled *Wall Papers*, included selections of her Versailles reportage as well as her etchings. Her artwork is in the collections of the Cooper-Hewitt, National Design Museum, Smithsonian Institution, and the Musée de Sens.

MARVIN ISRAEL (1924–84) was a painter, art director, graphic designer, and influential teacher. Born in Syracuse, New York, he briefly attended Ethical Culture School in New York City. He received a B.F.A. from Syracuse University in 1950 and in 1955 an M.F.A. in graphic design from Yale University. In 1950 Israel married the Cuban-born sculptor and ceramicist Margaret Ponce Israel (1929–87). Israel became art director at *Seventeen* in 1957. At *Harper's Bazaar* (1961–63) he replaced Henry Wolf, successor to Alexey Brodovitch with whom Israel had studied at Yale. Israel featured *Harper's Bazaar* star photographer, Richard Avedon, and also artists such as Arbus, Robert Frank, Lee Friedlander, Larry Rivers, and Andy Warhol, along with established masters such as Martin Munkacsi, Henri Cartier-Bresson, and

Walker Evans. From 1957 to 1963 he worked as a freelance art director for Atlantic Records, designing record covers for the label's roster of jazz and blues artists.

Israel taught design and painting at Parsons School of Design (1959–64), School of Visual Arts (1965–67), and Cooper Union School of Art (1968–69); and in 1967 he conducted a master class in photography with Avedon, to which Arbus was an occasional guest artist. Israel produced many photography publications, including *Nothing Personal* (1964), by Richard Avedon, with text by James Baldwin; Lee Friedlander's *Self Portrait* (1970); and the first two of Arbus's posthumous publications, *Diane Arbus* (1972) and *Diane Arbus: Magazine Work* (1984). In the 1970s and '80s Israel's long-term collaboration with Avedon expanded to include the exhibition design for most of the photographer's large shows including *Richard Avedon*, a retrospective at the Minneapolis Institute of Arts; *Portraits, 1969–1975* (1975), at the Marlborough Gallery, New York, and the Seibu Museum of Art, Tokyo (1977); and *In the American West* (1985), which opened at the Amon Carter Museum, Fort Worth, Texas, a year after Israel's death.

Israel designed Arbus's only portfolio, *A box of ten photographs* (1970). The portfolio box—manufactured of clear plastic—served both as safe storage for the prints and as an exhibition frame for any one of the ten photographs. His simple but effective design is credited with inaugurating a new style of acrylic exhibition frames that soon dominated the New York gallery scene in the 1970s.

For the last twenty years of his life, Israel devoted much of his creative efforts to his own artwork; his paintings can be found in the collections of The Museum of Modern Art, the Whitney Museum of American Art, and the Art Institute of Chicago, among others.

CLARENCE JOHN LAUGHLIN (1905–85) was born near Lake Charles, Louisiana, and in 1910 moved with his family to New Orleans where he lived for the rest of his life. In the mid-1920s he discovered the poetry and prose of the French Symbolists, as well as Edgar Allan Poe and Herman Melville, and began to write original poems and Gothic fiction, eventually earning a reputation as the "Baudelaire of the Bayou." Laughlin held a variety of jobs from 1924 to 1935, including a clerkship in a New Orleans bank, but by the late 1920s he was known regionally as an important bibliophile. By 1934 he had taught himself the rudiments of photography and soon began corresponding with a wide range of artists and writers from Margaret Bourke-White to Man Ray, André Breton, Eugene Berman, and Joseph Cornell. His photography also began to appear in *Photographie* (1939, 1954), *U.S. Camera* (1940), *Du* (1954), and *Life* (1942, 1960), among other journals and avant-garde publications.

Laughlin worked from 1936 to 1940 as a Civil Service photographer for the United States Army Corps of Engineers recording construction work on the Mississippi River levees between New Orleans and Vicksburg, Mississippi. He also began his thirty-year documentation of the region's nineteenth-century architecture. In 1936 he had his first one-person show of photographs at the Isaac Delgado Museum of New Orleans (now the New Orleans Museum of Art), then four years later exhibited his photographs of old New Orleans with Eugène Atget's photographs of Paris at the Julien Levy Gallery in New York City. Laughlin had in his lifetime more than two hundred solo shows at, among others, the Art Institute of Chicago and the Philadelphia Museum of Art.

Laughlin is perhaps best known for *Ghosts Along the Mississippi: An Essay in the Poetic Interpretation of Louisiana's Plantation Architecture* (1948), a book of his writings and photographs that blends documentary description with surrealism.

Arbus corresponded with Laughlin in April 1962 just after *Infinity* magazine published "The Full Circle," the reprint of her portraits of eccentrics, and around the time when a second edition of *Ghosts Along the Mississippi* was released. It is not known how they were introduced, but they likely met in person two years later when Arbus traveled to New Orleans to photograph Mardi Gras celebrations. Laughlin has been the subject of several monographs. His archive of master prints, negatives, papers, and correspondence is preserved by The Historic New Orleans Collection; the Louisiana State University in Baton Rouge houses his massive library of 30,000 volumes. Upon his request, Laughlin is buried in Père Lachaise cemetery in Paris.

HELEN LEVITT (B. 1913) was born in Brooklyn, New York, and had her first solo show of photographs at The Museum of Modern Art in 1943. For more than half a century she has explored the nature of life on her native city's streets in black-and-white and color photographs, and also in documentary films. James Agee provided the introduction to her first book, *A Way of Seeing* (1965).

Levitt began her career as a motion picture camera operator and film cutter while assisting Helen Von Dongen, one of several editors working for Luis Buñuel at The Museum of Modern Art during World War II making short, pro-democracy documentaries for the U.S. government. In 1945 Levitt collaborated with Janice Loeb on *In the Street*, a documentary set in Harlem. With the filmmaker Sidney Meyers, Levitt and Loeb also worked together on *The Quiet One* (1948–49), a feature-length documentary about a delinquent boy that won first prize at the Venice Film Festival, among many other honors including an Academy Award nomination for best story and screenplay.

In the 1950s and early '60s, while working in Hollywood, Levitt wrote a support letter for Arbus's first Guggenheim fellowship application. (The two artists did not meet until later in the decade and Levitt wrote her recommendation after reviewing a set of prints Arbus sent by mail to California at Walker Evans's suggestion.)

Levitt's photographs have been featured in hundreds of museum exhibitions in the United States and Europe, including the 1991 retrospective at the San Francisco Museum of Modern Art that traveled across the United States. Levitt has published two expanded editions of *A Way of Seeing*, as well as many other volumes of photographs, including *In the Street* (1987); *Mexico City* (1997); *Crosstown* (2001); and her most recent volume of photographs, *Here and There* (2003).

ALEXANDER LIBERMAN (1912–99) was born in Kiev, Russia, and schooled in England and Paris, graduating in 1930 with a degree in philosophy and mathematics from the Sorbonne. He studied painting with the cubist painter André Lhote, architecture at the Ecole des Beaux-Arts, then worked as an assistant to the renowned designer, Cassandre. From 1933 to 1936 Liberman was assistant art director at *Vu*, the progressive Paris-based magazine dedicated to photography that was Henry Luce's model for *Life*. He left the monthly in 1936 to devote himself to painting and writing, and after the Nazi occupation of France emigrated to the United States. In 1941 Liberman became art director of *Vogue*. He held this position for twenty-one years, until he was promoted to editorial director of all Condé Nast publications, a title he kept until his retirement in 1994. Under his leadership, *Vogue* integrated high art and culture with the world of fashion by regularly including serious art criticism in its pages alongside commissioned work by Marcel Duchamp, Salvador Dali, Marc Chagall, and Joseph Cornell.

Throughout his fifty-three years in fashion, Liberman made paintings, photographs, and ultimately sculpture. His work can be found in most public collections worldwide. Liberman is the author of numerous publications, including *The Artist and His Studio* (1960); *Dietrich: An Intimate Photographic Memoir* (1992); and a personal memoir, *Then: Photographs 1925–1995* (1995).

MARGUERITE LAMKIN LITTMAN (B. 1929) is a director of the Elton John AIDS Foundation and a member of the national council for amfAR.

Littman was born in Monroe, Louisiana. She went to Miss Finch's Finishing School in New York City, then Newcomb College at Tulane University in New Orleans where she studied philosophy. In 1949 she moved to Los Angeles, following her brother, Speed Lamkin, the novelist and playwright. Littman continued her study of philosophy at UCLA and soon became friends with Dorothy Parker and Christopher Isherwood, as well as Tennessee Williams. In 1955 she taught Barbara Bel Geddes how to speak "Southern" for her role as Maggie in Elia Kazan's original stage production of Williams's *Cat on a Hot Tin Roof;* three years later she coached Elizabeth Taylor in the film version. Littman was for many years a dialect coach for the stage and screen and worked on more than ten Hollywood films including Williams's *Baby Doll* (1956), and William Faulkner's *The Long Hot Summer* (1958) and *The Sound and the Fury* (1959).

After a brief marriage to the screenwriter Harry Brown, Littman moved to New York City around 1960 and became the arts editor at *Glamour* magazine. In February 1963, at the suggestion of their mutual friend Marvin Israel, Richard Avedon hired her to work with him on his current photographic project—taken on various trips from New York to Louisiana—of civil rights demonstrations, racist politicians, elderly former slaves, and members of the Student Non-Violent Coordinating Committee. With James Baldwin's text, the project was published as *Nothing Personal* (1964).

Through Marvin Israel, Littman met Arbus and subsequently assigned and published "What's New: The Witch Predicts," *Glamour*, January and October 1964. The story features uncredited texts by Arbus about the most famous Los Angeles soothsayers whose clients included, among others, Elvis Presley, Jayne Mansfield, and Littman's friend, Elizabeth Taylor.

In 1962 Littman adopted the pen name Daisy and started a column in *Glamour* that advised lovelorn young girls on how to win and keep their men. She married her third husband, the barrister and Queen's Counsel Mark Littman, and moved to London.

CARLOTTA MARSHALL (B. 1939) was born in Atlanta, Georgia, and raised in Jacksonville, Florida. She graduated in 1957 from The Ethel Walker School in Simsbury, Connecticut, and after living with her grandmother in Paris moved at age nineteen to New York City. She met Arbus during her first week in Manhattan.

In 1959–60 Marshall attended poetry classes at Columbia University and at the New School for Social Research, and, with a friend, opened a small shop called The Bead Studio. She held various odd jobs related to photography including work for film-maker Robert Frank, the French photo agency, Rapho Guillumette, commercial photographer David Attie, art director Alexey Brodovitch, and German-born photographer Hans Namuth. Marshall also modeled for an unpublished Diane Arbus feature for *Harper's Bazaar.*

She studied religion at New York's Union Theological Seminary, then in 1963–64 lived and traveled in Greece. Upon her return to New York City, Marshall met Sister Cora Brady, the distinguished professor of religion at Manhattanville College, a Catholic school run by the Society of the Sacred Heart in Purchase, New York. Sister Brady conceived and directed the Masters in Religious Education (M.R.E.) program.

In 1966 Marshall moved to Holland and married Louis Berger, a fellow theological student, and a year later gave birth to their son, Jamie. In the spring of 1968 Marshall visited New York and introduced Sister Brady to Arbus. While in Holland a few months later, Marshall developed encephalitis which triggered multiple sclerosis. She and Arbus corresponded steadily during the worst weeks of her severe illness.

In summer 1969, Sister Brady taught a Manhattanville College course for nuns, some from silent orders, who had recently left their convents. She invited Arbus to speak to her class and present slides of her work. Brady's objective was to introduce the sisters to life outside of the cloister. On July 14, 1969, six days before the historic moon walk and a month before the music festival at Woodstock, Arbus gave an evening lecture to the school entitled "The Still and All."

When Marshall's husband decided to pursue a monastic life in 1971, Marshall moved from Holland to London with Jamie who was then four years old. She became involved in childhood education, helping to facilitate the Early Education Project at the Froebel Institute. Marshall also supports the Campaign for Nuclear Disarmament (CND). She has lived in New York since 1997 and remains an active antiwar protester.

ROBERT MESERVEY (B. 1921) was born in Hanover, New Hampshire, and is a low-temperature physicist known for his research in superconductivity and magnetism at Massachusetts Institute of Technology (MIT). The son of a Dartmouth College professor, Meservey graduated from the college with a B.A. in physics in 1943 and was immediately drafted. A champion alpine skier, he became a rock climbing and skiing instructor in the Tenth Mountain Division, but by the end of 1944, instead of being sent overseas with the division, he was assigned to develop night-vision equipment at an army laboratory in Virginia, where he spent the rest of the war.

A lifelong devotee of photography, Meservey moved to New York City in the summer of 1946 to become second assistant to the fashion photographer Fernand Fonssagrives. Through Pati Hill, Meservey met and befriended Diane and Allan Arbus, who were just beginning their careers as fashion photographers. In early 1947 Meservey and Hill were married and left New York, traveling and working together on various photographic projects, including the contemporary photographs for Antoinette F. Downing and Vincent J. Scully, Jr.'s *The Architectural Heritage of Newport, Rhode Island, 1640–1915* (1952). Meservey and Hill separated in 1949, and for the next two years Meservey worked as a freelancer.

At the beginning of the Korean War, Meservey gave up photography for science and from 1951 to 1955 worked as a civilian physicist in night-vision research at the Army Research and Development Lab in Fort Belvoir, Virginia. In 1953 he married his present wife, Evelyn (Lyn) Miller Meservey, a painter then working in Washington, D.C., and two years later entered Yale University, where he earned a doctorate in 1961 in physics for an optical study of superfluid helium. After graduation Meservey conducted research on superconductivity at MIT's Lincoln Lab, then moved in 1963 to MIT's Magnet Lab (the Francis Bitter Magnet Laboratory). For more than thirty years he led a research team in low-temperature physics, superconductivity, and magnetism, and is known for the discovery of spin-polarized electron tunneling. Meservey retired in 1998, lives in Cambridge, Massachusetts, and continues to publish and write reviews as a visiting scientist at MIT.

JOSEPH MITCHELL (1908–96) was born on a tobacco and cotton farm in Robeson County, North Carolina, and attended the University of North Carolina for four years but left before graduating to take a reporting job in Durham. Mitchell moved to New York City in 1929 and spent his first decade there working as a newspaper reporter for the *Morning World*, the *New York Herald Tribune*, and the *New York World-Telegram*. In 1938 he moved to *The New Yorker* where he worked for fifty-eight years as a writer of "Talk of the Town" and of profiles of some of the city's most eccentric inhabitants and their milieu.

Mitchell's first book was a collection of his newspaper articles entitled *My Ears Are Bent* (1938). It was followed by, among others, *McSorley's Wonderful Saloon* (1943); *Old Mr. Flood* (1948); *The Bottom of the Harbor* (1959); and *Joe Gould's Secret* (1965). Arbus contacted Mitchell in early 1960, soon after reading *McSorley's Wonderful Saloon.* Although they never met in person, the two documentarians stayed in contact for almost seven years.

LISETTE MODEL (1901–83) was born in Vienna, Austria, and at age nineteen studied music harmony, counterpoint, and instrumentation with Arnold Schönberg, the influential Austro-Hungarian composer and theorist known for his atonal compositions. In 1926, after the death of her father, Model moved to Paris and eventually abandoned music for photography. In the summer of 1934 she produced her most famous series of photographs—intense, close-up studies of gamblers and pedestrians on the Promenade des Anglais in Nice, France. These and other photographs of Parisian vagrants soon appeared in the Communist periodicals *Regards* and *Lilliput*, and signaled the beginning of Model's career as a documentary street photographer.

After her marriage to the Russian-born painter Evsa Model, she emigrated in 1938 to the United States. She photographed on Wall Street, on the city's Lower East Side, and at Coney Island. Model worked for *Harper's Bazaar* from 1941 to 1953 and published her first photographs in the magazine in July 1941, a series of bathers presented in "How Coney Island Got That Way." Among her favorite subjects in the early 1940s were performers like Albert-Alberta, the half-man/half-woman at Hubert's 42nd Street Flea Circus, and the denizens of Sammy's on the Bowery, the infamous saloon and cabaret. The Museum of Modern Art presented her photographs in its survey exhibitions beginning in 1940, including *In and Out of Focus* (1948), *The Family of Man* (1955), and *Seventy Photographers Look at New York* (1957).

The Art Institute of Chicago organized Model's first solo museum exhibition in 1943, which was followed three years later by a show at the California Palace of the Legion of Honor, San Francisco. Model had career retrospectives at the New Orleans Museum of Art and the Folkwang Museum, Essen, Germany (1981–82).

She is the subject of numerous monographs, including *Lisette Model* (1979), designed by Marvin Israel, and Ann Thomas's retrospective book and exhibition *Lisette Model* (1990), based upon the artist's archive of negatives, papers, and related collections acquired by the National Gallery of Canada, Ottawa, in 1991.

Model taught photography at the New School for Social Research from 1951 through the 1970s in addition to giving private classes in her home. Arbus attended the first of several classes in 1956 and the two artists became friends. Model later served as a reference for Arbus's 1963 John Simon Guggenheim Memorial Fellowship. She also nominated Arbus in 1965 for the exhibition *10/10* at the Milwaukee School of the Fine Arts, University of Wisconsin. Although Model had applied unsuccessfully in 1949 for a Guggenheim Fellowship, Arbus encouraged her to reapply in 1964, and she was awarded a fellowship the following year for a project entitled "Glamour: The Image of Our Image."

In 1977 Graphics International published a portfolio of twelve photographs printed by Richard Benson. After thirty years of teaching, Model received an Honorary Doctorate in Fine Arts from the New School in 1981, and the following year the Medal of the City of Paris.

THOMAS B. MORGAN (B. 1926) is a political writer and novelist known for his nonfiction essays for *Esquire* and *Look* magazines in the late 1950s and '60s. Born in Springfield, Ohio, he graduated with a B.A. in English from Carleton College in 1949, then moved to New York City to work as a freelance journalist. He became Arbus's landlord and neighbor on Charles Street in the mid-1960s.

Morgan's compilation of essays commissioned by *Esquire* on famous people, *Self Creations: 13 Impersonalities,* was published in 1965. It includes a piece about Blaze Starr whom Arbus photographed for the original article. Morgan also wrote a novel, *Snyder's Walk* (1987), about a journalist covering the antiwar movement in the 1960s. For a long essay about a seven-hundred-mile peace march from Hanover, New Hampshire, to Washington, D.C., Morgan was paired with Arbus by Harold Hayes and Robert Benton at *Esquire*. For sixty-four miles and three days Morgan and Arbus recorded and observed thirteen pacifists on their march. When *Esquire* published "Doom and Passion Along Rt. 45" in November 1962, the essay included Arbus's photograph of the pacifists on a two-page spread.

HOWARD NEMEROV (1920–91) was a poet, novelist, playwright, and essayist, and the third poet laureate of the United States (1988–90). The author of fourteen volumes of poetry, he was the recipient of the Pulitzer Prize in 1978, as well as the National Book Award, for *The Collected Poems of Howard Nemerov* (1977). The oldest of three children of Gertrude and David Nemerov, he graduated from the Society for Ethical Culture Fieldston School in 1937, then received a B.A. in English from Harvard University in 1941. Nemerov served as a pilot in World War II in the Royal Canadian Air Force and in the U.S. Eighth Army Air Force, then returned to New York to work on his first book of poems, *The Image and the Law* (New York: Henry Holt & Company, 1947). He published poems in the *Nation*, essays in *Sewanee Review*, then became associate editor of the literary magazine *Furioso*. In 1946 he began his teaching career at Hamilton College, then two years later left for Bennington College, where he taught for two decades. From 1969 until his death he was distinguished poet in residence at Washington University in St. Louis.

Nemerov's poems and essays reveal a dramatic range of style and subject matter, from wartime terrors to football, to the fall of ginkgo leaves. The trope of the camera and photography appear frequently in Nemerov's writings, especially in *Mirrors and Windows: Poems* (1958).

RENÉE NEMEROV (B. 1928) is a painter of impressionist-style landscapes, portraits, and sculpture. The youngest and only surviving child of Gertrude and David Nemerov, she graduated from high school intent on becoming a sculptor. Nemerov continued her studies with the Mexican painter Rufino Tamayo and the Swiss experimental portraitist John (Hans) Hansegger. In 1947 she married Roy Sparkia, later a writer of popular fiction and the author of more than thirty books, including *Boss Man* (1954), *The Vanishing Vixen* (1959), and *Doctors and Lovers* (1960). In 1954 she and Sparkia moved to Michigan and adopted a child, Lisa. Nemerov collaborated with Sparkia, producing resin furniture embedded with shells, pebbles, and stones that they collected on beaches near their home. Nemerov's most acclaimed work remains an installation at the Empire State Building of public sculpture that exploits the varying refractive indexes of plastics. In 1963 the owners of the art deco landmark had commissioned Nemerov and Sparkia to produce a series of relief paintings depicting the Seven Wonders of the Ancient World.

Nemerov is now married to the painter Tom Brown and lives in Santa Fe, New Mexico.

PAUL SALSTROM (B. 1940) was born in Rockford, Illinois. He is currently associate professor of history at Saint Mary-of-the-Woods College in Indiana. A specialist in the history of the Appalachian region, he is the author of *Appalachia's Path to Dependency: Rethinking a Region's Economic History, 1730–1940* (1994). Before he received his doctorate in comparative history from Brandeis University in 1988, Salstrom, a lifelong Gandhian pacifist, homesteaded in West Virginia, raised goats, and from 1975 to 1978 was manager of Appalachian Movement Press.

Salstrom met and became friends with Arbus and the writer Thomas B. Morgan in May 1962 when they joined him and twelve other pacifists in New Jersey toward the end of the seven-hundred-mile "Walk for Peace" from Hanover, New Hampshire, to Washington, D.C. Salstrom had organized the event for the Committee for Non-Violent Action, one of three concurrent marches scheduled to converge on the nation's capitol from starting points in Hanover, Chicago, and Nashville. He is the hero of Morgan's November 1962 article for *Esquire* magazine, "Doom and Passion Along Rt. 45." Salstrom's friendship with Arbus continued throughout his three-year prison sentence for refusing to report for the selective service draft. In 1967 when she was at work on her second Guggenheim fellowship, Salstrom invited Arbus to San Francisco to stay at his house, then a haven for AWOLs and deserters from the Vietnam War. He then accompanied Arbus on a photographic excursion between San Francisco and Los Angeles, and from California to Oklahoma City.

AUGUST SANDER (1876–1964) was born in Herdorf, Germany, a small farming village east of Cologne. He began his photography training in 1896 while serving in the German army, and after World War I opened a photography studio, which he operated until 1944. In the 1920s he initiated a massive, unprecedented, lifelong portrait study of all classes of people known as "Menschen des 20 Jahrhunderts," or "People of the Twentieth Century." Although Sander died before seeing his project fully realized, he envi-

sioned its structure, organizing his portraits into seven broad categories representing the employment divisions and social structures of the day. Almost forty years after Sander's death, his grandson saw through the publication of *People of the Twentieth Century* (2002), a seven-volume opus that includes 619 photographs.

In 1929 Sander completed *Antlitz der Zeit* (1929), a preview of his grand project that became its first published expression. With a text by his friend Alfred Döblin, the German physician and author of the novel *Berlin Alexanderplatz* (1929), *Face of Our Time* remains one of the century's most distinguished publications. The straightforward documentary methods used by Sander to survey German society did not conform to the National Socialist ideal of a perfect society. After 1936 the Nazis confiscated all unsold copies and destroyed the book plates. But it was precisely the all inclusiveness of the work that attracted praise from multiple generations of artists and intellectuals from Walter Benjamin to Walker Evans to Arbus.

Sander did not have his first large show until 1951 at the Cologne Photokina where he exhibited his photographs of the city as it was before World War II. Three years later he met Edward Steichen, curator of photography at The Museum of Modern Art who was traveling in Germany researching for *The Family of Man* (1955). Steichen acquired eighty prints from Sander for the museum's permanent collection. It was this group of photographs that Steichen's curatorial successor, John Szarkowski, showed to Arbus in late 1962 when they first met at the museum. Arbus had already seen several of Sander's photographs in *The Family of Man* exhibition, which also included her and Allan's portrait of a father and son. She also owned the November 1959 issue of *Du* magazine, the illustrated monthly from Zurich which had published fifty-one portraits by Sander in a special feature on the artist.

The August Sander Archiv is preserved in Cologne at the Photographische Sammlung/SK Stiftung Kultur.

NEIL SELKIRK (B. 1947) is a photographer whose work has been published in magazines including *Esquire*, *Vanity Fair*, *Wired*, and *The New Yorker*. He maintains a studio in New York City and teaches photography at Parsons School of Design. Selkirk is also the exclusive printer for The Estate of Diane Arbus, a responsibility he has had since the year of her death.

Born in England, Selkirk graduated in 1968 from London College of Printing with a diploma in photography. From spring 1970 until summer 1971 he worked in the United States as an assistant to the fashion photographer Hiro. Selkirk met Arbus and Marvin Israel in Richard Avedon's studio and subsequently enrolled in her 1971 class taught at Westbeth in Greenwich Village. In the summer of 1971 he left the city to work for the German fashion photographer Chris von Wangenheim, shooting collections in Rome and Paris. After Arbus's death in July 1971 Selkirk returned to New York and helped Doon Arbus and Marvin Israel organize Diane Arbus's archive of negatives. As necessary, he made prints of original Diane Arbus photographs for the 1972 Museum of Modern Art retrospective and the Aperture monograph. The experience led him away from the commerical career he had been pursuing. He provided editorial portraits to Andy Warhol's *Interview* and *The New York Times Magazine*, where art director Ruth Ansel featured his full-page political portraits of Zbigniew Brzezinski, Jeb Magruder, and Henry Kissinger, among many others, during much of the early to mid-1970s.

In 1977 Selkirk opened his own studio where he began to produce advertising images and annual report illustrations for corporate clients. By the mid-1980s, Selkirk was concentrating on personal work. Around 1992 he completed *See No Evil*, an unpublished monograph designed by Yolanda Cuomo. In March 1998 the designer Tibor Kalman commissioned Selkirk to photograph pedestrians in Times Square. The portraits were at first transformed into posters that papered the scaffolding on 42nd Street, then reconfigured as *1000 on 42nd Street* (2000), a Photo District News award-winning book designed by Cuomo.

Selkirk is currently completing "Roundup," a book of photographs nominally about cowboys and cattle wrangling in Texas. He is also at work on a new portrait series, "Certain Women," using an 11x14 view camera.

MARY ELIZABETH SELLERS (B. 1936) was born in Philadelphia but spent her adolescent years in Stonington, Connecticut. After Sellers graduated in 1957 from Sarah Lawrence College in Bronxville, New York, she moved to New York City and began to write music. In 1958 she met Nancy Christopherson who introduced her to actor Robert Brown and his friends Diane and Allan Arbus.

Sellers, Christopherson, and Sellers often drove Arbus (who at the time did not have a driver's license) on various photographic expeditions. One of their earliest forays was a futile quest to New Jersey to find the Jackson Whites, an insular community of people of mixed descent (African, European, and Native American) living in the Ramapo Mountains near the New Jersey–New York state border.

In 1960, Sellers married Robert Brown and later moved to Los Angeles where he had been pursuing his theatrical, television, and film career. Arbus visited them in Malibu in summer 1962 and again in 1964. Sellers accompanied Arbus when she photographed the soothsayers featured in "What's New: Witch Predicts"; the nighttime photograph A castle in Disneyland; and during her Santa Barbara sitting with Bishop Ethel Predonzan of The Cathedral of the Creator, Omnipresence, Inc. Sellers and Brown also drove Arbus to photograph Mae West in her luxe Hollywood home.

In the early 1970s, after her divorce from Brown, Sellers went back to school and received a master's degree in social work (M.S.W.) from the University of Southern California–Los Angeles in 1975. Sellers is a psychotherapist and Licensed Clinical Social Worker (LCSW) in private practice in Los Angeles.

LAWRENCE SHAINBERG (B. 1936) is a novelist, nonfiction writer, and humorist. Born in Memphis, he graduated in 1958 with a B.A. in sociology from Columbia University, where he studied under C. Wright Mills. Shainberg met Arbus in the 1960s through their mutual friend Marvin Israel, and Shainberg's neighbors, Mary and Robert Frank. Shainberg is the author of numerous short essays, including "The Hot Hand Sutra," a sports commentary for the premier issue of the quarterly *Tricycle: The Buddhist Review* (fall 1991), and, for the same publication in winter 1996, "Wheels of Dharma," a rumination about automobile ownership in a Zen community.

Shainberg is the author of *Brain Surgeon: An Intimate View of His World* (1979); *Memories of Amnesia: A Novel* (1988); and *Ambivalent Zen: A Memoir* (1995), an autobiography that spans four decades of the author's life. Upon the publication of his first novel, *One on One*, a story about a 6'9" Jewish pro basketball player, Arbus pointedly gave Shainberg a print of one

of her photographs of the Jewish giant at home with his parents.

Shainberg lives in New York City and Wellfleet, Massachusetts, and is completing a novel.

EDWARD STEICHEN (1879–1973) and his family emigrated from Luxembourg to the United States in 1880 and settled in Hancock, Michigan. By 1968 he had taken up photography and within a few years had created a series of landscapes that were first exhibited at the Second Philadelphia Photographic Salon in 1899.

In 1900 Steichen moved to Paris to paint, stopping in New York at the Camera Club where he showed his portfolio to Alfred Stieglitz, already the preeminent force in photography in the United States. In 1902, he moved to New York City, rented a studio at 291 Fifth Avenue, and with Stieglitz became one of the twelve co-founders of the Photo-Secession, the premier organization in America dedicated to the art of photography.

Upon his return to Paris in 1905 Steichen lent his New York studio to Stieglitz as an exhibition space for the Photo-Secession. Known simply by its address on Fifth Avenue, 291, the gallery simultaneously introduced photography and modern French art to America. Steichen arranged exhibitions for Stieglitz of the works of Auguste Rodin, Henri Matisse, Paul Cézanne, and Constantin Brancusi, among many others.

Steichen lived on and off in France from 1900 to 1923, making paintings and photographs, and winning numerous exhibition awards. In 1920 he gave up painting altogether to devote himself to photography and by 1923 he was living in New York City making fashion and advertising photographs as chief photographer for Condé Nast Publications. He quickly became the era's preferred portraitist. In 1938, the year that Steichen retired from commercial photography, the Baltimore Museum of Art presented the artist's first of many retrospective exhibitions.

During World War II Steichen served in the U.S. Navy as a lieutenant commander and was placed in charge of all Navy combat photography. In the same period Steichen curated several large exhibitions for MoMA including *Road to Victory* (1942), with texts by Carl Sandburg, and *Power in the Pacific* (1945). He began his new career as director of the Department of Photography at MoMA in 1947. In the next fifteen years, until his retirement from MoMA in 1962, Steichen organized more than one hundred large and small exhibitions, including *The Family of Man* (1955), the era's most popular photography exhibition circulated by the U.S. Information Agency and seen by more than nine million people in thirty-eight countries. The show featured more than 273 photographers and 503 photographs, including one by Diane and Allan Arbus.

In 1963, the year after his retirement, he was awarded the Presidential Medal of Freedom by President John F. Kennedy, and published his autobiography, *A Life in Photography* (1963). The Edward Steichen Photography Center opened at MoMA in 1964 and is the repository for his complete archive.

STEWART STERN (B. 1922) is a screenwriter and author best known for his screenplay for *Rebel Without a Cause* (1955), the cult classic featuring James Dean. He received Academy Award nominations for *Teresa* (1951), a World War II story directed by Fred Zinnemann, and *Rachel, Rachel* (1968), directed by Paul Newman and featuring Joanne Woodward, about the life of a schoolmistress in a small New England town. He won an Academy Award for Best Short Documentary for *Benjy* (1951). In 1977 Stern

was awarded an Emmy for his television drama *Sybil* (1977), featuring Sally Field and Joanne Woodward.

Stern was born in New York City and attended Ethical Culture Fieldston School in the same graduating class as Arbus. He showed early acuity and interest in the visual arts. Through his uncle, Adolph Zuckor, the founder of Paramount Pictures, Stern was introduced to motion pictures. In 1941 he went to the University of Iowa to study painting, but graduated in three years with a degree in speech and dramatic arts. In 1943 he enlisted in the United States Army, was assigned to the 106th Infantry Division, and saw combat in December 1944 as a rifle squad leader during the Battle of the Bulge. Stern was hospitalized with frostbite and evacuated back to the United States in 1945. He received the Bronze Star for his role in the Ardennes Campaign.

After the war he worked briefly as an actor, appearing on Broadway in René Clair's production of the Joseph A. Fields and Jerome Chodorov comedy *The French Touch* (1945–46). In 1947 he moved to Los Angeles and for two years worked for Joseph Fields as a dialogue director at Eagle-Lion Studios. He worked for several years in television, writing teleplays for NBC and the Philco-Goodyear Playhouse, including *Crip*, a story about a boy with cerebral palsy, and *Thunder of Silence* (1954), an investigation of an American farm family who adopts a family of refugees saved from the concentration camps in Europe which starred then relatively unknown actor Paul Newman. They formed a close friendship that led to many subsequent projects, including the films *The Rack* (1956) and *Rachel, Rachel* (1968). Stern is also the author of *No Tricks in My Pocket: Paul Newman Directs* (1989).

Stern has many other writing credits, including screenplays for *The James Dean Story* (1957), *The Ugly American* (1963), and *Summer Wishes, Winter Dreams* (1973). In 1962 while Arbus was in Los Angeles visiting Robert Brown and his wife, Mary Elizabeth Sellers, Stern helped her gain access to the back lot of Universal Studios and other Hollywood locations. He taught screenwriting at the University of Southern California School of Cinema-Television and at the University of Washington in Seattle, where he lives with his wife, Marilee, a former dance teacher at the School of the Pacific Northwest Ballet. In the summer he now serves as creative adviser at the Screenwriters Lab at the Sundance Institute in Utah. Stern's papers are housed in the Special Collections Department in the library of the University of Iowa.

ALFRED STIEGLITZ (1864–1946) is widely considered the father of modern photography. Born in Hoboken, New Jersey, he moved to New York City in 1871. While studying at the Technische Hochschule in Berlin, Stieglitz acquired his first camera. Stieglitz worked in the photoengraving business from 1890 to 1895. In 1896 he became the founder and editor of *Camera Notes*, the journal of the New York Camera Club. In 1898 he published *Picturesque Bits of New York and Other Studies*, a photogravure portfolio of his own work, and the following year organized his first retrospective exhibition for the Camera Club.

In 1902 Stieglitz and eleven artists, including Edward Steichen, founded the Photo-Secession, the country's first modern photographic society. From 1903 through 1917 Stieglitz published *Camera Work*, the deluxe journal known for its gravure reproductions, poetry, satire, and commentary on the history of photography and contemporary art. Stieglitz frequently showed his own work as well as photographs by the other members of the Photo-Secession at 291. He also promoted paintings and watercolors by a generation of emerging American artists, notably John Marin, Marsden Hartley, and Arthur Dove. He first showed the drawings of Georgia O'Keeffe in 1916, then began to collaborate with her on an extended photographic portrait. Between 1917 and 1937 he made over 300 studies of O'Keeffe, whom he married in 1924.

For eight years following the demise of 291 in 1917, Stieglitz focused on his own career as a photographer and in 1921 began a new series of photographs of clouds that he called "Equivalents." In 1924 the Museum of Fine Arts, Boston, acquired a suite of his photographs for their permanent collection, as did The Metropolitan Museum of Art four years later. In the 1930s Stieglitz donated his collection of photographs by other artists to The Metropolitan Museum of Art and organized two retrospectives of his work at An American Place (1932, 1934). His last important series of photographs document the construction of skyscrapers in midtown Manhattan. In 1934 Stieglitz's friends commemorated his seventieth birthday with the publication of an influential volume of essays and photographs edited by, among others, Waldo Frank and Lewis Mumford: *America & Alfred Stieglitz: A Collective Portrait* (1934), which the Arbuses owned.

Steiglitz edited and/or published the monthly magazine *American Amateur Photographer* (1893–96); the quarterly *Camera Notes* (1897–1902); fifty issues of *Camera Work* (1903–1917); twelve issues of *291* (1915–16); and countless exhibition catalogs of gallery shows he organized from 1905 to 1946. In his lifetime he saw only one significant independent exhibition (and no such monographs) of his own photographs. The first major exhibition of his work, *An Exhibition of Photographs by Alfred Stieglitz* (1958), was held at the National Gallery of Art in Washington, D.C. This first show and its accompanying publication was followed by many others, most recently Sarah Greenough's *Modern Art and America: Alfred Stieglitz and His New York Galleries* (2001); and Greenough's two-volume compendium of the almost 1,600 photographs in the National Gallery's collection, *Alfred Stieglitz: The Key Set* (2002).

The Metropolitan Museum of Art is the custodian of his personal collection of other artists working in photography. Yale University preserves his papers in The Alfred Stieglitz/Georgia O'Keeffe Archive in the Yale Collection of American Literature at the Beinecke Rare Book and Manuscript Library.

JOHN SZARKOWSKI (B. 1925) is Director Emeritus of the Department of Photography at The Museum of Modern Art (MoMA) and one of the world's leading theorists and historians of photography. From 1962 until his retirement in 1991, he organized more than one hundred exhibitions and oversaw the dramatic expansion of the museum's photography collection, including the acquisition in 1968 of the Abbott-Levy Collection of Eugène Atget. Szarkowski curated landmark, monographic shows of such photographers as André Kertész (1964), Dorothea Lange (1966), Brassaï (1968), Walker Evans (1971), Diane Arbus (1972), William Eggleston (1976), Ansel Adams (1979), Eugène Atget (1981–82), Irving Penn (1984), and Garry Winogrand (1988). He also organized provocative survey exhibitions that integrated photographs by August Sander, Henri Cartier-Bresson, and Lee Friedlander with more functional, anonymous images that revealed the medium's vernacular traditions. From his first large museum show and publication, *The Photographer's Eye* (1964), to his last, *Photography Until Now* (1989–90), Szarkowski helped define and codify the language of photography.

Szarkowski was born in Ashland, Wisconsin, and graduated in 1948 with a B.S. in art history from the University of Wisconsin–Madison. From 1948 to 1951 he worked as a photographer at the Walker Art Center in Minneapolis, Minnesota, then for two years taught photography at the Albright Art School at the University of Buffalo, New York. While in Buffalo he became interested in the architecture and conceptual theories of Louis Sullivan, and in 1954 was awarded a John Simon Guggenheim Memorial Fellowship to produce the series of photographs in his first book, *The Idea of Louis Sullivan* (1956). Szarkowski was awarded a second Guggenheim Fellowship in 1961 to photograph the Quetico-Superior wilderness of Western Ontario, Canada. In 1962 Edward Steichen selected him to be his successor as director of the Department of Photography at MoMA.

Szarkowksi helped secure the reputations of many artists with his analysis of their work and its place in a historical tradition that was then in its infancy. He coauthored, with Maria Morris Hambourg, the four-volume treatise *The Work of Atget* (1981–85). Among Szarkowski's other books published by MoMA are *Walker Evans* (1971); *Looking at Photographs: 100 Pictures from the Collection of The Museum of Modern Art* (1973); *Mirrors and Windows: American Photography Since 1960* (1978); and *Winogrand: Figments from the Real World* (1988).

Szarkowski met Arbus in 1962 just after taking his post at MoMA. He became an early advocate for her work and in 1964 acquired seven photographs for the museum's permanent collection. In 1967 he organized *New Documents*, an exhibition that featured the work of Arbus, Lee Friedlander, and Garry Winogrand, and reflected his understanding of a shift in the poetics of the documentary tradition.

In 1970 Szarkowski hired Arbus to do preliminary picture research in the archives of the *New York Daily News* for a 1973 exhibition that eventually came to be called *From the Picture Press*. The exhibition was organized into seven sections defined by Szarkowski and Arbus as Ceremonies, Losers, Disasters, Alarums & Conundrums, Good News & the Good Life, Contests & Confrontations, and Heroes. For each of the photographs Szarkowski included the original newspaper captions.

In recent years Szarkowski has focused primarily on his own artwork. *Mr. Bristol's Barn* (1997) presents his photographs of the interior and exterior of a nineteenth-century wooden barn in East Chatham, New York. Szarkowski has also, in official retirement, revisited the achievements of three of his favorite artists in several books: *Alfred Stieglitz at Lake George* (1995), *Atget* (2000), and *Ansel Adams at 100* (2001).

Szarkowski has received numerous honorary degrees and has taught at many schools, including Harvard University, Columbia University, Cornell University, and at his alma mater.

SUZANNE VICTOR TRAZOFF (B. 1941) was born in Racine, Wisconsin, raised in Winnetka, Illinois, and graduated in 1963 with a B.A. in English from Hollins College in Roanoke, Virginia. Encouraged by her teacher Howard Nemerov, at the time the school's writer-in-residence, Trazoff moved to New York City and found an editorial trainee position at Random House. Through Nemerov she met Diane Arbus and shortly thereafter moved into her home to help take care of Amy Arbus, who was then nine years old.

After briefly moving in late spring 1964 to Iowa City to enroll in the master's program in creative writing at the University of Iowa, Trazoff returned to New York City in September to live and work in the Arbus household. She also assisted the essayist Thomas B. Morgan, who was their landlord and

neighbor. At the time Morgan was traveling abroad and doing research for a book on anti-Americanism, later published as *Among the Anti-Americans* (1967). Trazoff married in 1965 and worked as an assistant editor at Bantam Books.

After Arbus's death in 1971, Trazoff assisted Doon Arbus and Marvin Israel with the cataloguing and organization of Arbus's photographs. She also transcribed tapes from Arbus's 1971 master class for the text of the 1972 Aperture monograph.

From 1977 to 1981 Trazoff served as a writer and editor for Manpower Demonstration Research Corporation (MDRC), a nonprofit, nonpartisan social policy research organization. She left MDRC to work as a writer (1982–86), then as deputy administrator in the Office of Public Affairs in the New York City Resources Administration (1986–90).

In 1994 she moved to Maine and began a private practice as a consultant for nonprofit organizations on social services, health, and criminal justice policy issues. Since 1999 Trazoff has managed and represented the DaPonte String Quartet, a classical music ensemble based in Damariscotta, Maine.

JAMES VANDERZEE (1886–1983) is widely considered to be the most significant photographer of the Harlem Renaissance. His portraits from the late 1910s to the early 1930s of local celebrities, community leaders, and simple families helped forge a modern, urban identity among African-Americans in New York City and other communities. In 1924 he became the official photographer for Marcus Garvey and the Universal Negro Improvement Association.

Vanderzee was born in Lenox, Massachusetts, the son of the sexton of the town's Trinity Episcopalian Church. His parents had formerly been the maid and butler of Ulysses S. Grant in New York City. Around 1900 he acquired a camera and began to teach himself the rudiments of portrait photography.

Vanderzee moved to New York City in 1906 and worked as a busboy and elevator man while studying violin at the Carlton Conservatory of Music in New York. He became first violinist with the John Wanamaker Orchestra, formed the Harlem Orchestra, and taught piano and violin in Harlem. Music did not provide steady income and to support his wife and family he took a position in 1915 as the darkroom technician in Gertz's department store in Newark, New Jersey. After a year he opened his first portrait studio, Guarantee Photos, on 135th Street in Harlem. Vanderzee would operate a portrait studio under various names until 1969, when he retired. During his half century in photography he would photograph a cross section of Harlem residents from work-a-day shopkeepers and their families to such celebrities as Bill "Bojangles" Robinson and Adam Clayton Powell, Sr.

Outside of Harlem, however, Vanderzee was not well known until The Metropolitan Museum of Art featured his photographs in *Harlem on My Mind*, the controversial 1969 multi-media exhibition organized by Allon Schoener that presented the history of Harlem from 1900 to 1968. The show brought almost instant fame to the eighty-three-year-old artist and his photographs were soon featured in numerous monographs including Reginald McGhee's *The World of James Van Der Zee: A Visual Record of Black Americans* (1969), and *James Van Der Zee* (1973). With a foreword by Toni Morrison, *The Harlem Book of the Dead* (1978) focuses on Vanderzee's funeral portraits. In many postmortem photographs, Vanderzee added angels, biblical figures, and lifetime images of the deceased (often his own earlier portraits), which float like spirits over the open coffins. These last "double" portraits attracted Arbus, who visited

Vanderzee's studio on Lenox Avenue in 1963, six years before he came to public attention. Arbus acquired a few prints for her personal collection and became an early advocate of Vanderzee's work.

WEEGEE (Usher, later Arthur, Fellig) (1899–1968) is one of the world's most well-known tabloid newspaper photographers. He is the author of *Naked City* (1945), a book that includes nighttime portraits of criminals, lovers, victims, policemen, and the residents of the Bowery. The publication became a Hollywood film and quickly made Weegee an international celebrity.

Weegee himself made several short 16mm documentary films, including *Weegee's New York* (1948), *Cocktail Party* (circa 1950), and *The Idiot Box* (circa 1965). He also appeared as an extra in numerous Hollywood features, including the comedy *Every Girl Should Be Married* (1948) with Cary Grant. In 1963 the director Stanley Kubrick hired him as a special effects consultant for *Dr. Strangelove, Or: How I Learned to Stop Worrying and Love the Bomb*. Weegee also completed an autobiography, *Weegee by Weegee* (1961).

Weegee was born Usher Fellig in the city of Zlothev in the former Austrian province of Galicia, now part of Ukraine. In 1910 he immigrated with his family to the United States and lived in New York's Lower East Side. In the early 1920s, while living in boarding rooms on the Bowery, Weegee worked as a darkroom technician, first for *The New York Times*, then for Acme Newspictures, a major source of photographs for the *Daily News*, the *World Telegram*, and the *Herald Tribune*. One of his jobs was to squeegee wet prints and he became known as "Mr. Squeegee," possibly the origin of his adopted moniker. Another source may have been inspired by the Ouija board, an increasingly popular fortuneteller's game in which the Acme darkroom staff had quite an interest.

By the early 1930s Weegee was making his own photographs, and in 1935 he left Acme to work as a freelance police beat photographer. Two years later he published his first credited photographs in *Life* and *Popular Photography* magazines. In 1938 Weegee began to use his adopted name and to stamp his photographs "Weegee the Famous." From 1940 to 1945 he was staff photographer at the progressive evening newspaper *PM*.

In 1941 Weegee had two one-person exhibitions both entitled *Weegee: Murder Is My Business* at The Photo League, an organization dedicated to social and documentary photography. The Museum of Modern Art included his work in 1943 in the group show *Action Photography*, his first museum exhibition. Many more shows at MoMA would follow, including *Art in Progress* (1944), where his work was presented on the same wall with Lisette Model's, and *50 Photographs by 50 Photographers* (1948). Weegee then abandoned crime photography and devoted his talents to society, advertising, and to special effects motion picture photography, working in Hollywood, Munich, and Paris. He is the author of *Weegee's People* (1946), *Naked Hollywood* (1953), and *Weegee's Creative Camera* (1959).

He is also the subject of three documentary films, including *The Naked Eye* (1956) by Louis Stoumen.

Despite his success, Weegee was somewhat neglected at the end of his life when Arbus showed his work in 1965 to her students at Parsons School of Design. After his death, she discovered Weegee's archive, then in the possession of his common-law wife, Wilma Wilcox. Arbus brought the work to the attention of John Szarkowski while doing research for what became *From the Picture Press* (1973), an exhibition at MoMA on the tradition of news photography. She became an advocate of Weegee's work and introduced it to the gallerist Lee Witkin.

Weegee's work was posthumously the subject of many retrospectives at, among others, the Center for Creative Photography, University of Arizona, Tucson (1975) and the San Francisco Museum of Modern Art (1984). His photographs also appear in several major monographs, including John Coplans's *Weegee's New York: Photographs 1935–1960* (1982) and *Weegee's World* (1997), a comprehensive book by Miles Barth that accompanied a large exhibition at the International Center of Photography, New York.

GARRY WINOGRAND (1928–84) was born in New York City and raised in the Bronx. He graduated from high school in 1945 and subsequently served for two years in the Army Air Force as a weather forecaster in Georgia. He returned to the city, briefly studied painting at City University, then in 1948, on the G.I. Bill, entered Columbia University in the School of General Studies. His intention was to pursue painting, but after meeting the photographer George Zimbel he simultaneously began to photograph and make prints. In 1949 he left Columbia, and on a scholarship at the New School for Social Research, took classes with the art director Alexey Brodovitch, who helped him hone his mastery of the 35mm camera.

Winogrand received his first editorial assignment from *Harper's Bazaar* in 1951, the year he began his association with the Pix Photo Agency, soon followed by Henrietta Brackman Associates. He supplied the stock houses with a wide range of gritty images, including sweat-drenched boxers and dancers backstage at the ballet, street parades, and patrons and performers at the stylish El Morocco nightclub. His snapshot-style photographs began appearing in *Pageant*, *Sports Illustrated*, and *Redbook* and came to the attention of Edward Steichen, director of the Photography Department at The Museum of Modern Art (MoMA), who included two of Winogrand's photographs in his exhibition *The Family of Man* (1955). Steichen subsequently featured Winogrand in *Seventy Photographers Look at New York* (1957–58).

John Szarkowski, Steichen's successor at MoMA, included Winogrand in numerous important group exhibitions in the 1960s, including *Five Unrelated Photographers* (1963) with Ken Heyman, George Krause, Jerome Liebling, and Minor White; *The Photographer's Eye* (1964); and *New Documents* (1967) with Lee Friedlander and Arbus. The last show became a legendary exhibition of photographs—a focused analysis of the conceptual innovations and

formal traditions shared by the three artists. Nathan Lyons, curator at the George Eastman House in Rochester, New York, also featured Winogrand in several exhibitions, including *Photography 63* (1963) and *Toward a Social Landscape*, a 1966 show featuring four other artists, including Friedlander, that served in many ways as a preamble to *New Documents*.

His ironic study of caged animals and the captivated humans who stare at them became the subject for his first book, *The Animals* (1969), and a one-person show at MoMA. Winogrand compiled twenty years of his photographs of women in *Women Are Beautiful* (1975), later the subject of one of his four limited-edition portfolios.

Winogrand received three John Simon Guggenheim Memorial Foundation Fellowships (1964, 1969, 1978), a 1972 grant from the New York State Council on the Arts, and a National Endowment for the Arts Fellowship in 1975. His 1969 Guggenheim Foundation project "to study the effect of media on events" generated the book *Public Relations* (1977). Winogrand began his extensive teaching career in 1967 at New York's Parsons School of Design. He taught workshops worldwide and served on the faculty of many institutions, including the School of Visual Arts, New York (1968–71); Cooper Union for the Advancement of Science and Art, New York (1970, 1972); and the University of California, Los Angeles (1979, 1981).

Winogrand is the author of *Stock Photographs: The Fort Worth Fat Stock Show and Rodeo* (1980), his last book and a 1974 commission from the Fort Worth Art Museum. He is also the subject of numerous posthumous monographs, including *The Man in the Crowd: The Uneasy Streets of Garry Winogrand* (1999) and *Winogrand 1964* (2002). The Center for Creative Photography at the University of Arizona, Tuscon, is the custodian of the Garry Winogrand Archive.

HENRY WOLF (b. 1925) emigrated to the United States from Vienna in 1941. A designer, art director, teacher, and photographer, Wolf became art director of *Esquire* in 1952, then succeeded Alexey Brodovitch in 1958 as art director of *Harper's Bazaar*. In 1961 he left *Harper's Bazaar* to become the first art director of *Show*, the short-lived deluxe art magazine that featured Arbus, Robert Frank, and many of the most promising photographers of the generation. After the publisher Huntington Hartford sold *Show* to Hugh Hefner in 1965, Wolf left to become advertising director for Jack Tinker & Partners, McCann-Erickson, and ultimately Trahey/Wolf Advertising. He served as vice president of the Aspen Design Conference, president of the American Institute of Graphic Arts (AIGA), and was Mellon Visiting Professor of Art at Cooper Union School of Art. Among his many design awards is the Gold Medal from the AIGA in 1976. Wolf, author of *Visual Thinking: Methods for Making Images Memorable* (1988), is currently professor of art at Parsons School of Design, the New School, where he has taught since 1954. He heads Henry Wolf Productions, and is known for his photographic ad campaigns.

WITH ADDITIONAL ASSISTANCE FROM: MILES BELLAMY, JED BARK, ANDREA BAYER, LYLE BONGÉ, PHILIP BROOKMAN, ERIC BROWN, MALCOLM DANIEL, DOUG EKLUND, BARBARA FILE, MIA FINEMAN, LAURA T. HARRIS, TOBY HIMMEL, GALWAY KINNELL, CHRISTOPHER KOHAN, JOHN LAWRENCE, J.D. MCCLATCHY, FRED MCKISSICK, STEPHEN MAKLANSKY, LORI PAULI, STEPHEN PINSON, KELLYE ROSENHEIM, SHARON SNOW, JUDITH STEIN, NORMA STEVENS, DANIEL TALBOT, JEAN AND JOE TUCKER, JULIA VAN HAAFTEN

EXHIBITION VENUES

———

SAN FRANCISCO MUSEUM OF MODERN ART
OCTOBER 25, 2003 – FEBRUARY 8, 2004

❖

LOS ANGELES COUNTY MUSEUM OF ART
FEBRUARY 29 – MAY 30, 2004

❖

MUSEUM OF FINE ARTS, HOUSTON
JUNE 27 – AUGUST 29, 2004

❖

THE METROPOLITAN MUSEUM OF ART, NEW YORK
FEBRUARY 28 – MAY 29, 2005

❖

MUSEUM FOLKWANG, ESSEN, GERMANY
JUNE 17 – SEPTEMBER 18, 2005

❖

THE VICTORIA AND ALBERT MUSEUM, LONDON
OCTOBER 13, 2005 – JANUARY 15, 2006

❖

WALKER ART CENTER, MINNEAPOLIS
JULY 9 – OCTOBER 8, 2006

DIANE ARBUS REVELATIONS IS GENEROUSLY SPONSORED BY THE EVELYN D. HAAS EXHIBITION FUND AND CHARLES SCHWAB & CO., INC.

ADDITIONAL SUPPORT HAS BEEN PROVIDED BY CARLA EMIL AND RICH SILVERSTEIN, RANDI AND BOB FISHER, PRENTICE AND PAUL SACK, LINDA AND JON GRUBER, CAROLE AND ROBERT LIEFF, HARVEY S. SHIPLEY MILLER, AND ROBIN WRIGHT.

SUPPORT FOR THE EXHIBITION PUBLICATION IS PROVIDED BY THE KORET FOUNDATION.

Untitled (51) 1970–71

SPONSOR'S STATEMENT

———

It is with great pride that Charles Schwab joins the San Francisco Museum of Modern Art in presenting the work of Diane Arbus, a pioneer in photography who, with passion and integrity, pursued an artistic vision that has immeasurably enriched American culture. This exhibition, the first major international retrospective of the artist's work in over thirty years, offers viewers in San Francisco and around the world the opportunity to witness firsthand her bold exploration of the human experience.

At Charles Schwab, we understand that pioneering spirit and firmly believe that, whether in the arts or in finance, it is important to explore new ways of thinking and new approaches to help achieve your goals.

As a business, our mission is to provide the most useful and ethical financial services in the world. As a member of the community, our goal is to endorse artists and arts organizations by supporting and honoring both individual efforts and local programs.

Our hope is that both endeavors can help open the door to new opportunities for long-term rewards, artistically, socially, and economically.

charles **SCHWAB**

DIRECTOR'S LETTER

In capturing the unique nature of each individual that posed before her camera, the photographs of Diane Arbus challenge us to reconsider who we are and how we present ourselves to the world. It is our hope that this long-awaited exhibition and publication serve to document and celebrate the scope of her achievement. Such an ambitious undertaking requires the time, effort, and support of numerous people, and we would like to recognize their exceptional contributions here. Of course, no exhibition is possible without the lenders (listed on pages 322–325), who have entrusted us to care for their artworks as we make them available to the widest possible public. Equally vital is the financial support that has come to the Museum from a variety of sources. The Evelyn D. Haas Exhibition Fund stepped in to provide extraordinarily generous funding at a critical moment in the evolution of the project, and Charles Schwab & Co., Inc. sponsored the international tour with a major grant. In addition, a number of individuals from the SFMOMA community recognized the importance of this undertaking and made significant contributions toward it. They include Carla Emil and Rich Silverstein, Randi and Bob Fisher, Prentice and Paul Sack, Linda and Jon Gruber, Carole and Robert Lieff, Harvey S. Shipley Miller, and Robin Wright. Support for the exhibition publication was provided by the Koret Foundation.

Exhibitions are by nature collaborative, but this one is somewhat unique in that its successful presentation demanded the participation of virtually every staff member of the Museum. I would like to thank each one of them for their hard work and professionalism, and then to recognize a few individuals who merit special mention. It is appropriate to begin by acknowledging two friends, David A. Ross, former director, and Lori Fogarty, former senior deputy director, for their early advocacy of the project and for their care in shepherding it through its initial phases. Following their departure, Ruth Berson, deputy director for programs and collections, and Marcelene Trujillo, assistant exhibitions director, assumed responsibility for overseeing all aspects of the exhibition, and they executed their many duties with grace, wisdom, and unflagging dedication. Patricia McLeod, director of development, and the members of her department worked tirelessly to secure the funding necessary to stage the exhibition. Olga Charyshyn, exhibitions registrar, resolved the myriad complexities raised by the loans for this show with painstaking care. Suzanne Feld, curatorial associate for special exhibitions, and guest curatorial assistants Robin Clark and Elizabeth Grady provided vital research

and logistical support. Yolanda Cuomo, assisted by Kristi Norgaard, created the elegant and sensitive designs for the exhibition and accompanying publication. Kent Roberts, exhibition design manager, succeeded in translating their vision for the show into reality.

Other members of the SFMOMA exhibition team who deserve recognition and sincere thanks include Theresa Andrews, associate conservator; Libby Garrison, assistant communications manager; Keiko Hayashi, former design manager; Polly Winograd Ikonen, acting director of communications; Kara Kirk, former director of publications; Terril Neely, senior graphic designer; Rico Solinas, museum preparator; Lynda Sanjurjo-Rutter, associate director of development for individual giving; Stacey Silver, associate director of development for corporate partnerships; Peter Stevenson, manager of adult interpretive programs; Cara Storm, acting director of marketing; and Greg Wilson, senior museum preparator. We would also like to offer our gratitude to our colleagues from the institutions that collaborated with us to assemble the international tour for the exhibition.

We are very pleased that The Estate of Diane Arbus has partnered with Random House and SFMOMA to produce a publication that will continue to serve as an invaluable resource long after the show has concluded. I would like to thank an outstanding team of writers for providing essays that illuminate the artist's accomplishments. Mary Bahr, editor at Random House, and Chad Coerver, director of publications at SFMOMA, brought their considerable diplomatic skills and insight to the task of preparing the manuscript for publication. The complex process of producing a volume of such ambitious scale and high production values was undertaken by a number of gifted individuals, whose names can be found on page 327. The results of their excellent work are on display throughout this publication.

A particularly warm note of gratitude is extended to Doon and Amy Arbus, whose devotion to, and deep knowledge of, their mother's work has been evident at every stage in this process. It would be an understatement to say that their involvement has enriched and advanced the exhibition and publication in countless, fundamental ways. Finally, we are perhaps most indebted to the co-curators of *Diane Arbus Revelations*, Sandra S. Phillips, senior curator of photography at SFMOMA, and Elisabeth Sussman, guest curator. Their creativity and hard work have resulted in an exhibition that is a fitting, even poetic, tribute to an artist of remarkable vision.

—Neal Benezra
Director, San Francisco Museum of Modern Art

WORKS IN THE EXHIBITION

———

The catalogue below is arranged chronologically and records only those works exhibited at the San Francisco Museum of Modern Art; the presentations at other venues may vary. Unless otherwise indicated, all photographs are gelatin silver prints made by the artist. Measurements refer to the size of the photographic paper in inches followed by centimeters, height before width. Throughout the book an asterisk following the title indicates images first printed by Neil Selkirk. Numbers to the left of the titles refer to pages in the book.

19 Room with lamp and light fixture, N.Y.C. 1944
6⅝ x 4⅝ (17 x 11.8)
COLLECTION OF ALLAN ARBUS

15 Self-portrait pregnant, N.Y.C. 1945
7 x 5 (17.8 x 12.7)
LOS ANGELES COUNTY MUSEUM OF ART,
THE AUDREY AND SIDNEY IRMAS COLLECTION

284 Boy above a crowd, N.Y.C. 1956
11 x 14 (27.9 x 35.6)
THE ESTATE OF DIANE ARBUS LLC

— Boy in the subway, N.Y.C. 1956*
14 x 11 (35.6 x 27.9), print by Neil Selkirk
ROBERT MILLER GALLERY, NEW YORK, AND
FRAENKEL GALLERY, SAN FRANCISCO

20 Boy stepping off the curb, N.Y.C. circa 1956
14 x 11 (35.6 x 27.9)
THE ESTATE OF DIANE ARBUS LLC

21 Carroll Baker on screen in "Baby Doll"
(with silhouette), N.Y.C. 1956
7 x 10⅞ (17.8 x 27.8)
WHITNEY MUSEUM OF AMERICAN ART, NEW YORK,
PURCHASE, WITH FUNDS FROM THE PHOTOGRAPHY
COMMITTEE

141 Couple eating, N.Y.C. 1956
11 x 14 (27.9 x 35.6)
THE ESTATE OF DIANE ARBUS LLC

7 Fire Eater at a carnival, Palisades Park, N.J. 1956
14 x 11 (35.6 x 27.9)
COLLECTION OF EDWIN COHEN, NEW YORK

29 Kiss from "Baby Doll," N.Y.C. 1956
11 x 14 (27.9 x 35.6)
COLLECTION OF JOHN CHEIM

51 Lady on a bus, N.Y.C. 1956
14 x 11 (35.6 x 27.9)
THE ESTATE OF DIANE ARBUS LLC

255 Masked boy with friends, Coney Island, N.Y. 1956
14 x 11 (35.6 x 27.9)
THE ESTATE OF DIANE ARBUS LLC

141 Movie theater usher by the box office, N.Y.C. 1956
14 x 11 (27.9 x 35.6)
THE ESTATE OF DIANE ARBUS LLC

32 People on a bench, Central Park, N.Y.C. 1956*
20 x 16 (50.8 x 40.6), print by Neil Selkirk
ROBERT MILLER GALLERY, NEW YORK, AND
FRAENKEL GALLERY, SAN FRANCISCO

230 Woman carrying a child in Central Park,
N.Y.C. 1956
11 x 14 (27.9 x 35.6)
COLLECTION OF BRUCE VAN DUSEN

139 A Woman on the boardwalk, Coney Island,
N.Y. 1956
10 x 8 (25.4 x 20.3)
COLLECTION OF NORMA AND MARTIN STEVENS

25 Woman on the street with her eyes closed,
N.Y.C. 1956
11 x 14 (27.9 x 35.6), print by Neil Selkirk
THE ART INSTITUTE OF CHICAGO,
GIFT OF THE BOARDROOM, INC.

262 Woman on the street with parcels,
N.Y.C. 1956
14 x 11 (35.6 x 27.9), print by Neil Selkirk
ROBERT MILLER GALLERY, NEW YORK, AND
FRAENKEL GALLERY, SAN FRANCISCO

51 Woman with two men, N.Y.C. 1956*
11 x 14 (27.9 x 35.6), print by Neil Selkirk
ROBERT MILLER GALLERY, NEW YORK, AND
FRAENKEL GALLERY, SAN FRANCISCO

5 Child in a nightgown, Wellfleet, Mass. 1957
14 x 11 (35.6 x 27.9)
THE ESTATE OF DIANE ARBUS LLC

30 Kid in black-face with friend, N.Y.C. 1957
14 x 11 (35.6 x 27.9)
COLLECTION OF NORMA AND MARTIN STEVENS

— Woman in a bow dress, N.Y.C. 1957*
14 x 11 (35.6 x 27.9), print by Neil Selkirk
ROBERT MILLER GALLERY, NEW YORK, AND
FRAENKEL GALLERY, SAN FRANCISCO

141 Audience with projection booth,
N.Y.C. 1958
11 x 14 (27.9 x 35.6)
COLLECTION OF RICHARD GERE

54 Couple in silhouette watching burning cross
on screen, N.Y.C. 1958
11 x 14 (27.9 x 35.6)
THE ESTATE OF DIANE ARBUS LLC

147 Female impersonators in mirrors,
N.Y.C. 1958
14 x 11 (35.6 x 27.9)
COLLECTION OF YDESSA HENDELES

23 Female impersonators' dressing room,
N.Y.C. 1958
14 x 11 (35.6 x 27.9)
THE ESTATE OF DIANE ARBUS LLC

26 42nd Street movie theater audience,
N.Y.C. 1958
16 x 20 (40.6 x 50.8), print by Neil Selkirk
ROBERT MILLER GALLERY, NEW YORK, AND
FRAENKEL GALLERY, SAN FRANCISCO

— Movie theater lobby, N.Y.C. 1958
16 x 20 (40.6 x 50.8), print by Neil Selkirk
ROBERT MILLER GALLERY, NEW YORK, AND
FRAENKEL GALLERY, SAN FRANCISCO

142 Two girls on the beach, Coney Island,
N.Y. 1958
11 x 14 (27.9 x 35.6), print by Neil Selkirk
FRAENKEL GALLERY, SAN FRANCISCO, AND
ROBERT MILLER GALLERY, NEW YORK

144 Woman at a Puerto Rican dance,
N.Y.C. 1958*
14 x 11 (35.6 x 27.9), print by Neil Selkirk
ROBERT MILLER GALLERY, NEW YORK, AND
FRAENKEL GALLERY, SAN FRANCISCO

— Wrestler, N.Y.C. 1958
14 x 11 (35.6 x 27.9)
THE ESTATE OF DIANE ARBUS LLC

— Boy at a pool hall, N.Y.C. 1959
14 x 11 (35.6 x 27.9)
THE ESTATE OF DIANE ARBUS LLC

144 Woman and a dwarf backstage at the circus,
N.Y.C. 1959
14 x 11 (35.6 x 27.9)
THE ESTATE OF DIANE ARBUS LLC

56 Women on a sundeck, Coney Island,
N.Y. 1959
11 x 14 (27.9 x 35.6)
THE ESTATE OF DIANE ARBUS LLC

149 Woogie with snake, Hubert's Museum,
N.Y.C. 1959
14 x 11 (35.6 x 27.9)
THE ESTATE OF DIANE ARBUS LLC

2 Clouds on screen at a drive-in, N.J. 1960
16 x 20 (40.6 x 50.8), print by Neil Selkirk
ROBERT MILLER GALLERY, NEW YORK, AND
FRAENKEL GALLERY, SAN FRANCISCO

152 Coney Island, N.Y. 1960 [windy group]
11 x 14 (27.9 x 35.6)
THE ESTATE OF DIANE ARBUS LLC

238 Couple arguing, Coney Island, N.Y. 1960
14 x 11 (35.6 x 27.9)
COLLECTION OF THOMAS H. LEE
AND ANN TENENBAUM

149 A couple at a dance, N.Y.C. 1960*
14 x 11 (35.6 x 27.9), print by Neil Selkirk
ROBERT MILLER GALLERY, NEW YORK, AND
FRAENKEL GALLERY, SAN FRANCISCO

— Wax museum ax murderer, Coney Island,
N.Y. 1960
14 x 11 (35.6 x 27.9), print by Neil Selkirk
FRAENKEL GALLERY, SAN FRANCISCO, AND
ROBERT MILLER GALLERY, NEW YORK

28 Wax museum strangler, Coney Island, N.Y. 1960
14 x 11 (35.6 x 27.9)
COLLECTION OF YDESSA HENDELES

153 Woman shouting, Coney Island, N.Y. 1960
14 x 11 (35.6 x 27.9) print by Neil Selkirk
THE ROBERT MILLER GALLERY, NEW YORK AND
FRAENKEL GALLERY, SAN FRANCISCO

24 The Backwards Man in his hotel room,
N.Y.C. 1961
14 x 11 (35.6 x 27.9)
THE ESTATE OF DIANE ARBUS LLC

258 Elderly couple on a park bench,
N.Y.C. 1969
20 x 16 (50.8 x 40.6), *print by Neil Selkirk*
THE MUSEUM OF MODERN ART, NEW YORK,
MRS. ARMAND P. BARTOS FUND

292 Five children in a common room,
N.J. 1969
20 x 16 (50.8 x 40.6), *print by Neil Selkirk*
FRAENKEL GALLERY, SAN FRANCISCO, AND
ROBERT MILLER GALLERY, NEW YORK

283 Jorge Luis Borges in Central Park,
N.Y.C. 1969
20 x 16 (50.8 x 40.6), *print by Neil Selkirk*
FRAENKEL GALLERY, SAN FRANCISCO, AND
ROBERT MILLER GALLERY, NEW YORK

303 Man at a parade on Fifth Avenue,
N.Y.C. 1969
20 x 16 (50.8 x 40.6), *print by Neil Selkirk*
THE MUSEUM OF MODERN ART, NEW YORK,
MRS. ARMAND P. BARTOS FUND

304 Albino sword swallower at a carnival,
Md. 1970
20 x 16 (50.8 x 40.6)
COLLECTION OF CARLA EMIL AND
RICH SILVERSTEIN

108 Dominatrix embracing her client,
N.Y.C. 1970
20 x 16 (50.8 x 40.6), *print by Neil Selkirk*
FRAENKEL GALLERY, SAN FRANCISCO, AND
ROBERT MILLER GALLERY, NEW YORK

66 Dominatrix with a kneeling client,
N.Y.C. 1970
20 x 16 (50.8 x 40.6), *print by Neil Selkirk*
FRAENKEL GALLERY, SAN FRANCISCO, AND
ROBERT MILLER GALLERY, NEW YORK

243 Girl in her circus costume,
Md. 1970
20 x 16 (50.8 x 40.6), *print by Neil Selkirk*
THE GAY BLOCK COLLECTION, COURTESY
MUSEUM OF FINE ARTS, HOUSTON

300 A Jewish giant at home with his parents
in the Bronx, N.Y. 1970
20 x 16 (50.8 x 40.6)
THE MUSEUM OF MODERN ART, NEW YORK,
LILY AUCHINCLOSS FUND

247 The King and Queen of a Senior Citizens'
Dance, N.Y.C. 1970
20 x 16 (50.8 x 40.6)
THE MUSEUM OF MODERN ART, NEW YORK,
MRS. ARMAND P. BARTOS FUND

91 Masked woman in a wheelchair,
Pa. 1970
20 x 16 (50.8 x 40.6)
COLLECTION OF YDESSA HENDELES

66 Mexican dwarf in his hotel room,
N.Y.C. 1970
20 x 16 (50.8 x 40.6)
COLLECTION OF JASPER JOHNS

231 Tattooed man at a carnival,
Md. 1970
20 x 16 (50.8 x 40.6), *print by Neil Selkirk*
F. C. GUNDLACH FOUNDATION

— Untitled (1) 1970–71
20 x 16 (50.8 x 40.6)
COLLECTION OF CARLA EMIL
AND RICH SILVERSTEIN

— Untitled (2) 1970–71
20 x 16 (50.8 x 40.6)
THE ESTATE OF DIANE ARBUS LLC

65 Untitled (3) 1970–71
20 x 16 (50.8 x 40.6), *print by Neil Selkirk*
COLLECTION OF ROBERT MORTON

277 Untitled (4) 1970–71
20 x 16 (50.8 x 40.6), *print by Neil Selkirk*
NATIONAL GALLERY OF CANADA, OTTAWA,
PURCHASED 1974

— Untitled (5) 1970–71
20 x 16 (50.8 x 40.6), *print by Neil Selkirk*
THE MUSEUM OF CONTEMPORARY ART,
LOS ANGELES, THE RALPH M. PARSONS
PHOTOGRAPHY COLLECTION

115 Untitled (6) 1970–71 †
20 x 16 (50.8 x 40.6)
PRINCETON UNIVERSITY ART MUSEUM,
GIFT OF HENRY GELDZAHLER

290 Untitled (7) 1970–71
20 x 16 (50.8 x 40.6), *print by Neil Selkirk*
COLLECTION OF CARLA EMIL
AND RICH SILVERSTEIN

263 Untitled (8) 1970–71
20 x 16 (50.8 x 40.6), *print by Neil Selkirk*
THE MUSEUM OF MODERN ART, NEW YORK,
MRS. ARMAND P. BARTOS FUND

203 Untitled (10) 1970–71
20 x 16 (50.8 x 40.6), *print by Neil Selkirk*
COLLECTION OF FRISH BRANDT
AND AUGUST FISCHER

— Untitled (12) 1970–71
20 x 16 (50.8 x 40.6), *print by Neil Selkirk*
THE MUSEUM OF FINE ARTS, HOUSTON,
THE GAY BLOCK COLLECTION,
GIFT OF GAY BLOCK

204 Untitled (13) 1970–71
20 x 16 (50.8 x 40.6), *print by Neil Selkirk*
FRAENKEL GALLERY, SAN FRANCISCO, AND
ROBERT MILLER GALLERY, NEW YORK

205 Untitled (14) 1970–71
20 x 16 (50.8 x 40.6), *print by Neil Selkirk*
THE MUSEUM OF MODERN ART, NEW YORK,
MRS. ARMAND P. BARTOS FUND

— Untitled (15) 1970–71
20 x 16 (50.8 x 40.6), *print by Neil Selkirk*
THE MUSEUM OF FINE ARTS, HOUSTON,
THE GAY BLOCK COLLECTION,
GIFT OF GAY BLOCK

— Untitled (17) 1970–71
20 x 16 (50.8 x 40.6), *print by Neil Selkirk*
FRAENKEL GALLERY, SAN FRANCISCO, AND
ROBERT MILLER GALLERY, NEW YORK

— Untitled (18) 1970–71
20 x 16 (50.8 x 40.6), *print by Neil Selkirk*
FRAENKEL GALLERY, SAN FRANCISCO, AND
ROBERT MILLER GALLERY, NEW YORK

— Untitled (21) 1970–71
20 x 16 (50.8 x 40.6), *print by Neil Selkirk*
FRAENKEL GALLERY, SAN FRANCISCO, AND
ROBERT MILLER GALLERY, NEW YORK

204 Untitled (24) 1970–71
20 x 16 (50.8 x 40.6), *print by Neil Selkirk*
THE MUSEUM OF FINE ARTS,
HOUSTON, THE GAY BLOCK COLLECTION,
GIFT OF GAY BLOCK

65 Untitled (26) 1970–71
20 x 16 (50.8 x 40.6), *print by Neil Selkirk*
FRAENKEL GALLERY, SAN FRANCISCO, AND
ROBERT MILLER GALLERY, NEW YORK

65 Untitled (27) 1970–71
20 x 16 (50.8 x 40.6), *print by Neil Selkirk*
FRAENKEL GALLERY, SAN FRANCISCO, AND
ROBERT MILLER GALLERY, NEW YORK

— Untitled (29) 1970–71
20 x 16 (50.8 x 40.6), *print by Neil Selkirk*
THE MUSEUM OF FINE ARTS,
HOUSTON, THE GAY BLOCK COLLECTION,
GIFT OF GAY BLOCK

65 Untitled (31) 1970–71
20 x 16 (50.8 x 40.6), *print by Neil Selkirk*
THE MUSEUM OF FINE ARTS,
HOUSTON, THE GAY BLOCK COLLECTION,
GIFT OF GAY BLOCK

— Untitled (34) 1970–71
20 x 16 (50.8 x 40.6), *print by Neil Selkirk*
THE MUSEUM OF FINE ARTS,
HOUSTON, THE GAY BLOCK COLLECTION,
GIFT OF GAY BLOCK

282 Untitled (42) 1970–71
20 x 16 (50.8 x 40.6), *print by Neil Selkirk*
THE MUSEUM OF FINE ARTS,
HOUSTON, THE GAY BLOCK COLLECTION,
GIFT OF GAY BLOCK

— Untitled (50) 1970–71
20 x 16 (50.8 x 40.6), *print by Neil Selkirk*
THE MUSEUM OF FINE ARTS,
HOUSTON, THE GAY BLOCK COLLECTION,
GIFT OF GAY BLOCK

205 Untitled (58) 1970–71
20 x 16 (50.8 x 40.6), *print by Neil Selkirk*
THE MUSEUM OF FINE ARTS,
HOUSTON, THE GAY BLOCK COLLECTION,
GIFT OF GAY BLOCK

280 Blind couple in their bedroom,
Queens, N.Y. 1971
20 x 16 (50.8 x 40.6), *print by Neil Selkirk*
ROBERT MILLER GALLERY, NEW YORK,
AND FRAENKEL GALLERY, SAN FRANCISCO

302 Feminist in her hotel room, N.Y.C. 1971*
20 x 16 (50.8 x 40.6), *print by Neil Selkirk*
FRAENKEL GALLERY, SAN FRANCISCO, AND
ROBERT MILLER GALLERY, NEW YORK

66 A young man and his girlfriend with hot dogs
in the park, N.Y.C. 1971
20 x 16 (50.8 x 40.6)
THE ESTATE OF DIANE ARBUS LLC

351 A woman passing, N.Y.C. 1971
20 x 16 (50.8 x 40.6), *print by Neil Selkirk*
F. C. GUNDLACH FOUNDATION

† THIS PRINT IS INSCRIBED IN INK IN THE ARTIST'S HAND ON THE RECTO OF THE SHEET BELOW THE IMAGE: 3 WOMEN. (SCHOOL FOR THE MENTALLY RETARDED N.J.) ONE WATCHES, THE SECOND BEGINS A SOMERSAULT, THE THIRD LAUGHS. / 1969 DIANE ARBUS.

SUPPLEMENTARY EXHIBITION MATERIALS COURTESY OF: RICHARD AVEDON; MICHAEL FLANAGAN; FRED GURNER; LAWRENCE ISRAEL AND SHELLEY DOWELL FOR THE ESTATE OF MARVIN ISRAEL; SAUL LEITER COURTESY OF HOWARD GREENBERG GALLEY; GIDEON LEWIN; HARRY MATTISON; THE HOWARD NEMEROV COLLECTION, WASHINGTON UNIVERSITY LIBRARIES, DEPARTMENT OF SPECIAL COLLECTIONS; COSMOS SAVAGE; NEIL SELKIRK; PHILLIP STILES, THE ESTATE OF GARRY WINOGRAND COURTESY OF FRAENKEL GALLERY; ESQUIRE COLLECTION, SPENCER MUSEUM OF ART, UNIVERSITY OF KANSAS; JOHN SIMON GUGGENHEIM FOUNDATION; THE HAROLD HAYES COLLECTION, SPECIAL COLLECTIONS DEPARTMENT, Z. SMITH REYNOLDS LIBRARY, WAKE FOREST UNIVERSITY; CLARENCE JOHN LAUGHLIN ARCHIVE, WILLIAMS RESEARCH CENTER OF THE HISTORIC NEW ORLEANS COLLECTION; THE METROPOLITAN MUSEUM OF ART; THE MUSEUM OF MODERN ART; NATIONAL GALLERY OF CANADA.

EXHIBITION ACKNOWLEDGMENTS

———

CURATED BY ELISABETH SUSSMAN AND SANDRA S. PHILLIPS

Suzanne Feld   curatorial associate

Robin Clark   Elizabeth Grady   guest curatorial assistants

DESIGNED BY YOLANDA CUOMO AND DOON ARBUS

Kristi Norgaard   associate designer   Neil Selkirk   technical advisor

EXHIBITIONS AND COLLECTIONS

Ruth Berson   deputy director

Marcelene Trujillo   assistant exhibitions director

INSTALLATION BY KENT ROBERTS

Greg Wilson   Rico Solinas   preparators

Terril Neely   senior graphic designer

EXHIBITIONS REGISTRAR

Olga Charyshyn

ASSOCIATE CONSERVATOR

Theresa Andrews

INAUGURATED BY DAVID A. ROSS

additional advice and assistance from

Frish Brandt, Lori Fogarty, Jeffrey Fraenkel,

Richard L. Green, Royce Howes, Sherry Kerlin,

Keith Knight, John Pelosi, Paul Sack

supplementary exhibition materials

Janet Cross, Stuart Einhorn, Mariana Gruener,

Marion Misilim, Duggal Digital, Loupe Imaging

AND FOR THE INEXPRESSIBLE, THE UNDENIABLE, AND THE ESSENTIAL WITHOUT WHOM NOT...

BOOK ACKNOWLEDGMENTS

———

THE ESTATE OF DIANE ARBUS LLC

Doon Arbus Amy Arbus John Pelosi

RANDOM HOUSE

Mary Bahr editor Kathy Rosenbloom production manager Vincent La Scala copy editor

Jeff L. Rosenheim biographical research Elizabeth Grady research and permissions

and

Ann Godoff Howard Weill Katie Hall

SAN FRANCISCO MUSEUM OF MODERN ART

Chad Coerver director of publications

THE WYLIE AGENCY

Andrew Wylie Lisa Halliday

PHOTOGRAPHIC PRINTS BY NEIL SELKIRK

Jason Brownrigg Susan Spiller

PRINTS COURTESY OF
FRAENKEL GALLERY AND ROBERT MILLER GALLERY

Jeffrey Fraenkel   Betsy Wittenborn Miller
Frish Brandt   Robert Miller
Lizanne Suter   Royce Howes
Kim Schantz   Michele Heinrici

DUOTONE AND FOUR-COLOR SEPARATIONS BY ROBERT HENNESSEY

PRINTED AND BOUND IN GERMANY BY DR. CANTZ'SCHE DRUCKEREI

Klaus Prokop

CONCEIVED BY DOON ARBUS

DESIGNED BY YOLANDA CUOMO

Kristi Norgaard associate designer

DIANE ARBUS   *DIANE ARBUS: MAGAZINE WORK*   *UNTITLED*   ARE PUBLISHED BY APERTURE

ALLAN ARBUS AMY ARBUS RICHARD AVEDON MARVIN ISRAEL NEIL SELKIRK NORMA STEVENS

A family on their lawn one Sunday in Westchester, N.Y. 1968

ENDNOTES

THE QUESTION OF BELIEF
BY SANDRA S. PHILLIPS

Note: Unless otherwise stated, all Diane Arbus documents cited are in the possession of The Estate of Diane Arbus.

[1] *Diane Arbus: An Aperture Monograph* (Millerton, N.Y.: Aperture, 1972), published in conjunction with a major exhibition of the photographs of Diane Arbus at The Museum of Modern Art, 1972, p. 15.

[2] *Diane Arbus*. p. 15.

[3] Peter C. Bunnell, "Diane Arbus," *Print Collector's Newsletter,* vol. 3, no. 6 (Jan.–Feb. 1973), p. 129. Bunnell was the Curator of Photography, John Szarkowski's colleague, and a contemporary and friend of Arbus when he was at The Museum of Modern Art. He is currently the Emeritus David Hunter McAlpin Professor of the History of Photography and Modern Art and professor of art and archaeology at Princeton University.

[4] "The Full Circle," *Harper's Bazaar*, November 1961, p. 133. Diane also said, "Freaks...was one of the first things I photographed and it had a terrific kind of excitement for me...There's a quality of legend about freaks. Like a person in a fairy tale who stops you and demands that you answer a riddle" *Diane Arbus*, p. 3. John Szarkowski's wall text for the 1972 Arbus retrospective, which was included in the press release for the show (No. 116C, November 7, 1972), stated, "Diane Arbus's pictures challenge the basic assumptions on which most documentary photography has been thought to rest, for they deal with private rather than social realities, with psychological rather than historical fact, with the prototypical and mythic rather than the typical and temporal. Her photographs record the outward signs of inner mysteries."

[5] *Diane Arbus*, p. 13. To Ann Ray Martin, a journalist from *Newsweek* who interviewed her during the *New Documents* show in 1967, Arbus said, "Lisette [Model, her teacher] talked to me about how ancient the camera was, and she talked about light and that if light really stains the silver, or whatever the heck that stuff on film is, then memory can stain it, too." March 6, 1967, interview transcript, The Estate of Diane Arbus.

[6] From the wall panel (and a subsequent brochure derived from it) for *New Documents: Diane Arbus, Lee Friedlander, Garry Winogrand*, MoMA, 1967. See also the article "What's a Nice Girl Like You Doing in a Place Like This? Diane Arbus at The Museum of Modern Art," by Marta Weiss for *Critical Matrix* vol. 13, No. 1, which notes that Arbus's work was displayed in a separate room.

[7] From the wall panel for *New Documents*.

[8] I distinguish early from later additions to the library by the inscriptions in the books, from "Diane Nemerov" to "Diane and Allan Arbus." Later acquisitions usually have no inscriptions. The early reading shows an interest in philosophy and classical literature. Besides myth, she read extensively in French Romantic literature, Russian literature, especially the work of Dostoevsky, and the works of Melville, Hardy, and Joyce.

[9] She and Allan owned a copy of William Klein's first book, *Life Is Good and Good for You in New York Trance Witness Revels* (1956) and the second book, *Rome* (1959). Klein remembers that the Arbuses were conscious of his work, perhaps because they were both involved in the fashion world.

[10] *Diane Arbus*, p. 6.

[11] Not deliberately or with any self-consciousness, she and Allan also started to put together a small collection of prints and books. She acquired two Atget prints (one assumes from Abbott directly), one of the organ grinder and another which was a gift from Allan, and in the 1960s she obtained Riis pictures, including *Bandit's Roost,* from the Museum of the City of New York. She owned four Bellocq photographs printed by Lee Friedlander, some pictures by August Sander, James Vanderzee, Clarence John Laughlin, and also, later, Model. Model's reclining bather hung in Arbus's loft at Westbeth (p. 192).

[12] *Diane Arbus*, p. 1. See Doon Arbus's comments in "Diane Arbus Photographer," *Ms.*, November 1972.

[13] "Five Photographs by Diane Arbus," *Artforum,* May 1971, p. 64.

[14] 1960 Notebook (No. 4), with notes for "The Vertical Journey." Copyings from Baudelaire in the same notebook are also insightful: "Love may spring from a generous sentiment, the desire for prostitution, but it is soon corrupted by the desire for ownership. One of the two will always be cooler or less self-abandoned than the other. He or she is the surgeon or executioner, the other the patient or victim."
See also her letter to Israel, March 24, 1960: "If like you said one cannot know without being maybe there is another kind of knowing which has to do with outsides in which one cannot know without not being. (Like I know you, which is not to say I know you well, but that I know you much more stunning and sudden and visible than you will ever know yourself.) (Everyone is just as much locked in as locked out.)"

[15] See Thomas W. Southall's essay in *Diane Arbus: Magazine Work*, with texts by Diane Arbus, ed. by Doon Arbus and Marvin Israel (Millerton, N.Y.: Aperture, 1984), for a full discussion of her work in the context of New Journalism.

[16] Diane Arbus 1960 appointment book, April 19.

[17] "The Full Circle," *Harper's Bazaar,* November 1961, p. 133.

[18] "The Full Circle," *Infinity*, February 1962, pp. 10, 13. Arbus met Stormé around 1960 during the time she worked on "The Vertical Journey."

[19] Joseph Campbell, a mythologist Arbus read, was interested in examining the larger meaning of myth in contemporary society, at a historical moment when conventional belief and tradition appeared banal, or incomplete, or unimaginative. Campbell says, "Whatever may be thought of the detailed and sometimes contradictory interpretations of specific cases and problems, Freud, Jung and their followers have demonstrated irrefutably that the logic, the heroes, and the deeds of myth survive into modern times. In the absence of an effective general mythology, each of us has his private, unrecognized, rudimentary, yet secretly potent pantheon of dream." *The Hero with a Thousand Faces*, Bollingen Series 17 (Princeton University Press, 1973), p. 4.

[20] Both Hermaphrodite and Eros are described as two-sexed, as is Tiresius, the prophet who foresees Oedipus's fate. In his account of the origins of the sexes in Plato's *Symposium*, the character of Aristophanes describes androgyny as a third sex that, when split into two by the gods, became a pair of lovers, each desiring unity with the other. The ancient Kabbalistic writings and the sacred Indian texts also treat the hermaphrodite as a holy figure, a being of profound generative force, the embodiment of original creativity. See Campbell, *Hero with a Thousand Faces*, pp. 152–53. Arbus would have been familiar with all these references. On female impersonators in Arbus's work, see also Diana Emory Hulick, "Diane Arbus' Women and Transvestites, Separate Selves," *History of Photography*, vol. 16, no. 1 (Spring 1992), pp. 34–39; and Ariella G. Budick, *Subject to Scrutiny: Diane Arbus' American Grotesque* (Ph.D. dissertation, New York University Insitute of Fine Arts, 1996).

[21] Diane Arbus, Note on Female Impersonators, from the archives of Walker Evans, The Metropolitan Museum of Art.

[22] In 1959 the art magazine *Du* published a special edition of the work, and Arbus owned a copy ("August Sander photographiert: Deutsche Menschen," text by Golo Mann, Zurich: Conzatt & Huber, November 1959). She wrote about Sander to

her friend Marvin Israel on January 24, 1960, and then in the spring of that year: "Someone told me it is spring but everyone today looked remarkable just like out of August Sander's pictures, so absolute and immutable down to the last button, feather, tassel or stripe. All odd and splendid as freaks and nobody able to see himself, all of us victims of the especial shape we come in." She also later wrote Szarkowski asking for Sander's address and the name of the book with Kinsey's portraits of the loggers in Washington State with the trees they felled. He provided both. The Museum of Modern Art owns seventy-two prints by August Sander, who gave them to Edward Steichen for his use in the exhibition *The Family of Man* (1955). These seventy-two prints include many that Arbus would have found interesting in relation to her own work. The author would like to thank Peter Galassi and Sarah Hermanson for their help with the Sander material at The Museum of Modern Art.

[23] She repeatedly returned to this concept in her notebooks of the years 1962 and 1963. Arbus's poetic sensibility is suggested by a list of associative phrases gathered in 1962 Notebook (No. 8): "Transfix, Sleeping beauty, Butterfly collector, Kaleidoscope, Foreshortening, Human thing. Store windows."

See also a letter to her brother Howard Nemerov, circa November 1965: "To have believed in both the guilt and innocence of photographing (which I privately call the butterfly collection)."

[24] Marvin Israel, *Infinity*, "The Photography of Diane Arbus," November 1972, p. 8. See also p. 2 of *Diane Arbus*: "It was my teacher, Lisette Model, who finally made it clear that the more specific you are, the more general it'll be."

[25] "Five Photographs by Diane Arbus," p. 64.

[26] *Diane Arbus*, pp. 1–2.

[27] See Arbus's comments on nudists in *Diane Arbus* (p. 5): "They seem to wear more clothes than other people."

[28] From her "Plan for a Photographic Project," John Simon Guggenheim Foundation application, 1963.

[29] Letter from Diane Arbus to Marvin Israel, December 1960. See also 1960 Notebook (No. 5).

[30] "Five Photographs by Diane Arbus," p. 64.

[31] *Diane Arbus*, pp. 8–9.

[32] Cartier-Bresson's term *images à la sauvette*, which alludes to photographs taken hastily or by impulse, is related to another French phrase, *vendre à la sauvette* (sold in the street). Cartier-Bresson's term was meant to describe the process by which a photographer roamed the streets, responding to that which changed and vanished before his eyes. See David Travis, "André Kertész and His Contemporaries," in *André Kertész: of Paris and New York* (Chicago: Art Institute of Chicago, 1985), p. 87. It should be noted that Model used a 2¼ Rolleiflex to take the Nice pictures and many later works, and she cropped, often heavily, from the full frame. All this suggests that the 2¼ could, if willed, be voyeuristic.

[33] The author wishes to thank Allan Arbus for this information. He adds that after using the Graflex she also had a Deardorff 5x7 camera, which she could have used as early as 1941. The Rolleiflex facilitated a formal change of direction. Child with a toy hand grenade (p. 104) is made with the Rolleiflex.

[34] *Diane Arbus*, p. 2.

[35] Postcard from Diane Arbus to Marvin Israel, January 5, 1960.

[36] *Diane Arbus*, pp. 2–3. See also another relevant point she makes, "What I'm trying to describe is that it's impossible to get out of your skin into somebody else's...That somebody else's tragedy is not the same as your own."

[37] As Friedlander has said, "If you want information you need lots of light, especially if a shadow is covering what you want to see." Winogrand said, "Nothing is so mysterious as a fact clearly stated."

[38] The Instamatic advertised "instant loading film" as well as the flash. For a discussion of the Arbus photograph, see Life Library of Photography, *The Art of Photography*, 1971, p. 110: "The photographs {she made of this subject} were made with electronic flash—intentionally placed close to the camera to create a veiling reflection and harsh shadows. By her appreciation of amateur snapshots, she hoped to catch a flavor of 'total ordinariness'...The one...had a quality that she found deeply touching. It has the startling effect of looking like any father's snapshot of his wife and youngster."

[39] The author owes a debt of thanks to Peter Bunnell, who commented on the pictorial nature of Arbus's work in a letter dated August 20, 2002.

[40] *Mirrors and Windows: American Photography Since 1960* (New York: The Museum of Modern Art, 1978), p. 13.

[41] Szarkowski was examining Lange's photography in preparation for a show of her work that opened at The Museum of Modern Art in 1966.

[42] From a conversation with John Szarkowski, summer 2002. Szarkowski realized that by the early 1960s, "the development of the photo story had been toward greater aesthetic coherence at the cost of content." *The Photographer's Eye* was exhibited at the 1964 opening of the newly expanded Museum of Modern Art, but the catalogue was not published until 1966.

[43] From Louis Kronenberger, *Quality: Its Image in the Arts* (New York: Atheneum, 1969), p. 171. The first photograph in Evans's selection is Diane Arbus's Boy in a pro-war parade (p. 87).

[44] When Evans's retrospective, a show Arbus saw several times, was on view at The Museum of Modern Art, he refused to label himself a documentary photographer; rather, he said, "the term should be documentary style. An example of a literal document would be a police photograph of a murder scene...a document has use, whereas art is really useless." He added that a "photographer is a joyous sensualist, for the simple reason that the eye traffics in feelings, not in thoughts. This man is in effect a voyeur by nature; he is also reporter, tinkerer, and spy" (see Leslie Katz, "An Interview with Walker Evans," 1971, reprinted in Peninah R. Petruck, ed., *The Camera Viewed: Writings on Twentieth-Century Photography*, vol. 1 {New York: E. P. Dutton, 1979], p. 127). Although Evans and Arbus were not friends, they knew each other, and Evans was asked to write a letter of support for her first Guggenheim award. Arbus owned all of his books, including *American Photographs*, published in 1938 (an exhibition at The Museum of Modern Art) and *Many Are Called*, a volume of photographs made secretly on the New York subways published in *Harper's Bazaar* by Marvin Israel.

[45] News release, *From the Picture Press*, no. 4, January 30, 1973, p. 1.

[46] *From the Picture Press*, ed. by John Szarkowski. (New York: The Museum of Modern Art, 1973), p. 6.

[47] Diane Arbus 1962 Notebook (No. 9).

[48] From a research notebook in the exhibition files for *From the Picture Press*, The Museum of Modern Art, New York.

[49] Transcript of Diane Arbus master class, 1970. Brassaï's work was exhibited at The Museum of Modern Art in 1968. The introduction in the catalogue by John Szarkowski reads: "Brassaï...seems in contrast {to Cartier-Bresson} an angel of darkness. His sensibility dates from an earlier age, and delights in the primal, the fantastic, the ambiguous,

even the bizarre. Yet the most distinguishing characteristic of Brassaï's work is its profound poise and naturalness, its sense of easy permanence." Arbus also owned a rare volume of Brassaï's work, *Volupté de Paris*, published in 1937.

[50] *Diane Arbus*, p. 9.

[51] Letter from Diane Arbus to Allan Arbus and Mariclare Costello, circa November 1970.

[52] *Ibid.*

[53] Letter from Diane Arbus to Peter Crookston, January 1969.

[54] *Ibid.*

[55] Letter from Diane Arbus to Peter Crookston, December 1969. It should also be said that she was made anxious by the kind of misunderstanding and crude imitation her work generated. Szarkowski said this made her reluctant to exhibit the work. See also Peter Bunnell's essay "Diane Arbus," p. 129: "One of the things that disturbed Diane Arbus at the time of her death had to do with how misunderstood her work seemed to be, in the sense that it was thought of mainly in terms of the crudest subject of identification with no self-reflection. In terms of imitators of her photographs, these followers simply felt obliged to seek the bizarre in subject and secure a likeness on film."

[56] Letter from Diane Arbus to Allan Arbus, circa November 1969. See also *Diane Arbus: Magazine Work*, p. 171.

[57] Letter from Diane Arbus to Amy Arbus, circa summer 1969. See also Janet Malcolm's essay "Aristocrats," in her book *Diana and Nikon: Essays on Photography* (Millerton, N.Y.: Aperture, 1997), pp. 184–87.

[58] Letter from Diane Arbus to Allan Arbus, circa 1969.

[59] Letter from Diane Arbus to Allan Arbus and Mariclare Costello, circa November 1970.

[60] In the 1972 retrospective of Arbus's work, Szarkowski presented the prints in Kulicke plexibox frames, although the prints were matted according to conventional museum practice. The mats were cut to reveal the borders. The author is greatly indebted to Peter Bunnell for his insights into the Arbus portfolio.

[61] Letter from Diane Arbus to Peter Crookston, circa June 1968. About A family on their lawn one Sunday in Westchester, N.Y. 1968 (p. 329), she said, "They are a fascinating family. I think all families are creepy in a way."

[62] Postcard from Diane Arbus to Peter Crookston, circa May 1968.

[63] Peter C. Bunnell, "Diane Arbus," p. 129. See also Marion Magid's review of *New Documents* in *Arts Magazine*, April 1967, p. 54. "Because of its emphasis on the hidden and the eccentric, this exhibit has, first of all, the perpetual, if criminal, allure of a sideshow. One begins by simply craving to look at the forbidden things one has been told all one's life not to stare at...Then a reversal takes place. One does not look with impunity, as anyone knows who has ever stared at the sleeping face of a familiar person and discovered its strangeness. Once having looked and not looked away, we are implicated. When we have met the gaze of a midget or a female impersonator, a transaction takes place between the photograph and the viewer; in a kind of healing process, we are cured of our criminal urgency by having dared to look. The picture forgives us, as it were, for looking. In the end, the great humanity of Diane Arbus's art is to sanctify that privacy which she seems to have violated."

[64] From the wall text for the retrospective exhibition *Diane Arbus*, The Museum of Modern Art, New York, 1972.

A CHRONOLOGY 1923–1971
BY ELISABETH SUSSMAN AND DOON ARBUS

Unless otherwise stated, the originals of the material cited are currently in the possession of the initial recipient or his or her estate. The Archive of The Estate of Diane Arbus retains letters, photographs, and documents from Gertrude Nemerov's collection, letters from Diane Arbus to Marvin Israel, letters from Diane Arbus to Carlotta Marshall, and letters from Diane Arbus to Allan Arbus, Amy Arbus, and Doon Arbus. Fraenkel Gallery currently retains the original correspondence from Diane Arbus to Peter Crookston. All other original material, unless otherwise stated, is in The Archive of the Estate of Diane Arbus.

1. Frank Russek obituary, 1948, Collection of Gertrude Nemerov, Archive of The Estate of Diane Arbus.

2. Diane Arbus 1934 autobiography, seventh-grade class assignment, Fieldston School, original given by Elbert Lenrow to Howard Nemerov, Howard Nemerov Collection, Washington University Libraries, Department of Special Collections, St. Louis, Mo.

3. Diane Arbus 1940 autobiography, senior class assignment, Fieldston School, original given by Elbert Lenrow to Howard Nemerov, Howard Nemerov Collection, Washington University Libraries, Department of Special Collections, St. Louis, Mo.

4. Frank Russek obituary, 1948.

5. New York City telephone directory, 1924; also Diane Arbus 1934 autobiography.

6. Diane Arbus 1934 autobiography.

7. Howard Nemerov, *Journal of the Fictive Life* (Chicago: University of Chicago Press, 1965), p. 74.

8. Gertrude Nemerov note on verso of photograph taken in St. Mark's Place, and notation on photo of Gertrude with children in La Touquet, 1927, Collection of Gertrude Nemerov, Archive of The Estate of Diane Arbus.

9. Handbook of the Ethical Culture Fieldston School, 2001.

10. Elisabeth Sussman interview with Stewart Stern, February 2, 2002.

11. New York City telephone directory, winter 1929–summer 1930; also Diane Arbus 1934 autobiography.

12. Studs Terkel, *Hard Times: An Oral History of the Great Depression* (New York: Pantheon, 1970), p. 88.

13. Studs Terkel radio interview with Diane Arbus, WFMT Chicago, 1968.

14. Diane Arbus postcard to Marvin Israel, March 4, 1960.

15. New York City telephone directory, 1932.

16. Diane Arbus postcard to Marvin Israel, February 17, 1960.

17. Doon Arbus interview with Stewart Stern, February 1972.

18. Elisabeth Sussman interview with Stewart Stern, February 12, 2001.

19. *Ibid.*

20. Diane Arbus 1940 autobiography.

21. Elisabeth Sussman interview with Allan Arbus, April 12, 2001.

22. Doon Arbus interview with Allan Arbus, February 17, 1972.

23. Letter from Victor D'Amico to Katherine Frazier, head of the Cummington School, June 14, 1938, archives, Fieldston School, Riverdale, New York.

24. Elisabeth Sussman interview with Alex Eliot, May 1, 2001.

25. Doon Arbus interview with Alex Eliot, February 14, 1972.

26. Diane Arbus handwritten letter to Alex Eliot, November 1938. Collection of Alex Eliot and Jane Winslow Eliot.

27. Elisabeth Sussman interview with Stewart Stern, February 2, 2001.

28. *Ibid.*

29. Diane Arbus papers for Elbert Lenrow class, 1940, Fieldston School, copies in the Archive of The Estate of Diane Arbus.

30. Elisabeth Sussman interview with Allan Arbus, April 25, 2001.

31. Studs Terkel radio interview with Diane Arbus, WFMT Chicago, 1968.

32. Studs Terkel interview, quoted from Doon Arbus and Marvin Israel, eds. *Diane Arbus*, p. 5.

33. Typewritten letter from Howard Nemerov to Gertrude and David Nemerov, Collection of Gertrude Nemerov.

34. New York City telephone directory, summer 1940.

35. Newspaper clipping, *New York Times*, April 11, 1941.

36. Elisabeth Sussman interview with Allan Arbus, April 12, 2001.

37. Doon Arbus interview with Alex Eliot, February 14, 1972.

38. *Ibid.*

39. Elisabeth Sussman interview with Allan Arbus, October 17, 2000, and April 12 and 25, 2001.

40. Elisabeth Sussman interview with Allan Arbus, January 17, 2000.

41. Richard Ellmann and Robert O'Clair, eds. *The Norton Anthology of Modern Poetry* (New York and London: W.W. Norton and Co., 1988), pp. 1017–18.

42. Pati Hill, "Some Notes from My Life," pamphlet for *Wall Papers*, Hill's exhibition at the Bayly Art Museum, University of Virginia, Charlottesville, April 15–June 18, 2000.

43. Diane Arbus handwritten letter to Alex Eliot, May 1951.

44. Elisabeth Sussman interview with Allan Arbus, October 17, 2000.

45. Doon Arbus interview with Allan Arbus, February 17, 1972.

46. Alfred Stieglitz Collection, the Beinecke Rare Book and Manuscript Library, Yale University Library, New Haven, Conn.

47. Note to Pati Hill, 1945, Archive of The Estate of Diane Arbus, gift of Pati Hill.

48. Elisabeth Sussman interview with Alex Eliot, May 1, 2001.

49. Allan Arbus U.S. Army discharge papers, Allan Arbus Collection.

50. Nancy Newhall was Acting Curator of Photography at The Museum of Modern Art while her husband, Beaumont Newhall, was in the armed services during World War II.

51. Books in the Archive of The Estate of Diane Arbus.

52. Doon Arbus interview with Allan Arbus, February 17, 1972.

53. *Ibid.*

54. Elisabeth Sussman interview with Allan Arbus, April 25, 2001.

55. Doon Arbus interview with Allan Arbus, February 17, 1972.

56. Diane Arbus handwritten letter to Alex Eliot and Jane Winslow from Barcelona, July 26, 1951.

57. Doon Arbus interview with Allan Arbus, February 17, 1972.

58. Doon Arbus notes from a conversation with Nancy Bellamy, circa 1980.

59. Richard Ellmann and Robert O'Clair, eds. *The Norton Anthology of Modern Poetry*, pp. 1017–18.

60. *New York Times* announcement of the engagement of Renée Nemerov, circa August 1947.

61. Elisabeth Sussman interview with Alex Eliot, May 1, 2001; and interview with Allan Arbus, April 25, 2001.

62. *Ibid.*

63. Alex Eliot letter to Elisabeth Sussman, dated "first day of spring," 2002.

64. Doon Arbus interview with Allan Arbus, February 17, 1972.

65. Diane Arbus handwritten letter to Alex Eliot and Jane Winslow from Spain, June 22, 1951.

66. Alex Eliot letter to Elisabeth Sussman, dated "first day of spring," 2002.

67. Diane Arbus handwritten letter to Alex Eliot and Jane Winslow from Spain, June 22, 1951.

68. Diane Arbus passport. Elisabeth Sussman interview with Alex Eliot, May 15, 2001.

69. Diane Arbus typewritten letter to Alex Eliot and Jane Winslow Eliot on their honeymoon in Europe, 1951.

70. Doon Arbus interview with Robert Brown, February 1972.

71. Elisabeth Sussman interview with Stewart Stern, February 2, 2001.

72. Diane Arbus circa 1960 Notebook (No. 4).

73. Diane Arbus typewritten letter to Alex Eliot and Jane Winslow Eliot, May 30, 1952.

74. Edward Steichen, Director of the Department of Photography at The Museum of Modern Art (1947–62), organized the exhibition *The Family of Man*.

75. Doon Arbus interview with Allan Arbus, February 17, 1972.

76. Doon Arbus interview with Lisette Model, February 5, 1972.

77. From transcripts of tapes made by Ikko Narahara, a student in Arbus's master class who made the recordings to replay later in case he had trouble with the English. The class was given from January to March 1971 in a public room at Westbeth, the artists' residence where Diane lived in New York City. *Diane Arbus*, 1972.

78. Doon Arbus interview with Lisette Model, February 5, 1972.

79. Doon Arbus interview with Allan Arbus, February 17, 1972.

80. The following Lisette Model photographs were shown: Lower East Side N.Y., 1939–45; Coney Island Bather, N.Y., 1939–41; Sammy's, N.Y., 1940–44; World War II Rally, Lower East Side, 1942.

81. Application for fellowship, John Simon Guggenheim Memorial Foundation, New York. Received October 15, 1962. Archive, John Simon Guggenheim Foundation. Although many of these projects were dated in the Guggenheim application as originating in 1959, an examination of Arbus's contact sheets makes clear that most of these subjects were present in the work as early as 1956.

82. The thirteen appointment books (1959–1971) and a total of thirty-nine working notebooks are cur-

rently in the Archive of The Estate of Diane Arbus. The notebooks have been numbered by the Estate in an attempt to indicate their sequence and the years to which they apply. It is not clear whether these thirty-nine notebooks in Arbus's possession at the time of her death constitute a complete inventory of all the notebooks she had. There may have been others that were either lost or destroyed. The thirty-nine notebooks do, however, represent all years between and including 1959 and 1971.

[83] Diane Arbus 1959–1960 Notebook (No. 2).

[84] *Ibid.*

[85] In 1959 she includes in her notebooks (Nos. 1, 2, and 3) excerpts from writings and books including: *Howl*, by Allen Ginsberg; "A Secret Society," "The Web of Life," and "Beyond the Screen," by Howard Nemerov from his collection *A Commodity of Dreams and other Stories* (London: Secker and Warburg, 1960); Plato's *Symposium*; *The Art of Loving*, by Erich Fromm.

[86] According to her 1959 appointment book, other movies she saw during that year include Jean Cocteau's *Beauty and the Beast*, Ingmar Bergman's *The Seventh Seal*, Sergei Eisenstein's *Alexander Nevsky*, *Tall Story* (a comedy about college basketball with Tony Perkins and Jane Fonda, based very loosely on Howard Nemerov's novel *The Homecoming Game*), Akira Kurosawa's *Rashomon*, John Cassavetes's *Shadows*, and Robert Frank's *Pull My Daisy*.

[87] Typewritten letter from Diane Arbus to Lisette Model, September 25, 1962, Lisette Model Archives, the National Gallery of Canada, Ottawa.

[88] Elisabeth Sussman interview with Robert Benton, May 9, 2001.

[89] Typewritten letter from Diane Arbus to Robert Benton, circa October 1959. "Please get me permissions both posh and sordid...the more the merrier..." The *Esquire* Collection, Spencer Museum of Art, The University of Kansas, Lawrence.

[90] *Ibid.*

[91] List of permissions sought, with dates and indications of assignments completed, from Harold Hayes's office, probably maintained by his secretary, Toni Bliss. The Harold Hayes Collection, Special Collections Department, Z. Smith Reynolds Library, Wake Forest University, Winston-Salem, N.C.

[92] Harold Hayes letter to Deputy Police Commissioner Walter Arm, November 30, 1959. The *Esquire* Collection, Spencer Museum of Art, The University of Kansas, Lawrence.

[93] Diane Arbus typewritten letter to Robert Benton, circa October 1959.

[94] *Ibid.*

[95] It appears that only the letters from Diane Arbus to Marvin Israel during this period have survived, although it is clear from the nature of the letters that the other side of the correspondence existed. Her letters to Israel, mostly dated from 1959 through 1960 (although some later ones exist as well), are now in the Archive of The Estate of Diane Arbus, gift of Marvin Israel. The correspondence may have continued at this rate in later years, but is no longer extant.

[96] Diane Arbus handwritten letter to Marvin Israel, circa late January 1960.

[97] An examination of the 1959 appointment book suggests that this letter refers to the International Debutante Ball at the Astor Hotel on December 30, 1959.

[98] Diane Arbus typewritten letter to Marvin Israel, March 13, 1960.

[99] *Ibid.*

[100] In a postcard to Marvin Israel dated January 24, 1960, she writes parenthetically: "Maybe I will pho-

tograph Reverend Olford when I finish this Esquire thing. That will be like converting him (into 2 dimensions) (black & white magic)."

[101] Diane Arbus typewritten letter to Marvin Israel, January 29, 1960.

[102] Diane was given a portfolio of August Sander photographs published in the Swiss magazine *Du* in 1959, separated from the magazine and placed in a folder of its own by Marvin Israel.

[103] Diane Arbus postcard to Marvin Israel, circa April 1960.

[104] Working captions for *Esquire*, circa April 1960, from Harold Hayes's office, probably maintained by his secretary, Toni Bliss. The Harold Hayes Collection, Special Collections Department, Z. Smith Reynolds Library, Wake Forest University, Winston-Salem, N.C.

[105] Diane Arbus typewritten letter to Marvin Israel, circa April 20, 1960.

[106] From then unpublished 1965 article by Diane Arbus on the closing of Hubert's Museum entitled "Hubert's Obituary, or This Is Where We Came In." Published posthumously in *Diane Arbus: Magazine Work*, pp. 80–81.

[107] In a handwritten letter to Doon Arbus, circa 1960, Diane writes: "Hey Doon wouldja like me to make you curtains of this stuff?...it's like the scarves magicians pull out of tubes and make disappear...I have a dictionary of carnival lingo. A merry go round is a simp twister. Orange drink is Saniflush or internal douche. Candy apples are dentists' friends. Piggie bank is a fat girls stocking."

[108] A comparison between the contents of this letter and the 1960 appointment book suggests that Diane is describing Wirth's Circus in Hempstead, L.I., which she appears to have visited on April 5, 1960. In the original, the second sentence quoted here appears in the margin.

[109] Joe Loebenthal's name appears in this context in 1959 Notebook (No. 3), in the 1960 appointment book, and in a typewritten letter from Diane Arbus to Marvin Israel, August 27, 1960.

[110] Elisabeth Sussman interview with James Randi, June 21, 2001. James Randi is a professional magician (The Amazing Randi), author, lecturer, amateur archaeologist, amateur astronomer, and founding fellow of the Committee for the Scientific Investigation of Claims of the Paranormal.

[111] Diane Arbus typewritten letter to Marvin Israel, August 27, 1960.

[112] This novel was made into an eponymous movie (1947) about a geek, with Tyrone Power, Joan Blondell, and Helen Walker.

[113] Diane Arbus typewritten letter to Marvin Israel, August 27, 1960.

[114] The Stratoliners, a club for tall people, appears several times in her 1959 and 1960 appointment books and notebooks, but apparently never results in a photograph; she does, however, photograph on a number of occasions the giant she first encounters at Hubert's.

[115] Doon Arbus interview with Allan Arbus, February 17, 1972.

[116] Doon Arbus interview with Amy Arbus, August 2002. Amy recalls that Israel had a Nikon Rangefinder (which Amy now owns), and that this is almost certainly the camera that Diane borrowed from him. In the letter, Diane adds, "...I am much too slow with yours, lining up those two images infuriates me, like I am fitting them for a pair of shoes before I take their picture."

[117] Diane describes something of her camera dilemma to her brother as well. In an undated note to her Nemerov writes, "Fascinated with your camera problem; I'd never (of course) con-

sidered what a difference it might make. I hope you grow happily into the possibilities of the new one: is it a question of its vision rather than yours? Its handwriting? Frightening."

[118] Diane Arbus typewritten letter to Marvin Israel, November 13, 1960.

[119] Original typewritten letter in the Howard Nemerov Collection, Washington University Libraries, Department of Special Collections, St. Louis, Mo.

[120] "They just raised the price at Hubert's...to 40¢ which made them all glow with pride and I said how worth it they were and they were. The man who ties himself in knots is there whom I had been thinking I should find because he is really a perfect eccentric...and there is a wry sword swallower who is the son of sword swallowers...and next week there will be some knife throwers and soon after an eight foot tall giant." Letter to Marvin Israel, circa 1960–61.

[121] Diane Arbus appointment book, July 6, 1961.

[122] Diane Arbus 1961 Notebook (No. 5).

[123] Diane Arbus letter to Robert Benton and Harold Hayes about the Eccentrics project, circa November 1960.

[124] *Ibid.*

[125] *Ibid.*

[126] Harold Hayes letter to Diane Arbus, February 16, 1961. The Harold Hayes Collection, Special Collections Department, Z. Smith Reynolds Library, Wake Forest University, Winston-Salem, N.C.

[127] The date of this typewritten letter, in which she also refers to Moondog, is unclear.

[128] The legendary blind beggar, Moondog, is among the people she considers for the Eccentrics project.

[129] In her 1961 appointment book, Diane makes a note to herself that none of the six should be left out, and no text changes should be made without consulting her.

[130] Harold Hayes letter to Diane Arbus, August 25, 1961.

[131] Diane Arbus letter to Harold Hayes, August 28, 1961. The *Esquire* Collection, Spencer Museum of Art, The University of Kansas, Lawrence.

[132] Diane Arbus letter to Doon Arbus, circa August 1961.

[133] Diane Arbus 1961 Notebook (No. 7).

[134] The first mention of a twins convention appears in capital letters on a page of its own in 1959 Notebook (No. 3).

[135] *Diane Arbus*, p. 9

[136] Technical notes about the wide angle Rolleiflex camera, and about the Mamiyaflex camera appear on separate pages in her 1961 appointment book in March.

[137] Doon Arbus interview with Lisette Model, February 5, 1972.

[138] There are instances of Diane using both Rolleiflex and Nikon cameras in photographing people as well. One example, Girl on a stoop with baby N.Y.C. 1962 (p. 57) exists in both formats. The one she printed was the 2¼.

[139] Diane Arbus letter to Lisette Model, September 25, 1962. Lisette Model Archives, National Gallery of Canada, Ottawa.

[140] The actual text of the note says, "...I cant remember what you said about doing amy in clothes for Rae..." This is a reference to Rae Crespin, a fashion editor at *Harper's Bazaar*.

[141] These photographs, taken on June 26, were published in "Bill Blass Designs for Little Ones," *Harper's Bazaar*, September 1962, pp. 162–163.

[142] The full text of the The Silver Spoon project proposal, as sent to Nancy White, in 1962 Notebook (No. 8): "Silver Spoon (The Children of Good Fortune). I don't want to photograph the most distinguished and dazzling people of our time; I want to photograph their children. To discover the thousand ways they inhabit their rare and marvelous habitats, like princess and pirate (at once) in a predicament as poignant as it is pretty. Call it (perhaps) the Silver Spoon."

[143] The full text of the proposed Winners project in 1962 Notebook (No. 8) includes the following: "I guess there are four ways to win; by virtue of a test, or by an attribute, or to be chosen out of a hat, or immaculately conceived by a press agent without any contest at all. Even the Pope is a winner."

[144] Diane Arbus 1962 Notebook (No. 8).

[145] This project was originally intended for *Harper's Bazaar*. It is listed as "Seers" on Arbus's 1962 Guggenheim application. Application, courtesy of the John Simon Guggenheim Foundation. Ultimately, the pictures by Arbus appeared in *Glamour*, in January and October 1964, edited by Marguerite Lamkin for her column "What's New: The Witch Predicts." Elisabeth Sussman interview with Marguerite Lamkin Litman, April 2, 2002.

[146] Diane Arbus letter to Doon Arbus, summer 1960.

[147] In an interview with Doon Arbus on February 18, 1972, Bunny Sellers describes her first meeting with Diane Arbus, which took place around 1959.

[148] Bunny Sellers makes notes about fortune-tellers in Diane's 1962 Notebook (No. 10). The piece on fortune-tellers is published in Marguerite Lamkin's column "What's New: The Witch Predicts," in *Glamour*. Madame Sandra and Dr. George Darios are included on pp. 66–69 in the January 1964 issue, and Leslie Eliot and Doris Fulton are included in the October 1964 issue. The uncredited text accompanying the pictures is written by Lamkin, based on Diane's captions.

[149] Doon Arbus interview with Bunny Sellers, February 18, 1972.

[150] Diane Arbus letter to Lisette Model, September 25, 1962. Lisette Model Archives, National Gallery of Canada, Ottawa.

[151] Diane meets Lee Friedlander through Marvin Israel. In the early 1960s, Friedlander knew Israel when the latter was art director of *Seventeen* (1957–58). Diane knew Mary and Robert Frank from the mid-1950s. Mary Frank's name appears in her appointment books from 1959 through 1970. Elisabeth Sussman interviews with Lee Friedlander (March 6, 2002), Mary Frank (January 14, 2002), Allan Arbus (October 17, 2000).

[152] Diane Arbus letter to Lisette Model, September 25, 1962. Lisette Model Archives, National Gallery of Canada, Ottawa.

[153] In a letter dated October 30, 1962, Grace Mayer writes to Diane Arbus on behalf of Edward Steichen. She thanks Arbus for submitting a portfolio and the issue of *Infinity* containing her work. Mayer writes, "He finds your photographs 'good,' and feels that the *Infinity* piece did not do justice to your work, as you get the feeling of surrealism in the other subjects too. He has confidence in you, your undertaking and your ability to carry it out, and is, 'all for you on the strength of your portfolio.'" She concludes by saying he "will be glad to act as one of your sponsors..." Letter in Diane Arbus file, The Museum of Modern Art, New York.

[154] In the March 1962 issue of *Harper's Bazaar*, under the title "The Unposed Portrait," Israel publishes a group of Walker Evans photographs taken with a hidden camera while riding the New York City subways in 1938, 1940, and 1941. Walker Evans. Introduction by James Agee. *Many Are Called* (Boston: Houghton Mifflin Co., and Cambridge: The Riverside Press, 1966).

[155] Diane Arbus typewritten letter to Walker Evans. Walker Evans Archive, The Metropolitan Museum of Art, 1994. The date of receipt is marked on the letter, presumably by Evans, as 9/20/62. It reads as follows: "Dear WE, My grandmother was rather vulgar but superb, like a contemporary witch, and I often see something of her walking down Fifth Ave. although she is dead. In fact I am a bit enamored of vulgarity, excepting my own of course. When you asked about my literary tastes I forgot Celine... Meanwhile if you have news of Helen Levitt [the photographer] and she is anywhere near would you tell me?"

[156] Diane Arbus typewritten letter to Walker Evans, circa October 1962, with Guggenheim project proposal enclosed, "...for your criticism or approval." Walker Evans Archive, The Metropolitan Museum of Art, 1994.

[157] The earliest project that she lists is "children's games," from 1958; projects listed for 1959 are "movie theater interiors," "Vertical Journey (for *Esquire*)," and, "secret photos of steam bathers." She also lists more recent projects, such as "Female Impersonators," 1959–62; "photographs at the beach," 1959–61; and "sideshow," 1959–61. Application from the Archives of the John Simon Guggenheim Foundation and letter to Elisabeth Sussman from G. Thomas Tanselle, Vice-President, May 31, 2000.

[158] Included in her Guggenheim application, as required, is a list of people who will provide references (Guggenheim Fellows denoted by asterisk): "Richard Avedon, photographer; Leonard Bernstein, composer and conductor; Alexey Brodovitch, photographer; Victor D'Amico, Director of Education, The Museum of Modern Art; *Walker Evans, photographer; *James T. Farrell, writer; *Robert Frank, photographer; *Lee Friedlander, photographer; Marvin Israel, Art Director, *Harper's Bazaar*; *Helen Levitt, photographer; Lisette Model, photographer; Howard Nemerov (my brother) poet, novelist; James Thrall Soby, critic, Vice President and Trustee, The Museum of Modern Art." No letters were received from Brodovitch, Farrell, or Bernstein. Walker Evans did not write but spoke with Henry Allen Moe, chief executive of the Guggenheim Foundation at that time. Application from the Archives of the John Simon Guggenheim Foundation and letter to Elisabeth Sussman from G. Thomas Tanselle, Vice-President, May 31, 2000.

[159] The letter itself, in the Archives, Department of Photography, The Museum of Modern Art, has a handwritten note on it, probably written by John Szarkowski to his secretary, Pat Walker: "Pat: won't be back before October 15 deadline," and at the bottom of the page, in another hand, "telephoned September 28 to say not possible."

[160] Doon Arbus interview with John Szarkowski, February 11, 1972. Doon Arbus, "Diane Arbus, Photographer," *Ms.*, November 1972. Szarkowski's name appears in the 1961 appointment book on October 24, suggesting their meeting took place on that day.

[161] Szarkowski showed her Sander's book *Antlitz der Zeit (Face of Our Time,* 1929) and possibly *Deutschenspiegel (Mirror of Germans,* 1962).

[162] Pat Walker, John Szarkowski's secretary, responds on January 15, 1963, with the information Diane has requested. Diane Arbus file, The Museum of Modern Art.

[163] In the postcard she adds: "If what had to be done is still a problem I will try to help." The last line is probably a reference to her helping Model to write it.

[164] In light of the date of Model's recommendation, it appears that she did not take Diane up on the offer to help write the recommendation. Lisette Model Archives, National Gallery of Canada, Ottawa.

[165] See note 142 for complete text of Silver Spoon project from 1962 Notebook (No. 8).

[166] Letter to Paul Salstrom, Medical Center for Federal Prisoners, Springfield, Mo., January 9, 1963. Salstrom was one of the peace movement marchers Arbus had photographed for Thomas B. Morgan's "Doom and Passion Along Rte. 45" that appeared in *Esquire* in November 1962. Salstrom had written the leaflet about nonviolence that the marchers carried with them on their march from Hanover, N.H., to Washington, D.C. Salstrom was serving three years in prison for refusing to register for the draft. Elisabeth Sussman interview with Paul Salstrom, April 23, 2002. Collection of Paul Salstrom.

[167] Although the photograph of Penelope Tree was taken in 1963, the comment was made earlier, in 1962 Notebook (No. 8).

[168] Between 1962 and 1964 Arbus completes at least twenty-five assignments for magazines, including *Harper's Bazaar, Show, Esquire, Glamour,* and *The Saturday Evening Post.* For a more complete list and a discussion of Arbus's commercial activity, see *Diane Arbus: Magazine Work.*

[169] The Junior Interstate Ballroom Dance Championships take place in Yonkers, N.Y., on February 17, and a week later she photographs the winning couple. "Make sure children have trophies and formal clothes," she writes in her 1963 appointment book on February 25. Diane continues to work on the rituals and contests of everyday life as proposed in her Guggenheim fellowship application. Between January and October, she attends contests for "Mother of the Year," "Woman of the World," "Freckles," "spaghetti eating," and "Miss Lo-Cal."

[170] Doon Arbus conversation with Richard Avedon, June 2003.

[171] Diane Arbus letter to Henry Allen Moe, April 18, 1963, and his April 22, 1963, reply.

[172] Diane Arbus postcard to Walker Evans, circa April 1963. Walker Evans Archive, The Metropolitan Museum of Art, 1994. They appear to have remained in touch prior to this postcard. In another postcard to Walker Evans, circa February 1963, Diane writes, "Dear Walker, On Sunday on the radio (WRVR-FM 106.7, 8:30 P.M) they are playing the tape of J. Baldwin's appearance at the Y. I don't think the curious mass masochism of the audience will be audible but he will be and he is important and I remember one very magnificent thing he said about the sonnets of Shakespeare..."

[173] Diane Arbus postcard to Lisette Model, April 22, 1962. Lisette Model Archives, National Gallery of Canada, Ottawa.

[174] In 1965, Howard Nemerov wrote in his memoir, *Journal of the Fictive Life,* "Here is a poem I wrote months before my father's death, on first seeing him in the hospital and learning that he was seriously ill:

GROWING A GHOST

From the time he knew / He groomed his hair / In a gray pompadour / And made grim his smile / fitly to represent / all that would be meant / When he arrived by growing / To that great dignity / Nondenominational / But solemn all the same / And

showing forth a force.

the stone jaw / the sharp nose / the closed lids

dreaming / nightmares for all / who looked their last / looking his best / the ancestral look / in evening clothes / to go underground / and have at last / in his folded hands / the peace of the world

the red clay

As my sister wrote me toward the end, 'he looks more like everyman than himself.'" Howard Nemerov, *Journal of the Fictive Life,* pp. 171–172.

[175] Studs Terkel radio interview with Diane Arbus, WFMT Chicago, 1968.

[176] Diane liked Vanderzee's memorial photographs of the dead where he manipulated the image to show the living person rising from the coffin. Szarkowski visited Vanderzee's studio after Diane told him about the photographer. John Szarkowski, e-mail to Elisabeth Sussman, April 17, 2002.

[177] In the same 1963 Notebook (No. 11), under the heading "Mr. Vanderzee," Diane transcribes this quote: "If you stay in one place you become extinct."

[178] Sunshine Park is called Sunrise Haven in "Notes on the Nudist Camp," unpublished, 1965; later published in *Diane Arbus: Magazine Work*, pp. 68–69.

[179] *Diane Arbus*, pp. 4–5.

[180] Other photos Diane makes at the nudist camp at this time are A young waitress at a nudist camp, N.J. 1963 (p. 72); Husband and wife with shoes on in their cabin at a nudist camp, N.J. 1963 (p. 167); and Nudist man and his dog in a trailer, N.J. 1963.

[181] Although "Notes on the Nudist Camp" is written in 1965 in connection with an assignment for *Esquire*, it is largely based on notes from 1963 Notebook (No. 13). In 1965, she goes to a camp in Pennsylvania, but the *Esquire* assignment is never published. The complete article appears in *Diane Arbus: Magazine Work*, pp. 68–69.

[182] *Ibid.*

[183] Howard Nemerov was writer in residence at Hollins College in 1962–63, and Sudie Victor was a student of his in her senior year. In 1963 he received a one-year appointment as Poetry Consultant at the Library of Congress.

[184] *Harper's Bazaar*, April 1964, pp. 162–167. Five portraits of trendsetters Reed Buchanan, Mia Villiers-Farrow, Patricia Merle Silver, Maria Christine Drew, Cynthia Boves Taylor.

[185] *Harper's Bazaar*, April 1964, pp. 142–145. Text by Geri Trotta.

[186] Diane Arbus appointment book, January 13, 1964.

[187] Clarence J. Laughlin's name first shows up in Diane's 1962 appointment book in January, when she appears to have planned to call him and get his address in New Orleans. On April 15, 1962, she sends him the following postcard, apparently in response to his suggestion that they trade prints, and alluding to her difficulty changing from the Nikon to the Rolleiflex: "Dear Clarence, thanks for yr letter. Yes I wd like to exchange prints but may I wait a few months. I have been having serious growing pains changing cameras and relearning to photograph and progress has been so terrible slow that I hate to go back and print old things. So wd you wait until I know more where I am. Yes, I know which ones I want but I don't want to ask you for them yet. Thanks Clarence. I hope you are well. Diane." Original postcard in the Clarence Laughlin Archive, The Historic New Orleans Collection, New Orleans, La.

[188] Lee Friedlander discovered Bellocq's glass plate negatives in the late 1950s in New Orleans when they were in the possession of Larry Borenstein, who, with Al Rose (also from New Orleans), had bought the negatives after Bellocq's death. Friedlander told Arbus about Bellocq. Elisabeth Sussman interview with Lee Friedlander, December 2002. In her 1964 Notebook (No. 14), Diane attached Borenstein's card and copied Al Rose's address. She later acquired from Friedlander several of his prints of Bellocq's work.

[189] "Blaze Starr in Nighttown," *Esquire*, July 1964. Text by Thomas B. Morgan, photographs by Diane Arbus, pp. 58–62. On this trip, or on a separate one a few weeks later, also for *Esquire*, Diane photographs the atheist Madalyn Murray, a portrait published with an article by Bynum Shaw, "Nevertheless, God Probably Loves Mrs. Murray..." *Esquire*, October 1964, pp. 110–112, 168–171.

[190] Doon Arbus interview with Bunny Sellers, February 18, 1972.

[191] Diane Arbus typewritten letter to Marvin Israel, circa 1960.

[192] *Diane Arbus: Magazine Work*, pp. 48–53. In one of Diane's typewritten drafts of the text about the Bishop, she has included her own editor's note, which reads as follows, "The greatest stars of the human drama have always been the people who saw what no one else could see. Visionaries are by their very nature unbelievable...we (the editors) find ourselves unable to believe what the Bishop believes. But we ask your openmindedness, for if the Bishop can be believed this will indeed be a Holy Christmas."

[193] Dan Talbot claims to have been helpful in putting Diane in touch with Mae West. Talbot ran the New Yorker Theater, an art movie theater at W. 88th St. and Broadway.

[194] "Mae West: Emotion in Motion," *Show*, January 1965, pp. 42–45.

[195] Elisabeth Sussman interview with Robert Brown, April 2000. Robert Brown related that Diane went to see West for two days, and that at the end of the second day West gave her a hundred-dollar bill as a tip.

[196] "Mae West: Emotion in Motion," *Show*, January 1965, pp. 42–45.

[197] The opening spread includes a black-and-white portrait, and the next spread has two photographs, one of which is in color, of West in bed with her pet monkey.

[198] The title of the text as published in *Show*, "Mae West: Emotion in Motion," comes from the following West quote: "Sex is an emotion in motion." A variant photograph was also published in 1967 accompanying an article by Helen Lawrenson, "Mirror, Mirror on the Ceiling, How'm I Doin?" *Esquire*, July 1967, pp. 72–74, 113–114.

[199] Diane met Ruth St. Denis at a party with Stewart Stern. Elisabeth Sussman interview with Stewart Stern, February 2, 2001.

[200] Diane Arbus 1964 Notebook (No. 18).

[201] Diane comments in the same letter, "Partly I feel good like you do because it seems one thing is finished and what is next is vague enough to be at its most promising. If you see Bunny and Robert, ask them to show you the text of the Bishop..."

[202] Puerto Rican housewife, N.Y.C. 1963 (p. 60), and Sharon Goldberg, N.Y.C. 1965 (p. 175), are the only two photos of this series Diane actually prints.

[203] Diane Arbus postcard to Doon Arbus, August 5, 1960. She is reporting on Carlotta's car accident after she has been "quite decently sewed together."

[204] Diane Arbus 1964 Notebook (No. 15).

[205] Diane photographs the Red Shield Senior Citizens Club and its most renowned member, Mother Brown (born 1852) who turns 112 years old on November 17. In her 1964 Notebook (No. 15) she records a comment by one of the club members about Mother Brown: "It's terrible to live in the shadow of someone 112."

[206] Marguerite Lamkin, who is introduced to Avedon by her friend Marvin Israel, works on the book, arranging most of the sittings.

[207] In spite of John Szarkowski's enthusiasm for The Junior Interstate Ballroom Dance Champions, Yonkers, N.Y. 1963 (p. 40), this picture is not acquired by MoMA until 1969. Photography Department, The Museum of Modern Art.

[208] Diane Arbus artist file, The Museum of Modern Art.

[209] Diane Arbus 1959–1960 Notebook (No. 3). It is not clear what magazine she proposed this idea to but the format of it in the notebook suggests it was intended as such. Two out of the six pages of lists

following this project statement are reproduced on p. 236.

[210] Diane Arbus 1965 Notebook (No. 21) contains both quotes and a great deal more.

[211] The published article, "Fashion Independents: On Marriage," with text by Gerri Trotta (*Harper's Bazaar*, May 1965, pp. 151–161, 184), includes portraits of the following nine couples: Paul Lester and Ingeborg Wiener; Armando and Georgiana Orsini; Frederick and Isabel Eberstadt; John Gruen and Jane Wilson; Herbert and Eliette Von Karajan; Gilbert and Kitty Miller; Mr. and Mrs. Howard Oxenberg; Otto Preminger and Hope Bryce. Other names appearing in this context on the March 10th page of her 1965 appointment book are the Clay Felkers, the Marcel Duchamps, the Wyatt Coopers, Theodorocropolis, Toppings, Guests, etc.

[212] "Familial Colloquies," *Esquire*, July 1965, pp. 54–57. Apparently somewhat later she also photographed Susan Sontag and her son, David, possibly for this project, but for whatever reason the photograph was never published. There is reason to think that in a few cases she attempted to make the separate assignments overlap. Her fascination with Jayne Mansfield appears to have preceded—and perhaps given rise to—"Familial Colloquies." Jayne Mansfield's married name (Cimber Ottaviano) appears in one of the lists for *Harper's Bazaar*'s "On Marriage" assignment.

[213] The only other assignment she published in 1965 appears in the "Fashion Independents" feature in *Harper's Bazaar*, July, pp. 90–93, the same month as *Esquire*'s "Familial Colloquies." It consists of four photographs of the Philadelphia socialite Mrs. T. Charlton Henry (p. 116), with a text by Gerri Trotta. On April 14, where Mrs. Henry's name appears, there is also a sentence that reads like a quote from her: "I like everything unrefined."

[214] She begins to visit Kerista in April. Kerista was founded in 1956 by John Presmont, a businessman turned prophet. (See John Gruen, *The New Bohemian*, New Jersey: A Cappella Books, 1990, pp. 52–60). She also attends a motorcycle rally in Watkins Glen, Laconia, N.H., in June.

[215] "It was really remarkable. And I found it very scary. I mean I could become a nudist, I could become a million things. But I could never become that, whatever all those people were. There were days I just couldn't work there and then there were days I could. And then, having done it a little, I could do it more..." *Diane Arbus*, p. 12.

[216] *Ibid.* This description of her work in Washington Square is one she gave in her master class in 1971.

[217] The texts, sometimes two or three copies of each —original and carbons—are in a yellow spring lock binder. The binder itself is similar to the blue one (see p. 266) she later keeps in her darkroom that contains formulae and technical data.

[218] Unpublished typewritten text dated September 20, 1965. The names Jamie and Dexter appear on the July 5th page of her 1965 appointment book, suggesting this may be the day the events described occurred.

[219] *Ibid.*

[220] She may not have been the first of her era to employ the black borders, but we have been unable to determine who if anyone did it before her. For a complete discussion of this and various other Diane Arbus printing methods, see in this book, Neil Selkirk, "In the Darkroom," pp. 267–275.

[221] On July 17, in her appointment book, she makes note of an Eastern Sunbathing Association convention. She had been visiting Sunnyrest off and on throughout July.

[222] The letter begins, "Dear John, everything is so superb and breathtaking I am creeping forward on my

belly like they do in war movies. I have a foot in several worlds and I hope I can do what there is to do." She refers to the Elliot Erwitt Show as "absorbing and instructive" and ends with "my fingers are crossed." Diane Arbus artist file, The Museum of Modern Art.

223 Letter from Harold Hayes, August 9, 1965. The *Esquire* Collection, Spencer Museum of Art, University of Kansas, Lawrence. Puerto Rican housewife, N.Y.C. 1963 (p. 60), is one of the photos related to the project.

224 Israel continues to teach at Parsons School of Design. One of his students, Michael Flanagan, works for a time as Allan Arbus's assistant and recalls processing Diane's negatives and being with her on occasion in the darkroom when she was printing. Flanagan believes that she was using Agfa Portriga paper at this point—which it appears she had been doing for at least a year or two. Elisabeth Sussman interview with Michael Flanagan, May 2, 2002.

225 The exhibition takes place in October. The nudist camp picture of the married couple at home was subsequently retitled twice by Diane, first as Man and wife at home, nudist camp, N.J. 1963, then, Retired man and his wife at home at a nudist camp one morning, N.J. 1963 (p. 253). The photograph of the female impersonators was retitled Two female impersonators backstage, N.Y.C. 1961 (p. 58). Diane cites this exhibition as well as one earlier in the year, in March (*Invitational Exhibition, 10 American Photographers*) in her Guggenheim application, dated October 31, 1965, as the only two shows in which her work appeared. Archives of the John Simon Guggenheim Foundation, New York.

226 The show took place at the School of Fine Arts, University of Wisconsin, Milwaukee, in March 1965. Ten photographers each chose a younger photographer. Lisette Model chose Diane, who was represented by five works. Archives of the John Simon Guggenheim Foundation, New York.

227 *Ibid.*

228 *Ibid.* In a letter to Gordon Ray at the Guggenheim Foundation dated November 7, 1965, she writes, "Months ago you wrote me in the customary way asking if I knew any people who ought to be candidates for fellowships and at the time it didn't seem to me that I did. I'd like to correct that oversight. Mary Frank is a sculptor of tremendous passion and constancy. I am not a chauvinist about womanhood, but her imagery is so authentically feminine that I look at it with a feeling like recognition. I think she is strong and delicate enough to last and not many women are. She has applied for a fellowship this year. Would you add my name to the list of those who vouch for her?" The year before, in a letter to Ray dated September 18, 1964, she had recommended Lisette Model and Marvin Israel for fellowships, "Lisette Model...is a photographer whose work is so profound, so amazing and subtle, that a whole generation of photographers is indebted to her...I hope she can be persuaded to apply or that some of the many people who believe in her could apply for her because her qualifications exceed everybody's. And Marvin Israel is a painter dedicated and daring enough to reward any trust." As indicated in Ray's response, Diane had recommended Israel the year before also but he had never applied.

229 See Howard Nemerov, *Journal of the Fictive Life*, p. 146.

230 Original letter in the Howard Nemerov Collection, Washington University Libraries, Department of Special Collections, St. Louis, Mo.

231 Howard Nemerov, *Journal of the Fictive Life*, p. 80. He also acknowledges several pages later (p. 84) that his indictment of photography as opposed to writing is quite possibly a sophisticated version of what he and Diane used to do to one another as children, blaming each other and getting each other punished. Another example of Nemerov's preoccu-

pation with subjects also of interest to Diane (the relationship of the image to the thing itself, issues of authenticity and fraudulence) is evident in the final stanza of Nemerov's poem "To Clio, Muse of History: On learning that the Etruscan Warrior in The Metropolitan Museum of Art is proved a modern forgery": (*The Next Room of the Dream,* Chicago: University of Chicago Press, 1962)

For I remember how / We children stared, learning from him / Unspeakable things about war / that weren't in the books; / And how the Museum store offered for sale / His photographic reproductions in full color / With the ancient genitals blacked out.

232 In the letter to Howard Nemerov about *Journal of the Fictive Life*, she invites him to stay with her at Charles Street when he is in town. In her 1965 appointment book, a poetry reading of Howard's is noted on November 15.

233 *Ibid.* A subsequent letter to Nemerov, probably written around the end of November, refers to Sudie Victor's imminent wedding to Michael Trazoff, which is to take place at Charles Street on December 8.

234 *Diane Arbus: Magazine Work*, pp. 80–81.

235 *Ibid.*

236 *Ibid.*

237 Letter from G. Thomas Tanselle to Elisabeth Sussman, September 14, 2000, "I have now looked into Diane Arbus's file to see whether the titles of the photographs she submitted with her two successful applications are present. We have no lists of titles; in each case, there is just a receipt signed by her, in which she acknowledges that the material submitted has been returned to her. The one in 1963 says, '2 Magazines, 76 Photographs.'" The list of accomplishments submitted with her application for the Guggenheim Fellowship may be found in the Archive, John Simon Guggenheim Memorial Foundation.

The April 1966 issue of *camera* (the official organ of the International Federation of Photographic Art) is primarily devoted to essays and a photographic portfolio of the Guggenheim Fellows in photography 1937–65. The issue coincides with an exhibition at the Philadelphia College of Art of the work produced by the Guggenheim Fellows of this period. It includes A widow in her bedroom, N.Y.C. 1963 (p. 44) and Teenage couple on Hudson Street, N.Y.C. 1963 (p. 102).

238 Diane Arbus appointment book, February 8, 1966.

239 Archive, John Simon Guggenheim Memorial Foundation.

240 According to her appointment book entry, on January 6, 1966, she flies from La Guardia to Logan Airport on assignment for *Esquire* to photograph Brenda Frazier (Mrs. Chatfield Taylor), the 1938 debutante of the year, in her home in Medfield, Massachusetts. The portrait (p. 116) appears in an article by Bernard Weinraub, "Girl of the Year, 1938," *Esquire*, July 1966, pp. 72–77.

241 "James Brown Is Out of Sight," *Herald Tribune Magazine*, March 20, 1966, pp. 14–24, text by Doon Arbus.

242 Elisabeth Sussman interview with Ruth Ansel, February 15, 2002.

243 Elisabeth Sussman telephone interview, Lucas Samaras, New York City, February 18, 2002. Visiting Lucas Samaras, she saw his collection of antique French pornographic photography, which he subsequently brought to an Avedon workshop.

244 "Not to Be Missed: The American Art Scene," *Harper's Bazaar*, July 1966, pp. 80–85, text by Geri Trotta. A later portrait of Ad Reinhardt appears in "Ad Reinhardt, or the Artist as Artist," *Harper's Bazaar*, November 1966, pp. 176–177, text by Annette Michelson.

245 The article for *New York* was never completed. The dates and details of the Liddy raid vary in different accounts of the event. Leary was charged for possession of illegal drugs but the case was dropped on technicalities. Arbus gave a photograph she had taken at the Millbrook estate of members of The League for Spiritual Discovery, adding this inscription: "Dear Ralph [Metzner]. I hope these are of some use. Regards to tim and susan and rosemary and Eve and all. And you. Diane." The photograph, also inscribed "to Ro. Love Timothy, 7-22-95." This photograph is now in the collection of the San Francisco Museum of Modern Art.

246 Margaret Sanger Papers Project, Newsletter #22, Fall 1999.

247 Couple under a paper lantern, N.Y.C. 1966 (p. 112), Girl sitting in bed with her boyfriend, N.Y.C. 1966 (p. 239), Couple in bed, N.Y.C. 1966 (p. 62).

248 Letter from Ruth Ansel to Elisabeth Sussman, February 15, 2002.

249 Several years later, discussing the topic of sex and photography with her master class, she refers to "the greatest sex scene I've ever seen in my whole life." It is in a film called *Hunger*, based on the novel by Knut Hamsun. "The hero...looks through...a little crack in a door...and he sees his landlady who is a middle aged lady being fucked by her husband I guess...They've got their clothes on, except her skirt's up and his pants are open...there's like one movement you see...its like you never saw it before it's so accurate. It's really beautiful and there's nothing pretty about it...It's like you're there." "Authenticity" is the word she uses in her master class in 1971 in speaking of pornographic pictures and of the work of Tilo Kiehl.

250 Lyon and Davidson, who had photographed the civil rights movement in the South, were to be included (with Lee Friedlander, Duane Michaels, and Garry Winogrand) in a December 1966 show, *Toward a Social Landscape*, at the George Eastman House, Rochester, N.Y. Elisabeth Sussman interview with Bruce Davidson, April 22, 2002; Elisabeth Sussman interview with Danny Lyon, May 7, 2002.

251 Colin Westerbeck and Joel Meyerowitz, *Bystander: A History of Street Photography* (Boston: Bulfinch Press, Little Brown & Co., 1994), pp. 373–388.

252 From the wall label for the exhibition *New Documents*, curated by John Szarkowski, The Museum of Modern Art, February 28–May 7, 1967.

253 From a text by John Szarkowski sent by him on February 15, 1973, to Shoji Yamagishi at *Camera Mainichi, The Mainichi Newspapers*, Tokyo. Archive, The Museum of Modern Art. The text was presumably written to be published in connection with the posthumous Diane Arbus retrospective at Seibu Museum in Tokyo, organized by Yamagishi and curated by Doon Arbus and Marvin Israel. This exhibition, which subsequently toured throughout Europe, Australia, and New Zealand, took place at the same time that The Museum of Modern Art retrospective began touring the United States and Canada.

254 Archive, John Simon Guggenheim Memorial Foundation. Listed in her appointment book on June 13th are the following names of those who will require gamma globulin shots: "Amy, Doon, Allan, m[arvin]."

255 Letter from Diane Arbus to James Mathias, July 5, 1966. Archive, John Simon Guggenheim Memorial Foundation.

256 Note from James Mathias to Diane Arbus, July 6, 1966. Archive, John Simon Guggenheim Memorial Foundation.

257 Letter from James Mathias to Diane Arbus, July 29, 1966. Archive, John Simon Guggenheim Memorial Foundation.

258 Original letter is in the collection of Marilee and Stewart Stern.

259 Transcript of tape of master class at Westbeth.

260 Diane photographs the friend as well (Chronology, p. 181; Transvestite showing cleavage, N.Y.C. 1966, p. 82).

261 As she further explained, "She lives always dressed as a woman and she whores as a woman. I would never think she was a man. I can't really see the man in her...I have gone into restaurants with her and every man in the place has turned around to look at her and made all sorts of hoots and whistles. And it was her, it wasn't me." *Diane Arbus*, pp. 13–14. The subject of this narrative is Vicki, and her friend's name is Jean. In one of Diane's notebooks (No. 26) she records a number of Vicki's observations about her life, including, "You make your own heaven and hell on earth."

262 Transcript of tape of master class at Westbeth.

263 Letter to Stewart Stern, circa 1967.

264 Postcard to John Szarkowski that begins, "Dear John, what a good time I had..."

265 In the *Newsweek* research report by Ann Ray Martin who interviewed Diane for the magazine's March 20, 1967, review of *New Documents*, the idea of making the large prints is credited to Szarkowski, "[Arbus] uses either a 35mm or a two and a quarter camera and prints the pictures at whatever size appeals to her based on the subject. For the exhibit she blew some of them up to life size at John Szarkowsky's [sic] suggestion." This is supported by the fact that a few of the Friedlander and Winogrand photographs in the exhibition are printed in a large format as well.

266 Postcard from Diane Arbus to John Szarkowski, circa 1966. Archive, The Museum of Modern Art.

267 A print she eventually gives him, presumably of his choosing, is Young girl at a nudist camp, Pa. 1965 (p. 61), 16x20. Collection of The Museum of Modern Art.

268 Doon Arbus interview with Amy Arbus, January 17, 2003. These fashion pictures appear to be the first work she has done in color since the photographs of Mae West for the 1965 issue of *Show*: "Mae West: Emotion in Motion," *Show*, January 1965, pp. 42–45, text by Diane Arbus. Her 1967 appointment book suggests she may have returned to New York by January 3. On that page and the next of the appointment book she has written: "print."

269 "Children in the Sun," *The New York Times Magazine Part II*, March 12, 1967, text by Patricia Peterson. Cover plus eleven color and black-and-white photographs.

270 Postcard from Diane Arbus to Paul Salstrom in Berkeley, Cal., March 7, 1967. Collection of Paul Salstrom.

271 The postcard from Diane Arbus to Howard Nemerov concludes, "Didn't know you'd be so willing to come so far so briefly (opening). Don't feel obliged but I am glad you think of it."

272 The checklist for *New Documents* includes:

Burlesque comedienne, Atlantic City, N.J. 1963; Triplets, N.J. 1963 (p. 85); Girl with a cigar, Washington Square Park, N.Y.C. 1965 (p. 43); Young Negro boy, Washington Square Park, N.Y.C. 1965 (p. 114); Lady with swan sunglasses, nudist camp, Pa. 1965 (p. 176); Puerto Rican housewife, Jefferson St., N.Y.C. 1963 (p. 60); Young man on a sofa, E. 10th St. 1966 (p. 73); Transvestite at home, N.Y.C. 1966 (p. 250); Young man in curlers, W. 20th St., N.Y.C. 1966 (p. 46); Russian midget friends, 100th St., N.Y.C. 1963 (p. 100); Exasperated boy with toy hand grenade, N.Y.C. 1962 (p. 104); Transvestite with torn stocking, N.Y.C. 1966 (p. 291); Junior Interstate Ballroom Dance Champions, Yonkers, N.Y. 1963 (p. 40); Two female impersonators backstage, N.Y.C. 1961 (p. 58). Photography Department Archive, The Museum of Modern Art.

273 Doon Arbus interview with John Szarkowski, February 11, 1972.

274 *Ibid.*

275 *Ibid.*

276 *Newsweek* research report by Ann Ray Martin, March 6, 1967. Copy in Archives of The Estate of Diane Arbus. Excerpts used courtesy of Ann Ray Martin and *Newsweek*.

277 "An Interview with John Szarkowski," by Kelly Wise. *Views: The Journal of Photography in New England*, vol. 2, no. 4 (1982).

278 Doon Arbus interview with John Szarkowski, February 11, 1972.

279 List and letter from Diane Arbus to Pat Walker at The Museum of Modern Art, circa January 1967.

280 Diane Arbus 1967 appointment book, February 25 and February 26: "9 sasoon perm cut tips set $45; present for John, Bendel's party, etc."

281 Doon Arbus interview with John Szarkowski February 11, 1972. Szarkowski also recalls a present he received from the three photographers, although he suspects it was primarily Diane's doing. "I'm sure it was totally Diane's notion because it was the kind of thing a man wouldn't think of, certainly not Garry or Lee...They bought me a bathrobe. Lovely, really very handsome, camel's hair bathrobe, elegantly embroidered across the back it said *New Documents* and across one sleeve it had [each of] their names...Like a fighter [would wear]. An elegant fighter."

282 Elisabeth Sussman interview with Richard Avedon, August 22, 2002. Doon Arbus interview with Richard Avedon, February 14, 2003. Diane Arbus appointment book, February 28, 1967.

283 Twins postcard to Stewart Stern from Diane Arbus, March 5, 1967. The photograph of Identical twins was exhibited that year at the Fogg Museum in a show called *The Portrait in Photography*.

284 The rest of the postcard to the Meserveys reads: "Please Bob and Lyn get to The Museum of Modern Art between now and May 7 (30 of my photographs). It looks so good. Please call when you can come. Did you know my brother has moved to your town...Send me some word of you..."

285 Postcard from Diane Arbus to Paul Salstrom in Berkeley, Cal., March 5, 1967. Collection of Paul Salstrom.

286 "Showing It Like It Is," John Gruen's review published in *New York, The World Journal Tribune Sunday Magazine* with Teenage couple on Hudson Street, mistitled as 55th Street, says: "The New Document departs from the traditionally committed statement of the Thirties and Forties...in favor of observing, understanding and 'leaving alone' that which exists."

287 Jacob Deschin, "People Seen as Curiosity," *The New York Times*, March 5, 1967. The Diane Arbus photograph, Miss Surf Beauty Contest, Venice Beach, Cal. 1962 (p. 58), accompanies the review.

288 March 6 interview with Ann Ray Martin of *Newsweek*. A review by Martin, "Telling It as It Is," *Newsweek*, March 20, 1967, p. 110, reads in part, "She can capture the peacock pathos of a transvestite, the hygenic serenity of a nudist. She can evoke the scary sweetness of being a twin (or a triplet), the spotless sterility of a middle-class living room, the jaded grotesqueness of a burlesque queen, the togetherness of a trio of midgets."

She also receives a handwritten letter from Norman Mailer dated April 20, 1967, which reads: "Dear Diane, Saw your show. I think you're a remarkable photographer, splendid, extraordinary. My dear, you may select any word you wish in the Thesaurus. I'm so glad I saw it. All best to you, Norman Mailer."

289 Postcard from Diane Arbus to Stewart Stern, circa March 1967, begins, "Dear S, Your letter was so heartwarming and rending and felt..."

290 Letter from Diane Arbus to Peter Crookston, circa January 1969 (two years after Diane's first attempt to meet with Yaeger), proposing a story about Bunny Yaeger for *Nova*, a British magazine to which Crookston has recently been appointed editor in chief.

291 Postcard from Diane Arbus to Marvin Israel from Florida, circa March 1967. Referring to the photograph on the front, "the beautiful Aqua Maids of the Cypress Garden ski show," she writes: "Dear m. This is a pornographic postcard for your class in case I do not return on time. It goes to show how clean it can be...Tomorrow I go to an authentic Italian Miami palazzo. And in the evening to the lady wrestlers..." Original postcard in the collection of Michael Flanagan.

292 Postcard from Diane Arbus to Marvin Israel, circa March 1967. "The lady wrestlers were a little amazing, so emotional and vengeful and anguished. They plead and weep and sneer like hideous goddesses with orange and silver hair, but really they are housewives and mothers. They told me that there are midget women wrestlers who are 'adorable.' I was in Frank Sinatra's suite when he wasn't."

293 Postcard from Diane Arbus to Ruth Ansel, circa March 1967. Original postcard in the collection of Ruth Ansel.

294 Notes from Ruth Ansel to Elisabeth Sussman. February 15, 2002.

295 *Ibid.*

296 In April, two magazine assignments she began working on the previous year are published: a portrait of Thomas Hoving, director of The Metropolitan Museum of Art, for *Harper's Bazaar* ("Thomas Hoving Talks About the Metropolitan Museum," text by Gerri Trotta, pp. 108, 112, 178–179) and a portrait for *Esquire* of a transsexual who became a woman in 1958 ("The Transsexual Operation," text by Tom Buckley, pp. 111–115, 205–208). In the latter instance, she did some research, read New York endocrinoligist Dr. Harry Benjamin's book *The Transsexual Phenomenon* (New York: The Julian Press, 1966), and kept notes of her conversation with the subject of her portrait.

297 Diane Arbus 1967 appointment book, April, May, and June.

298 Postcard from Diane Arbus to Paul Salstrom at 591 Waller Street, San Francisco, circa June 1967.

299 Letter from Diane Arbus to Howard Nemerov, circa fall 1967, following her trip to San Francisco. Topless dancer in her dressing room (p. 257) is the only picture she prints from this visit.

300 Postcard from Diane Arbus to Paul Salstrom in Rock Island, Illinois, July 28, 1967. "Dear Paul, The drive was fun to Dallas and I got my money after a minimum of difficulty. which produced such an explosion out of me that the young man was rendered quite obliging and docile."

301 Letter from Diane Arbus to Howard Nemerov, circa fall 1967, on the subject of the publication of his book *The Blue Swallows*, which has one of her photographs on the cover.

302 Letter from Diane Arbus to Carlotta Marshall (Mrs. Louis Berger) in Holland, circa November 1967.

303 Letter from Diane Arbus to Amy Arbus at camp, Tanager Lodge, summer 1967.

304 "The New Life," *Harper's Bazaar*, February 1968, pp. 160–161, included a portrait of Anderson Cooper, infant son of Gloria Vanderbilt and Wyatt Cooper, and poems by Sandra Hochman. According to Diane's 1967 appointment book, this photograph appears to have been made on September 15 or 18.

305 "God Is Back—He Says So Himself," text by L. M. Kit Carson, *Esquire*, February 1968, pp. 104–105, published with a portrait of Mel Lyman, author of *Autobiography of a World Saviour*.

306 Diane made photographs at Camp Lakecrest during the summer of 1967 and her pictures were no doubt the inspiration for the subsequent publication by *The London Sunday Times Magazine* of an article by Hunter Davies entitled "Please Don't Feed Me," April 14, 1968, pp. 34–37, which included two of Diane's pictures.

307 One of her assignments from *Cheetah*, a young people's magazine devoted primarily to music, is a portrait of the actor Michael J. Pollard, which is published along with the article "An Autobiography of Michael J. Pollard" by her daughter Doon, composed entirely of the actor's own words during a two-hour taped interview they did together. Pollard had a small but noticeable part in the 1967 movie *Bonnie and Clyde*, written by Robert Benton and his partner from *Esquire* days, David Newman, and directed by Arthur Penn.

308 Elisabeth Sussman interview with Stewart Stern, February 2, 2001.

309 In her appointment book on September 26 beneath the name John Berendt (an editor at *Esquire* since 1961), she has written the following names: Krishnamurti, Mel Lyman (author of *Autobiography of a World Saviour*), Meher Baba, and L. Ron Hubbard. She does eventually publish in *Esquire* a photograph of Mel Lyman, accompanying an article by L. M. Kit Carson ("God Is Back—He Says So Himself"). Her appointment book also reflects a number of Scientology sessions she attends in September and October in an effort to become "a clear."

310 Letter from Diane Arbus to Howard Nemerov, circa October 1967 on the publication of his new book of poems, *The Blue Swallows*, on the cover of which a photograph of hers was used.

311 The letter from Diane Arbus to Carlotta Marshall circa November 1967 continues with a description of Roxianne Lancelot, a woman Carlotta had met on the street several years earlier and had arranged for Diane to photograph. "Roxianne turned up about 30 lbs svelter as a result of going to one of those fancy NY drug doctors who make people feel so good they don't have to eat. She is living with a mysterious art dealer in a menage which seems to include his wife and assorted mistresses and housekeepers and a sense of perversion much wilder than it probably is. She asked me to photograph her there which is very much fun. She is still mean and ugly but has learned more about transforming herself into a sort of splendid creature, half beast half woman. She has shaved her eyebrows off and paints them on with consummate skill and about a thousand strokes like a giant exclamation mark in an awesome sunset. And apparently she wears sunglasses in bed. Thank you for finding her."

312 Diane Arbus 1967 appointment book. There is a notation on October 24 that reads: "Peter Crookston... Room 403 Wentworth," and a second notation of his name for the evening of November 5. Also, see Peter Crookston, "Diane's all-devouring eye," *The Sunday Telegraph Review* (London), October 5, 1997.

313 "Pauline Peters on People: Dr. Glassbury's Widow," *The London Sunday Times Magazine*, January 7, 1968, pp. 30–31. "Pauline Peters on People: How to Train a Derby Winner," *The London Sunday Times Magazine*, March 21, 1968, pp. 44–48. Both articles had texts written by Pauline Peters.

314 It is not clear what photograph this refers to. It might be *A widow in her bedroom* (p. 44) or *Woman in a turban* (p. 63) or neither.

315 Typewritten letter from Diane Arbus to Peter Crookston dated "Thurs Nov 30" with handwritten annotations and numbered paragraphs. Paragraph 5 details her return visit to the diaper derby winner

where she "photographed lots more...I will send those as soon as I can print them as well as the ones of Mrs. Henry (the rich lady) [p. 116]."

316 Typewritten letter from Diane Arbus to Peter Crookston, dated by Diane "Dec 12 or so."

317 Diane Arbus 1967 appointment book, December 14 and 15.

318 Handwritten letter from Diane Arbus to Peter Crookston, December 19, 1967. The letter ends, "Happy New Year. Don't be sorry I'm not coming. When I see you I'll be glad. Uttermost thanks for your ingenuity, sweetness, zest, alacrity, generosity and smile..."

319 Note from Diane Arbus to Peter Crookston, circa early January 1968, accompanying enclosed prints for Diaper Derby and two of Mrs. T. Charlton Henry, and supplying her new address.

320 Note from Diane Arbus to Peter Crookston, circa late January 1968.

321 In a note from Diane Arbus to Peter Crookston, circa March 1968, she writes, "Yes, too bad about the republicans." This note follows publication (January 7, 1968) of *The London Sunday Times Magazine* piece on Dr. Glassbury's widow ("I like Pauline's Mrs. G") and precedes the publication of the Diaper Derby story ("How to Train a Derby Winner," March 21, 1968).

322 A 1968 notebook (No. 32) contains her customary record of the words of the subjects she encountered with Dr. Gatch on his rounds, as well as his account of some of his experiences.

323 Studs Terkel radio interview with Diane Arbus, WFMT Chicago, 1968. The description she gives apparently reminds Terkel of the Walker Evans and James Agee collaboration, *Let Us Now Praise Famous Men* (New York: Houghton Mifflin, 1939). The title of the published piece in *Esquire*, "Let Us Now Praise Dr. Gatch," June 1968, pp. 108–111, 152–56, makes the same comparison. Three of Arbus's photographs were published with the article.

324 The publication by *The London Sunday Times Magazine* of "Pauline Peters on People: Dr. Glassbury's Widow" (January 7, 1968, p. 37), and the 1963 photograph *A widow in her bedroom* (p. 44 in this book), prompts the widow herself to call twice, Diane reports in a May 18 letter to Crookston: "once in dismay and then again to say she found the story perfectly charming on reflection and so did all her friends and to please send Pauline her particular regards and thanks." "Pauline Peters on People: How to Train a Derby Winner" (March 21, 1968, pp. 44–48) uses three photos. "Please Don't Feed Me," (April 14, 1968, pp. 34–37), with text by Hunter Davies, uses two photos. Apparently she is unhappy with these pictures and asks Crookston in advance not to give her a credit. In a typewritten letter to Peter Crookston circa May 1968 she says after seeing the piece, "I think the fat girl looks nice which just shows how unreliable I am."

325 When *New York* became an independent weekly, Clay Felker remained the editor. Other founding staff members included Milton Glaser as art director and Gloria Steinem as contributing editor.

326 Typewritten letter from Diane Arbus to Peter Crookston, circa May 1968. "La Dolce Viva," *New York*, April 29, 1968, pp. 36–41. Two portraits of Viva were published with the article.

327 Dr. Frederick Wertham was a New York psychiatrist known for leading a campaign about the bad effects of comic and horror stories on children. His books *A Sign for Cain: An Exploration in Human Violence* (New York: Macmillan, 1966) and *Dark Legend: A Study in Murder* (Garden City, N.Y.: Doubleday, 1941) were in Arbus's library.

328 Dr. Frederick Wertham's phone number appears on the May 22 page of her appointment book "after 3 Wertham," along with the titles of two of his books.

329 The early photograph she made appears on page 153. In another letter a week or so later, she notes in a postscript, "The jewish giant is in calif having left his parents behind in ny for the present so forget that image I conjured up unless I can resurrect the old photograph." She does in fact return to this in 1970.

330 The same pair of postcards to Peter Crookston include other suggestions as well. "There are also frequently those stories in the Daily News about the largest family and an association who pick the mother of the yr. They meet before Mother's Day [May 12] so that is over but I can call them to find out who the mother of the yr is. And what her family is like. Usually she is someone fantastically self-sacrificing but might be geographically difficult...I think I am supposed to work on some poverty photographs for an agency that is advertising poverty for the city. (!) The slogan is 'Give A Damn.'"

331 On April 12 she calls the woman and eventually they make arrangements. She visits the family on June 16.

332 Typewritten letter from Diane Arbus to Peter Crookston, circa June 1968. On July 4, she writes Crookston, "I photographed the family in Westchester once and I must go back I think but they were fun and in August they will let me photograph at a party they are giving I will show you what I got when you come." The photograph she refers to having taken on June 16 is the photograph she eventually prints after all (p. 329).

333 *Ibid*. Her mother and her mother's new husband, Phillip Rosenberg, were married on June 24, 1968. They were divorced within about a year.

334 Typewritten letter from Diane Arbus to Peter Crookston, circa June 1968.

335 This may be a reference to Mary Stevens Baird, who does eventually help her secure permission to photograph in some New Jersey institutions.

336 Although it is clear she had conversations with several publishers over the years, including those she considered adding to the MoMA invitation list for *New Documents*, there isn't any information as to what publisher she is referring to in this instance.

337 Typewritten letter from Diane Arbus to Peter Crookston, May 18, 1968.

338 Typewritten letter from Diane Arbus to Peter Crookston, circa June 1968.

339 Although apparently written in the same month, this letter is different than the one previously cited.

340 Typewritten letter from Diane Arbus to Peter Crookston, dated July 4. Most of the first page of the letter is devoted to ideas, including the average American family, family week at the Concord Hotel in upstate New York ("...an extraordinary vulgar place with indoor iceskating rink and things like revolving dance floor and more food than you have ever believed in."), and her progress, or lack of it, with the the generations of women, and the Mother of the Year ("...a dud..."), and her attempts to trace sets of twins who married twins.

341 Typewritten letter from Diane Arbus to Amy Arbus, circa July 1968.

342 Handwritten letter from Diane Arbus to Amy Arbus, circa July 1968.

343 Letter from Diane Arbus to Carlotta Marshall, dated by her "Aug 4 or 5," 1968.

344 *Ibid*.

345 Letter from Diane Arbus to Amy Arbus, August 8, 1968.

346 That same day Allan goes to the apartment to prepare things for her departure from the hospital and notices that Ishmael—the seven-year-old family cat and an offspring of Marvin's cat, Mouse—is behaving strangely and Allan takes Ishmael to the

veterinarian. Apparently he was suffering from an incurable disease and died the next night.

347 Handwritten letter from Diane Arbus to Amy Arbus, August 8, 1968.

348 Four-page handwritten letter from Diane Arbus to Marvin Israel, circa mid-August 1968. Rene d'Harnoncourt died on August 13, 1968.

349 Letter from Diane Arbus to Stewart Stern, circa August 1968. Toward the end of the letter she remarks, "The hospital was wonderful. I learned Not to photograph and in the marvelous middles of the night walking the hospital corridors like a scene on TV I was both lost and found."

350 Typewritten letter from Diane Arbus to Carlotta Marshall, circa late August 1968.

351 Judging by her appointment book, the first class takes place on Friday, September 13, between 9 and noon.

352 Typewritten letter from Diane Arbus to Carlotta Marshall, circa October 1968, that begins, "I absolutely cannot bear to make you wait and I see it is a frustration for me not to answer everything you asked about in your letters."

353 The possibility of this job actually taking place persists for months and she meets with the producer, anticipating calls that are promised but are not made, followed by the unexpected arrival of the script. She remains ambivalent about the prospect throughout this period.

354 Crookston himself dates this letter—which is primarily devoted to information on the Brooklyn family—as "midsummer 1968," which may be correct although the letter also contains references to the *Catch-22* movie offer ("I don't know about the movie yet. I am to meet with the producer next week. He is rather fun but I have the oddest feeling I will blow the whole thing probably out of some deep snobbery which is quite uncalled for under the circumstances..."). She also mentions her efforts to locate the sets of double twins. ("There is an odd tidbit about these twins who marry twins. One set live in identical houses with identical furniture but they are in missouri or somewhere...The book in which I found all this is called Twins and Super Twins by Amram Scheinfeld, J.P. Lippincott pub.") Most of this suggests that the letter was probably written in the fall.

355 Probably on June 16.

356 Letter to Carlotta Marshall, October 10, 1968, about photographing Mrs. Martin Luther King on October 2. The picture is published in "On a Photograph of Mrs. Martin Luther King at the Funeral," *Harper's Bazaar*, December 1968, pp. 106–107.

357 Letter from Diane Arbus to Carlotta Marshall, circa November 1968. "I am supposed to do Agnew and McCarthy for Esquire." The Agnew sitting was never arranged. In a letter to Peter Crookston dated November 13, 1968, she writes, "*Esquire* hasn't been able to arrange it with Agnew in time for their deadline so as of yesterday they decided to use a caricature which I think (but didn't exactly say it like that because it seemed a bit sour grapes) looks awful since he IS a caricature and its sort of a vulgar looking one so you tend to assume it can't be true." The McCarthy photograph was not published. The image she printed appears in *Diane Arbus: Magazine Work*, p. 110.

358 Letter from Diane Arbus to Howard Nemerov, November 10, 1968. In a postscript to the letter to her brother she says, "I don't think it will do to mention you to Agnew...I will just have to resort to something more elementary." Then she adds: "It is quite extraordinary how I cannot seem to take a photograph of a person that makes them look good. I don't think I ever have and the few times Ive made a special effort the photograph was rotten."

359 "Tokyo Rose Is Home," *Esquire*, May 1969, photograph and text by Diane Arbus, pp. 168–169.

360 "How Fat Alice Lost 12 Stone (Yes 12 Stone— The Weight of an Average Man!) and Found Happiness, God and the Chance of a Husband," *The London Sunday Times Magazine*, January 19, 1969, pp. 8–15. In a letter to Crookston in early 1969, following publication, Diane writes, "Alice wrote that she met a 6ft blond handsome boy who had to go back to Vietnam but when he comes back they will take up where they left off. I nearly cried with a kind of incredulous trepidation."

361 Transcript of Diane Arbus 1971 master class, p. 18.

362 Typewritten letter from Diane Arbus to Peter Crookston, circa December 1968, about *The London Sunday Times Magazine* issue on the family.

363 Letter from Diane Arbus to Carlotta Marshall, circa November 1968.

364 Letter from Diane Arbus to Peter Crookston, dated November 12, 1968.

365 "Ready for Action," *The New York Times Magazine Children's Fashions* supplement, published March 16, 1969, cover and twenty-eight color and black-and-white photographs by Diane Arbus, with text by Patricia Peterson.

366 Letter from Diane Arbus to Paul Salstrom. The letter includes a reference to teaching her last class of the semester at Cooper Union, which appears to have taken place on December 5, indicating the letter was probably written that day.

367 Typewritten letter from Diane Arbus to David Halberstich, Division of Graphic Arts and Photography, Smithsonian Institution, Washington, D.C., circa January 1969. Diane Arbus file, National Museum of American History, Smithsonian Institution.

368 Typewritten letter from Diane Arbus to Peter Crookston, circa February–March 1969. "Let me do something about very rich people (beyond my wildest dreams) when I come over. Maybe at least some of the Wives of Famous Men should be Enormously Splendid..." In another typewritten letter from Diane Arbus to Peter Crookston, circa February 1969, she writes, "congratulations. how fine" with regard to his new job at *Nova* and later says, "Of course I'll come over. And do the wives and the Who." Neither of these two projects transpire, but several other ideas replace them.

369 Typewritten letter from Diane Arbus to Peter Crookston, circa late February 1969, also contains the following anecdote: "...did you hear the rather incredible reverberations caused in the Wall Street area several warm days last October when a very plain young girl from Bklyn whose bosoms measured 43 inches around gradually accumulated a crowd of 7000 men waiting to watch her walk from the subway station to work...She was swamped with offers to dance toplessly in nightclubs. What struck me about her was that I remembered several girls in school...who were sort of ugly and had enormous bosoms which they bore like an affliction...I remember how hard it was for them to walk, let alone run. Francine struck me as just such a girl and I have been quietly waiting for a little time to pass while she danced topless briefly, figuring that by March she would have gone back to being a keypunch operator and I would photograph her. But I just realized how it might very well have changed her life permanently and she might still be wandering downward through the fringes of show business and might look extraordinary. Would she interest you?" This idea is not pursued.

370 In October of 1968, she first made contact with Drs. Eberhard and Phyllis Kronhausen, experts in human sexuality and erotic art, and collectors of erotic art. They had published *Erotic Art: A Survey of Erotic Fact and Fancy in the Fine Arts* (New York: Grove Press, circa 1968). She makes note of the Kronhausens' other books, *The Sexually Responsive Woman* (New York: Grove Press, 1964) and *Pornography and the Law: The Psychology of Erotic Realism and Pornography* (New York: Bell Publishing Company, circa 1959).

371 Typewritten letter from Diane Arbus to Peter Crookston, circa late February 1969.

372 *Ibid.*

373 On March 25, after photographing F. Lee Bailey in early March in New York, she visits him in his Boston office accompanied by the intended writer of the piece, Lady Alma Birk.

374 The camera being advertised is manufactured by Zeiss Ikon and the color photograph taken by Diane Arbus is of a friend of hers, Bob Horowtiz, standing on a path in Central Park with the camera and a lot of pigeons.

375 Diane Arbus letter to May Eliot, circa mid- or late June 1969.

376 Judge Roy Mark Hofheinz. "The Greatest Showman on Earth, and He's the First to Admit It," *Sports Illustrated*, April 21, 1969, pp. 36–49.

377 Appointment book, April 7, 1969.

378 Typewritten letter from Diane Arbus to Peter Crookston, probably April 2, 1969. She asks him to send money for the airfare ($300) and advance expenses and an estimate of the number of pages she might do "because I use a particular film which I must bring." She adds, "If you do want to do that thing I wrote you about, about the stigma of Beauty, a marvelous example is Louise de la Falaise. I know her only slightly but she is marvelously perverse, headlong, doomed and wild. I think she's in Paris." The idea is not pursued.

379 "People Who Think They Look Like Other People," *Nova*, October 1969, pp. 66–71. Eight portraits of look-alikes by Diane Arbus with text by Pauline Peters and Margaret Pringle.

380 Peter Crookston, "Diane's all-devouring eye," *The Sunday Telegraph Review* (London), October 5, 1997.

381 This text of an ad appears in her handwriting on the April 22 page of her 1969 appointment book.

382 Letter from Diane Arbus to Amy Arbus in late April 1969 on Camden Court Hotel stationery. This project on the wax museum never appears in the magazine. Four of the photographs were published posthumously in *Diane Arbus: Magazine Work*, pp. 134–137.

383 "Get to Know Your Local Rocker," *Nova*, September 1969, pp. 60–65. Six photographs by Diane Arbus with text by Peter Martin.

384 Typewritten letter from Diane Arbus to Peter Crookston, circa October 1969. In a subsequent letter in November 1969 she asks Crookston to tell the art director of *Nova* to return any old prints of hers. "It might be prudent for me to acquire them. Just the Rockers and Lulu [a pop singer of whom nine photographs were published as "Lulu's Career Is Important," *Nova*, January 1970, pp. 30–33. Text by Helen Lawrenson]. I have J. Susann." The photographs were apparently not returned.

385 Typewritten letter from Diane Arbus to Peter Crookston, circa late February 1969.

386 Postcard from Diane Arbus to Ruth Ansel from London, circa late April 1969.

387 Postcard from Diane Arbus to Richard Avedon from London, May 4, 1969.

388 Typewritten letter from Diane Arbus to May Eliot, circa mid-May 1969.

389 Typewritten letter from Diane Arbus to Peter Crookston, circa May 1969.

390 May 25, travels to Florida, first to St. Petersburg to photograph old people in retirement homes living on Medicare, a project for the Social Security Administration. The photographs are published in the Social Security Administration's Public Information Circular on December 1, 1970, to be avail-

able upon request within the agency for promotional and public relations purposes.

[391] 1969 Notebook (No. 37) dates the visit to Ratoucheff and Krauze as May 26, 1969.

[392] Typewritten letter from Diane Arbus to Marguerite Lamkin Littman, circa June 1969. Diane had apparently visited with Marguerite and her husband, Queen's Counsel Mark Littman, during her stay in London.

[393] "But Ladies, I am 76 Years Old, 'The World's Most Perfectly Developed Man', Now Lives Among the Aged in Florida. But Age, to Charles Atlas, Does Not Mean Being Reduced to a Seven Stone Weakling Again." *The London Sunday Times Magazine*, October 16, 1969, pp. 26–31.

[394] The speech is at the University of Florida, Gainesville, under the auspices of photographer Jerry Uelsmann, who taught there.

[395] Handwritten letter from Diane Arbus to Allan Arbus, probably June 6, 1969. Her speech to nuns takes place on July 14. It is arranged by the dean of Manhattanville College, Mother Brady, a Sacred Heart nun, who is a friend of Carlotta Marshall's and has instituted a graduate program for nuns to introduce them to issues of contemporary life. Gives lecture at Manhattanville. Her 1969 appointment book records: "July 14: Manhattanville 7:30 lecture $100."

[396] The photograph of the Joan Crawford fan was taken in the summer but was never published by *The London Sunday Times Magazine*. The photograph was published posthumously in *Diane Arbus: Magazine Work*, pp. 138–139

[397] In June she begins to photograph women involved with the women's liberation movement for *The London Sunday Times Magazine*. These include Betty Friedan, Ti-Grace Atkinson, Roxanne Dunbar, Delores Alexander, Kate Millet, and the Red Stockings.

[398] Typewritten letter from Diane Arbus to Allan Arbus, circa mid-June 1969.

[399] Typewritten letter from Diane Arbus to Allan Arbus, circa late June 1969.

[400] *Ibid.*

[401] Typewritten letter from Diane Arbus to Allan Arbus, circa mid-June 1969. "I have $1656 unpd bills and 2000 in the bank...I have SOS ed to Peter [Crookston, at *Nova*] to estimate the # of pps I did in England and put through the bill for me, because the expenses are absolutely nil. I will call the Social Security today and bill them but the prints arent due till June 30. I have more work. For the London Times, the Feminists and a family portrait of total strangers this weekend. but none of it is much money. The museum owes me $750. I will bother them again, altho they say its in the works."

[402] *Ibid.*

[403] Typewritten letter from Diane Arbus to Allan Arbus, circa June 1969.

[404] Typewritten letter from Diane Arbus to Allan Arbus, circa July 1969. "Last night I dreamed I decided at last to go to a psychiatrist and I got to his great Oaken door and knocked and waited and at last the door opened and there he was...(guess who* see bottom of page for the answer.) [At bottom, upside down, she writes Richard Avedon.] This kind of thing is entertaining and appalling but I don't know what to do with it. In any event, the real situation is not bad."

In September, she begins seeing Dr. Helen Boigon.

[405] In a letter to Allan Arbus and Mariclare Costello, circa December 1970, she sends Allan a check from the account in the amount of $500 and encloses a stack of blank checks for his use, urging him to write his own whenever he needs any. "The account is still in your name, of course."

[406] The Metropolitan Museum of Art purchases Identical twins Cathleen and Colleen, Roselle, N.J. 1967 (p. 265), and Xmas tree in a living room, Levittown, L.I. 1963 (p. 92).

[407] Typewritten letter from Diane Arbus to Allan Arbus, circa late June 1969. Several years later the third photograph they intended to buy was included in the museum's collection as a gift from curator John McKendry's wife, Maxime de la Falaise, Boy in a straw hat waiting to march in a pro-war parade, N.Y.C. 1967 (p. 87).

[408] In February she sells five prints for a total of $125 to the Smithsonian Institution's History Photography Collection, part of the Division of Graphic Arts and Photography, the Museum of History and Technology. The prints are (in her shorthand): "Twins [p. 265], Westchester Family [p. 329], Boy and Girl (on 10th St.) [p. 102], Midgets [p. 100], Transvestite [Transvestite with a torn stocking (p. 291)]."

[409] In February, her work is included in the exhibition *Thirteen Photographers* at the Pratt Institute in Brooklyn.

[410] In her 1969 appointment book, for June 2, she writes, "Mask, Bruce Cath [Naked man being a woman (p. 98), which she crossed out], Xmas [p. 92], Vicki [Transvestite with a torn stocking (p. 291)]."

[411] During the course of the exhibition, which continues for four years at venues throughout Europe, Latin America, and New Zealand, her print of Waitress at a nudist camp, N.J. 1963 (p. 72) is stolen twice and she is obliged to provide the museum with replacement prints.

In 1969 John Szarkowski and The Museum of Modern Art organized an exhibition, *10 Photographers*, for the United States Information Agency's U.S. pavilion at the Japan World Exhibition in Osaka, 1969–70. Among the photogaphers represented by approximately a dozen works each are Ansel Adams, Garry Winogrand, Lee Friedlander, Will Garnett, Bruce Davidson, and Diane Arbus.

[412] Typewritten letter from Diane Arbus to Allan Arbus, circa mid-August 1969.

[413] Letter from Jean-Claude Lemagny, Bibliothèque Nationale de France, May 31, 1969. "Dear Mrs. Arbus, As keeper in the 'Cabinet des Estampes' of the French National Library, in charge of the collection of photographs, I have the task of increasing this collection...Unfortunately...we cannot purchase photographic prints at their real price. Therefore, I must rely on your liberality and ask you whether you would let us have your prints rather cheap...I should like about twenty prints...I let you make your choice among your best and most famous photographs. I think, for instance, to the marvelous Identical Twins... P.S. Of course the reproduction of your photographs from our collections is strictly forbidden. Your copyright will be preserved."

[414] Doon Arbus interview with John Szarkowski, February 11, 1972.

[415] Typewritten letter from Diane Arbus to Allan Arbus, circa mid-August 1969.

[416] She also owns another Goffman book, *Asylums: Essays on the Social Situations of Mental Patients and Other Inmates* (New York: Doubleday, 1961).

[417] Typewritten letter from Diane Arbus to Peter Crookston, circa late March 1969. "Think of this: That Beauty is itself an aberration, a burden, a mystery, even to itself. What if I were to photograph Great Beauties (I don't know quite how they'd look but I think, like Babies, they can take the most remorseless scrutiny.)...Often they hate their noses or find their chins too long. Sometimes they feel painfully valuable like objects..."

[418] 1969 Notebook (No. 36) and again in No. 38. The subjects listed appear in different order, but almost all are included in the separate lists.

[419] Letter from Diane Arbus to Eugene Ostroff, Division of Graphic Arts and Photography, Smithsonian, June 13, 1969. Her 1969 Notebook (No. 38) records that she photographs at Vineland from July 29 to 31.

[420] In 1969 Notebook (No. 38) the first page of the five-page entry bears the dates July 29, 30, 31 which correspond to the entries in her appointment book. It also includes a description similar to the following, which appears in an August 1969 letter to Amy: "One of the best times was when they played Simon Says in a field. Its a really a very serious game for them because when Simon Says Raise your hands high, some can some cant, some only just put their hands on their head. And when Simon says run in place the ones that can do it as if it was nearly impossible. Lots of them are pearshaped. Once during Simon says there was a pause and one girl sat down. Everyone knew it was important. She bent her head to her knees and with an odd shiver somehow the rest of her followed in what looked like the First Somersault."

[421] Typewritten letter from Diane Arbus to Allan Arbus, circa mid-August 1969. She continues on the same subject: "What I mean is of course that if I have to shoot at a 60th or a 30th so as not to underexpose the background too much...then if the figure moves and they are moving more...more lyrical and pastoral...then there is either a ghost or a total blur. if on the other hand I underexpose the bg too much it looks too violent and lit and nightlike...And what with trying more movement it is terribly tricky...I am going to look into fellowship possibilities...So I Have to make 20 prints of the NJ pix first next week."

[422] Five-page typewritten letter from Diane Arbus to Allan Arbus, November 28, 1969.

[423] Typewritten letter from Diane Arbus to Allan Arbus, circa early December 1969. She sends Allan a group of 8x10 prints from Halloween made on the Ektamatic Processor and apparently in answer to his comments about the quality of the prints, explains, "Those...were made on the machine, just roughs, and the machine paper is soft even [with] the hardest filter. They wont look like that." She continues to employ this method of producing rough prints for the rest of her career.

[424] Letter from Diane Arbus to Allan Arbus, circa November 28, 1969. "Talked more to Marvin. I think the portfolio will be a box of 8 or so prints (actual photographic prints) but he says and I think he's right, that I shouldn't make them, just supervise the making of them. it will be utterly simple. the pictures will be ones that have been shown like the twins, xmas, etc. no text except maybe a paragraph by me. an edition of a hundred or two, selling for, I dunno, 4 or 500 dollars or 3...it'll be a business proposition but pristine...and it wont conflict with the eventual book...I mean its like an edition of etchings or lithographs."

[425] Typewritten letter from Diane Arbus to Allan Arbus, November 28, 1969. Some of her concerns focus on the strategic issue of how to obtain funding for the project. "I think I could get backing. The subject is so little known and people like Mrs Sargent Shriver have a passionate interest in it. The only tricky thing is which steps to make first...Im not sure whether to pursue an agent. Laura [Kanelous, Richard Avedon's representative] said Peter Schub (however you spell him I dread him)...she said to talk to Penn about him (he handles Penn) but talking to Penn is like talking to a pencil. Maybe I'd do better to pursue a fellowship for the retarded book. But I suppose I need both."

[426] Letter from Diane Arbus to Allan Arbus, circa mid-November 1969. "In my relentless search for

business I called Pat Peterson this morning on a most flimsy excuse. She was about to call me she said to ask about going to Barbados over Xmas."

[427] Typewritten letter from Diane Arbus to John Szarkowski, November 6, 1969, The Museum of Modern Art. "What a nice lunch that was," she adds. They appear to have had a meeting on the subject on October 14.

[428] Typewritten letter from Diane Arbus to Allan Arbus, November 28, 1969.

[429] Typewritten letter from Diane Arbus to Allan Arbus, circa mid-December 1969.

[430] Letter from Diane Arbus to Allan Arbus, November 28, 1969. "...and of all things halfway through the sitting his wife (he is the Macys santa, the parade one, a colossal idiot but pleasant and obliging) his wife volunteered 'how 'bout if I sit on his lap and ask him for the $200 gold pants suit I saw at Macys today.' So she did. perhaps I will take all my magazine pictures that way. Someone said J. Susann is angry at me."

[431] Ground for the Westbeth building had been broken for the conversion in June 1968.

[432] Typewritten letter from Diane Arbus to Allan Arbus, circa mid-October 1969.

[433] Typewritten letter from Diane Arbus to Allan Arbus, early November 1969.

[434] According to her appointment books she leaves for Barbados on Christmas Day 1969 and returns after January 5, 1970.

[435] In the same letter she continues, "I swam in the rain yesterday. Our hotel is small and I have a marvelous air conditioned double room to myself...the rest of it is a bit seedy, that sort where you hear everyone's conversations and greet at breakfast, expressing attitudes about the weather."

[436] Typewritten letter from Diane Arbus to Allan Arbus, January 16, 1970. She adds about Peterson, "I had spared her any knowledge of the near disaster of several sittings having been as much as 3 stops underexposed, which was very good and no one knew the difference so my professionalism hasn't been marred."

[437] "Looking to Summer," *The New York Times Magazine Children's Fashions* supplement, was published on March 15, 1970, with text by Patricia Peterson, and cover as well as twenty-two photographs by Diane Arbus. The photograph she describes to Allan of a "black girl and a white boy about four years old holding hands" does not appear on the cover or in the magazine at all.

[438] Typewritten letter from Diane Arbus to Allan Arbus, January 16, 1970. "I managed to get [an apartment] very like mine for Mary Frank who is separated from Robert and got sick and was in the hospital so I wrote a letter explaining her dire straits and she got precedence over the whole waiting list."

[439] Typewritten letter from Diane Arbus to Allan Arbus, circa early February 1970. Among the items receiving the spray paint treatment are a set of wooden shutters which she makes silver and sets up as screens on either side of the alcove around her bed.

[440] Typewritten letter from Diane Arbus to John Szarkowski, The Museum of Modern Art, New York. The letter, although undated, appears to have been written in January 1970.

[441] Memo, John Szarkowski to Inez Garson, January 19, 1970, The Museum of Modern Art, New York. Szarkowski outlines the tasks required to "identify and locate the major sources of negatives and prints...retrieving original negatives, or of finding prints of quality adequate to produce good copy negatives."

[442] *Ibid.*

[443] Typewritten letter from Diane Arbus to Allan Arbus and Mariclare Costello, circa July 1970, "dunno what has happened about Chicago." And typewritten letter to Amy Arbus, circa early July 1970, "I haven't been able to get in touch with the Esquire editor about the Chicago job (the dying people) so I don't know what has happened about that, when or if I am going."

[444] Typewritten letter from Diane Arbus to Allan Arbus, circa mid-November 1969.

[445] Dr. Helen Boigon is a colleague recommended to her by Dr. David Shainberg, writer Lawrence Shainberg's older brother. Lawrence Shainberg is a friend of both hers and Marvin Israel's.

[446] Handwritten letter from Diane Arbus to Allan Arbus, circa September 1969.

[447] Typewritten letter from Diane Arbus to Marvin Israel, March 24, 1960. "You know what I hate? motivation and the whole notion that one does something BECAUSE of something and all of psychologic continuity and maybe historical continuity too."

[448] In March, she works with Peter Bunnell, a curator, Department of Photography at The Museum of Modern Art, to compile a list of museums that might potentially buy photographs.

[449] Her 1970 appointment book indicates a meeting with Lauro Morales on March 24, Eddie Carmel on April 10, and the Senior Citizens' Dance on May 22. On the practice sheet of vellum (p. 222) some of the titles are at variance with the way they finally appeared in the portfolio. About the twins: "notice their bobby pins and the difference in their stockings" and about the dwarf: "he is about thirty four or thirty eight, he has two girlfriends, one of whom he will marry."

[450] Typewritten letter from Diane Arbus to Allan Arbus, circa early February 1970.

[451] Handwritten letter from Diane Arbus to Allan Arbus and Mariclare Costello, circa June 1970. In a subsequent letter to Peter Crookston on June 28, 1970, she refers to Amy's departure in similar terms, "Amy has gone cycling in Europe with nine strangers who looked rather frightful at both our first glances. And she had babysat day and night to save $500 to make it possible."

[452] From The Picture Press files, The Museum of Modern Art, New York.

[453] One of these assignments is probably the feature on carnivals that takes her to Hagerstown, Maryland, on July 31 and is referred to in a letter from Hayes dated October 5, 1970, about payment for the story, which as it turns out is never published.

[454] Typewritten letter from Diane Arbus to Peter Crookston, June 28, 1970. The letter refers to the fact that she is leaving the following day for Minneapolis to attend Richard Avedon's retrospective there, which Marvin Israel designed, "a tiny edition of 10 prints, boxed, which I am going to sell for $1000 to museums and collectors, I hope."

[455] Letter from Diane Arbus to Peter Crookston, June 28, 1970. "Some of the things are glorious. Yesterday I found a picture of a lady looking lathered as if for a shave sitting cloaked in white between a doctor and a nurse. All for Beauty's Sake it is called...Harriet Heckman submits to plastic surgery by Dr. Nathan Smilee of Phila. as nurse assists. (5/21/35) Miss Heckman has asked for the perfect face and perfect figure and announces she is perfectly willing to face death to attain them. 'I want to do something about a body and face that have made me miserable' she says."

[456] Marvin Israel also designs a portfolio of prints for Richard Avedon in the same year.

[457] The project, which eventually became *The Sixties* (New York: Random House, 1999), began with

Avedon's use of the 8x10 camera and entailed his portraits of artists and political and social activists. Doon conducted taped interviews with each of the subjects. Although a number of the Avedon portraits were published in the intervening years, the results of the project as originally conceived did not appear until the 1999 Random House publication.

[458] Handwritten letter from Diane Arbus to Amy Arbus, July 2, 1970.

[459] Typewritten letter from Diane Arbus to Allan Arbus and Mariclare Costello, circa early July 1970. This is the same letter excerpted in the text that follows, "I'm a bit sad to be back..."

[460] Letter from Diane Arbus to Amy Arbus, circa late July 1970.

[461] Letter from Harold Hayes to Diane Arbus, October 5, 1970. He writes, "I have put through a check for $371 for your Senior Citizens photograph, and an additional check for $500 against the assignment on Carnivals. However, I am loath to pay you the full amount for four pages until...I'm closer to booking the feature into an issue."

[462] According to her appointment book she leaves for Florida on August 8 and returns sometime just before the 14th.

[463] Marvin Israel had taken it upon himself to ask Richard Avedon if Diane and Doon could spend a few days there alone, and Avedon may have gone so far as to disinvite some people in order to make this possible.

[464] Letter from Diane Arbus to Amy Arbus, circa late June 1970. "Meanwhile I'll enclose an article from the VV by Paul Goodman (unless I forget) about not going to experimental schools. That should confuse you further." The article that she refers to is "Against 'Liberated' High Schools," *Village Voice*, June 25, 1970.

[465] Typewritten letter from Diane Arbus to Carlotta Marshall, circa November 1970.

[466] Typewritten letter from Diane Arbus to Allan Arbus, circa early November 1970.

[467] Handwritten note from Diane Arbus to Allan Arbus, August 29, 1970.

[468] Letter from Diane Arbus to Allan Arbus, circa mid-September 1970.

[469] Handwritten note from Diane Arbus to Allan Arbus, August 29, 1970.

[470] *The London Sunday Times Magazine*, January 3, 1971, "The Affluent Ghetto," six photographs of planned communities in America, with text by Ann Leslie, pp. 8–15.

[471] Letter from Diane Arbus to Allan Arbus, circa early October 1970. She writes, "Detroit was a nightmare but it doesn't seem to matter." "Conversation: Ida Lewis and Rev. Albert B. Cleage, Jr.," *Essence*, December 1970, pp. 22–27. Includes one uncredited photograph of the altar of The Shrine of the Black Madonna and a portrait of its pastor by Diane Arbus.

[472] "American Society of Magazine Photographers, Honors and Awards for 1970," *Infinity*, September 1970, pp. 16–17. "Of her present work Diane Arbus has said, 'I am still collecting things—the ones I recognize and the ones I can't quite believe. I think when you look anything squarely in the eye, it is different from how you thought it was.'" For the article she chose a photograph for which she provided a handwritten title, Miss Mary King and her dog Troubles, Carnival, Md. 1964 (p. 171).

[473] Typewritten letter from Diane Arbus to Allan Arbus, circa early October 1970. She adds in describing the event, "Bruce was first and he was hilarious...like a kid at his birthday party...and he wants everybody to put on their paper hats and pay attention and stop talking while he makes a wish.

At one point he was blah blahing on about how this all wouldn't have been possible without all these people and he suddenly said, 'I had my visual Proust and visual Dustyuskey: W. Eugene Smith and Diane Arbus to name just a few.' Gene Smith was good. like an old sea captain, funny and honorable."

[474] *Ibid*.

[475] *Ibid*.

[476] Letter from Diane Arbus to Allan Arbus and Mariclare Costello, December 6, 1970.

[477] Typewritten letter from Diane Arbus to Allan Arbus, circa early October 1970.

[478] Typewritten letter from Diane Arbus to Allan Arbus and Mariclare Costello, circa late October 1970. In a subsequent letter to them sent in December she reports, "My mother is eyeing Palm Beach which means she is feeling better."

[479] Handwritten letter from Diane Arbus to Carlotta Marshall, circa November 1970. Carlotta is now living in London.

[480] Letter from Diane Arbus to Allan Arbus, circa early November 1970.

[481] Typewritten letter from Diane Arbus to Allan Arbus and Mariclare Costello, December 6, 1970.

[482] Letter from Diane Arbus to Allan Arbus and Mariclare Costello, circa late October 1970.

[483] Typewritten letter from Diane Arbus to Allan Arbus and Mariclare Costello, December 6, 1970. "Both Dick and Hiro's assts use the cold light mostly. Of course they make harder negs..."

[484] *Ibid*. Later in the same letter she adds, "One of Hiro's assts. [Neil Selkirk] is working with an 11x14 camera. He found two old ones in London. I saw a negative which looked gorgeous. Not tempting to me though. hardly." A subsequent letter in mid-December reveals that the film issue rages on, "Must call Ilford. They have something called Pan F but I don't think its made in 120. Would probably be good (ASA 50). There is one rated at 125 and another like Tri x but Id like a slower one. And then there is the problem of getting it. At this point I have in the cabinet 10-50 rolls of all sorts of different films. Must get that settled."

[485] Typewritten letter from Diane Arbus to Gail Lineback, December 13, 1970. Lineback, unsolicited, sent a copy of this letter to Doon Arbus in 1972 suggesting it might prove to be of interest.

[486] Letter from Diane Arbus to Allan Arbus and Mariclare Costello, December 6, 1970.

[487] Letter from Diane Arbus to Peter Crookston, January 25, 1971.

[488] *Ibid*. This refers to *The London Sunday Times Magazine*, January 3, 1971, "The Affluent Ghetto," six photographs of planned communities in America, with text by Ann Leslie, pp. 8–15.

[489] Letter from Diane Arbus to Allan Arbus and Mariclare Costello, circa late January 1971.

[490] The account of this event that she gave to her master class in 1971 appears on pages 6 and 7 of *Diane Arbus*.

[491] Letter from Diane Arbus to Allan Arbus and Mariclare Costello, circa late January 1971.

[492] The name Bob Masochist appears several times in her 1970 appointment book in December.

[493] Letter from Davis Pratt to Diane Arbus, January 28, 1971. The letter goes on to say, "From the prints you kindly showed me here are the ones I would like to borrow for the exhibition. I will also attempt to purchase them for the Fogg." These are the images he lists: "Vicki (version 1. my notes say?), Man in curlers, Woman with accessories...Family on lawn, Giant, Dwarf, King & Queen."

[494] Letter from Diane Arbus to Davis Pratt, February 4, 1971.

[495] Letter from Davis Pratt to Doon Arbus, November 22, 1972.

[496] *Diane Arbus*, p. 3. "Sometimes I can see a photograph or a painting, I see it and I think, that's not the way it is. I don't mean a feeling of, I don't like it. I mean the feeling that this is fantastic, but there's something wrong. I guess it's my own sense of what a fact is. Something will come up in me very strongly of No, a terrific No. It's a totally private feeling I get of how different it really is. I'm not saying I get it only from pictures I don't like. I also get it from pictures I like a lot. You come outdoors and all you've got is you and all photographs begin to fall away and you think, My God, it's really totally different. I don't mean you can do it precisely like it is, but you can do it more like it is." This description was given by her to the class in the context of her response to the Walker Evans retrospective.

[497] Letter from Diane Arbus to Allan Arbus and Mariclare Costello, January 31, 1971.

[498] Transcript from Diane Arbus 1971 master class, p. 28.

[499] Transcript from Diane Arbus 1971 master class, pp. 16–17, 32–33. In the context of a discussion about various photographers she says of Cartier-Bresson, "In general I find the whole lyricism in Bresson...that sort of gentle sort of radiant pale silver that he photographs with—I just find it begins to separate out from the subject for me. I don't get that terrific kick that I get from say, Brassai, who has this kind of darkness that thrills me." About Brandt she says, "If you go through a hundred of his photographs you can really separate out that light [he has] and it's in the interior pictures, it's in the exterior pictures, it's in the lit ones, it's in the unlit ones, it's in the blackout pictures, it's extraordinary...It has something to do with the way he prints or something...[but] it comes from some mysterious deep place." About Ansel Adams, "One quarrel I've got with Adams is that—he's never lied in a photograph or even exaggerated—it's just that his prints are so sort of magnificent, he renders everything so incredibly...I mean I never saw a tree like an Adams tree...they're all silver and glowing and, you know, that sky...like something you might give for a wedding present, but not like trees. Not that I know trees very well." And about Robert Frank, "He is probably, well maybe outside of Cartier-Bresson, the most influential contemporary photographer there is. There's a funny thing in [his work] and it isn't even something I especially like but it always strikes me. It's a thing like a kind of hollowness in his work. I don't mean hollow like meaningless...I mean his pictures always involve a kind of nondrama...a drama in which the center is removed. There's kind of a question mark at the hollow center of the sort of storm of them, a curious existential kind of awe...It hit a whole generation of photographers terribly hard, like they'd never seen that before."

[500] The portfolio, titled *Walker Evans: Fourteen Photographs* (New Haven, Conn.: Ives Sillman, 1971) is printed by Thomas Brown, has an introduction by Robert Penn Warren, and is published in an edition of 100 on February 15, 1971. Fewer than a dozen are purchased during Evans's lifetime.

[501] Letter from Diane Arbus to Allan Arbus and Mariclare Costello, January 31, 1971. She adds, "Started to feel kind of grim: money, the sources drying up, Essence hasn't paid ($1000) and gives me a run around, I threatened them and finally asked Jay [Gold, lawyer, friend of hers and Marvin Israel's] to write em."

[502] Letter from Diane Arbus to Allan Arbus and Mariclare Costello, January 31, 1971.

[503] Note from Diane Arbus to Allan Arbus, February 2, 1971.

[504] *Ibid*. "Oh, Jay [Gold] got my ESSENCE money! it came this morning...AND my camera arrived from Japan. Going to Hiro's to get it."

[505] Letter from Davis Pratt to Diane Arbus, January 28, 1971.

[506] Letter from Diane Arbus to Davis Pratt, February 22, 1971.

[507] Postscript to a letter from Diane Arbus to Allan Arbus and Mariclare Costello, January 11, 1971. This is probably a reference to the pugilist Max Schmeling who was the heavyweight world champion from 1930 to 1932 and who defeated Joe Lewis in 1936. There is no information about which magazine was involved.

[508] Letter from Diane Arbus to Allan Arbus and Mariclare Costello, circa late February 1971.

[509] *Ibid*.

[510] Postcard from Marvin Israel to Diane Arbus, March 9, 1971.

[511] Letter from Diane Arbus to Allan Arbus and Mariclare Costello, circa late February 1971. The party following the last Westbeth class takes place in her apartment.

[512] *Ibid*.

[513] Letter from Diane Arbus to John Szarkowski, February 27, 1971.

[514] Szarkowski's letter of recommendation is dated March 24, 1971.

[515] Henry Geldzahler's letter of recommendation is dated March 8, 1971.

[516] It seems likely that her use of the phrase "quiet minorities" was a play upon the phrase "silent majority" which is often attributed to Richard Nixon. In fact, it appears John F. Kennedy actually originated the phrase in *Profiles in Courage* (New York: Harper, 1956). Nixon used the expression in a November 3, 1969, speech: "If a vocal minority, however fervent its cause, prevails over reason and the will of the majority, this Nation has no future as a free society...And so tonight—to you, the great silent majority of my fellow Americans—I ask for your support."

[517] The quote continues, "Yet when you start talking about the different races, different racial qualities, you're paying allegiance to Hitler—so the conversation is verboten. Hitler was an extraordinary agent of the technological society, because for two or three decades he made it impossible to think politically about the nature of people."

[518] Some of these contacts were initiated by the curators themselves, nonetheless it seems as though all the major institutional acquisitions that occurred during her lifetime were the result of personal contacts. These include John Szarkowski at The Museum of Modern Art, John McKendry and Henry Geldzahler at the Metropolitan Museum of Art, David Halberstich and Eugene Ostroff at the Smithsonian Institution, Jean-Claude Lemagny at Bibliothèque Nationale (one of the largest single institutional acquisitions), and Davis Pratt at the Fogg Museum.

[519] According to her appointment book, she flies to Portland, Maine, on May 7 and returns on the 9th. Among the photographs she takes of the yurts and the members of the Study Travel Community School is one of Amy perched on the roof of her yurt.

[520] Letter from Diane Arbus to Allan Arbus and Mariclare Costello, circa late April 1971.

[521] *Artforum*, May 1971. A Jewish giant (p. 300); Xmas tree in a living room (p. 92); Young Brooklyn family (p. 8); Mexican dwarf (p. 66); Identical twins (p. 265).

522 Apparently Diane first hears this joke at a dinner in 1960 with Allan and a friend of his. She gives Marvin Israel an account in a letter circa early November 1960. "Allan brought someone to dinner and we had a feast...his friend told a joke {which she recounts}...(How gorgeous. That is the real secret of these people I am pursuing, Uncle Sam, who I spent another afternoon with, and the lady who drinks Coca-Cola under water, and on and on. That joke would make me weep under water.)" She uses this joke in her November 1961 *Harper's Bazaar* piece "The Full Circle."

523 Letter from Diane Arbus to Allan Arbus, circa mid-May 1971.

524 *Ibid.* "This was her mistake. It made Marvin so mad he called and must have given her what for. In any event she called last night said she would stand by me and...would go to the top if necessary, totally changed in tone. He had somehow managed to transform it from a picayune, carping nuisance to an issue involving her own selfishness and indifference and she felt really ashamed because she knew he had done a lot for her."

525 The photograph of Germaine Greer for *New Woman* is never used either, although it is published posthumously in *Diane Arbus: Magazine Work*, p. 151. Following the first prints Diane submits to art director John Gerbino, she sends around a dozen more with a quick note saying she likes them better. None include the photograph that appears in *Magazine Work* or in this book (p. 302).

526 Letter from Diane Arbus to Allan Arbus, circa mid-May 1971.

527 Letter from Diane Arbus to Allan Arbus and Mariclare Costello, January 11, 1971.

528 Letter from Diane Arbus to Allan Arbus, circa mid-May 1971.

529 Diane Arbus completed the prints for eleven or twelve sets of the portfolio but did not sign them or prepare the individual title sheets until the sets had been sold. After her death, the remaining sets were designated by The Estate of Diane Arbus, on the advice of Marvin Israel and others, as artist's proofs. One was given by Doon and Amy Arbus to Allan Arbus as Diane had intended. One was purchased by the Fogg Art Museum in 1972. It remains unclear what happened to the two sets that would have been numbered 3/50 and 4/50. The probability is that they were set aside in anticipation of sales to specific purchasers that subsequently fell through and are included among the sets of artist's proofs.

530 This letter is written after May 13, the date that she attempts to retrieve 500 rolls of film from Pan Am Cargo building, described as follows: "Finally got the 500 rolls of isopan after such scenes as only maybe you can imagine. Hours in the cargo bldg, pd the freight chges, then they couldn't find the package, many phone calls, the hiring of an agent to facilitate matters, no receipt, filing a claim for restitution, warnings that it may have been x-rayed (I still don't know about that) (some of Dick's Vietnam film was ruined) and suddenly I came home and there was the postman by chance and looking idly among his packages, there it was. Even PanAm doesn't understand how it got to the postman..."

531 All previous correspondence between Davis Pratt and Diane Arbus on the subject of this exhibition refers to seven prints, and Boy with a straw hat (Bomb Hanoi) is not among them. This letter from Pratt, however, dated May 21, 1971, refers specifically to the return of eight prints and to the Bomb Hanoi print as having been damaged.

532 He goes on to say, "Thanks once more for loaning us your stunning prints and all agreed they were the guts of our smal exh. here." On August 11, 1971, Pratt sends a letter to The Estate of Diane Arbus expressing regret over her death and noting that, "During the spring we exhibited some of Diane's prints at Harvard. We had correspondence about the prospect of acquiring same when funds were available. This is now possible, so I wanted to learn whom I should contact." The Fogg subsequently acquires from the Estate a set of the artist's proofs of *A box of ten photographs* at the original purchase price of $1000.

533 Letter from Diane Arbus to Peter Crookston, circa mid-June 1971.

534 The photographs she takes at Tricia Nixon's wedding are apparently never published, nor do the negatives or contacts appear to have survived.

535 Letter from Diane Arbus to Peter Crookston, circa mid-June 1971.

536 1971 Diane Arbus Notebook (No. 39).

537 Her June appointment book indicates that she goes to Hampshire College in Amherst, Massachusetts, from June 20 to 27.

538 Doon Arbus interview with Lisette Model, February 5, 1972.

539 *Ibid.*

540 Letter from Vineland State School, dated June 14, 1971.

541 These photographs appear on several contact sheets numbered in the 7400s.

542 Elisabeth Sussman interview with Carlotta Marshall, March 27, 2001, and Doon Arbus interview with Carlotta Marshall, May 15, 2003.

543 Diane Arbus handwritten letter to Carlotta Marshall, circa late October 1968.

ADDITIONAL CREDITS

pp. 12–13 Photograph of items from collage wall; p. 16 photograph of pile of notebooks © Neil Selkirk.

pp. 122, 159, 176, 333, 335, 336 Excerpts of text by Howard Nemerov courtesy The Estate of Howard Nemerov.

p. 124 Photograph of Hooverville by Nat Norman, courtesy The Museum of the City of New York Print Archives.

p. 124 Interview with Studs Terkel used by permission of Donadio & Olson, Inc.

p. 138 *Family of Man* spread, The Museum of Modern Art Library, The Museum of Modern Art, New York. Photo of man hugging boy by Bob Jackobsen, courtesy the *Los Angeles Times*.

p. 139 Photograph of Lisette Model by Raymond Jacobs, courtesy Eleanor Jacobs, The Estate of Raymond Jacobs.

p. 139 Photograph of Alexey Brodovitch by Maurice Tabard, courtesy The Estate of Tabard.

p. 145 Photograph of Marvin Israel © Michael Flanagan.

p. 147 "The Vertical Journey" spread, used by permission, *Esquire* magazine.

p. 148 Photograph of Schmierenschauspieler by August Sander © 2003 Die Photographische Sammlung/SK Stiftung Kultur, August Sander Archiv Cologne/ARS, NY.

p. 151 *Death on the Installment Plan*, copyright © 1952 by Librairie Gallimard. Translation copyright © 1966 Ralph Manheim. Reprinted by permission of New Directions Publishing Corp.

p. 165 *The Next Room of the Dream* jacket photo courtesy the University of Chicago Press.

p. 165 Excerpt of letter from Lisette Model to the Guggenheim Foundation, The Lisette Model Foundation, Inc. Used by permission. Courtesy of the National Gallery of Canada.

p. 184 *New Documents* installation photo, The Museum of Modern Art, New York.

p. 185 *New Documents* opening photograph © George Cserna, The Museum of Modern Art, New York.

p. 186 Three photographs of Avedon/Israel class © Gideon Lewin.

p. 189 Photograph of Diane in Central Park by Garry Winogrand, The Estate of Garry Winogrand, courtesy Fraenkel Gallery, San Francisco.

p. 192 Photograph of Coney Island Bather, The Lisette Model Foundation, Inc. Used by permission.

p. 202 Photographs of Diane in Central Park © Fred Gurner.

p. 207 Cover of *The New York Times Children's Fashions* supplement, courtesy *The New York Times*.

p. 208 Photograph of Diane at Rhode Island School of Design in 1970 © Stephen Frank.

p. 213 Photograph of Diane in front of collage wall in 1970 © Saul Leiter, courtesy Howard Greenberg Gallery, New York.

p. 216 Photograph of Marvin Israel and Diane at Westbeth class, pp. 268, 272, 275; Photographs in Diane's darkroom in 1972 © Cosmos Savage.

p. 219 Postcard of Marvin Israel diptych, birthday card courtesy The Estate of Marvin Israel.

p. 219 J. H. Lartigue photograph © Ministère de la Culture—France/AAJHL

p. 219 Portrait of Dwight David Eisenhower © Richard Avedon 1964.

p. 220 Jacob Riis photograph, courtesy The Museum of the City of New York.

p. 220 Photograph of Diane in front of collage wall in 1971 © Eva Rubinstein.

p. 223 Photograph of Diane at Hampshire College in 1971 © W. T. Graham.

A CHRONOLOGY 1923–1971 WAS COMPILED WITH ADDITIONAL ASSISTANCE FROM: RUTH ANSEL, ALLAN ARBUS, AMY ARBUS, RICHARD AVEDON, BERT BEAVER, ROBERT BENTON, MICHAEL BLACKWOOD, IRVING BLUM, ROBERT BROWN, PETER BUNNELL, ROBIN CLARK, WENDY CLARKE, ADRIAN CONDON (ALLEN), BERNARD CRYSTAL, BRUCE DAVIDSON, BETTY DODSON, SHELLEY DOWELL, ALEXANDER ELIOT, MAY ELIOT, SHIRLEY FINGERHOOD, LARRY FINK, MICHAEL FLANAGAN, MILES FORST, MARY FRANK, LEE FRIEDLANDER, ELIZABETH GRADY, JOY HART, NICKY HASLAM, SARAH HERMANSON, PATI HILL, TOBY HIMMEL, JANE HOZER, LAWRENCE ISRAEL, ELEANOR JACOBS, RICKY JAY, JASPER JOHNS, CAROL KISMARIC, MARAGUERITE LAMKIN LITTMAN, RICHARD LAMPARSKI, SAUL LEITER, GIDEON LEWIN, JEROME LIEBLING, DANNY LYON, CARLOTTA MARSHALL, SUSAN MEISEL, ALEXANDER NEMEROV, RENÉE NEMEROV, MICHAEL PUTNAM, JAMES RANDI, CHARLES REYNOLDS, PAUL SALSTROM, LUCAS SAMARAS, ALLON SCHOENER, MARY SELLERS, LARRY SHAINBERG, EVE SONNEMAN, JUDITH STEIN, STEWART STERN, LOUIS STETTNER, NORMA STEVENS, JOHN SZARKOWSKI, JACQUELINE TAESCHLER, DEBORAH WILLIS, HENRY WOLF, LAMONTE YOUNG

Somewhere at the very end there is a joke

and even though I forget it there are moments when

I have fancied I knew just for a second what the punch line was.

—FROM A LETTER TO PETER CROOKSTON, MAY 1968

A house on a hill, Hollywood, Cal. 1962

INDEX

———

A woman passing, N.Y.C. 1971

This edition published by Jonathan Cape 2003.

The moral right of Diane Arbus to be identified as the author of this work has been asserted.

First published in Great Britain in 2003 by
Jonathan Cape, Random House, 20 Vauxhall Bridge Road, London SW1V 2SA

The Random House Group Limited Reg. No. 954009
www.randomhouse.co.uk

ISBN 0-224-071831

Printed in Germany